RWBC   LIBRARY
NA96
Pevsner, Nikolaus, S.
North-east Norfolk, Norwich / by Niko

CTURE

DATE L

WITHDRAWN
FROM THE
WILLIAMS UNIV
LIBRARY

D1091705

WITHDRAWN
FROM THE
... LIBRARY

THE BUILDINGS OF ENGLAND
NORTH-EAST NORFOLK
AND NORWICH
NIKOLAUS PEVSNER

N.W. & S. Norfolk

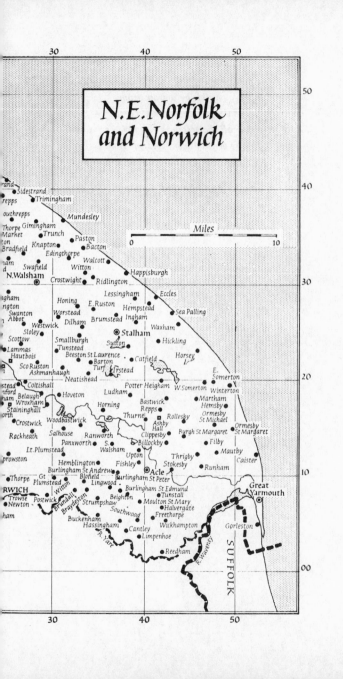

*The publication of this volume has been made
possible by a grant from*
THE LEVERHULME TRUST
*to cover all the necessary research work and
by generous contributions from*
ARTHUR GUINNESS, SON & CO LTD
and
ABC TELEVISION LTD

★

North-East Norfolk and Norwich

BY

NIKOLAUS PEVSNER

*

ROGER WILLIAMS COLLEGE LIBRARY

PENGUIN BOOKS

6-20-85

Penguin Books Ltd, Harmondsworth, Middlesex, England
Penguin Books, 625 Madison Avenue, New York, New York 10022, U.S.A.
Penguin Books Australia Ltd, Ringwood, Victoria, Australia
Penguin Books Canada Ltd, 2801 John Street, Markham, Ontario, Canada L3R 1B4
Penguin Books (N.Z.) Ltd, 182–190 Wairau Road, Auckland 10, New Zealand

—

First published 1962
Reprinted 1970, 1973, 1976, 1979

—

ISBN 0 14 071023 X

—

Copyright © Nikolaus Pevsner, 1962

—

Made and printed in Great Britain
by Butler & Tanner Ltd, Frome and London
Set in Monophoto Plantin

NA
969
N6
P4
1979

FOR MICHAEL

ROGER WILLIAMS COLLEGE LIBRARY

This book is sold subject to the condition
that it shall not, by way of trade or otherwise,
be lent, resold, hired out, or otherwise circulated
without the publisher's prior consent in any form of
binding or cover other than that in which it is
published and without a similar condition
including this condition being imposed
on the subsequent purchaser

CONTENTS

*

*

Map References

★

The numbers printed in italic type in the margin against the place names in the gazetteer of the book indicate the position of the place in question on the index map (pages 2-3), which is divided into sections by the 10-kilometre reference lines of the National Grid. The reference given here omits the two initial letters (formerly numbers) which in a full grid reference refer to the 100-kilometre squares into which the country is divided. The first two numbers indicate the *western* boundary, and the last two the *southern* boundary, of the 10-kilometre square in which the place in question is situated. For example, Mannington (reference 1030) will be found in the 10-kilometre square bounded by grid lines 10 and 20 on the *west* and 30 and 40 on the *south*; Thrigby (reference 4010) in the square bounded by grid lines 40 and 50 on the *west* and 10 and 20 on the *south*.

The map contains all those places, whether towns, villages, or isolated buildings, which are the subject of separate entries in the text.

FOREWORD

Norfolk is no doubt the biggest county job I have had to do so far. According to the late Munro Cautley it contains 659 churches earlier than the year 1700. It also contains Norwich, which is my biggest town job up-to-date, apart of course from London. The first of our journeys coincided with the best weather for two hundred years, the second to a certain extent corrected the earlier impression of nothing but bliss by cold and biting winds and occasional driving rain. Norfolk is an exposed county, but it is also a curiously secluded one, with many stretches and patches so remote and unvisited that one cannot believe that one is only 100 miles from London. The improbable pronunciations of village names fall into place when one sees them: Cley pronounced like sky, Costessey like Cossy, Stiffkey like Stewkey (as in Irish stew), Happisburgh like Haysbro' (as in haystack), Garboldisham like Garblesham, Hunstanton like Hunston, Wymondham like Windham, Tacolneston like Tackleston, and so on. Buildings are just as stubbornly unexpected, and on some at least the following pages will alas not provide the elucidation users may hope for.

In spite of Munro Cautley, Norfolk is little researched into. Cautley had to be brief on Norfolk and could not go all out, as he did in Suffolk. The more strictly architectural problems of certain churches he hardly touched. The local archaeological journal is on the scanty side, and the lists of the Ministry of Housing and Local Government are what we historians of art call an early work. On the other hand the photographic survey of the National Buildings Record is prodigious. I counted 232 boxes, and that should represent about 20,000 photographs.

Norfolk had to be divided into two volumes, the first containing North-East Norfolk and Norwich, the second North-West and South Norfolk. The boundary runs as follows: from Wells to Fakenham along the main road (B1105 and B1388), and then along the Wensum and the Yare to Yarmouth and Gorleston. All places on the boundary, including Norwich, are taken into the first volume.

The volumes contain and miss out what their predecessors have. Or, at least, they are meant to. In fact, the state of research and publication being what it is, it is more than likely that of the many ancient, interesting, and attractive farmhouses, cottages, and barns a large number have been left out simply because I never saw them, or in seeing them did not realize their significance. The rules of inclusion and exclusion, however, remain as before: all churches prior to 1830, selected ones after that date, all country houses, town houses, etc., provided they are of more than purely local architectural interest, no movable furnishings in houses (exceptions excluded), no bells, hatchments, and chairs in churches, brasses after the Reformation only occasionally, chests only occasionally, early decorated coffin-lids only occasionally, church plate only if of silver, and after 1830 only rarely, no village stocks, and only here and there one of the characteristic ploughs preserved outside churches.

The geological notes in the introduction were provided as usual by Mr Terence Miller, the notes on prehistory and Roman antiquities both in the introduction and the gazetteer by Mr J. V. S. Megaw. The Ministry of Housing and Local Government (here abridged MHLG) *have once more kindly put at my disposal the lists compiled by the Chief Investigator and his staff. I wish to thank them, and also Mr Cecil Farthing and the staff of the National Buildings Record (abbreviated* NBR) *for their helpfulness. The sign* GR *means, as in previous volumes, that information comes from the Goodhart-Rendel list of Victorian churches at the Royal Institute of British Architects, the sign* TK *refers to Sir Thomas Kendrick's lists of Victorian glass which he kindly allowed me to use. The sign* PF *means Mr Peter Ferriday's index of Victorian restorations. I am most grateful to Mr Ferriday for making this index permanently accessible to me.*

I also want to thank as usual the many rectors and vicars who answered questions and read galleys, and the owners and occupiers of houses who showed me round and answered letters. Mr P. Hepworth and Miss Mary Alexander of the Norwich Library have untiringly been at work to help me and to answer difficult questions. Mr A. A. C. Hedges of the Great Yarmouth Library and Mr C. H. Senior of the library at King's Lynn have also found answers to quite a number of questions, and the same is true of the Norfolk and Norwich Archaeological Society and its Secretary, Mr I. Cresswell. The Director-General of the Ordnance Survey and Mr A. L. F. Rivet have generously given their help to Mr Megaw. In addition, of individual people who put their knowledge of Norfolk generously at my disposal I want to mention in the first place Mr Rainbird Clarke of the Castle Museum, Norwich, Mr R. W. Ketton-Cremer, Mr A. B. Whittingham, formerly surveyor to Norwich Cathedral, Mr A. Stephenson, Headmaster of Norwich School, the Rev. C. L. S. Linnell, Mr B. Cozens-Hardy, and Lady

Cholmondeley of Houghton. I also owe a debt of gratitude to the Right Rev. the Lord Bishop of Norwich, to Mr E. Croft-Murray for allowing me the use of his unpublished corpus of painting of the C16 to C19 in England, to Mr D. J. C. King for information on motte-and-bailey castles, to Mr John Harris for information on drawings at the R.I.B.A., to Mr Rex Wailes for help on windmills, to Mr Herbert Tayler of Tayler & Green, the architects, for detailed information on their estates in the Loddon Rural District, to Mr David Percival, City Architect of Norwich, for information on his work at Norwich, to Mr A. B. Whittingham for most valuable stop-press comments on Norwich Cathedral, to Mr A. Paget Baggs and Mr D. M. Young of the Bridewell Museum for equally valuable, equally last-minute addenda on all kinds of matters, chiefly Victorian, and last but by no means least to my wife, whose eyes are sharper than mine, and to my former secretary, Mrs P. Mayes, and present secretary, Miss M. Tims, for patience in crises.

INTRODUCTION*

IN size, Norfolk is the fourth among English counties. In population it comes twenty-ninth: that is, it is not an industrialized county. Norwich of course has its industries, Colman's, Boulton & Paul's, Jarrold's, and so on, but even Norwich has no more than 120,000 inhabitants (1961) and has hardly more than doubled them in a hundred years. And after Norwich there are Great Yarmouth with 53,000 and King's Lynn with 27,500, and then nothing over 7,000, though plenty of little country towns of between 2,000 and 7,000. They are one of the signs of the great riches of Norfolk in the past.

Another is the prodigious number of parishes and of parish churches built before the C19. Norfolk has 607 ecclesiastical parishes (696 civic ones) and more than 650 pre-Victorian parish churches,‡ not including nearly 100 ruined ones§ or any of those of which we know but which have completely disappeared, or any of the more than fifty monastic houses which survive in more or less conspicuous ruins or which are recorded to have existed. No other county in England can compete with these figures. Many of today's ruined churches were already ruinous when a survey was made in 1602, a proof of a greater need before than after the Reformation. The need before the Reformation reflects Norfolk's golden age, the great age of sheep-rearing and cloth-making, stimulated by the arrival of many Flemish weavers under Edward III. When in the mid C16 Norfolk's light began to dim, more immigrants were encouraged, again from the Netherlands and this time the victims of Spanish Counter-Reformatory persecution, with the result that even Defoe as late as 1722 could speak of Norfolk as a county thriving on its weaving trade. Then, when, with the Industrial Revolution and the shift of

* This introduction deals with the architecture of Norfolk in general, including North-West and South Norfolk, to which a separate volume of *The Buildings of England* is devoted. For the borderline, *see* Foreword, p. 9. In plate references, E refers to plates reproduced in this volume, W to those reproduced in the volume on North-West and South Norfolk.

‡ Cautley counts 659 of before 1700.

§ Specially many in the w, from SE of Lynn and S of Swaffham N to Hunstanton, Walsingham, and Wells.

cloth-making from s to N, and also from wool to cotton, Norfolk weaving declined beyond hope of recovery, the county was lucky in having some of the leading agricultural reformers, foremost among them Turnip Townshend (of Raynham Hall) and Coke of Norfolk (of Holkham), and thus creating for itself a more moderate but once again stable prosperity. Today Norfolk appears indeed, as one travels through the county, to be busily employed on husbandry – at least as far as it is not busily if seasonally employed on tourists.

The scenery of Norfolk is not on the whole eventful, but it is certainly varied. Nor is it, as strangers to the county seem to think, flat. Much of it is rolling country, and the chalk ridge running from Thetford N to Hunstanton is a prominent feature, as are to a surprising degree the hills immediately s of Norwich and the hills N of Norwich, which behind Sheringham rise to just over 300 ft. The most characteristic landscape features, all caused by the geological history of the county or by more recent history, are the Broads, Marshland, Fenland, and Breckland. The Broads are probably the outcome of Anglo-Saxon peat-digging round the rivers Bure, Yare, and Waveney, the rivers on E2a which Coltishall, Hoveton, and Horning, Norwich, Reedham, and Yarmouth, and Diss, Bungay, and Beccles are situated. Sails sliding silently among fields against the low horizon are as much a recurrent sight of the Broads as expanses of reeds behind which one does not at once see the water. There are more windmills than can be counted, the majority of them serving the purpose of drainage. Indeed Norfolk is the county of windmills more than any other, and the recent decision of the County Council to preserve permanently at least eighteen out of the hundreds whose tapering brick towers penetrate the skyline is a telling token. Tower-mills are the rule, wooden post-mills a rarity.*

Marshland is the area s of Lynn, and w of Lynn into Lincolnshire, Fenland the area around Downham Market and Wisbech and into Cambridgeshire. Marshland is the outcome of periodical flooding by sea-water, Fenland of flooding by fresh water. Fenland before the Great Draining of the Fens, which took place gradually from the C17 to the early C19, was a country fertile in the summer, swampy in the winter, and rich in reeds, eels, and wild fowl; Marshland was outstandingly good land for sheep-rearing. Breckland is the area round Thetford, sandy, of wild

* Those to be preserved are Berney Arms (Ministry of Works), Billingford, Blakeney, Burnham Overy (National Trust), Caston, Cley, Denver, E4b Horsey, Hunsett, Paston, Potter Heigham (High's Mill), Ringstead, Stracey Arms, Sutton, Thurne Dyke, Tottenhill, Walpole Highway, Worstead.

heaths in the past, impressively afforested now with some of the wɪʙ largest coniferous plantations of England, a landscape reminiscent of North Germany and Denmark and in its own way visually as rewarding as the Broads.

GEOLOGICALLY the foundation of Norfolk, as we see it to-day, is the Chalk, but comparatively little of the countryside resembles the familiar South-Eastern English downland. Nevertheless, the general line and character of the Chilterns and the Cambridgeshire Gog Magog Hills stretches northwards through West Norfolk, from Thetford to Castle Acre, Massingham Heath, and Ringstead Downs, to the sea at Holme. Unlike the true Downs, these East Anglian Heights rarely rise above a couple of hundred feet, and in Breckland they are covered over with a skin of sand and gravel. Similar, but thicker, layers of glacial clay, silt, sand, and gravel conceal the Chalk over most of Norfolk E of the Peddar's Way. The Chalk surface slants very gently underground to the E, so that in the valley-floors about Norwich, and again on the coast at Sheringham and Trimingham, it can still be seen. Only to the W of a line through Hunstanton and Stoke Ferry is there no substratum of Chalk. Here, a narrow strip of lower, older rocks – Red Chalk, Carstone, and Gault Clay – intervenes between the low Chalk scarp and the Fenland silts and clays. With the Wash and the Fens on one side, and the North Sea on the other two, Norfolk seems only just able to keep above water, and there can be very little difference between the exposed surface of the county and the invisible sea-floor beyond its coasts.

There is thus little in the way of primary indigenous BUILDING STONE in Norfolk. The Chalk is of little use for unprotected outside work: it is seen occasionally – as 'clunch' – in interiors. The Carstone of Snettisham, a variety of the Lower Greensand of the Weald, has been used quite extensively in the King's Lynn–Sandringham–Hunstanton strip. It is a 'gingerbread' stone, dark-brown, gritty, and rather soft, so that it needs to be protected by a good ashlar when exposed to wear. The curious Red Chalk which lies above the Carstone in the triple-banded cliffs at Hunstanton, although a good deal harder than the normal white Chalk, never seems to have been much quarried, although lumps of it appear in some walls.

There is, however, one ubiquitous material – flint. The glacial sands, gravels, and 'crags', and the river-deposits of a similar kind, contain great quantities of flint pebbles and cobbles, originally embedded as concretions in the Chalk, and subsequently weathered out. Flints have been used, either more or less directly, as rubble, in many villages (Weybourne and Cley are examples) and in most churches.*

The only other partly native building material is of course, *faute de mieux*, brick, for which the glacial clays, loams, and brick earths, and the Jurassic clays round the Fens, provide the raw stuff. Norfolk is full of fine brickwork; yet for the most part, the great houses, both religious and lay, and the few castles relied upon stone brought in from outside the county. The famous quarries of Barnack, Clipsham, and Ancaster, in the Middle Jurassic Limestone formation of Northamptonshire, Rutland, and Lincolnshire, could provide plenty of good stone, and the Fenland rivers – Welland, Nene, and Great Ouse, and their cross-channels – were an easy carriage-route. Thus the familiar buff-coloured, shelly, oölitic limestone that can be seen in its many varieties from Normandy to the Scottish Border turns up in Norfolk – in the churches of the Marshland, in castle and cathedral at Norwich, and a host of others.

Now for PRE- and PROTOHISTORY. For an area so important as East Anglia was in this period, Norfolk has only few visible structures of dates earlier than the Middle Ages. Nevertheless, and though much of what has already been written in the Introductions to *The Buildings of England: Suffolk* and *Cambridgeshire* applies in general terms to Norfolk as well, the main cultural signposts of the prehistoric ages must be indicated here.

The evidence of man in East Anglia as a whole is slender indeed prior to the coming of the first ice sheets of the Pleistocene; the vast flakes of yellow-stained flint which perhaps accompanied the flora and fauna of the Cromer Forest Beds, deposited in the delta of a great northward-flowing river, are by no means certainly the work of man. These deposits, indicative of a generally warm phase, are dated to the First Interglacial Period; the earliest in-contestable evidence of man comes from the Second, or Great Interglacial Period (*c.* 400,000 B.C.), when the county was covered with well-stocked forest and parkland. The evidence consists of pear-shaped flint hand-axes of the so-called Acheulian type, occurring at riverside knapping sites such as Whitlingham and connected with various temporary hunters' encampments. Throughout the successive phases of the Palaeolithic, occupation seems in general to have been concentrated on the valley gravels.

* Sometimes one finds the mortar mixed with bits of flint, a technique called galleting.

This deduction is, however, based on the tools alone; no human bones can with certainty be ascribed to this period.*

About 8000 B.C., the ice sheets having retreated, the climate became comparatively mild. At this time East Anglia was joined to the Continent by a series of fens which must have looked rather as the Broads do today. At Kelling in the N and Thetford in the S W small encampments of this Mesolithic phase have yielded core-axes as well as flake tools of flint which show that they belonged to the Maglemosian hunting groups of Scandinavian origin. Contemporary with the last stages of the Mesolithic, c. 3000 B.C., fresh occupation of Breckland, the chalk ridge of W Norfolk, and the sandy E regions by pottery-using farmers heralds the Neolithic. Their bag-shaped pottery, found at such sites as Edingthorpe, marks them as belonging to the general 'Windmill Hill' group of cultures of South England, though certain features of their ceramics indicate relations with, and indeed perhaps direct settlement from, the Low Countries. The large-scale mining of flint to make axes for more extensive deforestation is another feature with analogies in Belgium. Primitive industrialization occurred on quite a large scale, and there were mines at Lynford, Great Massingham, and Whitlingham. The peak is reached, however, with the 366 shafts of Grime's Graves, Weeting, worked by such simple tools as antler picks and ox-shoulder-blade shovels; the final products were worked up on the site with a skill not exceeded by the knappers of present-day Brandon.

No actual Neolithic dwellings have been discovered in Norfolk, but another hint as to possible north-eastern origins is given by three wedge-shaped unchambered burial mounds or long barrows characteristic of the Windmill Hill Culture; their closest Continental parallels are in Poland. Two of the Norfolk examples lie near the Icknield Way, the natural route to the Wessex downlands: Windmill Hill pottery has been found on the surface of the long barrows on Harpley Heath and at Ditchingham, and excavation of another at West Rudham disclosed evidence of ritual similar to that found on Wessex sites.

Another Neolithic group was the 'secondary' cultures formed from local Mesolithic communities who acclimatized themselves to the new farming techniques and other features. One such group, the Peterborough Folk, named after the Northamptonshire

* Remains from Hunstanton have been shown to be later than the deposits from which they were previously supposed to have come.

type site,* can be detected by their coarse impressed pottery. This has been found in Breckland and at one north-eastern site, Edingthorpe, where a hollow may have formed part of a hut. Grime's Graves, Weeting, seems to have been worked by these people also; for there is evidence of their distinctive Mesolithic-type techniques.

About 2000 B.C. or a little later a final Neolithic group arrived from the Low Countries and Middle Rhine – the 'Beaker' people. These were pastoralists who, with their characteristic S-profiled, bell-shaped pots and archer's equipment, seem on the Continent to have been connected with the earliest exploitation of copper. They were concentrated in Breckland and West Norfolk. Burial was as a rule in flat graves, and the occurrence of a small round barrow over such an inhumation at Cley-next-the-Sea suggests the influence of a more warlike north-eastern barrow-using group. As can be seen from a typical battle-axe found at Langley and made of stone indigenous to Schleswig-Holstein, these barrow-using people also made the journey across the North Sea. To a small degree this group may have been responsible for a British variant form too, the necked beaker, likewise concentrated in Breckland. They were also predominantly pastoralists, and no settlement structures have been found. At Trowse Newton, amongst a number of mounds was a double-ditched round barrow with necked beaker inhumations. Near by at Arminghall is a large circular 'henge' monument with a single entrance into an enclosure defined by an outer bank and slight ditch and a larger inner ditch. The central horseshoe setting of oak posts recalls Stonehenge, with whose earliest phase such monuments are contemporary.

This brings us to about 1700 B.C. and the beginning of a bronze-using age. Contemporary with the latest evidence of the beaker folk, a northern culture characterized by the so-called 'Food Vessel', whose form suggests an ancestry in Peterborough Ware, filtered into Breckland. Besides finds at Needham, Swannington, and Wereham, the inhumation of a young girl with a copper and jet bead necklace found at Methwold probably belongs to this group. There are no noteworthy structures, however, until the succeeding phase, and these are again funerary: the ditched round barrows of the 'Wessex' culture,‡ the wealthy warrior traders who set out c.1500 in a north-easterly direction via the Icknield Way, from their central area astride trade routes

* *See Buildings of England: Northamptonshire, p. 15.*

‡ Only the most important barrow groups are noted in the gazetteer.

from the Continent and the metalliferous regions of Ireland. The Wessex Culture – also pastoral – now has only its barrows, in particular the bell and disc forms, to remind us of the adventurousness of a group which left its mark even on the wind-swept islands of Orkney. Such barrows occur at Rushford, West Rudham, Great Bircham, Weasenham All Saints, and Little Cressingham. At Little Cressingham a contracted male burial was found with two daggers, a necklace of Baltic amber beads, and gold work, which point to the same early date as the Bush Barrow 'Founder's' burial of the Normanton group to the w of Stonehenge. On the other hand a barrow at Reffley, King's Lynn, contained a number of urns filled with cremated bone and, in one case, a ring and segmented bead of faience paste imported from the Eastern Mediterranean some time in the fifteenth millennium B.C.

At this time the urn with cremation as the common rite was general. The urns often had a collared or overhanging rim; they are, like the Food Vessels, of Secondary Neolithic descent. Sometimes these cremations were merely insertions in earlier burial mounds, although Norfolk has some dozen or more sizeable barrow groups which may belong to this period. Towards the latter part of the Bronze Age, c.1200, when metal finds are restricted to what seem to have been private hoards (Downham Market) or the discarded stock-in-trade of itinerant smiths (e.g. two groups from Norwich), flat cemeteries occur but rarely, although there is a strong contrast with the large urnfields of South-East Anglia; at Salthouse Heath for example a number of tiny mounds was added to the earlier barrows constructed from Beaker times. The most spectacular evidence for structures belongs, alas, to the days before scientific excavation. In Breckland, as at Mickle Mere, artificial islands, a sort of poor man's version of the famous Somerset lake villages, were found with their attendant domestic rubbish. After 1000 B.C. new bronze types, such as leaf-shaped swords (e.g. at Caistor St Edmund), gold dress-fasteners of Irish origin from Caister-by-Yarmouth, and a group of objects of West European manufacture, suggesting a re-awakening of foreign contacts, although for much of the Bronze Age Norfolk seems to have been a cultural backwater.

About 500 B.C. or earlier, farming groups from the region of the Low Countries once more appeared in East Anglia. One group, connected with others in Cambridgeshire and Northamptonshire, settled in Breckland, avoiding the Fens, which had again been rendered uninhabitable by a rise in sea-level. At this time, the dawn of the Iron Age, there was a certain amount of new coastal occupation, e.g. at Stiffkey where there is a single Iron Age barrow. Evidence from Snettisham and elsewhere indicates co-existence with the Late Bronze Age inhabitants, but remains are again slight, except for the range of coarse pottery types.

One settlement outside the area of the Late Bronze Age must be mentioned, the only Early Iron Age site in Norfolk whose complete plan has been recorded. This is Micklemoor Hill, West Harling (excavated between 1932 and 1953), overlooking the river Thet. It consisted of three enclosures, two with circular houses (one of these with a central open area and external ditch) and one with a rectangular building which is closer in plan to the simple type of farmhouse of contemporary northern Europe. By 300 B.C. a slight smoothing off in the profile of the local pottery indicates a general evolution of local craftsmanship which was to remain more or less unchanged until well into the Roman occupation. In this later phase rectangular huts have been deduced from excavations at Snarehill, but only in the c3 B.C., with the arrival in Breckland and Western Norfolk of a more warlike group from Northern France, do we get visible evidence of large-scale construction. The hill-forts of Narborough, Tasburgh, and South Creake may have been constructed in this disturbed period; the extended burial at Shouldham of a man with an iron sword is a typical grave of these 'Marnian' warriors.

Some tribal system is deducible from Caesar's accounts of his campaigns in Southern Britain. At that time a third Iron Age group, the Belgae, Celts of trans-Rhenish origin who had arrived c.100 B.C., were establishing themselves round a number of tribal centres or *oppida*. Of the earlier, non-Belgic, groups, the 'Ceni-magi' who sent tribute to Caesar may in fact represent the Iceni, Boudicca's tribe, an amalgam of a sw group perhaps with its headquarters in Cambridgeshire and an e group centred round Tasburgh; the first coinage issue of the Iceni dates from the late c1 B.C. The society of the day can best be judged from such rich hoards as those at Ringstead with its decorated horse bits, Ken Hill, Snettisham, with its famous gold alloy torcs found with Franco Belgic coins probably imported as scrap, and c1 A.D. Santon, with linch pins and iron nave bands. At Arminghall a considerable amount of later Iron Age pottery suggests a possible re-use of the Neolithic sanctuary. The rise to supremacy in the se of the Belgic Catuvellauni centred on Camulodunum (Roman Colchester) is reflected in the fact that Norfolk pottery began to imitate certain features of Belgic wheel-turned wares. The outworks of Thetford Castle, too, may represent an emergency strengthening of the frontier of the Iceni at this time, as may the construction of the larger hill-forts at Holkham and Warham – although Warham has been taken in another context (*see* below, p. 23).

The Belgic threat was postponed by the Claudian invasion of A.D. 43. Realization that this timely respite might only be the prelude to fresh domination led however to the abortive native uprising of A.D. 47–8, although Prasutagus, the king of the Iceni, managed to direct local affairs without undue Roman pressure. Coins and pottery are indeed the only substantial signs of Roman infiltration. The violation of his family after Prasutagus's death, however, and the climax of provincial Roman rapacity, resulted in the, at first, all-successful revolt under the king's widow, Boudicca (A.D. 60–1). But the Iceni were finally defeated, and harsh retribution followed at the hands of Suetonius. There was mass deportation to the then deserted Fens; hoards such as that at Santon and a temporary native camp at Thornham may be a result of this troubled time.

This is the background to the improvements in tactical communications undertaken by the Romans. From c. A.D. 70 we have evidence for the earliest part of the comprehensive road network, although Norfolk never became a much Romanized area even at the height of the occupation. The first highway was the Pye Road, the trunk route from the now Roman *colonia* of Camulodunum via a posting station at Scole* to Caistor St Edmund, which as Venta Icenorum became the new cantonal capital.‡ At first a simple affair with a network of streets running between wattle huts, it was much improved in the C2 and early C3 A.D. by the addition of public buildings and the surrounding masonry wall which can still be seen enclosing the central area. Another important route was the Fen Road from the industrial centre of Caistor-on-Nene (*see The Buildings of England: Northamptonshire*, p. 19) via Denver to Smallburgh and perhaps on to Caister-by-Yarmouth. Here, c.125 – when Venta Icenorum was first enlarged – a small defended port was constructed. The Fen Road had at least two timber bridges, one by the Old Bedford River and a second across the Wensum at Worthing. Peddar's Way (of the late C1 A.D.), running from Stanton in Suffolk via Castle Acre, near the junction with the Fen Road, continues on to Holme-next-the-Sea, where there may have been a ferry to link with the

* Possibly the Villa Faustina of the Antonine Itinerary.
‡ Identified also as Icinos in the Itinerary.

roads to Lincoln. In contrast to these military routes, more or
less parallel with Peddar's Way, the old prehistoric Icknield Way
seems to have been used for local traffic from Thetford to
Hunstanton; the Good Sand region formed the centre of the most
Romanized area, with small settlements such as Snettisham and
Narford. Here too are Grimston and Gayton Thorpe, two of the
major villas in the county. In contrast, Woodcock Hall and
Brettenham are by Peddar's Way, and on the heavier soils of the
s Lopham and Tivetshall are also sizeable villas. Among other
routes, a road ran from the coast at Holkham linking settlements
at Sculthorpe and Toftrees, and another, a short gravel stretch,
additional to the main plan of Venta Icenorum, possibly ran NE
down to a staithe on the river Yare.

Now back to the general history of construction. There is
evidence for industry in the North and West from the late C1 A.D.
with salt-works at Denver and Runcton Holme, a typical local
settlement where Romanization only really begins to show in the
reign of Hadrian (117–38). Pottery kilns have been found at
Morley and also around Hevingham. Ranworth offers the first
certain evidence for exploitation of the local iron ores; by the C2
Ashwicken had six shaft furnaces. Local agriculture in the region
of the Fen Road can still be seen in the pattern of rectangular
fields s and w of Downham Market, while another area is centred
on a Roman building at Hockwold-cum-Wilton in the Little
Ouse valley. In the religious sphere barrow burial continued
(Burnham Thorpe, excavated in 1862), but in the C3 three
Romano-Celtic temples were constructed in and near Venta
Icenorum.

By the close of the century inundations caused widespread
destruction in the Fens. At the same time, increasing Saxon raids
led to the construction of a chain of forts from the Solent to the
Wash: Burgh Castle (Gariannonum; *see The Buildings of England:
Suffolk*, p.116) and Brancaster (Branodunum), whose site is now
more than a mile from the coast, once commanded the Wash
approaches. Situated between Peddar's Way and the Toftrees
road, it was a square of 6¼ acres. Its walls were 11 ft thick, and it
had an internal rampart and an external ditch. It also had internal
angle towers and central gateways. The main occupation can
be dated to the late C3 A.D., although the ditch and gates are
typical of C2 forts, and some of the pottery supports an earlier
date of occupation. From the crossing at Worthing 18 miles SE
come two C3 ornamented cavalry helmets of probable Danubian
manufacture; c.400 there was a Dalmatian unit stationed at

Brancaster. Such villas as Gayton Thorpe and Appleton were deserted *c.*320, and the cantonal capital suffered a considerable eclipse. Following a disastrous defeat in 367, the shore defences were strengthened, and, as a desperate measure, *foederati* were introduced, mercenary settlers from the Saxon homelands of North Germany, whose pottery has been found at Caister and in the W of the county. The forts seem to have been garrisoned until 407–8, but by 425 Britain was left to work out her own salvation with only the *foederati* to act as dubious protection; the rich Fenland farms were completely deserted. The sub-Roman population of the early C5, continuing to strike their own copies of Roman coinage, may, in an effort to control the newcomers, have constructed the various stretches of linear earthworks after 390, as we know them from excavations of the Foss Ditch and Launditch. The latter barred traffic on the Fen Road.

Evidence for early ANGLO-SAXON settlement is really limited to the cremation cemeteries at such sites as Castle Acre, Pensthorpe, and the large cemetery outside Caistor St Edmund. By *c.*525 the spread of inhumation shows the influence of the Danish Wuffingas dynasty (to one of whose members the Sutton Hoo cenotaph was raised). From the close of this period date a few squalid huts at Postwick, Snettisham, and Thetford – the last example preceding the important C9 township. A few inhumations under barrows occur, e.g. at Sporle. Christianity was given considerable support by the last of the Wuffingas, Aelfwald (d. *c.*740), and as early as 673 North Elmham was declared a separate see. For the latter part of the early Saxon period (*c.* 650–850) the best we have for a settlement plan is the scatter of huts within the ruins of Roman Caister-by Yarmouth, and round and rectangular houses at Sedgeford. At Norwich there is as yet no evidence of a township as early as late C7–early C8 Ipswich.

The main historical feature of the late Saxon period (to 1066), when probably began the extensive peat digging which was to form the Broads, is the commencement of the Danish raids in 841. In 865 the 'Great Army' landed on the East Anglian coast, attacked York, and ravaged Mercia. Wintering at Thetford, they probably established the earliest widespread occupation on the site. Despite the indisputable historical facts, however, there is little or no tangible evidence for the Danish settlement to A.D. 920, although the circular camp at Warham has often and wrongly been claimed to be a Viking military centre because of its superficial similarity to such Danish sites as Trelleborg and Fyrkat. One result of the late C9 Danish settlement seems to have

been a considerable increase in trade and population; there were
townships of up to 5,000 inhabitants. It is unfortunate that subsequent occupation has destroyed the early structural history of
Norwich, the largest town with dense Danish settlement to the
E and S. At Thetford ('Ðeodford' = the chief ford) on the other
hand, which established itself on the Icknield Way crossing of the
Thet and Little Ouse, houses of the C10–11 have been found.

Finally, concerning ANGLO-SAXON CHURCH ARCHITEC-
TURE, there are really only two facts in need of recording here:
the only survival in England of a Saxon cathedral, and the problem
of the Norfolk round towers. North Elmham was a see till 1075,
when the see was removed to Thetford, where it stayed for only
nineteen years finally to establish itself at Norwich. The cathedral of Elmham, preserved in a state sufficiently good to under-
stand its plan and elevation, is a disappointment as far as size is
concerned. It is a small building and, moreover, was reconstructed towards the end of the Saxon period so that nothing
earlier than the late C10 remains. In its final form of the early C11
the cathedral had an interesting plan, unusual for England but
not without Continental parallels. It is distinguished by an apse
immediately attached to a relatively far-projecting transept, i.e.
what one calls a T-plan and what is an Early Christian and early
medieval type, and it has, in addition to a W tower, two thin
towers in the angles between transepts and aisleless nave. This
grouping of towers is a remote reflection of customs of the Holy
Roman Empire rather than of earlier Anglo-Saxon customs.

W3		For the ROUND TOWERS also one ought to look to the Con-
tinent for precedent or parallels. They have been explained – on
the material plane – as the natural result of having to build in
flint rather than stone, and hence being at a loss what to do to
produce firm corners. But it should also not be forgotten that the
round tower seems to have been a motif of Italy as well as the
Empire in the C9 and C10. The earliest datable example exists on
parchment only: the two detached round towers on the famous
plan of c. 835 for the monastery of St Gall. Italian examples of
brick may be earlier, but current scholarship does not accept the
detached campanili of Ravenna as of the same time as the
churches to which they belong. They are supposed to date only
from the C9. The type, however, is likely to be older, and St Gall
the result of Italian influence rather than the other way round.
About the year 1000, cathedrals in the Empire liked round
towers, but they were in pairs, not detached (Gernrode, Augs-
burg, Mainz, etc.). For the round towers of Ireland experts

again tend to discount an origin before the C9, and as regards East Anglia Cautley wishes to take their introduction back to the C9 and C10 and pleads for their being at first detached structures for defence. Of all the round towers of England – a total of just under 180 – Norfolk possesses 119, Suffolk 41, and Essex 8. In Norfolk there are distinctly more in the E than in the W half. Of these round towers the majority is no doubt Norman, but there are good arguments in favour of an Anglo-Saxon dating in about twenty cases. Most of the round towers are completely plain, but Thorpe-next-Haddiscoe, Kirby Cane, and Tasburgh have flat blank arcading of different kinds. The bell-openings are of the familiar twin type with a dividing column set far back and the heads of the openings either round or often triangular. In addition there are circular windows, in naves as well as towers, an Anglo-Saxon feature not universally English. They may, like so many Saxon motifs and customs, have been carried on after the Norman Conquest, as workmen do not change when rulers change. Gissing certainly seems Norman, in spite of its round windows, and there is one wholly mysterious round window in the E wall of the W range of the cloister of Norwich Cathedral. Normal oblong round-headed windows of before (and perhaps after) the Conquest are characterized by double splays as against the single splays of the Norman style. Long-and-short work also can serve as a recognition mark. Herringbone laying of stone or flint on the other hand, and also the use of carstone in square blocks, seem to be common features of the C11, before and after 1066. Apart from round towers central towers occur, the most impressive at Weybourne, with blank arcading, another formerly at Guestwick is probably of the Saxo-Norman overlap, and a third at Great Dunham definitely of after 1066. For Anglo-Saxon decoration it is sufficient to mention one cross, at Whissonsett, whose head in a circle is preserved, the strange coffin-lid at Rockland All Saints with two cross-heads and interlace carved in, and that most remarkable survival, the arms of the Bishop's Throne in Norwich Cathedral. They seem to come one from a bishop's throne, the other from stalls. Both appear to date from the C8 and will therefore have been made for North Elmham. The arrangement there was no doubt that of Early Christian churches in the Mediterranean area such as Parenzo, i.e. with the stalls semicircularly along the apse and the throne on a raised platform in the middle facing W. The arrangement of the throne was repeated when it was put up at Norwich. The decoration of the arms with coils and beasts unfortunately is almost effaced.

Of NORMAN DECORATION Norfolk does not yield much
more. There are in fact about seventy doorways left with some
decoration,* but in a survey of Norman doorways in England
hardly more than half a dozen of them would find a place, say,
w6 Hales, Heckingham, and Larling, and Wroxham, glorious and
w5b barbaric, and Haddiscoe, because it has an image above, Barton
Bendish and Burlingham St Edmund because of the beakhead
motif used.‡ This motif occurs more plentifully in the portal of
the keep of Norwich Castle. A peculiar motif of bobbins is to be
found at Hales, Heckingham, Castle Acre, Ashby St Mary, Hell-
ington, and Langford. Tympana are of extreme rarity, and,
where they appear, they are modest in their decoration: just a
cross at Tottenhill and just a pattern of lozenges inside Norwich
Cathedral.

B5   Norwich Cathedral is of course the centre of NORMAN
ARCHITECTURE in Norfolk, but it was originally accompanied
by four major abbey churches, Binham, Castle Acre, Wymondham, and Thetford. Of all four much survives, even if not all.
They were all large, the cathedral 407 ft long, Norman Wymondham about 250 ft, Norman Castle Acre about 200 ft. The cathedral was begun in 1096, Castle Acre and Binham about 1090,
Wymondham and Thetford in 1107. Of the Norman cathedral
nearly all is preserved, of Wymondham and Binham mostly the
w4 naves, of Castle Acre and Thetford only ruins. In Norwich
B20 building must have gone on consistently and without a break so
& 6a that by about 1140 all was complete, except perhaps the crossing
towers. What we see of Wymondham, Castle Acre, and Thetford
follows in the wake of Norwich and is work of c.1120–50. At
B21 Binham the surviving details are close to the w end and point to
as late a date as c.1175. In plan the five buildings represent the
two principal types of Romanesque planning: the type with the
staggered E chapels and the type with the chapels radiating from
an ambulatory. The latter is what we see at Norwich, the former
what we know of Binham, Castle Acre, Thetford, and Wymondham. The staggered plan means a chancel with apse flanked by
chancel aisles with apses and a further apsed chapel E of the N
and E of the s transept. The plan with the radiating chapels is
varied at Norwich in a curious and typically English way by not
letting the NE and SE chapels face NE and SE, but adjusting them
by means of a visually confusing arrangement of ante-chapels so
that they can face due E. As far as elevation is concerned, Nor-

* And a few chancel arches.
‡ At Burlingham left unfinished.

wich, Binham, Castle Acre, and Wymondham had a big gallery with entirely unsubdivided openings, the system of St Étienne in Caen and Old St Paul's in London. Thetford and Wymondham had façades with two w towers and a crossing tower, Norwich and Binham no prominent motif to enhance the dignity of the façade. But Norwich has of course the most swagger and at the same time the most individual and idiosyncratic of all Norman crossing towers. It is highly decorated, but decorated entirely by means of bold, easily recognizable and easily remembered geometrical motifs, chiefly circles or bull's eyes and lozenges. Otherwise Norwich Cathedral is remarkably averse to ornament, with the exception of one moment in its history, about 1120, when the plan was changed and circular piers introduced decorated with the splendid, large incised motifs which are best known at Durham. At Norwich they were soon given up again and a return to the original plan proclaimed. But Castle Acre took them over. Still, Norwich appears to us perhaps more rigid in its refusal to accept ornamental enrichment than it appeared in the C12. For there exists, not *in situ*, a group of extremely prettily and vividly decorated capitals of about 1140 which probably belonged to the Norman cloister. The only comparable thing in Norwich itself is the main portal of the keep, which also has small figures. This dates from about 1160. Only one more piece of Norman figural sculpture in Norwich can supplement this evidence: the statue of a bishop outside the N E40b transept, which has convincingly been suggested as being the funeral effigy of Bishop Losinga who began the cathedral and was after his death in 1119 buried in the chancel. If that is so, the figure would be the earliest funeral effigy in England.

Norwich Cathedral is one of the MONASTIC cathedrals of England. The monks and prior were Benedictines. Benedictine also were Binham and Wymondham. Castle Acre and Thetford were Cluniac. Norfolk is astoundingly rich in monastic foundations, and though no others are as well preserved as these five, of many more substantial fragments survive, and a few words must be said about them. The Benedictines, the oldest monastic order, had establishments at Horsham St Faith, where the chief remaining fragment is the Norman entry to the chapter house, at Blackborough (Middleton) and Winnold, where nothing worth speaking of is preserved, and also ceils at King's Lynn, where the church of St Margaret perhaps owes its (excavated) hexagonal chapter house and its two-tower w front – an unusual thing for a parish church – to their vicinity, and at Great Yarmouth, and

in addition, nunneries at Thetford and Carrow just outside
Norwich. At Carrow the plan incorporated a straight Norman E
end like that of the nunnery church of Romsey in Hampshire.
At Thetford the church was aisleless and had a s transept with a
grand arch leading into it. Thetford was altogether remarkably
rich in monastic houses. Apart from the Cluniac priory and the
Benedictine nunnery there was a house of the Augustinian
Canons, which had more settlements in Norfolk than any other.
Of Great Massingham, Hempton, Old Buckenham, Peterstone
Priory (Burnham Overy), and Weeting little is to be seen,
of the C13 buildings of Flitcham and Weybridge (Acle) hardly
more. C13 remains are at Hickling, at Weybourne, interestingly
mixed up with the pre-existing Anglo-Saxon parish church,
at Beeston Regis, where the straight-ended chancel with tall
blank arcading is the token of the priory, at Coxford (Tatter-
sett), where there is no more than some big arches, and at Creake
w22a Abbey (North Creake), where the E and W crossing arches as
well as the chancel walls remain. West Acre had a front wider
than nave and aisles, as excavations have shown. Of the famous
shrine of Little Walsingham there is mainly the dramatic late C14
E wall. Of Cluniac houses other than Castle Acre and Thetford
E23awe need only note one more, Broomholm (Bacton), as famous as
Walsingham and even less eloquently preserved. The Cister-
cians and Premonstratensians had little impact on the county.
No more exists of the former than the fine C13 s wall of the
church of the nunnery of Marham, no more of the latter than
insignificant bits at West Dereham and Wendling and one substantial fragment of Langley. In addition only the Gilbertines at
Shouldham (c1190)* and the Trinitarians at Ingham (1360)
need a passing reference, and then we come to the friars.
The Franciscans (Greyfriars) had a house at King's Lynn,
and here the impressive tower survives which, according to
the curious custom of England, was built above the dividing
E13a space between nave and chancel. The Dominican (Blackfriars)
church of Norwich is impressively large (265 ft) and preserved
completely, except for the tower, a unique survival in a county
in which hatred against the friars ran so high in the C16. Lynn
also had Austin Friars and Carmelites (Whitefriars). The Carmelites moreover had a house at Burnham Norton to which
reference will be made presently, and one at Blakeney (founded
in 1296) which has almost disappeared. At Great Yarmouth
there were Franciscans, Dominicans, and Austin Friars, the

* Nothing preserved.

latter across the river at Gorleston, at Thetford Dominicans and Austin Friars, at Walsingham Franciscans, and finally at Norwich Franciscans, Dominicans, Carmelites, and Austin Friars. Of all these houses little survives, and in one or two cases nothing. The remains worth looking for are those of the Blackfriars church at Thetford, the Blackfriars cloister at Norwich, the Whitefriars gatehouse at Lynn, and the unusual Little Cloister of the Greyfriars at Walsingham.

But monastic living quarters must be kept separate from churches, and nothing has yet been said of those of the older orders. There the record is this: first of all of course the Norman refectory, infirmary, and parlatorium at Norwich Cathedral, then the excavated plans and remaining crags at Thetford, including the infirmary with a small cloister, then the E.E. dormitory undercroft and refectory with pulpit at Walsingham and the strangely small and domestic refectory of the Benedictine cell at Great Yarmouth, then the cellarium at Langley Abbey, the tunnel-vaulted chapter house and the extensive lavatory arrangements at Castle Acre, the Prioress's House at Carrow Abbey, E49a and finally the many surviving gatehouses, preserved because so obviously useful even after the Dissolution. Of St Benet's Abbey (Ludham) e.g., one of the leading abbeys of Norfolk, there is little more than the gatehouse, and others are at Binham, Broomholm, Burnham Norton, Castle Acre, Pentney, Thetford, w49b and West Acre.

This annotated list of monastic buildings has taken us far beyond the Norman style: in fact with the prioress's house at Carrow and the gatehouse at Castle Acre to the very end of the Middle Ages. We must now, however, return to the C12 and examine what is notable of NORMAN PARISH CHURCHES. There is of course much – doorways have already been mentioned – but most of it is of no more than local interest. Hales e.g. is a perfectly preserved village church of round tower, nave, and chancel. There are also quite a number of Norman central towers, and of these the central space is best preserved at Gillingham, but on a larger scale are only the central towers of Attleborough and, decorated with several tiers of blank arcading, of South Lopham. To these ought to be added the s w tower of St w5a Margaret King's Lynn.* That leaves us with three major parish churches, all three Late Norman: Walsoken, Tilney All Saints, and Castle Rising. Walsoken is grand indeed. Its arcades of seven wooa

* Chedgrave incidentally has a NE tower, which is a very uncommon thing.

bays have alternating circular and octagonal piers (cf. Peterborough Cathedral). Tilney All Saints, although more mixed in
appearance, is also to its full extent Late Norman. Here the piers
of the seven-bay arcade are all round, and the original clerestory
is preserved. At Castle Rising the most interesting parts are the
rib-vaulted space under the central tower and the w façade with
its blank arcading. This was a motif much favoured in England,
and it is also used to enrich the appearance of larger surfaces,
and indeed whole major façades. So it is at Castle Acre Priory,
so up the walls of whole parts of the keep of Castle Rising Castle
and nearly the whole of the keep of Norwich Castle.

w48b
E46

These two are completely exceptional among the NORMAN
CASTLES of England, and indeed the Romanesque castles of
France, in applying such extensive external decoration to what is
after all a severely functional building. The Norwich and Castle
Rising keeps belong to the type for convenience's sake called hall
keeps, that is keeps longer than they are high. Both are among
the largest in England, Norwich being only a little smaller than
the White Tower in London, and both were consequently subdivided into two main rooms on each of the two principal floors.
At Castle Rising the most interesting part is the forebuilding; at
Norwich this has gone, but there are the remains of the chapel
partly fitted into a corner of what appears to be a vaulted private
cabinet of the governor. The Norwich keep stands on a mound
partly natural but mostly artificial, and it is one of the most impressive of Norman earthworks in England. At Castle Acre,
where not much else except the earthworks remains, they are just
as impressive. The remains of the bailey here are interesting too.
At Norwich they do not exist any longer. To these castles must
be added among the so-called MOTTE-AND-BAILEY CASTLES
Old Buckenham, with an enclosure of a most unusual oblong
shape, New Buckenham, with big mound and ditch and the
featureless ruin of a round keep, and also Thetford, Bessingham,
Horsford, Mileham, Morley, Swanton Morley, and Wormegay.

w48a

New Buckenham was built about 1145–50 etc. to replace Old
Buckenham. Its round keep may therefore well be the earliest in
England. At the same time probably the little town was laid out.
It is a rare case of the survival of a town plan of that date. Norwich received its first stone walls in the C12 too. But their present appearance – and they are remarkably extensive – dates from
between 1294 and c.1320. Long stretches survive, though with
little detail, and a number of towers. The area enclosed is as large
as that of the City of London, a reminder of the importance of

Norwich as one of the three or four largest towns of England.*
No civic structure of so early a date stands in Norwich, but
Great Yarmouth has its Tolhouse, which is at least largely of the
late C13, though it may originally have been a private house and
not a public building. Norman secular remains in Norwich are
confined to the small Lazar House in outer Norwich and the
interesting, even if not very telling, late C12 Music House at
Norwich, unless one wishes to supplement this scanty evidence
by the equally scanty remains of Norman work in the Bishop's
Palace. Much more impressive are the late C13 hall windows of
the prior's lodgings (later deanery). The C13 in Norfolk is on the
whole, however, also poor in secular remains, whether house or
castle. When the undercroft of Stranger's Hall in Norwich and
the gatehouse of Castle Acre are mentioned, all is said that needs
saying.

It is different with regard to EARLY ENGLISH CHURCHES.
Here there is plenty. The first building to be mentioned is West
Walton, another Marshland church, and as splendid in the C13
style as Walsoken was in the style of the late C12. It must be the
work of masons trained at Lincoln, and its round piers with four w2ob
and even eight detached shafts and exciting stiff-leaf capitals are w21a
unforgettable. The clerestory is original too, and so is the power- w7
ful detached tower. The motifs of West Walton find their parallels in other Norfolk churches. A detached tower was e.g. built
at Terrington St Clement, and in addition Norwich Cathedral
received a massive detached 'clocher' in the C13 which was
placed to the NW of the front at some distance, and of which not
a stone is visible any more, and East Dereham has an early C16
tower to the S of the E end. A Suffolk example like Beccles may
also be added, as the identity of Norfolk and Suffolk features will
have to be referred to quite often. Other prominent E.E. towers
in Norfolk are Walsoken, Tilney All Saints, and St Nicholas
King's Lynn. To these one ought to append a sentence on octagonal towers; for already in the C13, perhaps as an encasing job
of an earlier round tower, occasionally a tower was built octagonal from the ground. This is the case at Toft Monks and Old
Buckenham.‡

The PIERS of West Walton have their closest parallels at
Grimston (four shafts) and at St Margaret King's Lynn (four as

---

* A reference to the TOWN WALLS of Great Yarmouth and King's Lynn
must not be forgotten. Lynn has kept at least one of its town gates, though
this is of the C16.

‡ And later at Billingford, Edgefield, and Kettlestone.

well as eight shafts). But this is not a customary design in Norfolk. The majority of E.E. arcades have round piers (Weybourne, and about ten other churches) or round alternating with
octagonal piers, i.e. the arrangement chosen in the later C12 at
Walsoken, Aylsham, Reymerston, Thornham. Quatrefoil sections
also occur, with semicircular foils (Letheringsett, Great Massingham), or with hollows between the foils so deep that it looks
almost like four detached shafts (Northwold, with rich stiff-leaf
capitals, and some others in the neighbourhood), or with thin
shafts inserted in the diagonals, a motif more of the C14 than the
C13 (Yaxham) or an alternation of quatrefoil and circular (Burnham Overy). Arches are on the whole simple and have hollow
chamfers more often than the normal chamfers.

w8   Of other elements or motifs the SOUTH PORCH of Great
Massingham (with open side arcading) and the CHANCELS of
E22a Burgh-next-Aylsham, Great Cressingham (with mighty wall-
arches), and Wramplingham (as late as about 1280) should be
E22b looked at, and that of Blakeney emphatically also, because it is
rib-vaulted. At Norwich Cathedral incidentally there is hardly
anything to represent the E.E. style. The former Chapel of St
Catharine (now Dean's Vestry), also rib-vaulted, is all that remains, as the mid-C13 Lady Chapel was pulled down except for
the double arch which led into it. This has dog-tooth decoration,
but Norfolk on the whole possesses very little of E.E. decoration;
the finest pieces perhaps are the double PISCINAS of Harding-
w21b ham and Pulham St Mary, both of the delightful composition of
Jesus College, Cambridge, that is with an arch intersected by two
half-arches.*

Norfolk has two major E.E. WEST FRONTS. That at Great Yar-
E7 mouth introduces to the largest of all English parish churches,
of the C13 certainly and perhaps of the whole Middle Ages, a
church, however, which unfortunately was badly damaged in the
Second World War and restored or internally rebuilt not as it
had been, but in an imitation-Gothic style. The other major E.E.
E6b façade is that of Binham Priory, splendid even in its ruined state,
and of the greatest historical interest in so far as it can be firmly
dated to before the year 1244 and yet has bar tracery on the
grandest scale. Westminster Abbey was begun in 1245 and is
usually considered the first example of this new, airier kind of
tracery created at Reims in the design of 1211 and amplified from
a two-light to a four-light pattern at Amiens after 1220. In this

---

* The angle piscina at Baconsthorpe has bar tracery. From about 1300
onwards angle piscinas become frequent in Norfolk.

particular connexion, to compare the very small with the very large, the fragment of a figure at West Acre Priory ought to be introduced, as it clearly formed part of the decoration of the voussoirs of a portal and thus also links up with Westminster Abbey.

The w window of Binham is the paradigm of Geometrical tracery at its purest: four lights and two small and one large foiled circle, all kept clearly separate. Later in the century composition and motifs grew more varied and more restless. Examples are the following. First the s side of the nave of Marham Abbey, which has round instead of oblong windows. The priory was founded before 1249. Then, valuable as a dated instance of the turn away from perfection, the E window of Trowse Newton, inscribed so as to make a date before 1288 certain. Here quatrefoils appear unencircled and also placed diagonally. Other instances of the same tendency, a little later still, are the E windows of North Creake, with unencircled trefoils and an unencircled w22a quatrefoil, and Carbrooke, with barbed trefoils and quatrefoils and so-called daggers. The chancel of North Creake was completed by 1301. Nowhere in this group are Geometrical motifs abandoned yet in favour of motifs including ogee curves.

This change established the DECORATED STYLE. Its first and most sumptuous monument is the portal of the cloister into E8 the s aisle of Norwich Cathedral. The cloister was rebuilt from E10b, 1297 onwards, and this portal must have come c.1310. It has 11,24, extremely good statuettes, matched in style and quality at Norwich in the adjoining bays of the E walk of the cloister and also in the portal to the Carnary Chapel begun in 1316, and it has E9 prominent ogee arches. The date 1301 makes the chancel of North Creake specially interesting: for here too, side by side with the cusped intersected tracery current in Late Geometrical work about 1300, are again ogee arches (Sedilia). Late Geometrical forms and motifs were not given up for a long time to come, and it is a sobering thought for the student who all the time tries to make up his mind about the dates of buildings and parts of buildings that Rushford College was founded in 1342, yet that all the details of the church look as if they were of about 1300. Moreover the chancel of South Lopham cannot have been started before 1361 and may well be a little later, and yet is wholly and unquestionably Dec. So while the student learns that Dec runs from 1300 to c.1350 and is then replaced by Perp, the actual dates in a county may well shift these ideal figures considerably.

The best examples in Norfolk of the fully matured Dec style in all its richness and luxuriance are the following. First Snet-
w9 tisham, complete with a Dec w front, a Dec spire,* and a clere-story with alternating two-light windows and circular windows –
E12a a motif to which we shall have to return. Secondly Cley, again with such a clerestory, with a s chapel with very wilful tracery and a crocketed gable, and also with very lavish doorways with cusped and subcusped ogee arches, a motif repeated at Ashill, Carbrooke, Elsing, Harpley, and the cloisters of Norwich Cathedral, and, with odd arches, other than ogee, at St Nicholas King's Lynn.‡ In the third place Elsing itself, built by Sir Hugh Hastings, who died in 1347. This is an aisleless church, spacious in nave as well as chancel, a type which was much favoured in Norfolk and carried on throughout the Perp style. Elsing has the widest of all naves – 40 ft. Cautley gives as others Winterton and East Tuddenham with 34 ft and Tittleshall and Bunwell with over 32. Number four: the Carnary Chapel in the cathedral precinct at Norwich, founded by Bishop Salmon in 1316. Its vaulted undercroft with foiled, cusped, and subcusped circular windows survives, and the upper chapel, though not with the original window tracery.§ Number five: Harpley, built between 1294 and 1332. This, apart from all other attractions, has a rib-vaulted vestry. Number six: the Blackfriars church (now St Andrew's Hall) at Norwich, which is mainly mid-c15, but whose s aisle windows and grand E window belong to the building erected after the house had moved to its present site in 1307 and may well be *in situ*. Number seven: Ingham, built before 1344, with fine flowing tracery in the E window. On the whole Norfolk is not a county for the most daring fantasies of flowing tracery. For that one must go to Lincolnshire. But there are fine examples, especially Syderstone, Watlington, and St John Maddermarket at Norwich. Number eight: Hingham, built by a man who was rector from 1319 to 1359, and num-bers nine and ten: the lavish Slipper Chapel at Houghton St Giles, close to the Shrine of Walsingham, and the parish church of Great Walsingham. Great Walsingham has two motifs which
w14b occur in other places: again a clerestory with circular windows,

* Norfolk is not a spire county – in spite of the memorable spire of the cathedral. Stone spires are scarce, and even lead-covered timber spires far from frequent.

‡ Doorways at Little Walsingham, Oulton, and Rollesby have cusped and subcusped normal arches.

§ For Bishop Salmon's Hall *see* the summary of medieval secular architec-ture on pp. 43–4.

and a particular detail in the window tracery which can be w14b
described as small reticulation inside a large reticulation unit.
This is to be found quite a bit round Walsingham and also at
Hilborough, Thompson, and in some other churches. Another
favourite motif, not confined however to the Dec style, is what is
here called the motif of the four-petalled flower, i.e. two figures
of eight, cusped and intersecting at r. angles. This is the *leitmotif* of Attleborough, which, from heraldry, seems as late as the w14a
late C14.

After tracery we must examine piers, arches, and vaults. Of
PIERS there is a great variety, and no details need to be given.
Generally it can be said that the quatrefoil shape and variations
on it (foils with fillets, thin round shafts or spurs or polygonal
shafts in the diagonals) are popular. Octagonal piers are equally
common and rarely of interest.* As for arches, double chamfers,
double-hollow chamfers, and especially sunk quadrant mouldings and sunk wave mouldings occur often. Where enrichment
was desired we find fleurons or shields or crowns up one hollow
of jambs and arch. This is done on an unusually large scale in
an arch thrown across the large chapel of St Thomas Becket at
Wymondham, over its w end. VAULTING before the C15 was,
it seems, confined to small compartments. The most usual pattern is the tierceron-star. This is the pattern of the Norwich
cloister, begun in 1297, and it was never changed until the four
walks were at last complete by *c.*1430. It is also the pattern of
many porches, especially in Norwich parish churches, of the w
tower of St Gregory Norwich, where it is repeated below the
gallery subdividing the space under the tower, and of the Greyfriars tower at King's Lynn (late C14). The earliest lierne-vaults,
that is vaults with subsidiary ribs not issuing from either the
springing point or the centre of the bays, are inside the Ethelbert Gate of Norwich Cathedral of 1316. It had few Norfolk
successors. The sumptuous flushwork along the top of the Ethel- E10a
bert Gate was heavily restored in the early C19, but is not a C19
addition.

FLUSHWORK is indeed a chief speciality of Norfolk, or rather
Suffolk and Norfolk. Flushwork is the patterning of a surface by
the contrast of freestone and knapped flint, i.e. flints split in half
so that smooth surfaces result which are thus exposed. The
pattern may be simply chequer or diapering, or initials or indeed
whole tracery motifs. The chancel at Wiveton, with complete

---

* Except for those with concave sides and little arches at the top of each
side (Dersingham, Narborough).

blank windows done in flushwork, must be as early and may
be earlier. But it has no known date. Similar blank windows
occur in the gatehouse of Butley Priory in Suffolk which can
be dated to *c*.1320. The earliest datable example in Norfolk
is the Ethelbert Gate with its flushwork rose-window at the top.
The next dated piece of flushwork in Norfolk is the gatehouse
of the Carmelite Friary of Burnham Norton. The date is 1353.
The tower of Elsing, begun, as we know, some time before
1347, has flushwork-panelled battlements. This was going to be a
set manner of enrichment for dozens of Norfolk towers. The *nec
plus ultra* of flushwork decoration in Norfolk are the tower of
w12a Redenhall and the s aisle and chancel N side of St Michael at
316a Coslany, Norwich, and these are definitely Perp work.

Altogether it must by now be clear that no sharp boundary can
be drawn between the Dec and Perp styles in Norfolk. The great
prosperity of the county came with the time of Edward III and
remained to the end of the Middle Ages. The large parish
churches, especially round King's Lynn, along the coast near
Yarmouth, and at Norwich, may be Dec or Perp. Their size,
their slender piers and wide aisles, or their wide naves without
aisles, are the same throughout the c14 and c15. Due to these
centuries of prosperity is of course also the existence of so many
parish churches in the county, more than in any other. Totals
have already been given. Here it might be added as one particular
illustration that in half a dozen or more cases two parish churches
lie in the same churchyard,* and in one case, Reepham, three. It
might also be added that this past prosperity is reflected nega-
tively in the many parish churches without an adjacent village –
some of them as grand as Terrington St Clement – and the sadly
many ruined parish churches.

Even if not significant in every respect, the boundary line between Dec and Perp, or rather the zone of overlap, is important
all the same – notably as a change of style. So the earliest examples of the PERPENDICULAR STYLE must be collected. They
E20 are as follows: the clerestory of the chancel of Norwich Cathedral rebuilt in the 1360s, and, exactly contemporarily, the nave,
three-storeyed s porch, and w tower of Ingham, for which licence
to rebuild was obtained in 1360. A three-storeyed porch is
unique in Norfolk, but two-storeyed porches are very frequent,
especially at Norwich, where they are often attached to, instead
of placed in front of, the aisle. The w tower of Ingham has

---

* Suffolk has one case: Trimley; Essex one: Willingale; Cambridgeshire
one: Swaffham Prior.

plenty of flushwork decoration, traceried sound-holes – a Norfolk speciality * – and Perp windows. Swanton Morley was rebuilt by Lord Morley c.1378, Worstead, a spectacularly large church, from 1379, Cawston from a date before 1414.

The junction of Dec and Perp has just been called a zone of overlap rather than a boundary line. The truth of this is patent in the interesting cases where, obviously as part of one design and one build, definitely Dec and definitely Perp tracery motifs appear side by side. Such is the case at Aldborough, at Belaugh, at Brandiston, Catfield, St George Tombland Norwich (c.1445), Tuttington, and Walcott. We shall see something similar later in fonts.

Now some general remarks on Late Medieval churches in Norfolk, and then some remarks on details. Generally, the most conspicuous fact is the large size of the parish churches of some parts of the county, of St Nicholas King's Lynn (a chapel of ease in fact!), of the Marshland churches around such as Walpole St Peter and Terrington St Clement, of some of the churches of Norwich and in particular St Peter Mancroft, St Stephen, St Laurence, and St Andrew, of some on the coast such as Blakeney, Salthouse, Cromer, Winterton, and of some others such as Salle and Redenhall. The Perp style, as a style of middle-class prosperity, benefits from being displayed big. Mr Theodore Gumbril knew this when he said: 'Perpendicular at its best – and its best is its largest – is the finest sort of English Gothic.' Not everyone will be with him in the second half of this statement; its first half is undeniable. So after large naves and chancels big and tall TOWERS in Norfolk: Cromer 160 ft, North Walsham originally 147 ft, Wymondham 142 ft, Winterton c.130 ft, and Hingham and St Giles Norwich c.120 ft. Spires, as has already been said, are rare. The tallest of them is of course that of the cathedral, which rises to 315 ft. This is followed by Snettisham, 175 ft from the ground. After Snettisham come Oxborough 150 ft (but spire and tower collapsed some years ago) and Methwold c.120 ft. A few churches have, instead of a spire, a pretty little spike or spirelet on top, lead-covered and held by flying buttresses. Such it is at St Peter Mancroft Norwich, and with more charm at Shipdham and East Harling. St Peter Mancroft has a processional way through the tower from S to N, the same arrangement as at Diss, Holme Hale, and Metton, and in addition a passage below the chancel, possibly because the ground

* They are in fact not sound-holes, but windows into the bell-ringers' room.

falls away here. This is repeated at Walpole St Peter and at St
Gregory Norwich. St Gregory also has a w porch, an exceptional
feature, as nearly all church porches are on the s and n sides. It is
however also to be found at Little Walsingham, Dec not Perp,
Garboldisham, North Elmham, and Swaffham. These porches
lead into w towers, and most towers in Norfolk as anywhere in
England, are at the w end of the nave. Norfolk has a number of
towers in other positions, but relatively speaking few, all the
same. Most of them are at the sw corner (e.g. St Nicholas Lynn
and Harpley), a few at the nw corner (e.g. Cley), and fewer still
on the s side E of the sw corner (e.g. Hardingham) or on the n
side E of the nw corner (e.g. St Stephen Norwich). In this context the two oddities of Wymondham and Blakeney must be
remembered. Wymondham has two mighty towers in axis, a w
tower belonging to the parochial and a crossing tower belong to
the monastic part of the church. At Blakeney, in addition to the
w tower, there is a slim beacon tower attached to the church on
its n side.

The Norfolk CLERESTORIES with circular windows or windows alternating between circular and a normal shape have been
referred to earlier on. There are many instances, both Dec and
Perp, and the circles are either foiled or traceried (at Snettisham
e.g. with three spherical triangles).* The majority is Dec, Shrop-
ham perhaps even c13, but Heacham and Terrington St Clement e.g. are Perp for certain. At Cley the circular windows are
cinquefoiled and the foils trefoil-cusped. At Stalham the normal
two-light windows between are feigned in flushwork. In some
cases the clerestory, often a later raising of the height of the
church, is so much higher than the chancel arch that an E window
becomes possible. One of the chief thrills of the great Perp
churches in Norfolk and the whole of East Anglia is the clerestory with very closely set windows, double the number of the
arcade bays below. These long even rows are as impressive from
outside as they are from inside, especially in conjunction with
the spectacular roofs that were at the same time installed. For
clerestories the score is as follows: St Peter Mancroft 17, St
Stephen Norwich 16, Loddon 15, Terrington St Clement 14,

----

* This is the place to remember circular windows in other parts of
churches – again a Dec rather than a Perp speciality. There is one in the w
wall at Shelfanger, one between chancel and vestry at East Harling, one in
the w wall of the s aisle at Woodrising, and the porch at Gooderstone has
circular windows too. At Brancaster and North Creake the porch windows
are quatrefoils, and next to the n doorway at Ringland there is a quatrefoiled
lozenge-shaped window.

EI2a

WII

EI5

Swaffham 13, Walpole St Peter 13,* Shelton (nave only) 9; for w17 roofs a simple scoring is impossible.

Norfolk is among the counties richest in, and most ingenious at, church ROOFS, even if unquestionably second to Suffolk. The most lavish types are the hammerbeam (Trunch, Wymondham, w24 Cawston, etc.) and double-hammerbeam roofs (Knapton, Gissing, E27b and Swaffham), the roofs with alternating major and minor &w23 hammerbeams (Fincham) or alternating major-beams and tie-beams (Outwell, Upwell, Emneth, Methwold, Northwold, etc.), or alternating hammerbeams and arched braces running up direct to the ridge or to collar-beams (Necton, Great Cressingham, St Giles Norwich), or indeed arched braces exclusively, a specially noble, because more restrained type (Salle, Stody, several E27a churches at Norwich). Special tit-bits are the roofs of St Peter Mancroft and Ringland, where (as at Framlingham in Suffolk) w25 the hammerbeams are hidden behind a ribbed coving such as are familiar from rood-lofts, the arched braces of St Mary at Coslany E28a Norwich, St Peter Hungate Norwich, and Stody, meeting at a crossing to form what seems a quadripartite rib-vault, and the panelled roofs of the s chapel at East Dereham with the ever-recurring motif of the lamb in a wreath and of the chancel of the Great Hospital at Norwich, with a painted black eagle in every panel.

Chancels and their surroundings need little comment. Some, once more as in Suffolk, have VESTRIES attached to their E, not their N wall. Thus it is at St Peter Mancroft and St Peter Permountergate Norwich, at Shelton and Wighton. At Blakeney and Yarmouth the vestry is inside the chancel behind the altar, at Tunstead a low tunnel-vaulted chamber is placed somewhat mysteriously below a raised E platform, and at Rollesby there is an odd corner chamber built into the chancel. PRIEST'S DOORWAYS into the chancel do odd things occasionally in Norfolk (and Suffolk). The one at Knapton has a little porch, and those of Trunch and Warham St Mary have a porch on which stands a buttress. LOW-SIDE WINDOWS are too many even for a mere inclusion in the gazetteer, let alone for listing in this introduction. They are only mentioned here to contradict the popular idea that they were provided for lepers to get a peep of the service. They were instead in all probability meant to allow for the Sanctus bell to be rung so that those outside the church knew when the moment of the Sanctus had been reached in the service.

* This compares with Suffolk as follows: Southwold 18, Blythburgh 18, Long Melford 18, Lavenham 12.

An argument in favour of this interpretation is that at Scarning, just inside, attached to the E side of the rood screen, is the wooden frame for the Sanctus bell. The low-side window at Melton Constable has a seat and book-rest. Special SANCTUS-BELL TURRETS exist in many places. Their usual position is on the E gable of the nave. It is sufficient to name Swaffham and Walpole St Peter and West Lynn. At Methwold and Upwell they are at the SE corner of the nave.

A motif much liked by the masons of Norfolk is BLANK ARCHES along the walls of an aisle or a chancel to embrace the windows. The earliest instance of this, at Great Cressingham in full C13, has been listed before. At Ellingham there is C13 evidence as well. Howe seems to be of c.1300, Rushford is of 1342 etc., Attleborough also Dec. Norwich has particularly many Perp examples. Of piers and window TRACERY there are too many varieties to discuss them in detail. As for tracery, apart from the limited number of national standard patterns, there are a few favourite motifs, and most in evidence that of a stepped and embattled transom high up, just where the head of a window starts. It may be stepped up and down for three lights, or up-down-up-down for five lights. That ARCHES are two-centred first, four-centred later, is a very rough-and-ready rule and would be borne out by statistics. But it does not apply always – not for instance in Gloucester Cathedral at the very start of the Perp style. In Norfolk a similar case is Swanton Morley, datable, as we have seen, to c.1378, and yet consistently using four-centred arches. Arches with straight shanks, if they can be called arches, also occur occasionally (e.g. Lyng) and tracery incorporating straight arches as well (e.g. Sporle).

PIERS continue in most of the previously accepted shapes, but many new ones are added to the repertoire. As for the old types, the octagonal is kept even in churches proud enough otherwise to have been more imaginative in this detail (Worstead, Cley, Cawston). The Dec quatrefoil pier is also kept, but one can watch how its moulded capitals turn Perp by turning polygonal, or how the foils of the quatrefoil turn polygonal altogether. The general tendency of the Perp pier is to go slenderer and to intensify this visually by going a lozenge shape, however detailed, with the longer axis in the N–S direction. Thus e.g. the piers at Didlington and Deopham are elongated octagons. Otherwise there are octagons with thin shafts in the main directions and very elongated diagonals made concave (St Andrew Norwich, Emneth). The same design in the more normal, duller, more even four-shafts-and-four-hollows way is that of St Peter Mancroft Norwich, of Salle and Salthouse. More complicated designs with elongated polygonal members without capitals towards nave and aisle and thin round polygonal shafts with capitals towards the arch openings are frequent (North Lopham, Fincham). A more elaborate moulding is that with two shallow hollows in the diagonals (Methwold) or a hollow and a wave (Shelton, St Martin- w22b at-Oak Norwich).

All these are variations of details. In general shape the Perp parish church is normal throughout in Norfolk, with only one EXCEPTION, the Red Mount Chapel at King's Lynn which was w13a begun in 1485 and is an octagon with the chapel proper elevated and reached by ingenious staircases and with an undercroft below. The centre of the chapel is fan-vaulted, again a great rarity in Norfolk.* VAULTING altogether recedes in the Perp centuries; for parish churches in England have no stone vaults. If it were not for the cathedral nothing would have to be reported, but the lierne-vaults of the cathedral, designed about 1450-60 for the nave and then carried on without change of plan in the chancel, the Bauchun Chapel, and the transepts (and also taken over in the s transept of the church of the Great Hospital) are spectacular enough.

The Red Mount Chapel introduces another point into this story. It is BRICK, and brick was then still a comparatively new material in England and one more readily accepted, at least in Norfolk, for domestic than for ecclesiastical building. The earliest datable use of brick in the county is at Norwich between 1370 and 1380, in the undercroft of what is now the Bridewell Museum, and in the Cow Tower, the strongest of the towers of E47a the town wall. The sudden surge into fashion however is a matter of the Early Tudor decades. In Norfolk churches by far the most memorable example is Shelton, a major church begun with w22b plenty of money shortly before 1487. With this we may join the churches of Wiggenhall St Mary and Wiggenhall St Mary Magdalene, the w tower of Walpole St Andrew, that of Wheatacre, w12b which is brick and flint in chequerwork, such porches as at Needham, and the n chapel at Outwell (of before 1527). Potter Heigham, true to its name, has even a Perp font of brick.

But where Norfolk is incomparable in England is in its SECULAR BRICK ARCHITECTURE of the later c15 and early c16.

---

* But the s porch of St Gregory Norwich is fan-vaulted and that of Shelton was at least intended to be fan-vaulted.

Brick, it will be remembered, was an exceptional material in England before that time, and in the earlier Middle Ages had been forgotten. It is true that recently Anglo-Saxon bricks have been found by Dr Jope at Oxford, that Polebrook in Suffolk has Norman bricks, Little Coggeshall in Essex and Little Wenham Hall in Suffolk E.E. bricks, and that the use of bricks in the C14 substantially increased. Holy Trinity Hull is the example of a major C14 brick church. But only the vigorous influence of the Netherlands and France in the C15 turned a utilitarian into a fashionable material. The best mid-C15 example in Norfolk is E47b Caister Castle of 1432-5. Second place is due to the mid-C15 gatehouse of Middleton Towers. Tattershall in neighbouring Lincolnshire is of 1431-9, Herstmonceaux of c.1445-50, Faulk-bourne in Essex of some time before 1440, Bishop Waynflete's tower at Farnham Castle in Surrey of c.1470-5, the Bishop's Palace at Hatfield of c.1480, the Bishop of Lincoln's palace at Buckden in Bedfordshire of 1480-94, Kirby Muxloe Castle in W50 Lincolnshire of 1480-5, Oxburgh in Norfolk of 1482. With Oxburgh the great line of grand and ornate brickwork in the county begins. Work in Suffolk cannot be separated. In Norfolk W51b the principal buildings are Great Cressingham, Northwold, E50a Denver Hall, East Barsham, Great Snoring. East Barsham Manor is *facile princeps* of the group. It is to a certain extent fairly recent rebuilding, but there was enough original work there to secure the correctness of the additions and re-instatements, and in any case the *ensemble* is a picture-book Tudor mansion. No eager child could wish for a more suggestive. The chief motifs of this group of brick houses are initials (Denver Hall), emblems (Great Cressingham), profiles (Great Snoring), or busts (East Barsham). The latter two motifs are definitely inspired by Early Renaissance, not by Late Gothic precedent, and we have still a long way to go before we can turn our attention to this pheno-menon. Members of the Norfolk group not yet mentioned are Barnham Broom Hall, Church Farmhouse Caston, Fincham Hall, Snore Hall Fordham, Kenninghall Place, Thorpland Hall, Upwell Rectory, and Watlington. Upwell Rectory has turrets with brick-built spiral staircases, a motif which also exists at Oxburgh and at Faulkbourne Hall. Great Cressingham has the unique feature of Perp panelling all over whole walls. Other C15 motifs were carried right through the Elizabethan and Jacobean decades without being adapted at all to Renaissance taste. This applies first and foremost to stepped gables. These and the polygonal angle shafts (e.g. Kenninghall) which take the place of buttresses became in fact the Elizabethan and Jacobean hallmark in Norfolk.

However, this group of lavish brick buildings is only one group. There are other brick houses which do not share its ambitions, such as Hales Court and Beaupré Hall Outwell, and secular architecture in flint and stone of course also continued. We must link it up now with the few early CASTLES which are all that have so far been discussed. Later CASTLES are few and far between. What remains of Claxton, Dilham, and Weeting Castles hardly deserves attention here, and though Baconsthorpe and Gresham must once have been major buildings, there is not enough left of them to detain us. Both were of the quadrangular type, and this is also the type of Sir John Fastolf's castle of Caister, which, being of brick, has been referred to once before. E47b Its brick is pink and yellow, and it has a specially interesting arrangement for the arrival of boats and barges.*

Unfortified, or only secondarily fortified, DOMESTIC BUILDINGS include the gatehouses of Hunstanton Hall, Middleton Towers, St Mary's Hall Wiggenhall St Mary, and the more or less telling external or internal remains of Mannington Hall, Rainthorpe Hall, Elsing Hall, and Manor Farm Pulham Market. Then there are the town houses of Norwich merchants. The undercroft at the Music House in Norwich is of the late C12 and rib-vaulted, that of the Strangers' Hall of the late C13 and rib-vaulted, the kitchen of the Bishop's Palace and the adjoining rooms are also C13 and also vaulted. The undercroft of *c.*1370 in the house of the Appleyards, now the Bridewell Museum, has been mentioned. Similar undercrofts exist in other houses (e.g. the former Tolhouse, now inside the Guildhall, No. 35 St Giles Street).‡ At Suckling House and the Master's Lodge in the Great Hospital the vaulted chamber seems to have been the buttery. Suckling House and the Strangers' Hall have their halls complete, with a bay window of the early C16. A fine kingpost roof, about 30 ft wide, is in King Street. To this must be added the Prioress's Lodging at Carrow Abbey Norwich, with hall, E49a parlour, and upper bedchamber. This is of the time of Henry VIII and so worldly that one can feel the Dissolution approach. But the grandest hall of Norwich was that of the bishops, added

---

* From Caister comes a specially good C15 chimney-piece, now at Blickling.

‡ Brick-vaulted rooms of the C15 to the early C16 are also preserved at the Blakeney Guildhall, King's Lynn (Clifton House), and at East Barsham Manor House. A chapel of the Blackfriars at Norwich is brick-vaulted too.

to the Norman palace by Bishop Salmon in 1318 etc. It does not
survive, except for the porch, but that gives sufficient impression
of the splendour of the whole. Then there are the gates to the
E10a cathedral precinct: apart from the early c14 Ethelbert Gate al-
E14a ready mentioned, the Erpingham Gate of 1420 with its many
& b statuettes on the buttresses and in the arch, the Bishop's Gate,
and the interesting Water Gate towards the river Wensum, and
there is, also inside the precinct, a certain amount of Bishop
Salmon's Carnary College, other than the chapel which has been
referred to. The final detail is Bishop Lyhart's picturesquely
vaulted staircase up to the chapel, work of c.1450–70.

Apart from the merchants' and the cathedral buildings civic
building at Norwich flourished as well. The most important
example is the Great Hospital, founded for decayed chaplains
and all sick people by Bishop Suffield in 1249 and built just like
a monastic infirmary with a large infirmary hall and a long chapel
E of it, i.e. looking exactly like an aisleless church with a chancel.
The composition is complicated by the later tower set at the
s w corner, by a long s porch of the c13, and by the fact that the
centre of the building served as a parish church. Moreover, at
the time of Elizabeth I the hall and chapel were both horizontally
subdivided to form more wards. A cloister was added in the c15,
the Master's Lodge has just been mentioned – in short the whole
is picturesque as well as impressive.

Picturesque as well as impressive are also the c15 Guildhalls
which survive in Norfolk, that of Norwich of 1407–13 with the
E48 delightful s front completed in 1535 and that of King's Lynn of
W49a 1421. Lynn has also a second more altered guildhall of 1406 etc.
Rather indistinctly outside, but more unmistakably in the woodwork inside the s part of the Norwich Guildhall, Renaissance
forms again appear.

Norfolk is an outstandingly good county for woodwork inside
buildings and especially churches; outside – i.e. in TIMBER-
FRAMED HOUSES or timber porches to churches – it has con-
tributed little. Timber-framed domestic architecture can in no
way compete with Suffolk and Essex. While there is much, there
is little of any ambition, and even carved angle-posts or brackets
are a rarity. A fine example is at Diss. The best timber-framed
houses which survive are perhaps the Greenland Fisheries
Museum at King's Lynn, Blo' Norton Hall, Saxlingham Old
Hall, and so on to Lovell's Hall Terrington St Clement, which
carries a date 1548. As regards TIMBER CHURCH PORCHES,
Shimpling is the only one deserving notice here.

But for CHURCH FURNISHINGS the natural beginning is not wood but stone. At the start of all stone furnishings stands of course the Bishop's Throne in Norwich Cathedral, but that has been dealt with some way past. Apart from this there are some stone screens, also in Norwich Cathedral, and otherwise there are mainly FONTS. With the exception of the one highly characteristic (and late) brick font at Potter Heigham, on which *see* above, and one C13 font of lead at Brundall, they are of stone and they range through the whole Middle Ages, starting with such Norman pieces as those at Fincham with figures and whole little w27a scenes under arches – the Nativity, the Magi, the Baptism, and Adam and Eve – and at Breccles also with figures under arches on one side. They are both square, and another dozen or so square Norman fonts are in the county. Burnham Deepdale has w27b the Labours of the Months (as had Warham All Saints), Toftrees has rams' heads, knot patterns, and angle colonnettes, Shernborne four human faces, knot patterns, and angle colonnettes, South Wootton has monster faces at the corners, Castle Rising big human faces looking up. Then there are the familiar square fonts made of Purbeck marble and having, rather unimaginatively, just flat arches as their only decoration. They must have been a standard article of export; for they occur in most counties. Norfolk has six and one E.E. one. The industry carried on, however; only in the C13 an octagonal was preferred to the square form, and octagonal C13 fonts of Purbeck marble or in imitation of the Purbeck type are in over thirty churches. One of them, at Didlington, is Norman, yet octagonal. A much more aesthetically valuable Purbeck font is at Wymondham, unfortunately left a fragment. This has beautiful stiff-leaf capitals.

Another type, starting apparently in the late C13 and going on into the C15, has what can only be described as flatly carved blank windows, as if they were taken from pattern books. The only C13 examples are Bressingham and Hockham, and even they – considering what has been said of conservatism in tracery – may of course be a little later. At Frenze all the motifs are of the late C13 to early C14, at Threxton, Tibenham, and perhaps Thompson they are all Dec, but at Marham pre-Dec, Dec, and Perp motifs are demonstrated side by side, and at Sea Palling Dec and Perp ones – a parallel to those cases listed higher up, where real Dec and Perp windows were designed as part of one composition.

When and where the so-called East Anglian type of font originated, we do not know. It is the type with four lions, or

more rarely four or eight standing figurines, against the stem,
and, against the bowl, the Signs of the four Evangelists and four
lions or four demi-figures of angels holding shields or even only
four flowers, or perhaps two flowers and the Emblem of the

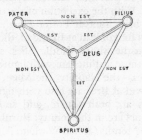

SYMBOL OF THE TRINITY

Trinity and the Instruments of the Passion. The earliest dated
w28a examples in Norfolk are of between 1402 and 1419 at Caistor St
Edmund, of 1410 at Acle. An even more elaborate variety of the
w28b East Anglian font is that with the Seven Sacraments in relief
against the bowl. The Seven Sacraments are Baptism, Confirmation,* Ordination, Penance, Matrimony, Mass, and Extreme
Unction. For the eighth side the Baptism of Christ or the Crucifixion might be chosen. Only one font – at Blofield – has scenes
from the Life of Christ instead of the Sacraments. Cautley
counts twenty-five Sacraments fonts in Norfolk, thirteen in
Suffolk. Dated Sacraments fonts are at East Dereham 1468 and
Walsoken 1544.‡ The best preserved one of all of them is
E29 at Sloley. Some of these East Anglian fonts are placed on steps,
the top one sometimes in the form of a Maltese cross, and the
face of the steps or step might have a frieze of quatrefoils or an
inscription.

FONT COVERS are invariably of wood. Norfolk has no example
as spectacular as some in Suffolk, but it has two of the four
FONT CANOPIES in England, that is timber structures on piers
forming a baldacchino above the font. The two are at St Peter
E30 Mancroft Norwich and at Trunch. To continue with wooden
church furnishings there are STALLS often with MISERICORDS.

* Of quite small children. Cautley refers to the Synod of Exeter in 1287 as
demanding Confirmation within three years of birth.
‡ But the font at Mutford in Suffolk is of 1380 and seems to have had the
Seven Sacraments originally. The donor of the Salle font died in 1489.

Here the splendid set of over sixty at Norwich Cathedral dating E34
from c.1420, c.1480, and c.1515 eclipses all others. Somewhat
unusual and probably of the C14 are the stalls at Hevingham.
Good misericords are at Salle. BENCHES are a pride of Norfolk.
There are churches with complete sets, with openwork traceried
backs,* blank-traceried fronts, poppy-heads, and little figures l. E33a
and r. of the poppy-heads or on the arm-rests. The best are those & b,
of Wiggenhall St Mary and Wiggenhall St Germans, followed w33b
by Feltwell, Gooderstone, Marham, Shingham, Wilton. A w32
straight top to the ends is quite unusual (Holme Hale is the only & 33a
example), whereas it is the rule in south-west England. Benches
were apparently not provided in churches before the C15.‡
Traceried DOORS may be allowed one sentence, and IRONWORK E36a
on doors, mostly of the C14, would deserve more. In places like w37
Tunstead it is splendid, and the door-knocker at St Gregory E37b
Norwich of the same century is one of the most thrilling in E37a
England. As in the case of doors, the interest in LECTERNS is
divided between wood and metal. The three memorable wooden
lecterns are at Shipdham, Ranworth, and Shelton. Ranworth has w35b
music painted on. For BRASS LECTERNS East Anglia must have & E36b
been a centre for export far beyond England. Examples occur at
St Mark's in Venice, at Urbino Cathedral, and as far apart in
England as Exeter and Newcastle. Of a total of forty-two, eleven
have remained in Norfolk, four in Suffolk, and seven in Cambridgeshire, Lincolnshire, and Northamptonshire together. Of
these Oxborough is datable shortly after 1489, St Gregory Norwich 1496, and Wiggenhall St Mary 1518.§

While we are considering metalwork and before we return to
timber, the odd fact must be recorded that Norfolk possesses
more PATENS of before the Reformation than all other counties E39a
together. The total is 48, and quite a number of them are gilt.
They often have the face of Christ in the middle in a circle
set in a lobed depression. Perhaps the most beautiful is that at
Beeston Regis. Their dates range from c.1350 (Beighton) to
just before the Reformation, with most of them made in the
last fifty years. Foxley is an early one. Hockham has a London
hallmark and the date 1509–10. Against all these patens there
is only one chalice, Thornage. But the earliest and most beautiful

* This is not a Suffolk motif.

‡ Wooden CHESTS should not strictly come into *The Buildings of England* w34
at all, but a reference to the fine chest at Dersingham may be permitted.

§ Redenhall has the unusual feature of twin heads to the eagle. A propos w36a
brass, the German brass CHANDELIER of c.1500 at St John Baptist, Tim- E38a
berhill, Norwich ought to be mentioned, an exceedingly pretty piece.

piece of plate in Norfolk is not ecclesiastical at all. It is King
w38 John's Cup of the mid C14, which forms part of the regalia of
King's Lynn.

Back now to WOODWORK and what is the most familiar
wooden ornament of East Anglian churches, the ROOD SCREENS.
Cautley says that 202 Norfolk churches have screens or parts of
w30 them. The earliest of them are of the C14 and have shafts instead
of mullions and little, rather bold, flowing tracery. Mullions seem
to have replaced shafts before the Dec style was quite over, as is
indicated by such screens as those of Griston and Shelfanger.
However, by far the majority of Norfolk screens are Perp, of the
E31b C15 and early C16. They cannot compete with Devonshire in
richness of decoration, but they are in their greater restraint just
as impressive. The rule is one-light divisions with ogee arches.
Some have close and sometimes very pretty tracery above them,
others have a ribbed coving in the spandrels between the arches
to support the loft, yet others are content with dainty cusping
and subcusping along the arched head, often even in two layers,
one to the w, the other to the E. Surprisingly few have doors.*
The two winners in any screen competition would be Ranworth
w31a and Attleborough, both with ribbed coving for the rood loft, and
Attleborough even with the loft parapet. Ranworth moreover
has arms coming out in two places, serving as side-pieces to
w31b subsidiary altars. And both have PAINTED PANELS in the dado
E32a and some of the upper spaces as well. Painted panels in the dado
were the rule in Norfolk (and to a lesser degree Suffolk), while
they are the exception in south-west England. The quality of
PAINTING varies enormously, and it must be admitted that –
even taking defacement and effacement fully into consideration –
the aesthetic value of the majority of them must always have been
slight. The late C14 and the C15 and the early C16 were altogether
not a period of thriving painting in England. Norwich could do
very well indeed: the retables in the cathedral, one of c.1380, the
other of c.1430, are as good as anything of their date in England,
even if nothing like as good as Beauneveu or Master Francke,
not to mention Italy. No paintings on screens are of such quality,
though some might be, if they were cleaned. Good examples are
e.g. at Edingthorpe and North Elmham. Specially bad examples
are not to be referred to in this introduction. As a rule single
figures, mostly Saints, are represented, but Loddon has the Life
of Christ and portraits of donors, and Sparham a Dance of
Death. Among paintings of before 1400 those at Hempstead and

* Only nine according to Cautley, and only two in Suffolk.

Lessingham ought to be noted, of the C15 and early C16 the
following are dated or datable: Litcham 1436, Thornham 1488,
Ludham 1493, Aylsham 1504, Cawston c.1505, Worstead 1512,
Edgefield 1526, Horsham St Faith 1528, Wellingham 1532.

Whether WALL PAINTINGS were on the whole as artistically E40a
indifferent, or whether they were better, it is difficult to say; for &W40
most of the wall paintings in Norfolk are in too faint a condition
to have kept any impact. The earliest are the architectural painting in Norwich Cathedral of c.1100–10 and the figural work in
the S aisle of c.1175. Then there are, also in the cathedral, the
beautiful, if again faint, figures in the N chancel aisle above the
tribune, and they date from about 1300. If some more must be
listed here, they ought to be the mid-C14 Tree of Jesse at Weston
Longville, the splendid St Georges at St Gregory Norwich and
Fritton, and the large scenes above the chancel arch at Attleborough. The rare cycle of the Life of St Christopher at Hemblington, the Seven Works of Mercy and the scene of the Three
Quick and the Three Dead, both at Wickhampton, and the sin
of Gossip at Colton and Little Melton * may be admitted into the
introduction for iconographical reasons.

Of the other arts of figural representation in the flat TEXTILES
need not detain us,‡ nor FLOOR TILES, except for a reference to
the tiling in the form of a rose window at North Barningham, but
STAINED GLASS must; for Norwich in the C15 had one of the
most flourishing schools of glass-painting in England. But the
earliest panels are not of the C15 or from Norwich: they are the
beautiful French roundel of the C13 in Oxborough R. C. church,
the four roundels also of the C13 at Saxlingham, and the small
C13 trefoil at Carleton Rode. Then the best and best preserved
C14 work, which is again at Saxlingham, and at Elsing and Mileham, both of c.1350. For the C15 the two figures at Framingham
Earl are exceptionally good. At East Harling are twenty panels W41
datable to c.1475, and at St Peter Mancroft the whole E window
is full of C15 glass, though not *in situ*. There are forty-two panels
all told. In addition, North Tuddenham has many panels, one
of them with the date 1467. They come from another church.
And Shelton, begun about 1480–90, has most of its original glass
preserved. To conclude, there is much interesting foreign glass

* And formerly at Seething and Stokesby.
‡ One pre-Reformation piece is at St Gregory Norwich. There is also,
although not figural, the late C15 CORPORAS CASE at Wymondham. No
banners are preserved, though in E Norfolk and E Suffolk a number of
BANNERSTAFF LOCKERS. They are simply tall narrow wall recesses,
originally closed by doors, and they exist hardly anywhere else in England.

in Norfolk churches, thanks partly to the activities of one J. C. van Hampp, who bought in 1802 plenty of glass from Rouen, the Rhineland, Nuremberg, and also the Netherlands. Through him e.g. and through Lady Beauchamp Proctor foreign glass reached Chedgrave, Langley, and Thurton, and probably also Earsham, Hingham, and Kimberley. The best glass on the whole is German: late C15 at Hingham, of 1511 at St Stephen Norwich (from Mariawald in the Rhineland), of 1540 at Stradsett (from Munich).

Church furnishings have taken up several pages; CHURCH MONUMENTS of the Middle Ages in Norfolk require no more than a couple of paragraphs. It is curious how little of more than local interest there is in so wealthy a county. The earliest and most interesting funeral effigy, if it is an effigy, has had its due, E40b that of a bishop of c.1120 at Norwich Cathedral, perhaps Bishop Losinga. After that there is nothing until one comes to a mid-C13 priest at West Walton, Purbeck work connected with what survives e.g. at Ely, to the late C13 couple at Wickhampton, the late C13 Knight at East Tuddenham and Lady at Fersfield, to the three fine early C14 oaken effigies at Banham, Fersfield, and South Acre, the excellent little mourners against the tomb-E41 chest of Sir Roger de Kerdiston † 1337 at Reepham, and so to the one real glory of medieval funeral art in Norfolk, the Hastings brass at Elsing, and the Walsoken brass and the Braunche brass at St Margaret King's Lynn. Sir Hugh Hastings died in 1347; the corresponding dates for Walsoken and Braunche are 1349 and 1364. The Hastings brass is the largest in England. It is English and includes, apart from the effigy, six lively smaller figures arranged up the buttresses of the canopy and the Coronation of the Virgin at the top. The two brasses at King's Lynn are also exceptionally long. They are Flemish, i.e. plates with the figures etc. engraved, not cut-out figures as in English brasses. Their quality of draughtsmanship is extremely high. The Walsoken brass has to the l. and r. small figures of prophets and apostles and at the foot horsemen and a windmill. At the foot of the Braunche brass is the Peacock Feast given to Edward III in 1349. To the l. and r. are again small figures, and at the top seated figures, angels, and little souls. The best later brasses are at Felbrigg (c.1380), South Acre († 1384), Reepham († 1391), Blickling († 1401), Great Fransham († 1414), and Hunstanton († 1506). On the whole the best period of brass engraving was over by the mid C15. Effigies also tend to be larger before that time, i.e. wealthier clients chose brass.

Of alabaster monuments the best unquestionably is that at
Ashwellthorpe († 1417), of stone effigies the most interesting, w42a
also unquestionably, are the two at Reepham († 1337) and Ingham († 1344), recumbent on a bed of pebbles. But the best stone
monument, as against stone effigy, is, again unquestionably, the
Morley Monument at Hingham. Lord Morley died in 1435, but w42b
the monument cannot have been erected at once. It is one of the & 43
most ambitious funeral compositions in England and ought to be
much better known. It reaches right up to the roof of the chancel
and contains a large number of statuettes, up the buttresses, on
the top cresting, and against the back wall of the recess. It has
been compared with the Erpingham Gate at Norwich, but the
style of the figures is very different. Most of the more ambitious
monuments from the C14 to the C16 take the form of a tomb-
chest with a recess above and a top cresting. Some are of Purbeck
marble (Outwell, Brockdish, etc.), others of freestone. Of the
late C13 and the early to mid C14 are those at Wickhampton,
Raveningham, and Kelling, the latter an Easter Sepulchre. The
lavish Easter Sepulchre of Northwold, with soldiers in relief
against the tomb-chest, is of the late C15, but the best of the later
C15 stone monuments, apart of course from the bishops in Norwich Cathedral, is that of Sir William Chamberlain † 1462 at
East Harling, and that was erected free-standing between chancel
and chancel chapel. It has ogee arches standing partly on pendants. This motif was retained in the most interesting and,
nationally speaking, most important group of early C16 monu- w44a
ments in Norfolk, the Bedingfield Group, as it might be called, & b
and they are of terracotta and in all their details à l'antique.

So now at last we can leave the Middle Ages and focus our
attention on the COMING OF THE RENAISSANCE. When and
where did the new forms of Italy enter Norfolk? How did the
county take to them? In what materials and for what jobs were
they accepted and were they rejected? The terracotta monuments
are in fact the earliest dated evidence we have. They are not
entirely confined to Norfolk. The Marney Monuments at Layer
Marney in Essex of 1523 and 1525 are closely connected with
them, and so are the terracotta details of the windows at Layer
Marney Tower and at Barsham and in other places in Suffolk.
The centre of the group in Norfolk is the Bedingfeld Monu- w44a
ments in Oxborough parish church. They are of about 1525. By
the same craftsman must be the Jannys monument at St George
Colegate Norwich of 1533/4, the monument to Abbot Ferrers w44b
at Wymondham, who was elected in 1532 and died after the

Dissolution in 1548, and an undated (Berney?) monument at
Bracon Ash. These monuments have pilasters with applied
balusters, lively foliage in the panels, and pendants and little
turret-like superstructures also fully decorated with foliage. The
fact that Great Snoring Rectory of the Early Tudor group of
brick houses introduces Renaissance motifs such as heads in profile may be attributed to the influence of such monuments but is
more probably inspired by Early Renaissance woodwork. In
woodwork the first dates which we have are c.1535 for the panelling etc. of the Council Chamber in the Norwich Guildhall,
with arabesques side by side with the old linenfold, before 1536
(in all probability) for the panelling of a room from St Benet's
Abbey now in the Bishop's Palace at Norwich, and with the very
E32b profile heads just referred to, and 1537 for the pulpit at Catton,
with balusters instead of buttresses. In addition there are the
little genre scenes in some panelling at Swannington Manor
which are connected with a mayor of Norwich of the 1540s,
the entertaining and instructive bench ends at Bressingham,
where the Perp elements are preserved but gently converted into
Renaissance forms: buttresses into balusters, etc., and the extremely Mannerist little allegorical figures on a chest at East
W35a Dereham, in all probability Flemish. In church plate the earliest
piece with Renaissance forms is a chalice of 1543-4 at St Peter
Mancroft Norwich.

On the other hand the Perp style was still kept entirely or
essentially e.g. at St Stephen Norwich in 1550 with its hammerbeam roof and in the tower of the same church even in 1601, and
in the font at Ashwellthorpe with its quatrefoils, the standard
Perp motif when nothing more elaborate was asked for, as late as
1660. These and similar cases are not part of a revival – to this
problem we have to turn a good deal later – but a long and perfectly healthy survival, in opposition to new fashions. For the
Renaissance appears at first as a fashion. It took a long time before it was understood as a style, that is a matter of plans and
elevations and not just ornamental motifs.

The ELIZABETHAN STYLE is in fact the victory of the English Perp tradition over the new fashion, but a victory made
fruitful by not squashing but absorbing the new fashion. This is
what ought to be called the Elizabethan Settlement in architectural history. Its complete expression in Norfolk is houses such
W52a as Morley Old Hall, Thelveton Hall, or Kirstead Hall. The
motifs are easily remembered: brick, the E-plan, mullioned and
transomed windows, stepped rather than straight gables, poly-

gonal angle shafts, and pediments above the windows. Several of
these motifs we have found to date back to before the Reformation. The E-plan also, though not in Norfolk, was developed at
the beginning of the c16 – see e.g. Barrington Court in Somerset.
Only the window pediments are a Renaissance contribution, and
they were established for England at Somerset House in London
in 1550. The brick look-out tower at Freston in Suffolk has them
in the fifties, and probably the early fifties, and Bisham, a brick
mansion in Berkshire, has them in 1552–62.* In Norfolk the
earliest inscribed date – admittedly not in the original figures – is
the 1569 at Channonz Hall Tibenham. This is followed by
Gowthorpe Manor Swardeston 1574 (on the porch, though 1669
on a gable), the Manor House Bracondale, Norwich, 1578, Wood
Hall Hilgay 1579, Heydon Hall 1581–4, Breccles Hall 1583. The E50b
type then continues without any break far into the c17.‡ A specially famous example was the Pastons' principal mansion, Oxnead; but of this, alas, only a subsidiary range remains. A
few dated c17 examples are Kirstead Hall of 1614, and then W52b
Wroxham Manor House 1623, Bawburgh Hall 1634, Rokeles
Hall Watton 1653, and stepped gables even still at Colton in 1660
and 1666, Marlingford in 1679, and Hindolveston in 1722. But
here the other gable is not stepped but shaped. Shaped gables
appeared later in Norfolk (as indeed everywhere) than stepped
gables. The first dated example is an unusually early one, the
Manor House Bracondale, Norwich, of 1578. The next after that
is the gatehouse of Merton, 1620, and they go on into the c18,
especially in the form of end-gables to otherwise classically regular façades. Dated examples are at Bawdeswell Hall 1633,
Wiveton Hall 1652 and 1653, Chedgrave 1669, Hevingham 1675,
and then Silfield Lodge Wymondham 1709, Hedenham Lodge
1711, a house at Shotesham 1712, Gateley Hall 1726, Thurgarton
Old Hall 1733, and Ashby Hall Ashby St Mary 1736.

Back to Elizabeth I and James I. Norfolk possesses only one of
the 'prodigy houses' of the period, to use Sir John Summerson's
term: Blickling. This was built about 1616–27 and had a closed E52
courtyard on the entrance side with a gatehouse in the middle of
one side and the hall in the middle of the range opposite, and
then, beyond, two far-projecting wings. It has angle turrets, a tall
turret with cupola over the entrance, and shaped gables. Inside.

---

* Hardley and Porch House, Brooke have the curious motif of two
pediments side by side over the same window.

‡ It also occurs in timber-framed houses – see Saxlingham Old Hall, with
pedimented windows.

E53 the long gallery is one of the most impressive apartments of the
&54a time, and the staircase, though remodelled, was clearly originally
E54b a sister to that at Hatfield. The architect is in fact the same,
E49b *Robert Lyminge*, buried at Blickling. There are also splendid fireplaces. The office wings, dated 1624, have Dutch, not shaped,
gables, i.e. shaped gables ending in a proper pediment, a form
introduced in England from Holland only a few years before – in
1618, it seems. They also went on for a long time (Surlingham
1736) but, from the point of view of this Introduction, belong in
a different context (*see* p. 60).

Not on the scale of Blickling, but also major and also memorable for certain particular features, are Stiffkey Hall of *c.*1575–
1600 which, with its round angle towers and its long wings, continues an earlier tradition rather than accepting a new one, Barn-
E51a ingham Hall of 1612, with its impressive two-storeyed dormers,
E51b and Felbrigg Hall of about 1620, with the lettering along its
parapet – such as was done at the same time at Castle Ashby in
Northamptonshire. A supplement to these are a few buildings of
exceptional shape and function: Drayton Lodge outside Nor-
wich, a C16 plaisance, the summer house of Bawburgh Hall of
*c.*1634, also outside Norwich, the Tower House in Bracondale,
Norwich, the very similar tower at the back of Clifton House,
King's Lynn, and the Standing or Look-out Tower at Melton
Constable. All these participate more or less in the motifs of the
Elizabethan and Jacobean style.

The best interior elements are the stucco work in the Long
Gallery and the South Drawing Room at Blickling of the 1620s,
E55 in No. 4 South Quay Great Yarmouth of 1596, and in Nos 1–2
South Quay and the Old Merchants' House as well, and also
in Rainthorpe Hall and in Barnham Broom Hall, the latter of
1614. There are characteristic chimneypieces at Great Yarmouth in Lloyds Bank (1598) and the Duke's Head, again
at Blickling, especially one of wood dated 1627 in East
Barsham Manor House, and in Great Witchingham Hall, dated
1609.

The decorative material for domestic interiors and for funeral
monuments in churches is so similar that ELIZABETHAN AND
JACOBEAN MONUMENTS may suitably find their place here.
There is in fact an Early Elizabethan type of funeral monument
which does entirely without effigies and is even shy of any demonstrative ornament. In the case of the Lovell Monument
(† 1567) at East Harling there is neither Early Renaissance nor
strapwork decoration. It is a remarkably dignified piece. Also

non-representational are the monuments † 1571 at Waxham,
† 1579 at Ranworth, and † 1584 at Reedham (with an ogee top
which may be a survival but might even be self-conscious
Gothicism). Where effigies are admitted, the standard types are
the reclining effigy, as had been the custom almost without exception before the Reformation, and the kneeling effigy, a Renaissance newcomer from France via the Netherlands. For small
monuments two kneeling figures facing one another across a
prayer-desk are the most usual thing, and they are not even always listed in the following gazetteer. Major examples are e.g.
the Heydons at Baconsthorpe † 1593, Bridget Coke † 1598 at
Tittleshall, with beautiful alabaster ribbonwork, and the Mapes
at Rollesby † 1619. The Pastons at Oxnead † 1597 are represented so that she kneels but he lies on a half-rolled-up mat,
again a motif of Netherlandish origin. The earliest Renaissance
monument with recumbent effigy is Sir Robert Southwell † 1563
at Woodrising, again very subdued in its use of ornament, but a
six-poster with Roman Doric columns. That six-poster or four-
poster was to become the most ambitious type. There are typical
four-posters at St Andrew Norwich († 1613) and St Peter
Permountergate Norwich (1623) and a typical six-poster at
Marham († 1604). They are Jacobean, as are a number of other
good alabaster monuments with coffered arches and flanking
columns (North Walsham 1608, by *John Key*, Snettisham † 1612, E42
Little Walsingham † 1612, Hethel † 1612, Wiggenhall St Mary
1625, Paston 1629).

Only three further comments are called for. A monument at
North Tuddenham has a recess framed by backs of books. Black-
letter for inscriptions is kept in a few cases even in the c17
(Syderstone 1605, Elsing † 1623). And, heralding a new type of
the second third of the c17, the frontal bust is occasionally introduced. This is the case in a very unusual monument at St
Peter Mancroft Norwich † 1592 and in one at St Andrew Norwich † 1613. *Nicholas Stone*, the leading English sculptor between 1620 and 1650, uses the bust (Oxnead), the kneeling effigy
(Holkham), the recumbent effigy (Emneth, Tittleshall), and the
semi-reclining effigy (Paston), but he endows his effigies with a
new feeling and therefore belongs to a new age.

CHURCH FURNISHINGS of the same years are ample, but
rarely spectacular. In quantity church PLATE easily holds first
place. With the Elizabethan Settlement chalices and patens were
required everywhere, and had all of a sudden to be supplied.
How the Norwich silversmiths could cope remains a mystery,

E39b but it is a fact that about 275 pieces date from the years 1567–8.*
Many of them are inscribed with the names of the villages for
which they were made, often in bewildering spellings, and it is
another mystery why, not all that rarely, the church of one village has a vessel inscribed for another. Only very few date from
between 1543–4, the date of the chalice cover at St Peter Mancroft already mentioned because of its Renaissance detail, and
1566 (1551 Hunstanton, 1559? Hethel, 1562 Hoveton, 1563
Thornage (Paten), 1564 to 1566–7 twenty-eight), and after 1568
the flow receded at once (1568–9 to 1571 fifteen). One of the
beneficiaries of the great rush is known to us by name, *Peter
Peterson* of Norwich, who made about fifty chalices in those
few years. He became a freeman of the city in 1553 and died
in 1602.‡ Next in order of frequency, if we leave out foreign
glass, which mostly came in, as we have seen, only after 1800,
is PULPITS. They usually have the short, broad, blank arches
familiar from Elizabethan and Jacobean domestic woodwork as
well, and in addition perhaps some arabesque or studding,
etc. Dated examples are Beeston 1592, North Elmham 1614–26,
Moulton St Mary 1619, Walpole St Peter 1620, Thwaite 1624,
Wiggenhall St Germans 1631, Thornham 1631, Edingthorpe
1632, Necton 1636, Aylsham 1637. The pulpit at Runcton Holme
is specially ornate, and back panel and tester are preserved.
w36b Some HOURGLASS STANDS are still attached to pulpits,
needed to keep a watch on the length of sermons. A rough
READER'S DESK at Edingthorpe is dated 1587. Much WOOD-
WORK was provided at Wilby after a fire of 1633, including
benches with fleur-de-lis poppy-heads. Poppy-heads are on the
bench ends of 1627 at Wretton too. Much woodwork of *c.*1635
is at Tibenham, including a family pew. The family pew of 1640
at Little Barningham has a gruesome little figure of Death.
COMMUNION RAILS, as a rule an addition of the years of Archbishop Laud, i.e. *c.*1635–45, have balusters of the shapes fitting
their date. Only one has fretwork instead (West Acre). SCREENS
were put up or renewed infrequently. There are examples at St
Margaret King's Lynn of 1584 and after 1603, at Tilney All
Saints of 1618, at St Nicholas King's Lynn, Walpole St Peter,
and North Elmham. FONT COVERS on the whole are finer and
bolder than other woodwork. The most splendid of all is at

---

* For the purpose of this count a chalice counts one, a paten counts one,
but a chalice and paten also count only one.

‡ Peterson's pieces are only occasionally quoted with his name in the
gazetteer.

Walpole St Peter. That at Terrington St Clement is Gothic, yet w29
more probably C17 than early C16. There are a number with
columns and openwork obelisks in Norwich churches, e.g. at St
Andrew, where it is dated 1637. The cover at Saham Toney is
dated 1632. The FONTS for which they were provided were as a
rule medieval, and it has already been pointed out that the font
at Ashwellthorpe, though dated 1660, is medieval in its design.
The same applies to Tilney All Saints. Strapwork, i.e. the ornament of the day, appears only at St Nicholas King's Lynn (1627)
and Terrington St Clement (1635). Among the most impressive
and, for our own taste, most attractive pieces of the later C16 and
early C17 in churches are the painted ROYAL ARMS of Queen
Elizabeth at Kenninghall and Tivetshall, both enormous and w39a
both originally above the screen. A few ODDMENTS to conclude
this section: the sexton's wheel, to work out fast days, at Long
Stratton (cf. Suffolk), the collecting shoes, i.e. little square
shovels, at Blo Norton (1610), Bressingham (1631), Morston,
North Tuddenham, St Peter Hungate Norwich, and South
Lopham, and the *cuir bouilli* cases for church plate at Starston
(1567) and Thompson.*

It may seem strange that church furnishings have been summarized before the churches themselves. But there was a good
and simple reason. No churches or parts of churches were built
in Norfolk between 1550 and 1700, except for the few posthu-
mously Perp items already listed. If one wants to follow the
development of style in Norfolk architecture and decoration one
must keep to the houses and the monuments. The church no
longer dominated people's lives. Monuments are the better in-
dicators for small and quick changes, houses for large and more
thorough ones.

So we return to MONUMENTS first. A new elegance and court-
liness, and also a new awareness of European events after the
heavy provincialism of most of the Jacobean work, even when
done by sculptors from the Netherlands, appears around the
year 1620 in such monuments as those at Riddlesworth † 1617
and North Barningham † 1621, with splendid Mannerist angels
lifting up curtains. Classical composition without any strapwork
or other Jacobean embellishment appears at the same moment in
the modest tablet at Aylsham commemorating Bishop Jegon
† 1617. The monument to Sir Edmund Paston † 1632 at Paston
is by *Nicholas Stone*, and so faultlessly classical that it might have
been designed by Inigo himself. A conceit which this age of

* There is incidentally also a leather case of the C14 at Cawston.

concettismo adored was to portray the dead person in a shroud, preferably rising out of the coffin. So it is done for Mrs Calthorpe † 1640 by the *Christmas Brothers* at East Barsham. At Stratton Strawless † 1638 are comfortably reclining effigies, but also in their shrouds and in proximity to a gruesome charnel-house still-life below. A similar panel appears at the foot of a monument at E43a South Acre † after 1623. *Edward Marshall* at Spixworth † 1635 keeps the shrouded effigies recumbent. But they are now endowed with all the signs of death. Another typical C17 conceit is used at Stiffkey as early as about 1610. Here a black marble cloth is carved over a white marble sarcophagus. It could well be by *Maximilian Colt.* Busts or demi-figures now become fashionable and are placed in oval recesses: see North Barningham † 1639, Honingham † 1642, and Dickleburgh † 1659, where the architectural forms are not classical but display the mannerisms in which the more provincial artisans revelled about the middle of the century.

The second half of the C17 did not in Norfolk contribute much beyond these innovations. It is sufficient to comment on four or five monuments. For the continuation of *concettismo* it would not be easy to beat the monument, † 1680, at Mulbarton, with a copper diptych with inscriptions on a wooden bible. Busts go on at East Bradenham, † 1684. A bust is placed on a plinth between columns, a Georgian rather than a Stuart conception, at Caister, with a date of death as early as 1668, and a bust is at the top of a monument at Colton † 1715, and that also is decidedly Georgian. A monument † 1675 at St Nicholas King's Lynn modernizes the type with kneeling figures by placing them nearly frontally, a monument † 1693 at Stow Bardolph modernizes that with the semi-reclining figure by dressing it up in Roman armour.* More important is the early appearance of the standing figure in the Clement Spelman † 1672 at Narborough. This is by *Cibber.* A standing figure was also used by the Suffolk sculptor *Robert Singleton* in a monument at West Dereham († 1706). Of other sculptors of national importance working in the late C17 *Grinling Gibbons* is also represented in Norfolk, even if only with an ornamental tablet (Felbrigg † 1686). However, it was in ornamental rather than figure work that he was at his best. The *Stantons* have four monuments in Norfolk (*Edward* at Gissing † 1710, *William* at Thursford † 1666, in Norwich Cathedral † 1702, and at Hethersett † 1704), but they are unim-

W45 * A good monument with semi-reclining figure is that to Lady Williamson † 1684, at Loddon. It comes no doubt from a leading London workshop.

portant. So are the two at Norwich by *Thomas Green* (both † 1715), one of the believers in the standing figure, where major monuments are concerned. Finally two more conceits to round off the picture of monumental sculpture about 1700: the single column as the centre of a monument placed before an obelisk or a back panel (Guist † 1699, Marlingford † 1727, Horstead † 1728, St Peter Mancroft † 1731 and 1732, Colton † 1741, Dersingham † 1743), and the use of little piles of books as an ornamental element (Denton † 1684, Barnham Broom † 1707).

How does DOMESTIC ARCHITECTURE FROM CHARLES I TO QUEEN ANNE express these changes? The greatest and most sudden change in all English architecture was that brought about between 1615 and 1620 by Inigo Jones. It was far deeper than the change of a hundred years earlier. Inigo's buildings are fully classical, those of Henry VIII's court had no more than antique trimmings. Among those who fully understood what Inigo was about was *Sir Roger Pratt*. He was a Norfolk man and retired in 1667 to Ryston in Norfolk. But the house he built himself there has been so entirely changed that hardly anything of his design remains. It was a classical design, but crowned by a big, top-heavy, semicircular pediment, a solecism of French origin that Inigo would not have committed nor, one feels, would Pratt, as long as he was working in London. The house which introduced the Inigo Jones style to Norfolk, Raynham Hall, was built forty years before Ryston, and in it also Palladian w54 purity was sacrificed to a sense of greater ease and warmth. Raynham Hall, which was begun in 1622, has, it is true, a giant attached portico with pediment on the garden side, and that would have been impossible without Jones's designs for the Banqueting House in Whitehall and the King's House at Newmarket. But the house has, besides Dutch gables (cf. Blickling, 1624; *see* above), on the entrance side a very Baroque composite gable, and these gables display Ionic pilasters bent like dough to accompany the curves of the gables. So Raynham still has much of the gaiety and carefree play with motifs which had been the great asset of Jacobean architecture; and the fact that Jacobean grossness has been overcome is another asset. The moment of Raynham was a happy one. Pure classicity, of a domestic nature, not as display, i.e. façades with a hipped roof, very little decoration, and regularly placed upright windows, originally with a stone or timber cross of a mullion and a transom, is achieved at Melton Constable in the wing said to have been begun in 1664, but quite B57 probably begun somewhat later, and at Felbrigg in the wing built

E56b by *Samwell* in 1674–87. Both have splendid plasterwork dated 1687 and with the inimitable, completely detached fruit and flower garlands of the Grinling Gibbons era.

But such purity was still the exception in 1680 and 1685. As a rule Norfolk architects and bricklayers tried to come to terms with the new style by accepting some of its refined elements but mixing them with more robust ones of their own.*A case in point, and a very superior one, is the well-to-do, much travelled gentleman-architect and wit *Henry Bell* of King's Lynn, whose
N55a Customs House of 1683 deviates from the new rules of restraint only in that it has pilasters in two superimposed orders all along its fronts. But his Duke's Head at Lynn of 1683–9 piles on its top a big broken segmental pediment, derived no doubt from Raynham but curiously heralding the Baroque of Archer. The bricklayers took to the superimposed pilasters and, often in conjunction with flat raised surrounds of windows or alternatingly rusticated surrounds, they characterize local art of the 1670s. It is
N53b enough to mention the White Hart Inn at Scole, as large and ambitious as the King's Head, and the two farmhouses at Brockdish near by whose dates, 1672 (Grove Farmhouse) and 1676 (The Grange), establish the date of the Scole inn. One of them and the inn incidentally still have Dutch gables. Stalham Hall also has pilasters in two orders, and here one finds to one's surprise even stepped gables. At Horsham St Faith is a group of houses and a proud barn typical of the same date, and Bramerton Grange and Street Farmhouse Bergh Apton also belong in this context. Another favourite motif of the more traditional brick-
N53a layers of the later C17 was the giant pilaster, taken over from Jones by Peter Mills, bricklayer to the City of London, and others (especially in Surrey), and then quickly accepted in the provinces. It is represented in Norfolk by Hoveton House, the
E19a porch of Thurton Hall,‡ and the Old Meeting at Norwich. But the latter is of 1693, and the pilasters have a new grandeur, reminiscent of John Webb at Greenwich rather than the provinces.

By 1693 indeed the time of hesitation was over. The simplicity of Felbrigg and Melton Constable is taken up by a house of 1682 in the Close at Norwich and then by Aylsham Old Hall in 1689 and The Limes Coltishall in 1692. The two latter have doorways with segmental pediments on pilasters. The sturdy twisted

B56a * The sculpture of the Samson and Hercules House at Norwich is certainly robust enough.

‡ Compare the porch of Christchurch Mansion at Ipswich of *c*.1675.

balusters of the staircase of Aylsham Old Hall are as characteristic of this date as the dumb-bell balusters of Grove Farmhouse Brockdish are of theirs. These staircases lead us back for a moment to CHURCH FURNISHINGS. There is not much to report. In 1684 *Henry Bell* designed the reredos for St Margaret King's Lynn which is now at North Runcton. It is in the style of the fittings of Wren's City churches, with which everybody was then familiar. This is also reflected in the panelling, the reredoses, and other fitments of the Norwich churches of St George Colegate, St George Tombland, St Peter Mancroft, and also the Octagon Chapel. Then there are fine royal arms of William III at E28b Ingworth and Shelton, the very Baroque statues at Trowse w39b Newton, probably from a Norwich organ case, the former &E35 Communion Rail at St Margaret Norwich with its dumb-bell balusters, dated 1707, and splendid Early Georgian pulpits at St Margaret King's Lynn, St George Colegate at Norwich, and St Nicholas Yarmouth. The latter comes from St George, built in 1714–16 by *John Price*, and one of the only two bigger E17 CHURCHES of the time with which we are concerned at present. It is a naive design. The other is *Henry Bell*'s (?) North Runcton w19 of ten or twelve years before. No other churches come into our story,* nor any other church furnishings; for the big screen right across the church of Terrington St Clement is of 1788, and we must not go that far yet.

About 1720 a new fundamental change of fashion took place in DOMESTIC ARCHITECTURE, the change from a comfortable domestic plainness on the one hand and a serious or less serious Baroque on the other to the grand, official display of pure Palladianism. We have seen both the tendencies develop which the new doctrine opposed. To carry on with them beyond 1700 it is enough to refer the reader to the plain, but eminently satisfying façades of Ditchingham Hall of 1702 or Hanworth Hall or Cavick House Wymondham of *c.*1710 or Honing Hall of as late as 1748 on the one hand, and on the other to the barley-sugar columns of Clifton House King's Lynn of 1708 (and the monument by *Stayner* at Morning Thorpe which commemorates a death in 1723 and has the same columns), the restless composition of No. 74 South Quay Yarmouth, and to the giant pilasters of houses of the first half of the C18 in Colegate Norwich, Coslany Street Norwich, Magdalen Street Norwich, Pitt Street Norwich, of houses at Aylsham (The Knoll, Bank House), North Walsham (Aylsham Road, Bacton Road), Wymondham (Caius House), w61a

* Except St Augustine Norwich for its brick tower of 1726.

62	INTRODUCTION

Coltishall (Old House), and of Hall Farm Bergh Apton, Dial
House Emneth, Hardingham Hall, Hedenham Hall, and two
houses at Swafield.

The complete statement of the new or renewed Palladian discipline formulated by *Colen Campbell* himself, the architect who
had established it, is Houghton, begun by him in 1721, and in its
present appearance made more human by the corner domes introduced by *James Gibbs* instead of the square pedimented corner
eminences planned by Campbell on the pattern, not of Palladio,
but of Inigo Jones's Wilton House. Houghton was built by Robert
Walpole, George I's and George II's 'prime minister'. It is enlarged, like a villa of Palladio, by quadrant wings ending in
pavilions, and the village of Houghton was rebuilt on a new site
w58a as a model village. The interiors are very splendid and were
w56 largely designed by *Kent*. The design for Holkham goes back to
1725, though building did not start until 1734. The client was
the first Lord Leicester, the architect *William Kent*, protégé of
Lord Burlington, who had made himself the mouthpiece of Palladianism. After Kent's death *Matthew Brettingham* carried on.
Holkham has four wings and a centre more severely correct than
Houghton, with a detached pedimented portico and again raised
angle pavilions. It is of white brick unrendered and has the most
w57a consistently palatial interiors of any mansion in England, cul-
& b minating in the entrance hall which runs through two storeys.
It ends in an apse, and the staircase to the state rooms runs up
inside the hall into the apse. Various temples and an obelisk
complete the setting of Holkham. The composition of Houghton
and Holkham with the raised angle pavilions was repeated at
Langley Park by *Brettingham* about 1740–50 and at Kimberley
Hall by *Thomas Prowse* about 1750, both in red brick. In both
cases also houses had been there before and were merely remodelled and enlarged. By another of the Palladian fanatics,
Thomas Ripley, is Wolterton, built in 1727–41. He was a dull
architect, and the interiors are more rewarding than the exterior.*
Of the great names after 1750, few appear in Norfolk, and those
that do, appear with minor works. By *Robert Adam* is the delight-
e18a ful little church opposite Gunton Park (1769), a house of white
brick by *Brettingham* enlarged by *James Wyatt* about 1780, by
e43b *Bonomi* is the monument and taciturn memorial pyramid of 1793
in the grounds of Blickling. *Soane* worked in Norfolk before he

* The best feature of the exterior, the terrace and arcade on the garden
side, is by *G. S. Repton*, 1828. Ripley was also the architect who actually
built Houghton.

was made architect to the Bank of England and achieved fame in London in his own brilliant and idiosyncratic style. But such buildings as Shotesham Park, the Music Room at Earsham, the w63a parsonage at Saxlingham, all three of about 1785, and the hall and staircase of Letton Hall of 1785–8 are very fine all the w62 same, in a Holland rather than a Soane way. Soane's Gaol at Norwich is not preserved.

For Georgian interiors other than those already mentioned one must go to Narford for its hall with the wall paintings by *Pellegrini*, which form part of European rather than English art, to Gillingham Hall for its staircase of *c*.1710–20, to Raynham Hall for splendid interiors by *Kent*, to Langley Park for the w58b Kentian dining room, to Felbrigg for its dining room of *c*.1750, to Hilborough Hall also for its dining room, and to Langley Park w59 and Gateley Hall for exuberant Rococo plasterwork.   w60

Norwich was a populous city in the C18. It was also a wealthy and a civilized city, and this is reflected in its merchants' houses, its public buildings, and also in the existence of excellent local architects and sculptors. As one examines GEORGIAN CHURCH MONUMENTS in Norwich and the whole of Norfolk, one is struck by the perfectly metropolitan quality of the large or smaller tablets commissioned from *Thomas Rawlins*, *Robert Page*, and the *Ivorys*. There was no demand for really swagger monuments, and what the county has of works by the leading London sculptors is not on the largest scale, except for the elder *Horsnaile*'s *magnum opus* at Langford († 1727), with one semi-reclining and two standing figures. Otherwise *Scheemakers*'s monument at Stow Bardolph († 1741) has a semi-reclining figure, *Sir Henry Cheere*'s at St Giles Norwich († 1742) is an architectural tablet, *Roubiliac*'s at Narford (1753) and Tittleshall († 1759) are busts in settings provided by others, *Wilton*'s at Horsford († 1777) and West Harling (*c*.1780) are busts again, *Nollekens*'s at Tittleshall (1805) has a fine relief, at Felbrigg (1813) once w46 more an excellent bust. Messrs *Coade & Sealy* provided monuments at Thorpe outside Norwich († 1810), at St Stephen Norwich († 1812), and at Melton Constable († 1812), the Justice at the Thetford Guildhall (1799), and also the monumental figure of Britannia on top of the Nelson Column at Great Yarmouth, put up in 1817 and one of the earliest of such columns in England. *Banks* did a relief at Holkham Hall. *Flaxman* was responsible for the Cowper monument at East Dereham (1802), a monument at Burnham Thorpe (1803), and one at Ketteringham († 1825), *Westmacott* for monuments at Ketteringham

(1807), Little Walsingham († 1804 and 1819), Catton outside
Norwich († 1820), and Stradsett († 1823) and a relief at Holkham Hall, the younger *Bacon* for about half a dozen including
E44 excellent ones at Ormesby St Michael, Sheringham, and Sprowston (Norwich), and *Chantrey* for the curious Woodcock at
Holkham Hall, for a relief in the same house, and for the seated
figure of Bishop Bathurst in Norwich Cathedral (1841).* To the
funeral monuments two notes must be appended: one on the
curious, completely asymmetrical Rococo tablets at St Giles
Norwich († 1767), Melton Constable († 1768), and Witton near
E45a North Walsham († 1769); the other on the plentiful headstones
& b
w47b in Norfolk churchyards, fully investigated by Mr F. Burgess.‡

Here we must leave sculptors, as we are on the verge of the
Victorian Age. It was the Norwich sculptors who caused this di-
gression, and the most interesting family of them has not yet been
commented on, the *Ivorys*. They were sculptors, joiners, architects, and timber merchants. *Thomas Ivory* (1709–79) bought the
freedom of Norwich in 1745, was appointed carpenter to the
Great Hospital in 1751, built some houses attached to the Hospital in 1752 etc., probably the Assembly Rooms in 1754, the
Norwich Theatre nearby (which does not survive) in 1757, the
E19b Octagon Chapel in 1754–6, various houses, and in 1771–2 the
& 28b Artillery Barracks. *William Ivory* (1746–c.1801) was the designer
of the Norwich and Norfolk Hospital (1770–5) and the pretty
family pew in St Helen's, the church of the Hospital (1780).
John Ivory († 1805) was a sculptor, not an architect. Resident in
Norwich also was *Matthew Brettingham*, whose name, as we have
seen, is connected with some of the greater Georgian houses of
Norfolk.

The Octagon Chapel and the Old Meeting of 1693 are far and
E19a away the most interesting NONCONFORMIST CHAPELS in Nor-
& b
& 28b folk. There are few others of before 1830, and they are minor.
Only two will be quoted here, the Presbyterian Chapel at Hap-
ton, because its date 1741 is uncommonly early, and the Friends'
Meeting House at Norwich by *J. T. Patience* (1825), because it
attempts a composition of some dignity. Nor do CHURCHES need
E18a more space, once Gunton has been remembered. The only other
church-building event of interest is the rebuilding of the nave of
St Margaret King's Lynn by *Brettingham* in 1745–6, because this

---

* *Rysbrack* did no funeral monuments in the county; he did however provide the statues outside Houghton and chimneypieces inside.

‡ *Monumental Journal*, March–October 1954.

is a remarkably early essay in Gothicism, i.e. a self-conscious handling of the Gothic style, no longer the unselfconscious continuation we have had earlier on. But for the GOTHIC REVIVAL also Norfolk is of slight interest. The *Ivorys*, in adding to Blickling, kept to its Jacobean style, and on the remodelled staircase placed two strangely historicizing statues in relief in niches. *William Ivory*, as just noted, designed and made a Gothick family pew for St Helen in Norwich, the church of the Great Hospital, in 1780, and he may also have designed and made the Gothick Bishop's Throne in Norwich Cathedral now dethroned. Beeston Hall Beeston St Laurence of 1786 is Gothick too and castellated; Gothick also, of the ending Georgian Age, were the stables at Felbrigg of 1825 and Cromer Hall outside Cromer of 1827–8, both by *Donthorne*. Gothic finally is the façade of the grotto in the grounds of Denton House. This is dated 1770 and has a wholly delightful interior.

But all these C18 houses so far have been country houses. Norfolk, and especially Norwich, is rich in GEORGIAN TOWN HOUSES too. Of those in Norwich Thomas Churchman's house in St Giles Street is *facile princeps*. Its Rococo interiors are E58 splendid.* Other notable and enjoyable town houses are at Great Yarmouth and King's Lynn, but hardly fewer in the small towns such as Swaffham, Aylsham, Wymondham, Harleston, Reepham, and the charming little places 'next-the-sea' such as Wells and Cley, and even in certain villages like Coltishall and Hingham. They are almost without exception of red brick. Brick had been the favourite material in the countryside ever since the time of Henry VIII. In the towns timber-framing carried on, and Celia Fiennes could still write of Norwich in 1698 that of the houses 'none [are] of brick except some few beyond the river which are built for some of the rich factors'. This was the exact moment when things changed, and we have seen earlier on that the houses selected to represent the style of about 1700, with their giant angle pilasters and parapets, were of brick. So were of course those by Brettingham and the Ivorys also mentioned before. It is hard to select among the other fully Georgian houses. At Great Yarmouth the most lavish one is that of a great fish merchant in South Quay. At King's Lynn there are plenty, even if none of them is outstanding. At Wymondham the best is Caius House of *c.*1750 (already mentioned), at Harleston the w61a Early Georgian Candler's House.

* He died in 1742.

But town architecture is not complete without PUBLIC BUILDINGS, and these have not so far been collected systematically. So we must for a moment go back to Queen Elizabeth I and the Stuarts in order to place on record the gay extension to the King's Lynn Guildhall,* the market houses of North Walsham, Wymondham (1617), New Buckenham, and, to jump into the
w61b later Georgian decades, Swaffham (1783). Then Almshouses. Those of Castle Rising (1614) are unusually extensive, as are those for fishermen at Great Yarmouth (1702), a fine, animated composition with a big steep pediment and a turret. The Cus-
w55a toms House at Lynn of 1683 needs only a reminder. It is one of the best public buildings of its date in England. The same munificent merchant who had it built also paid for the building of the Duke's Head, for gentlemen to have somewhere to stay when they came to Lynn on business. Norfolk has two more inns of about that time, equally spacious and architecturally ambitious:
w53b the White Hart at Scole, half-way on the Norwich–Ipswich road (on which see above), and the Swan at Harleston, which is in a plain Queen Anne style but has a front of nine bays.

The other public buildings to be summarized all date from after 1750. The first is the Assembly Rooms at Norwich – of 1754, probably by *Thomas Ivory* (*see* above) – one of the most accomplished assembly rooms of the C18 in England. Originally a Theatre Royal went with it, but that has alas been replaced. The 1760s are represented by the Paston School of North Walsham (1765), the 1770s by the Norfolk and Norwich Hospital at Norwich (1770–5; *see* above), both pedimented brick houses. Then two more hospitals must be recorded: the Naval
E59 Hospital of 1809 at Great Yarmouth by *Edward Holl*, very large, of four blocks of twenty-nine bays each, and the mental hospital of 1811–14 outside Norwich, which is by *Francis Stone*, the county surveyor. It consists of a centre block with lower wings. Pedimented again, and with long lower wings, are the former Cavalry Barracks of 1791 in Norwich. The Arsenal at Gorleston (Southtown), also three ranges, two of them with pediments, is of 1806 and was designed by *James Wyatt*. Soane's Gaol in the castle at Norwich does not exist any longer, but King's Lynn has a not very memorable gaol of 1784. Then two

---

* The REGALIA of King's Lynn later than the Cup of King John ought not to be forgotten, nor those of Norwich, one of the finest collections in the country, nor those of Thetford either. In this context a word must be said
E38b also of the numerous wrought-iron SWORD and MACE RESTS in Norwich churches and the Octagon Chapel.

very remarkable early FACTORIES, both at Norwich, of 1836 and 1834 etc. one in King Street, the other, now Jarrold's, in Cowgate. E60 This latter, by the County Surveyor, *John Brown*, is one of the best of its date, if not the best, in England, both functional and dignified. Finally the WORKHOUSES, starting in a purely Georgian mood with those of Hales 1764, Wicklewood 1776, Gressenhall 1777,* and getting into their stride with the many provided after the reform of the Poor Law in 1834: Hindringham, Lingwood, Pulham Market, Swainsthorpe, Thetford, Tivetshall, Yarmouth, all of 1836–8 and all Latest Classical, and then Downham Market, Aylsham, and Beckham of *c.* 1850, turning Tudor.‡ This is the turn from the Georgian to the Victorian Age, and we can now at last take the turn.

The VICTORIAN AGE has done comparatively little to Norfolk. The county was not industrialized; even the city of Norwich remained manageable, and small towns remained small towns. There were on the whole enough churches, and there were not many *nouveaux riches* who clamoured for super-mansions. So the record is brief. To begin at the beginning, *John Brown* designed some churches, including South Runcton of 1839, which is Norman, and New Catton, Norwich, of 1841–2, which is E.E. *Pugin* did the bold and heavily picturesque alterations at West Tofts (1849–50). The furnishings at or from West Tofts are his too. *Penrice* did the super-Norman church at Gillingham as late as 1858–9. The only other noteworthy church prior to the Late Victorian decades is Holkham, rebuilt and enlarged by *Street* in 1870. This was a big job, but nothing like as big as *Charles Barry Jun.*'s Bylaugh Hall of *c.*1850, a descendant of Wollaton, now happily a ruin, and *S. S. Teulon*'s prodigious Shadwell Park of 1857–60, in a Gothic externally and internally which no-one but Teulon would have dared. Sandringham by *A. J. Humbert* (1870 etc.) is Old English. It is restrained by comparison, a judgement nobody would make for its main gates, designed by *Thomas Jekyll* and shown at the Great Exhibition of 1862. Jekyll of Norwich was an interesting, erratic architect. His w63b church at Hautbois (1864) is of no interest, his Methodist church at Holt (1862) and his church at Thorpe outside Norwich (1866) are terrible.

The last quarter of the C19 is represented in Norfolk church architecture by Booton (*c.*1875–91), the design of the Rev. *Whitwell Elwin*, admirable in his zest, less admirable in his

* These remarkably early dates are matched in Suffolk.
‡ But Gayton of 1836 is in a minimum-Tudor too.

E18b results, and by the Catholic church of St John Baptist in Norwich, which was designed by *George Gilbert Scott Jun.* and continued by his brother *John Oldrid Scott*. It was begun in 1884 and completed in 1910. It is in its entirety the gift of the Duke of Norfolk, of cathedral size, solidly built in the E.E. style and in its internal effect infinitely enhanced by the stained glass designed by *John* and *Dunstan Powell* in 1895 etc. This is imitation C13 work and very good of its kind, though it takes no notice of the innovations brought about more than thirty years earlier by the Pre-Raphaelites and consolidated by William Morris. The Pre-Raphaelite style is excellently documented in Norfolk: at Sculthorpe in the early sixties, where the work is by *Morris* and his friends, at Thursford in 1862, where it is by the almost unknown Rev. *Arthur Moore* (one of outstanding quality), and at North Pickenham in 1864, where it is by *Powell's*.*

The Pre-Raphaelites and Morris are the fountain-head of the ARTS AND CRAFTS movement in England, and the architects believing in its tenets have left some of their most significant work in Norfolk: *Lutyens* in The Pleasaunce Overstrand of 1897–9 and Overstrand Hall of 1899,‡ *Detmar Blow* in a large house of 1900 at Happisburgh, and *E. S. Prior* in the unbeliev-
E61 able Home Place Holt of 1903–5, with its wild mixture of local building materials.

That is one trend of the Edwardian decade. There were two others, equally significant. One of them is the unashamed Baroque of public and commercial buildings, and in this trend
E63a few in England could beat *G. J. Skipper* of Norwich. His Nor-
E62 wich Union in Surrey Street of 1903–4, though not large, seems vast. The elements of it are colossal and the spirit Piranesian. The other trend was that of functionalism, and that also has a representative at Norwich as perfect in its diametrically opposed way as Skipper's Norwich Union: the factory now of Messrs
E63b Roberts, the printers, in Botolph Street. This was built in 1903 too, and the façade is entirely a grid of wide brick pilasters and the mullions and transoms of spacious seven-light windows. It is in its modest way as logical as Sullivan and perhaps inspired by Mackintosh's Glasgow School of Art. It established a bridge

* No other church furnishings need recording, and only one church MONUMENT: that by *Watts* at Blickling of 1878.

‡ *Lutyens* also designed the Methodist Church at Overstrand (1898), and this and young *Sir Giles Gilbert Scott*'s Catholic church at Sheringham, begun in 1910, are the only latest C19 and C20 churches of note in Norfolk, until Mr *B. M. Feilden*'s Presbyterian Church of 1954–6 at Norwich is reached, an example of the characteristic mid-C20 revived Expressionism.

to MODERN ARCHITECTURE, but few in Norfolk went across it. The *Smithsons*' Hunstanton School of 1950–3, ruthlessly per- w64b fect and ruthlessly symmetrical, remained an alien body and an irritant. Norfolk is more truly represented by the City Hall of E64 Norwich, 1932 by *C. H. James & S. R. Pierce*, and by the rural housing of 1947 etc. at and around Loddon by *Tayler & Green*. w64a The City Hall is the most successful public building of between the wars in England, although, or perhaps because, it is so frankly dependent on Ostberg's Stockholm Town Hall. With this pattern, a building after all designed in 1909, it is pre-modern, but not the worse for it. *Tayler & Green*'s rural housing on the other hand can almost be called post-modern, if by modern one still understands what is now familiar as the International Style of the 1930s. It is far more accommodating and gentle, it uses local materials, it is pretty and varied in an unobtrusive way in its details, it makes use of terraces of houses, of closes, and of other compositional means not usual in rural council housing, and it is remarkably sensitive to landscape and contours. In Norwich a new City Architect, *David Percival*, has also within the last three years or so given municipal housing a turn to this new pleasant, unregimented, unradical domesticity.

It suits Norfolk, and in this mood we can happily leave the county. It is a domesticated county; even its largest and proudest houses, Houghton, Holkham, Blickling, Raynham, Felbrigg, are truly inhabited, and the many medium-sized ones are often still in the hands of the families who built them, the Bacons of medieval descent, the Barclays and Birkbecks and Buxtons and Gurneys of Georgian mercantile descent. The land is made use of as it should be, except where it has been given over to the roaring airfields, British and American, with their weird and sinister machinery. The hundreds of churches are trying hard or not so hard to keep going. Churchyards grow crops of nettles unmatched in their profusion. Struggling vicars rush in their secondhand cars from one of their churches to the other to arrive in time for the next service. Their congregations are small and scattered and often live away from where the church was built, long before the Black Death or an improving C18 squire had removed the original village. There is plenty of change and disturbing change under the grandiose, ever-changing and yet eternal East Anglian sky.

No wonder that the rebirth of Western landscape painting in the early C19 was an East Anglian affair, with Constable in Suffolk and Crome and Cotman in Norfolk. Constable's and

Crome's skies are the greatest monument to the landscape of East Anglia, but Cotman also drew, sketched, and etched the buildings of his county.* So to the DRAWINGS and then the books for those who wish to study Norfolk buildings beyond the narrow compass of this book. Norfolk has been served unusually well by its draughtsmen. Apart from Cotman's series there are the Ladbrooke drawings, published in six volumes in 1823–30, and the views of Norwich by J. Sillett, published in 1826, and there is the Dawson Turner collection of drawings at the British Museum (Add. 23024–62).

Then BOOKS AND PAPERS. This list must of course be headed by Francis Blomefield's unfinished *Essay towards a Topographical History of the County of Norfolk*, inadequately completed in five volumes and finally published in 1739–75. He did himself the first two and three-quarter volumes, mainly in the southern parts of the county, and was then, as his monument in Fersfield church says, 'snatched away in the midst of his Labors'. The late Munro Cautley made a survey of Norfolk churches as complete (and with the same limitations) as that he had made before of Suffolk, but it was published (in 1949) rather more briefly. The introduction to his volume is, within his own terms, without doubt more useful and knowledgeable than mine. Similar surveys were made by J. C. Cox (*County Churches*, 2 vols, 1910–11) and by T. H. Bryant (published in the press and collected at the Norwich Central Library). Then there are of course, not only for churches, the volumes of the *Little Guides* (by W. A. Dutt and E. T. Long, 9th ed., 1949) and the *Shell Guides* (by W. Harrod and C. L. S. Linnell,‡ 1957). The county antiquarian journal is *Norfolk Archaeology*. In the volumes of this (vols IX–XXIV) appeared e.g., a catalogue of Norfolk church plate. Other indispensable surveys are R. Rainbird Clarke's *East Anglia* (1960) in the *Ancient Peoples and Places* series which covers the whole field of archaeology from earliest times to the later medieval period and has a most useful bibliography, Dean Woodforde's *The Norwich School of Glass Painting in the Fifteenth Century* (1950), E. Farrer's survey of heraldry in Norfolk churches (3 vols, 1887–93), and Miss A. Baker's of painted screens (thesis, London University, 1937; unpublished). In addition there are, needless to say, the books dealing with such subjects for the whole country: I am thinking of F. Bond on screens and A. Vallance on screens

---

* His *Architectural Etchings of Norfolk* were published in 1838.

‡ Mr Linnell has also written a number of exemplary guides to churches around Letheringsett.

in major churches, Mill Stephenson on brasses, E. W. Tristram on wall painting of the twelfth, the thirteenth, and the fourteenth centuries (1944, 1950, 1955), of Howard Colvin's and Rupert Gunnis's indispensable dictionaries of architects and sculptors respectively, and the volumes of *Country Life* with their equally indispensable articles on country houses. Houses also, though in exemplary interaction with people and events, form the subject of Mr R. W. Ketton-Cremer's three books called *Norfolk Portraits* (1944), *Norfolk Gallery* (1948), and *Norfolk Assembly* (1957).* These few titles must be enough to guide users into further reading.

* B. Cozens-Hardy: Some Norfolk Halls (*Norf. Arch.*, vol. 32, 1960) could only be used immediately before going to press.

NORTH-EAST NORFOLK AND NORWICH

*

ST EDMUND. Round tower, the top storey of the C13, octagonal, with long lancets. Yet later battlements with flushwork panelling and figures as pinnacles. Bits from a Norman doorway have been reassembled so as to look like a blocked fireplace. They are two shafts with scalloped capitals, a zigzag arch, and another scalloped arch moulding. Nave and chancel much renewed. The windows point to an early C14 date. The chancel Sedilia are in order, and they have ogee arches. They are incidentally of the dropped-sill type so that the arches are blank against the back wall below the window. The S doorway of the nave also was not interfered with, and that bears out the date of the nave windows. Two two-storeyed porches, that on the S side simple, that on the N side with flushwork panelling on the façade; in the spandrels of the entrance two praying people (donors?) and a leaf motif. Above the entrance two windows and a niche. C16 brick and flint rood turret. – FONT. On two steps, the upper with quatrefoil decoration. Inscription, not revealing the name of the donor, but the year of the donation: 1410. Against the stem four lions and four wild men. Against the bowl four angels and the Pietà, the Trinity, and further angels with the Emblem of the Trinity and the Instruments of the Passion. – FONT. Miniature model of a font, perhaps really made as such. Stone, only 11 in. high, octagonal, with plain panelling against the stem and heads supporting the rim. – SCREEN. Tall and exceptionally good. Two-light divisions with ogee heads. Tracery in two tiers, i.e. a transom with tracery below and in addition the ogee arches at the top with thin tracery. Dado with ornamental motifs, especially IHS and E with crossed arrows for St Edmund. – STALL. With two bench ends with poppy-heads. – INSCRIPTION. Below a chancel N window painted on the stone an early C15 inscription starting: 'Nota. O mors mesta nimis, quamplures mergis

in imis. Nunc hos, nunc illos, nunc rapis undique, mors.' –
PLATE. Cup and Cover, London, 1656; Paten, secular, London, 1776; Chalice, London, 1802. – MONUMENTS. Brass to John Swanne † 1533, a 13 in. figure. – Jeremiah Berry † 1767. By *W. Lane* of Norwich. Of coloured marbles. Obelisk with a shield in a cartouche.

Several nice HOUSES by the cross-roads, especially one of three bays and two storeys with four Venetian windows, one arched window, and a doorway with broken pediment.

BRIDGE HOTEL, 1 m. NE. Attached to the house the ruin of a circular structure of flint supposed to form part – the only surviving part – of WEYBRIDGE PRIORY, a small Augustinian priory founded at the time of Henry III.

(The BRIDGE is of three segmental arches. NBR)

1030   ALBY

ST ETHELBERT. Mostly Dec, but the chancel Perp. The W tower has a three-light window with cusped intersected tracery. Traceried sound-holes, Dec bell-openings. In the nave cusped Y-tracery and Dec tracery proper. The church has a clerestory, although there are no signs of aisles having ever been built. Arched braces to support the nave and the S porch roofs. – FONT. Octagonal, plain, with shields. – Of the SCREEN only the dado is preserved. – Some old BENCH ENDS. – PLATE. Norwich-made Chalice of 1567–8.

1030   ALDBOROUGH

ST MARY. Nave, chancel, and N aisle. In addition a quaint bell-turret of 1906. The W quoins of the nave and also the SE quoins halfway to the E are of carstone and suggest a Norman date for the nave. The windows however are C14. As in other churches, of the three on the S side the l. and r. ones have purely Perp, but the middle one has Dec tracery. Above the S doorway a little vaulted niche. The N arcade is very rough, partly just cut through the wall with responds instead of proper piers. Here also the extent of the Norman nave can be surmised. – FONT. Octagonal, with quatrefoiled circles and tracery. – PLATE. Chalice and Paten by *John East* of London, 1716. – BRASSES (nave). To Robert Herward † 1481 (2 ft 2 in. figure), to Anne Herward † 1485 (2 ft 2 in. figure), to a Civilian, *c.* 1490 (3 ft figure).

ALDERFORD

1010

ST JOHN BAPTIST. Of the early C14. Small W tower with a small w window (cusped Y-tracery). In the nave one big three-light Dec window. The tracery is repeated in a narrower three-light window in the chancel. The former N arcade also goes with an early C14 date. There is no chancel arch between nave and chancel. – FONT. Octagonal. With statuettes against the stem and the Seven Sacraments and the Crucifixion against the bowl. On the underside of the bowl the Signs of the Evangelists and four angels. – SOUTH DOOR. The plate for the knocker with cross-wise fleur-de-lis extensions, C13 to C14. – STAINED GLASS. Some original glass in one S and the W windows. – PLATE. Norwich-made Chalice and Paten Cover of 1567.

BELL INN, E of the church. Nice castellated house, probably of the late C18, with short castellated retaining walls l. and r.

(FARMHOUSE, E of the church. Georgian, but in the gable of an outbuilding below the chimneystack the date 1666 in brick. NBR)

ANTINGHAM

2030

ST MARGARET. In the same churchyard with St Mary. In ruins. The NW quoin of the nave is of big blocks of carstone, i.e. probably Norman. W tower standing up, nave and chancel fragmentary and overgrown.

ST MARY. The windows almost exclusively of three lights with reticulated tracery, i.e. a unified job of *c*.1330–50. The W tower has one of these windows, the nave has them, and the chancel, which follows the nave without structural division. Arch-braced roof. – FONT. Octagonal, of Purbeck marble, with two shallow pointed arches on each side; C13. – STAINED GLASS. The SE window of 1868, good; probably by *Powell*. The angels in a N window could be by the same. – The NE window by *Kempe*, 1891. – (SCULPTURE. Two head corbels inside; good. NBR) – BRASS Richard Calthorp † 1562 and wife; 17 in figures.

ANTINGHAM HALL. The house is of the C17, with a two-storeyed porch with a shaped gable. The rest is old in its walling too, but has no features preserved.

ASHBY HALL

4010

1 m. E of Thurne

Nice Georgian front of three bays with a doorway with broken pediment on fluted attached columns. At the back an outbuilding still with shaped gables.

ASHMANHAUGH

3020

ST SWITHIN. Small. The round tower rebuilt in 1849. Nave
and chancel. Dec windows. – BENCHES. Ends with poppy-
heads. Also a back with ten shields, five with the Wounds of
Christ, five with initials and the date 1531. – PLATE. Chalice,
made in Norwich, 1567. – MONUMENT. Honor Bacon † 1591.
Tomb-chest with shields.

ATTLEBRIDGE

1010

ST ANDREW. Slim, unbuttressed W tower without datable details. Nave and chancel apparently of *c.*1300 with Perp additions. The E window has three stepped lancet lights under one
arch. The N arcade must be later. It has three bays, and piers
and arches have two continuous chamfers. – (LECTERN. A
bulbous baluster of *c.*1700 with leaf growing up the lower
parts. NBR) – PLATE. Chalice, made in Norwich, 1567. –
BRASS. George Conyngham † 1525, with a chalice (S of communion rail).

AYLMERTON

1030

ST JOHN BAPTIST. Round tower, but bell-openings with Y-
tracery and flushwork panelling on the battlements. Small
doorway from the S into the tower; altered. Tall Perp two-
storeyed S porch. Small niche above the entrance. Dec nave
W windows, but tall Perp S windows differing in their tracery.
Dec chancel, the E window with flowing tracery and Sedilia and
Piscina with nodding ogee arches – SCREEN. Fragmentary.
Each division with two pendant ogee arches. – STALLS.
Traceried ends with poppy-heads. – PLATE. Norwich-made
Chalice, 1567.
CROSS, 1 m. S. Square base and part of the shaft. The top parts
restoration.

AYLSHAM

1020

ST MICHAEL. A large church, immediately N W of, and partly
visible from, the market place. The interior is older than the
exterior. The six-bay arcades with their alternation of circular
and octagonal piers look early C14. The tower arch is later, apparently Dec, and that date is borne out by the exterior of the
tower. Late Dec W window of four lights with tracery of a
shape not quite reticulation. Dec bell-openings. Pretty lead-
covered spirelet, probably early C17. Lavish two-storeyed S
porch, built in 1488. Faced with knapped flint. Above the en-

trance flushwork panelling and cusped panels with shields.
The upper floor with a niche flanked by two-light windows.
The s aisle is also faced with knapped flint. Flushwork-
panelled battlements. Nicely decorated buttresses. Perp transepts and Perp chancel chapels of two bays. The pier has the
usual section of four shafts and four hollows. The church was
drastically restored in 1852. – FONT. If it is Perp, it was much
retooled in 1852. – REREDOS. Made up of bench ends by
J. Adey Repton in 1833. – SCREEN. With an inscription to a
man who died in 1507. Dado with sixteen painted figures,
two of them the donors. The paintings are by two hands.* –
PULPIT. Unusual. C17, with square balusters framing blank
arches in perspective (cf. Itteringham).‡ – BENCHES. A few
in the transepts. (MISERICORDS: a bearded head, a man with
a club. NBR) – WEST GALLERY. Supported on arched braces
with tracery in the spandrels. – STAINED GLASS. Much is
preserved of the time of the restoration of the church. The
different styles ought to be observed. The makers are unknown except for the pictorial glass in the s chapel (Brazen
Serpent), which is by Clutterbuck, 1857 (TK). The same
maker is clearly responsible for the s aisle w window, the
Repton family window of 1855. The maker of the chancel E
window took his inspiration from the partly genuine German
St John in the other s chapel window.§ – PLATE. Chalice
and Paten, Norwich, 1567; Flagon, 1701; oval Dish, London,
1752; two Cups, London, 1807. – MONUMENTS. Brasses to
T. Tylson, rector, c. 1490, 24½ in.; Robert Farman and wife,
c.1490, 16 in.; Richard Howard † 1499 and wife, in shrouds,
19 in.; (Civilian and wife, c.1500); Thomas Wymer † 1507
(a worsted weaver who gave the screen), a 32 in. figure in a
shroud. – Bishop Jegon † 1617. Small standing alabaster
monument. Below a classical pediment, in a niche, a shield
and the mitre over. No effigy, but at the foot a skull and rib-
bons. – Clement Francis † 1792. By John Ivory of Norwich.
Neo-classical, with an urn in front of an obelisk. – Repton
family, Gothic, outside the chancel. The monument recalls
Humphry, the most famous gardener of his day, † 1818, his

* Mr J. Sapwell, who kindly amended the entry on Aylsham, tells me that
parts of the upper part of the screen and some MISERICORDS are incorporated in the REREDOS.

‡ Mr Sapwell also tells me that the pulpit can be dated 1637 from the
church wardens' accounts.

§ He was, according to Mr Sapwell, a Mr Yarrington of Norwich, and
the date is 1842.

wife and family. Repton lived at Sustead Hall when he was
newly married. His sister married John Adey, an Aylsham
solicitor. The epitaph composed by Repton reads as follows:

> Not like Egyptian tyrants consecrate,
> Unmixed with others shall my dust remain;
> But mold'ring, blending, melting into Earth,
> Mine shall give form and colour to the Rose,
> And while its vivid blossoms cheer Mankind,
> Its perfumed odours shall ascend to Heaven.

The date of the monument must be considerably later than
that of Repton's death.

THE TOWN. The houses worth recording are mostly of the C18
and all of red brick. The centre is the MARKET PLACE, just S
of the church. At the SE corner a five-bay house of two and a
half storeys with a pedimented doorway on pilasters. At the
NE corner a house typical of several at and around Aylsham:
six bays with giant angle pilasters and a half-storey above the
cornice. Probably c.1710-20. On the W side the BLACK BOY,
much altered, but with giant pilasters framing the centre bay.
Also Queen Anne or a little later. On the same side a chemist's
shop with a delightful front with fluted columns.

We must now make sallies in various directions, and first to the
NW because in BLICKLING ROAD is the best house in Aylsham.
On the way to it THE KNOLL, five plus three bays, but apparently of one build. Again giant angle pilasters. The gable
ends still with shaped gables. The staircase has three slim
twisted balusters to the step. The date about 1700-10. The
porch is later C18. AYLSHAM OLD HALL, dated on a chimney
1689, is a perfect specimen of its date. Seven bays, two storeys,
hipped roof. The first and last two bays project. Brick quoins,
elongated wooden cross-windows (preserved only on the NW
side). Doorway with brick pilasters and a broad segmental
pediment. Staircase with sturdy twisted balusters.

Secondly to the SE, along NORWICH ROAD. Here at once two
good houses on the l., Bank House and the Manor House.
BANK HOUSE has a five-bay front with a recessed centre bay.
Pedimented doorway. Giant angle pilasters, parapet with sunk
panels, shaped gables, i.e. once more c.1710. The MANOR
HOUSE has a long eleven-bay front with a middle porch.
Doorcase with broad Doric pilasters and a segmental pedi-
ment. Wooden cross-windows. All this is clearly late C17, but
the brickwork is equally clearly Tudor. (Good interior.
MHLG)

To the NE first RED LION STREET. Here, next to the Red Lion Inn, a seven-bay house with shaped gables and wooden cross-windows. Then, across the end, No. 1 WHITE HART STREET, five bays with giant pilasters. Later doorway with broken pediment. More minor Georgian houses in White Hart Street. The continuation is MILLGATE STREET, where No. 56 is mid-Georgian. Five bays, two and a half storeys. Good doorcase with Doric pilasters, guilloche on the frieze, and a pediment.

Further out the following buildings ought to be listed: the WINDMILL, ⅝ m. SW, the stump of a brick tower-mill; the former WORKHOUSE (Hospital), ⅝ m. WSW, built by *Donthorne* in 1849, Tudor, with a surprisingly ambitious centre (four polygonal turrets, one very large, many-transomed window) and lower wings; DAKIN'S FARMHOUSE, ¾ m. SE, on the Wroxham Road, of four bays, with angle pilasters in two orders and shaped gables, probably late C17; and ABBOT'S HALL, 1½ m. NE, of the early C17, with a flat, long front of which the l. half is ruinous at the time of writing. Brick with dark-brick diaper. The first-floor windows all with wooden mullions.

BRAMPTON PIECE, near Bolwick Hall. A rectangular ditched area where Iron Age pottery was found. In the same area there are badly robbed remains of ROMAN FARM BUILDINGS, including a large timber-framed barn(?). There were also two flint-walled buildings, one with a lime kiln attached; the other was demolished in the late C4.

BACONSTHORPE

1030

ST MARY. The best thing about the church is the double Angle Piscina of the chancel, with a quatrefoiled circle that dates it securely *c*.1260–80. The chancel was of the same date, but is over-restored. The tower looks Perp but is a Victorian rebuild. Perp aisle windows, but the arcades (three bays, octagonal piers, double-chamfered arches) probably earlier, at least the s arcade. Perp one-bay chancel chapels. Perp Easter Sepulchre. Four-centred arch below a crocketed ogee gable. Castellated cresting. – SCREEN. Under the tower arch. Probably made up of bench-backs. – PLATE. London-made Chalice and Paten, 1767; Flagon, 1773. – MONUMENTS. Brass to Anne Heydon † 1561; small (E wall of s aisle). – Standing monument to Sir William Heydon † 1593 and wife. Alabaster with two kneeling figures, both now facing s.

BACONSTHORPE CASTLE, 1 m. NW. Begun about 1450 and
completed in 1486. Quadrangular building in a moat (cf. e.g.
the contemporary Kirby Muxloe in Leicestershire). The walls
remain to a certain height, and several towers. The only building of which more is preserved is the gatehouse. This is faced
with knapped flint. It is three-storeyed, and the passage
through was vaulted. Within the wall to the r. also a big
living-house of the later C17 with a symmetrical front; mullioned and transomed windows. (Outside, about 50 yds to the
s remains of an outer gatehouse with flanking octagonal turrets. B. Cozens-Hardy)

To the s of the gatehouse remains of BACONSTHORPE HALL, a
C16 house made by conversion of an outer gatehouse of the
castle. Of this the inner archway and the prominent E staircase
tower are left. The corresponding W tower as well as the whole
W half of the house has collapsed. The house has a doorway
with four-centred arch and mullioned and transomed windows, still with arched lights. The tower has an ogee cap.

3030   BACTON

ST ANDREW. Perp. W tower with strong batter. W doorway with
shields and tracery in the spandrels. Two niches in the W
buttresses. Sound-holes with shields on tracery. – FONT. On
two traceried steps (renewed). Against the foot four animals.
Against the stem attached shafts and nodding ogee arches
bending round them, a decidedly Dec motif. Against the bowl
demi-figures of angels below, and, above, the Signs of the four
Evangelists and four angels with shields. – BENCHES. With
poppy-heads (at the W end). – SCULPTURE. Large demi-
figure of an angel with a scroll. It is said that it came from one
of the niches in the tower buttresses. – PLATE. Norwich-made
Chalice, inscribed 1568.

BROOMHOLM PRIORY. Founded from Castle Acre in 1113.
About 1195 the priory came under Cluny direct. In the C13,
thanks to a relic of the Holy Cross, it became very famous.
Henry III visited Broomholm quite frequently. The ruins
are impressive but not easily read, especially because the most
interesting fragment, that of the N transept of the church, suf-
fers from later cross-walls not yet removed. The site is entered
through the ruined GATEHOUSE, which was two bays deep. To
its E a long stretch of the precinct wall. Towards the s, i.e. the
priory, it was faced with knapped flint and had a four-centred
arch and in the spandrels flushwork decoration with shields.

To the SE now appears the outer wall of the NORTH TRAN- 23a
SEPT, Late Norman with flat buttresses, round-arched upper
windows, and a small doorway leading out to the N. Of Norman
work remain the very similar arches from the transept to
a former E chapel, c.1300 replaced by a larger chapel (the date
to be deduced from a remaining shaft), and from the N aisle to
the transept. Responds with decorated scallops. In the NE
corner a spiral staircase. Inside the transept conspicuous E.E.
work. Of the nave and aisles there exists no more than a
stretch of the S aisle wall. Further S the most prominent piece
is the S wall of the S transept, which also forms the N wall of
the CHAPTER HOUSE. This is E.E. and has tall blank arcading
on its N and S walls. To its S the DORMITORY. This lay of
course on the upper floor. The lower floor was vaulted, see the
springer in the SW corner. The dormitory windows to the E
can still be recognized. Of the S range of claustral buildings
there is only the wall dividing the REFECTORY from a chamber in the SE corner which could have been the Warming
Room. The WEST RANGE is represented by no more than a
lump of masonry close to the aisle wall.

THE VILLAGE of Bacton is one of the prettiest in this part of
Norfolk.

BALE   0030

ALL SAINTS. Most memorable perhaps for the ilexes in front of
it. W tower with a niche below the W window. Chancel of
c.1300, with straight-headed side windows of two lights and
a very fine E window with fully cusped tracery heads, a form
no longer Geometrical and not yet flowing. The roof, which is
single-framed, could be contemporary. Nave and N transept
Perp. Nave roof with arched braces. – FONT. Octagonal with
the Instruments of the Passion, four flower panels, etc., all
severely re-cut. – PAINTING. Three crosses surrounded by
loose trails (nave E, N transept). – STAINED GLASS. Much
original and good glass is reassembled in a S window. The
earliest and best pieces are two apostles of the C14. They are
set against a dark red ground and hold scrolls. Much glass of
the C15. – PLATE. Parcel-gilt Chalice, Norwich-made, 1567;
Paten, London, 1717.

BANNINGHAM   2020

ST BOTOLPH. Dec and Perp. Dec the chancel (but the E window
is Victorian), the arcades with quatrefoil piers with thin

shafts in the diagonals and double-chamfered arches (but the
polygonal abaci make a date after 1360 or 1370 likely), the
chancel arch, the s doorway, the s aisle E bay (one window has
a segmental arch), and the N aisle E window. Perp the other
windows, the s porch (with curious recesses l. and r. inside
divided by a detached shaft), and the w tower. The tower is
tall and has flushwork panelling on base and battlements,
traceried sound-holes, and a tall arch towards the nave. Steep
nave roof with hammerbeams. Much tracery and demi-figures
of angels. The ROOD BEAM is preserved, a rare survival. Arch-
braced N aisle roof. – FONT COVER. Thin, later C17, with attenuated Tuscan columns and ogee cap. – BOX PEWS in the
aisles. – PAINTINGS. On the nave N wall a St Christopher and
a St George. – STAINED GLASS. In one s aisle window and one
N aisle window. In the latter an Annunciation. – PLATE. Pre-
Reformation Paten, parcel-gilt. In a lobed depression a circle
with the face of Christ. – Chalice, Norwich, 1567–8.
RECTORY. With shaped gable-ends but later fenestration. The
house itself probably of the late C17.

9030   BARNEY

ST MARY. Over-restored. s doorway of c.1200, pointed arch on
(formerly) one order of colonnettes. Roll moulding. Blocked
N doorway simple. Chancel of the late C13, see the Angle
Piscina. The windows (pairs of lancets) cannot perhaps be
trusted. Dec chancel E window with minor, but nicely unusual
tracery. Also Dec the s transept E and w windows with segmental arches. Perp w tower and several windows. Nave roof
with arched braces to the ridge and some bosses. In the s
transept also arched braces. – PULPIT. Jacobean. – BENCHES.
Three with poppy-heads. One Jacobean bench with a high
back on knobs. – PLATE. Chalice with an inscription, 1697.

1030   BARNINGHAM

LITTLE BARNINGHAM, see p. 184.
NORTH BARNINGHAM, see p. 200.
ST MARY, Barningham Town or Barningham Winter. In the
grounds of Barningham Hall. Partly in ruins. What remains is
the chancel, now in use as the parish church, a Victorian w
addition to it, and the ruinous Perp nave and w tower. The
chancel is Dec with familiar tracery. Sedilia and Piscina

arched with continuous mouldings. – PLATE. Chalice and two
Patens without marks. – BRASS. John Wynter, early C15. The
figure is 3 ft 9 in. long (s wall).

BARNINGHAM HALL. Built for Sir Edward Paston and dated on 51a
the porch 1612. Red brick with stone dressings. The side with
the porch (W) has polygonal angle buttresses; so has the porch
itself. The most unusual feature is the two-storeyed dormers.
The upper parts of the porch are developed to match. The
windows are all mullioned, transomed, and pedimented. Little
decoration round the doorway. The fine chimneys are polygonal with star tops. The s front was remodelled by *J. A. Repton* in 1805. He altered the windows and added the bays. The
polygonal buttresses and the stepped gables, however, are
original on the l. and simply carried on on the r. More stepped
gables at the back (E). Inside, the staircase with simple cast-
iron railing is evidently Repton's. Two Flemish statuettes of
saints, carved in oak, on the staircase newels.

BARTON TURF
3020

ST MICHAEL. Amid old trees. Big W tower with flushwork
chequer on the base. Traceried sound-holes. Flushwork panelling on the battlements. Two-storeyed N porch with big flushwork panelling. Entrance with spandrels exhibiting shields on
traceried fields. Three niches above. Battlements with flushwork panelling. Tierceron-star vault inside. Perp aisles and
chancel. Early C14 arcades with octagonal piers and double-
chamfered arches. Perp s chapel of two bays. The pier has the
well-known Perp section of four shafts and four hollows. –
FONT. Is it old at all? Stem and bowl with the same motif of
flatly carved ogee-arched panels. – SCREENS. Of the rood
screen dado with three painted saints and the Heavenly 32a
Hierarchies (cf. Ranworth), in style mid C15, and exceptionally good in quality. Of the s aisle screen dado with four
kings; not so good. Also two good tall isolated panels. –
BENCHES. Some, with poppy-heads. – WEST DOOR. Tra- 36a
ceried; Perp. – PAINTINGS. Virgin and Child attended by
angels; Late Mannerist; Netherlandish. – Also a copy of
Rubens's Descent from the Cross, which belonged to Dawson
Turner. – STAINED GLASS. Fragments in a N aisle window. –
(Two brass CHANDELIERS, one of them of *c*.1725. NBR) –
PLATE. Chalice and Paten, London, 1805, neo-Elizabethan. –
MONUMENTS. Brass to Thomas Amys † 1445, without effigy.
He 'made' the s chapel, as he says in the handsome inscription

with some foliage to complete the lines: 'I beseche all people far and ner to pray for me, Thomas Amys, hertely', etc. – Anthony Norris, the antiquary, † 1786. Tablet with pilasters and pediment. – Mrs Norris † 1787, by *Ivory & de Carle*. Pink and white marble. Mourning putto seated by a broken column.

BARTON HALL. Georgian, of red brick, two-storeyed, the w side of seven bays with three-bay pediment, the s side of seven bays also, if one counts a canted bay window as one, the e side only of three with a pedimented one-bay projection and a door surround (no doubt altered).

4010

BASTWICK

¾ m. NE of Repps

CHURCH. Only the tower remains, now in a private garden. Unbuttressed; the bell-openings with cusped Y-tracery. In the garden also the base of a pier and the bowl of the FONT (with a small quatrefoil frieze).

0020

BAWDESWELL

ALL SAINTS. 1953–5 by *J. Fletcher Watson*. A curious but in its way convincing church. It is debatable whether in the 1950s one had any justification for imitating a past style. But if one did, the Neo-Georgian is as good as the Neo-Gothic (*see* e.g. Yarmouth), and it is handled here with pleasure and originality. The material and its treatment is what distinguishes the church: flint pebbles laid herringbone-fashion with occasional bricks forming a loose chequerboard pattern, and all dressings of fawn brick. Nave, w tower, and apse. The apse flanked by Tuscan columns inside. In the middle of the s front outside a broad porch with Tuscan columns. On the tower a shingled lantern. In the church even a three-decker PULPIT. The appreciation of bygone styles has come full circle indeed.

At the w end of the village a nice group including the BELL INN and SOUTH VIEW. Midway down the main street, near the church, CHAUCER HOUSE (much restored), with timber-framed oversailing upper floor. At the e end of the village the METHODIST CHAPEL of 1829, small, with arched windows and a pyramid roof.

BAWDESWELL HALL. With big shaped gables of the type starting with an ogee curve and ending with a semicircle. The importance of the house is that it carries the date 1633.

BAYFIELD
0040

1 m. s of Glandford

BAYFIELD HALL, the house of the Jodrells (*see* Glandford).
Plain, sizable C18 house.* Seven bays, two and half storeys,
brownish brick. Parapet; no pediment. Doorway with pediment on Ionic columns. Inside Elizabethan masonry survives
– a small mullioned window was found by chance recently.

ST MARGARET. Parish church of a lost village. In ruins; just to
the E of the Hall. Nave and chancel and later bellcote. Also a S
chapel or transept. No features survive. The church was still
in use in 1603 but in ruins at the end of the C18.

BECKHAM
1030

ST HELEN AND ALL SAINTS. 1890–1 by *Habershon & Faulk-
ner*. This replaces the former church, which had been ruinous
already in 1602 and of which remains can be seen ¾ m. to the
E. The new church consists of nave and chancel and bellcote.
Pebble outside and inside. (Is that unique?) A few pieces from
the old churches of East Beckham and West Beckham are re-
used. – PLATE. Norwich-made Chalice of 1567.

SW of the church four wireless PYLONS, very high and extremely
graceful.

WORKHOUSE (now Hospital), ¾ m. SE. 1851 etc. Tudor, by
Donthorne. The centre projects a good bit and has the surprising feature of a very large five-transomed window between
polygonal embattled towers. Lower wings to the l. and r. and
behind. The same design was used at Aylsham.

BEESTON REGIS
1040

ALL SAINTS. Alone above the sea, on a bluff – or no longer
quite so alone now that it overlooks a large caravan site. Unbuttressed W tower with cusped Y-tracery in the bell-openings. Parapet with a frieze of flushwork panelling and another
of quatrefoils.‡ Most windows Perp, including those of the
clerestory, which is faced with squared knapped flint. Only the
chancel E window is Dec. Dec also the arcade inside. Three
bays, octagonal piers, double-chamfered arches. W of the
chancel arch two head brackets. The chancel Sedilia with
pretty Perp shafting, but in all probability not an original arrangement. The porch is paved with knapped flint. – SCREEN.

---

* Mr Cozens-Hardy says of before 1788.
‡ The original now in the SW corner of the churchyard.

Of one-light divisions with twelve painted Saints. Nice carvings in the spandrels. – COMMUNION RAIL. Straight, clumsy balusters; C17. – STAINED GLASS. In two chancel windows *Kempe* glass of *c*.1905. – PLATE. Paten *c*.1450, silver-gilt with a sexfoil. In this circular band and in this the Head of Christ set on a cross. – Chalice 1567. – MONUMENTS. Brass to John Deynes † 1527 and wife, 22 in. figures (chancel). – (Also C15 Signs of St Luke and St Mark.) – The sanctuary is paved with the black ledger-stones of the Cremer family.

PRIORY. The ruins of the Augustinian priory, founded *c*.1216, lie to the W of the church, by ABBEY FARMHOUSE, a handsome C18 flint house with stone dressings. Door and window surrounds with rustication of alternating sizes. Of the priory, the church stands in an impressive condition. It was *c*.130 ft long. The monastic quarters have not been excavated. The cloister is now a back garden S of the nave of the church. The W wall still shows, though shapelessly, with the doorway and the window above. This seems to have had C14 tracery. The nave had no aisles. The chancel ended in a straight wall, and this as well as the side walls have tall E.E. blank arcading comprising the former windows. There was a N transept but no S transept. On the other hand there was a bell-turret at the junction of the nave and chancel S walls. To the N an early C14 chapel N of the nave and another, larger, N of the chancel.

BEESTON ST LAURENCE

3020

ST LAURENCE. Round tower, with much carstone below. Nave early C14; see e.g. the windows with three stepped lancet lights under one arch. Perp chancel; broad flushwork panels below the E window. The interior received a shallow coved ceiling with sparse ribbing in the early C19. Wall panelling Gothick too. – PAINTING. Monochrome copy of *Benjamin West*'s 'Last Supper'. – PLATE. Gilt, nicely embossed Chalice, made in Norwich, 1635; Apostle Spoon, inscribed 1655; two Patens, London, 1807 (but inscribed 1749); silver-gilt Knife, London, 1809; Flagon, London, 1812. – MONUMENTS. Many to the Preston family. Tomb-chest to Jacob Preston † 1673. With shields and garlands l. and r. of the inscription. – Of the tablets one ought to note Alicia † 1743 (sarcophagus and urn in arched recess with pediment) and Sir Thomas † 1823 (urn in front of obelisk).

See BEESTON HALL. Built in 1786. Gothick, of seven bays, faced p.
389 with squared knapped flint and castellated. Pointed windows.

Polygonal angle shafts with pinnacles. No other enrichments. The Entrance Hall has a ceiling coved and ribbed just like that in the church. In the middle of the garden side handsome central entrance passage apsed at both ends.

BEIGHTON

3000

ALL SAINTS. Short W tower. The arch towards the nave proves a C14 date. The top parts of the tower date from 1890. Nave and clerestory thatched. The windows are all renewed. They represent the Dec style, and the original doorways bear this out. The chancel seems to be of the same time: see the Sedilia with good ogee arches, luxuriously crocketed. The arcades inside are Perp (four bays, octagonal piers, double-chamfered arches). The nave roof is single-framed with scissor-bracing at the top. – FONT. Of stone, but of the familiar C13 Purbeck type, with eight sides, each with two shallow pointed arches. – (BENCH ENDS, with many animals. NBR) – (CHEST. C17, with pokerwork. NBR) – CHANCEL DOOR, in the S wall. Traceried arch with a band of fleurons around. – STAINED GLASS. In the chancel N and S windows of 1849, and characteristic of that date. – PLATE. Mid or late C14 Paten. Sexfoiled depression with the Hand of God against a cross in a circle. – Chalice, made in Norwich, 1567.

MANOR HOUSE, ⅜ m. SW. Brick, Early Georgian. Five bays, two storeys, with a slightly projecting one-bay centre. This and the whole house have brick quoins. The doorway and the middle window are segment-headed.

BELAUGH

2010

ST PETER. Norman nave and chancel: see one N window in the chancel, built up of blocks of carstone, the carstone NE corner of the chancel, and – a very curious, unexplained feature – the remains of blank arcading outside the S wall of the nave. It looks Saxon rather than Norman, if it is original. In the nave doorway and windows of c.1300, also one larger Perp window. Of c.1300 also the N arcade of four bays with octagonal piers and double-chamfered arches. Dec to Perp W tower with a tower arch dying into the imposts, traceried sound-holes, flushwork-panelled battlements. The three N aisle windows must also be called Dec to Perp; for they have the none too rare feature of a Dec tracery pattern being flanked by two Perp ones. The aisle roof has arched braces. – FONT. Of cauldron shape, Norman, made of a blue stone. The bowl rests on a thick centre shaft and four slightly projecting columns which carry raw blank arches against the sides of the cauldron. – SCREEN. One-light divisions. Ogee-headed panels. Against the dado twelve painted Saints. The style suggests the early C16, and the quality is unusually good. – PLATE. Chalice of 1670, hall-marked London, but the cup of Norwich shape. – Paten Cover without date-mark. – BRASS. John Feelde † 1508, a chalice brass.

BERNEY ARMS MILL
see REEDHAM

1030
BESSINGHAM

ST MARY. Round tower, Anglo-Saxon, see the twin bell-openings with triangular heads and a deeply recessed strong carstone shaft between. The tower is essentially built of carstone, not of flint like most of the round towers. Towards the nave unmoulded arch on simple (Early Norman?) imposts. Above, a triangle-headed doorway. Nave and chancel under one tiled roof. Most of the windows Perp, but all severely restored in 1869. Roof with arched braces and collar-beams; a little tracery above the collars. – STAINED GLASS. On the s side by *Kempe*, c.1897 and c.1906. – PLATE. Norwich-made Chalice, 1567; Paten, date mark illegible.

MOAT YARD, ¼ m. NW. This large area may be the site of a castle.

0020
BILLINGFORD
Near East Dereham

ST PETER. Octagonal W tower. Battlements panelled in flint and stone. Nave and chancel of the early C14, see the windows with cusped Y-tracery and the N and S doorways. Arcades of four bays, quatrefoil piers with thin shafts in the diagonals, but polygonal capitals. Clerestory windows encircled quatrefoils placed above the spandrels, not the apexes of the arches. – FONT. Octagonal, with pretty arcading, probably of c.1300. – SCREEN. Some tracery re-used in the front benches. – LECTERN. Brass, with an eagle at the top. Early Tudor. The same type as King's Lynn St Nicholas, Venice St Mark's, and others (*see* Volume 2, King's Lynn, p. 227). – PLATE. Elizabethan Chalice and Paten; Spoon, London, 1715–16; Chalice, London, 1802–3; two Patens, London, 1804–5.

BILLOCKBY

ALL SAINTS. In ruins except for the chancel. The tower is pre-
served, but not to the top. The nave had big Perp windows.
The chancel was still in good repair in 1762 and is in use now.
It has a big three-light E window with intersected tracery. –
FONT. Octagonal, Perp, with very simple panels. – PLATE.
Chalice and Paten Cover, Norwich-made, 1567–8.
WINDMILL. Stump of a tower-mill, 1¼ m. SW.

BINHAM

BINHAM PRIORY was founded about 1091 by Peter de Valoines
for Benedictine monks and made dependent on St Albans. The
remains of the church are considerable and include the present
parish church of ST MARY. Of the monastic buildings less survives. The church is Norman in style with an E.E. front, the
monastic buildings range from the C12 to the C15. The site is
reached by the GATEHOUSE, NW of the church. Of the entrance
the outer jambs of the carriageway and the pedestrian entrance
are still visible. To the inside there was no special pedestrian
exit. Having entered, one had on one's r. outbuildings.
WEST FRONT. Though not first in time, it is looked at first and
comes first in architectural interest. The special archaeological
interest hinges on the date. According to Matthew Paris it was
built by Prior Richard de Parco, who ruled from 1226 to 1244
(Chron. Maj., R.S. LVII, vol. VI, 90: 'Frontem ecclesie a
fundamento usque ad volsuram construxit'), and if what we
now see is really of before 1244, i.e. before Westminster Abbey, it is the first example of its style in the whole of England
and amazingly up-to-date even from the French point of view.
A description will help to explain this statement. The façade
falls into three parts with three doorways, two minor and one
major, and the middle part, corresponding to the nave, falls
again into three. The size is not big but the treatment is remarkably lavish. Much dog-tooth is used to enliven mouldings, and in the middle portal also a very pretty stiff-leaf variety
of dog-tooth. The portal has five orders of shafts charmingly
grouped so that three stood in a diagonal row and the other
two recessed in shallow hollows. The capitals are of the crocket
type. To the l. and r. are twin pairs of tall blank arches, the
outer pair projecting as part of the buttress. The spandrels between the twins have almond-shaped octofoiled recesses, the
main spandrels sunk pointed trefoils and, l. and r. of the portal,

sunk cinquefoiled circles. The aisle fronts are narrow and chiefly remarkable for their two-light windows. They are really windows in two tiers, the lower, of two simply chamfered lights, connected with the upper by descending mullions. The upper windows have quatrefoiled circles in their heads, with the spandrels sunk if not yet pierced. Yet the middle window has just that, i.e. what we call bar tracery, and bar tracery was invented at Reims Cathedral, in the chancel, which was begun in 1211 and consecrated in 1241. In England its first appearance has always been connected with Westminster Abbey. Moreover, at Binham the w window is of four lights with two sexfoiled circles and one very large octofoiled one. That is an enrichment which appears in the nave at Amiens (1220–39) and again at Westminster Abbey. Whatever the date, the window must have been very beautiful when it was intact. To its l. and r. tall pairs of blank arches with trefoiled heads. Modest bellcote probably later than the c13.

NAVE, TRANSEPTS, CHANCEL. This splendid w front was the end of a building activity of well over a hundred years. Too little is preserved of the E end, which, one may assume, came first. It had the plan best known as that of the second building at Cluny and also familiar from such buildings as Durham. St Albans represents an enriched variety of it. It is the type with a chancel (two bays at Binham) ending in an apse, chancel aisles ending in apses, and transepts with E apsidal chapels, resulting in a staggered arrangement of five apses. The lengthening of the chancel, the straight E wall, and the addition of chancel aisles belong to the Perp style.

The chancel and the other E parts were demolished in 1540, and the elevation of the chancel can only be reconstructed by the stumps of the piers and by comparisons with transepts and aisles. The transepts tell us more, the nave still a great deal. In the transept one can see that there was a gallery and, in front of the clerestory, a wall passage with a stepped tripartite arcade, the type of elevation familiar from Winchester or Ely. The capitals of the wall passage are of the two-scallop kind. There is not enough here for any tentative dating.

21   What is clear, however, is that the nave was built later. The nave and aisles survive sufficiently to enable us to reconstruct their appearance fairly fully. The nave was nine bays long. Seven of these, deprived of their aisles, are now the parish church of Binham. The other two read with the ruins of the E parts. In fact they were always separated from the rest; for the

present E wall (with its domestic window) represents the
PULPITUM. The two doorways are original. The wall was of
course decorated, but we do not know how. Above the arcade
in the nave was a gallery, and it is here evident that this was
unsubdivided, i.e. as at St Étienne in Caen and at Norwich or
Colchester or St Paul's or Blyth. The wall passage is the same
as in the E parts, but the details differ. The scallop capitals are
decorated a little, and there is even quite close to the crossing a
waterleaf capital on the gallery; unless this is a later re-making,
it would push the nave or this part of the nave right on to
c.1170–80. The arcade has (as in the chancel) two shafts,
rising side by side, uninterrupted, from floor to roof, and a
compound arrangement to the arches. The aisles were groin-
vaulted. The arches have decoration with zigzag, billet, and
other geometrical varieties – nothing, however, that could
force one to go beyond, say, 1130 in date. The gallery arches
are undecorated.

The architectural evidence suggests that the nave remained
unfinished for a long time, and that Richard de Parco's *novum
opus* was novum indeed. The joint of Norman and E.E. will be
seen at once, and it runs, as building joints usually do, diagonally, i.e. more was ready on the ground floor than on the upper
floors when building stopped. On the ground floor the w bay
was only in need of w responds and vaulting, which was now
done of course with rib-vaults. On the gallery floor there are
two E.E. bays on the N, one and a half on the s. On the clerestory level three bays are E.E. and have in fact very good stiff-
leaf capitals, richer than those of the w portal.

FURNISHINGS. FONT. Octagonal, Perp, on two steps. The
upper step with panel and quatrefoil decoration. Statuettes
against the stem, the Seven Sacraments against the bowl. –
SCREEN (now near the w end). The dado panels with black-
letter texts faintly revealing former figures of Saints. – STALLS.
Two with MISERICORDS. Heads with twisted beards. –
BENCHES. With openwork-traceried backs and poppy-heads.
– PLATE. Chalice, 1567; Flagon, 1741 (London), and Cover
inscribed 1741. – BRASS. Civilian and Wife, c.1530, three-
quarter figures.

MONASTIC QUARTERS. The parts round the cloister are
easily recognizable: the straight-ended chapter-house s of the
s transept, the dormitory undercroft and the warming house
with its big fireplace to its s, the now divided refectory (or its
undercroft) in the s range, the kitchen with ovens to its w, and

the two-naved w range with Norman wall-piers. The extension
to the s w was probably the guest house. It projects w beyond
the w front of the church and has slender piers and a vault.
THE VILLAGE. In the centre CROSS (base and the major part of
the shaft). Close to it MANOR FARMHOUSE, with a porch
with pinnacles (in decay at the time of writing), and a house
with a shaped gable.

0020

BINTREE

ST SWITHUN. Early C14 w tower, see the w window and the
tower arch. Dec s transept s window (reticulated tracery with
smaller tracery in the reticulation units). Late Perp s aisle.
Chancel of 1806, but re-gothicized. – FONT. Dec, very attractive, with thinly and shallowly carved tracery patterns, including a mouchette wheel, cusped intersected tracery, flowing
tracery, and a circle with three spherical triangles inside. –
PAINTING. Small study on wood for the Transfiguration
painted by *Douglas Guest* in 1809 for St Thomas at Salisbury.
– PLATE. Norwich-made Chalice and Paten, 1567; London-
made Paten on foot, 1721. – MONUMENTS. Chalice Brass to
Thomas Hoont, rector, † 1510 (near the font). – Lord James
N. B. B. Townshend † 1842. By *Sievier*. Tablet without
figures but with very sturdy Greek Doric columns.

WATTS NAVAL TRAINING SCHOOL, 1½ m. wsw. Built in
1871–4 as the Norfolk County School. Designed by *Giles &
Gough*. The chapel was added in 1883. The style was progressive for its date. There were, it is true, still two towers, one
with a higher stair-turret, as a reminder of a gloomier scholas-
tic past, but the gabled dormers and the white casement windows show the effects of Norman Shaw and the London Board
Schools. Quite extensive and well placed on the ridge of the
Bintree Hills, but out of action at the time of writing.

0040

BLAKENEY

ST NICHOLAS. A large, masculine, somewhat forbidding
church. Refaced with a fair amount of knapped flint in the
1880s, and hence rather dark. The church lies outside the little
town, to the s, on an eminence overlooking the marshes and
the sea. Its distinguishing feature, odd rather than beautiful, is
the tall, slender polygonal beacon tower at its NE end, trying a
little perkily to compete with the mass of the w tower. The w
tower is 124 ft high; Perp. Panelled base, originally, it seems,

done in flushwork, a doorway with shields in the spandrels, shields against the N and S buttresses with the arms of the see of Thetford and Norwich, and a deliberate plainness in its upper parts. The decoration of the buttresses continues into the N aisle. At the NW corner the Instruments of the Passion and the defaced date 1435. Large four-light Perp aisle windows, three-light Perp clerestory windows. The chancel externally forms a disappointing contrast to the loftiness of the nave. Internally it is lower still, but far from disappointing. It[22b] turns out to be rib-vaulted, and the nobility of its E.E. forms comes as a surprise after the tall and wide nave. The vault is low indeed (so low as to allow for a chamber above which has a Perp window to the E), yet not in the least depressing. The vaulting is done in four bays, with very elegant ribs and two generously large stiff-leaf bosses. Simple sedilia. Group of seven stepped lancet lights under one arch at the E end (the top of the arch being left blank). Hood-mould with stiff-leaf stops. The window is placed a little higher up than may be expected, but there is a narrow sacristy space behind the altar, accessible from the sanctuary by two plain doorways and lit by one S lancet. Easter Sepulchre with Victorian canopy.*

The nave is very wide in comparison with the chancel and so high as to allow for E openings above the chancel, both now blocked. The upper is a quatrefoil. The Perp arcades are of six bays and have broad, flat projections to the nave, two wave-mouldings (without capitals) in the diagonals, and a demi-shaft to the arches. Roof with long wall-posts, longitudinal arched braces, hammerbeams and subsidiary horizontal beams starting from the apexes of the longitudinal braces, horizontally placed angel figures against both kinds of beams, and traceried spandrels.

FURNISHINGS. FONT. Octagonal, Perp, with the Signs of the Evangelists and four seated Prophets. Against the stem three shields with the Instruments of the Passion and one with a sun. – SCREEN. Mostly recent. – STALLS. With MISERICORDS exhibiting leaves, a monster, a bird, etc. Heads or leaf motifs on the arms. – BENCHES. A few with original poppy-heads. – STAINED GLASS. Some old glass in one N aisle window. – All S windows by *Powell's*, c.1910–30. – PLATE.

---

* The Rev. C. L. S. Linnell's guide to the church mentions as also E.E. a corbel at the E end of the N aisle, two shafts built into the N aisle window recesses, and some fragments in the walls of the chamber above the chancel. He suggests that they come from the C13 nave.

Chalice, 1715–16; Paten, 1731–2; Chalice, 1781–2; Paten, in-
45a   scribed 1802. – MONUMENTS. A fine lot of tombstones in the
churchyard.

THE TOWN is tiny, and mostly built of flint with brick dressings.

THE QUAY overlooks the marshes and, in the summer, the gay
and confusing picture of sailing-boats in the water and outside.
The best individual house along the front is at the very W end:
RED HOUSE, looking E. It is Georgian, low, of brick, seven
bays and two storeys with a three-bay pediment. Close to the
N end of the High Street, as the back part of the so-called
GUILDHALL, a stone-built, brick-vaulted undercroft. The
pillars are octagonal, the ribs unmoulded. The date is probably the C15. In the HIGH STREET nothing of note until Nos
86 and 88 are reached, the former facing away from the street
with an early C19 façade of yellow brick (Tuscan porch), the
latter, though small, with a full supply of door and window
surrounds with rustication of alternating sizes – mid-C18, if
original.

To the N of the church, some distance N of the A-road, the old
FRIARY, i.e. a house incorporating remains of a Carmelite
friary founded in 1296. The remains include a buttress and
some fragments of window surrounds.

WINDMILL, E of the former. A brick and flint tower-mill with
Gothick windows and the sails in disorder (at the time of
writing).

WIVETON HALL, yet further E. See p. 347.

(BLAKENEY CHAPEL, 1¼ m. NE. Only low courses of walling;
no details. MHLG)

1020   # BLICKLING

ST ANDREW. Externally the church seems entirely Victorian,
and partly indeed it ïs. The E window is by *Butterfield*, 1851,
and the W tower and the S porch are by *Street*, 1876. The
oldest surviving piece of the church is the S doorway, which is
E.E. It has one order of colonnettes. The plain N doorway
looks early C14. The arcades (of four bays) are Perp. They
have four shafts and in the diagonals two thin rolls without
capitals. Roof with arched braces supporting the principals.
The aisle roofs follow the same principle, but have traceried
spandrels. In the chancel a handsome angle piscina. – FONT.
Perp, octagonal, with four lions against the stem and eight
lions in panels against the bowl: altogether twelve self-satisfied

Blickling church, brass to Sir Nicholas Dagworth † 1401

lions. – PULPIT. Jacobean, with back panel. – STAINED
GLASS. In the E window by *Hardman*, 1851. – PLATE. Silver-
gilt Chalice, made in Norwich, 1568–9; Norwich-made Paten,
1631. – MONUMENTS. Quite a number of brasses, namely:
Bust perhaps of James of Helveston († 1378; S aisle). – Sir
Nicholas Dagworth † 1401, fine, large figure (5 ft 8 in.; S
aisle). – Roger Felthorp † 1454 and wife (12 in. figures; N
aisle). – Cecily Boleyne † 1458 (18 in., with long hair; chancel). – Anna Boleyne † 1479 (18 in., without head; at chancel
entrance). – Isabel Boleyne † 1485 (27 in., with butterfly
headdress; chancel). – Anne Wood † 1612 (small; S aisle). –
Elizabeth Gurdon † 1582. Small, standing wall-monument
with kneeling figure of a girl. – Sir Edward Clere. Late Elizabethan tomb-chest, now without its effigy. Against the chest
sixteen shields under arches. They represent a fanciful pedi-
gree reaching back to 1066. – Seventh Marquess of Lothian
† 1841, and wife. Big Gothic recess without effigies. – Mar-
chioness of Lothian † 1901. By *A. G. Walker*. White marble
relief with angels at her bier. – Eighth Marquess of Lothian.
By *G. F. Watts*, 1878. Recumbent effigy in ample shroud and
with ample beard. At his head and feet two standing angels.
All figures in the round.

BLICKLING HALL. Built between 1616 and 1627 for Sir Henry
Hobart, Lord Chief Justice, by *Robert Lyminge*, who had designed Hatfield House some twelve years before and appears
at his death in 1628 in the church registers of Blickling as 'the
architect and builder of Blickling Hall'. The date 1616 represents the purchase of the manor, 1619 appears in the courtyard,
1620 on the façade, and 1627 on the dining-room chimneypiece. The house, though designed in the same year as Inigo
Jones's Queen's House at Greenwich, is still entirely un-
affected by the new Palladian trend. It is one of the major
Jacobean houses in England, in scale and otherwise. It mea-
sures *c.*120 by 220 ft and has the square corner turrets with
ogee caps of Syon House and Osterley Park. Originally, i.e. up
to *c.*1770, it was open to the N, the two wings forming a deep
courtyard of the type of Melford Hall, Rushbrooke Hall, and
Cobham – all much older houses.

See
p.
389

The house is of brick with stone dressings, two and a half
storeys high, but three in the shaped gables and three and a
half in the turrets. The principal sides face S and E. The S side
contains the entrance. It has seven wide bays, bays one and
seven belonging to the turrets. The main floor is the first, with

52

tall windows with two transoms. They and the windows in the gables have strapwork decoration above the lintels. The main windows in the turrets however have pediments, and this chaste motif (which might be an alteration of *c*.1770) also occurs on the long E front, which is punctuated by five bay windows, three canted and two straight-sided. The climax of the S façade is the doorway, the window above it, and the three-storeyed lantern turret which completes this middle axis. The doorway has detached Tuscan columns, Victories in the spandrels, and heraldry above the entablature. The window is given Ionic pilasters intermittently blocked, and the turret has intermittently blocked pilasters, then tapering pilasters, and finally an octagonal, open-sided lantern. These details look convincing enough, but the turret was rebuilt about 1820–30 and hardly according to original evidence. The bold chimney-stacks have polygonal shafts with star tops.

The N side was filled in by *Thomas*, *William*, and *John Ivory* of Norwich between 1767 and 1779, in harmony with the original. The first, second, sixth, and seventh bays are Jacobean, the Ivorys' three centre bays have pedimented windows. The Ivorys also rebuilt the W side. A tablet on it records the date 1769 and the fact that the then owner's young wife, the Countess of Buckinghamshire, bequeathed her jewels towards the expense of building this front.

As one entered through the S doorway one found oneself originally in a square courtyard with four projecting or extruded corners. The two in the NE and NW corners belonged to the hall, which was then placed in a traditional position. In 1767, however, these two disappeared, and the recessed wall between them was pushed forward so as to create a fresh front. At the same time the hall as such was abolished and the space taken by it given to a grander staircase, rebuilt with the materials of the old staircase, which had been placed to the E of the hall (where the Smoking Room now is). All we know of the old hall is that it was entered in the middle, not, in the medieval and still the Tudor way, close to one end. In this Blickling is not unique for its date, but exceptional. The central entrance became the standard in the Inigo Jones and altogether the classical style, but Thorpe e.g. in his drawings also experimented much with it. The STAIRCASE, before it 54b was altered, had the shape of that of Hatfield, and is in fact also in its details much like that predecessor – with the same oblong tapering balusters, the same daintily decorated square newel posts with short, squat tapering top pieces and supporter figures, and even the same bits of strapwork between the balusters at their foot. Some of the supporters are Jacobean, others (e.g. the Highlander), and of course the other work of enlarging the staircase, are by the *Ivorys* and done with remarkable tact and gusto. Of 1767, needless to say, also the two charming, life-size Rococo-Tudor figures in relief of Anne Boleyn (a relative of the Hobarts) and Queen Elizabeth. They are placed in two shallow niches above one of the intermediate landings of the staircase.

Along the E front the most remarkable room on the ground floor is the DINING ROOM at the SE end. It has a grand wooden chimneypiece with coupled tapering pilasters and fancy caryatids flanking the panels of the overmantel. The date 1627 occurs below these. The rest of the room was redecorated by the Ivorys. Above it lies the SOUTH DRAWING ROOM, with an even grander chimneypiece – there are coupled columns here below as well as above – and a gorgeous plaster ceiling with broad bands forming star or flower shapes and short pendants. To the N of the Drawing Room the ANTEROOM, with a big central pendant. This is where the staircase originally was. Then follows the crowning glory of Blickling, the GALLERY, again with a broad-banded plaster ceiling. The room is 127 ft long. The frieze at the top of the wall was remodelled by *John Hungerford Pollen* in the High Victorian years.

Of other rooms all that needs mentioning is the PETER-THE-GREAT ROOM to the W of the N end of the Gallery and the STATE BEDROOM to the W of this, i.e. at the NW corner. The latter has the alcove for the bed screened off from the rest of the room by fluted Ionic columns. The decoration of both rooms is very restrained. Of fitments in yet other rooms the most interesting is the Early Tudor fireplace which comes from Caister and went from there first to Oxnead and then to Blickling, where it was re-set by the Ivorys (see the surround). It is in the Brown Drawing Room on the ground floor, and has magnificent spandrels with splendidly composed seraphim.

In front of the S façade a deep turfed forecourt, and to the l. and r. of it STABLES and OFFICES looking a little later than the house, with their big Dutch gables, i.e. shaped gables ending in pediments. Yet the W range carries the trustworthy date 1624. So the Dutch gables are among the earliest in existence.

The GARDENS extend chiefly to the E of the house. The parterre received its present form only in 1930. But the two

symmetrical groves beyond, with their crosses of diagonal rides,
are older than 1729, the year of a map containing them. Between them runs a straight walk up to the TEMPLE, a small
C18 building of three bays with Tuscan columns, a metope
frieze, and a pediment. Behind the temple and the plantations
runs the BASTION WALK. In the parterre stands a C16 or early
C17 FOUNTAIN bought from Oxnead. It is a basin on a base.
Also from Oxnead comes the STATUE of Hercules by *Nicholas
Stone*, now in the ORANGERY. Nicholas Stone did a number
of statues for Oxnead. The Hercules was made in 1632. The
Orangery is placed to the E of the church. It dates from about
1785. Seven bays with pilasters plus angle bays with arched
windows and pediments.

MAUSOLEUM, 1 m. NW. A grand pyramid, 45 by 45 ft in plan. 43b
Designed by *Joseph Bonomi* and built in 1793. The pyramid
commemorates the Earl and Countess of Buckinghamshire,
who had employed the Ivorys. Doorways with coat of arms in
a frame. In a similar frame the inscription at the back. Domed
interior with coved angle recesses.

RACECOURSE STAND.* Castellated, with a tall, thin circular
turret against one wall, and some ogee-headed niches in the
wall opposite.

In the village the BUCKINGHAMSHIRE ARMS, late C17. Six
bays, cross-windows, hipped roof with dormers.

BLOFIELD
3000

ST ANDREW AND ST PETER. The largest church in the imme-
diate neighbourhood. It has a big, tall later C14 W tower with
flushwork panelling, spandrels with shields, a four-light W
window, a lofty arch to the nave, sound-holes with a grid of
Perp panel units, and pinnacles in the form of figures. Later
C14 also the five-bay arcades inside. They have quatrefoil
piers with polygonal capitals. In the arch a hollow chamfer
and a wave. The clerestory was probably built at the same
time. The aisle windows are all new, but all Perp in style. Two-
storeyed N porch. The chancel arch belongs to the arcade piers
in its style, and the chancel windows are also Perp, as is the
traceried Angle Piscina. – FONT. Octagonal, with scenes in
relief on the bowl, oddly enough all scenes from the Life of
Christ, a cycle not in general connected with fonts: Nativity,
Flight into Egypt, etc., to the Crucifixion, Resurrection, and

* Take the road to the W from the front gates, follow it for about ¾ m., and
then turn r. (sign-post to the golf club).

Ascension. – SCREEN. On the dado of the rood screen twelve painted Saints. – BENCHES. Ends with poppy-heads. Four arms with figures or animals. The best are a kneeling man with a rosary and a seated bishop. – BOX PEWS. Raised at the back. – MONUMENT. Edward Paston † 1630. Small alabaster tablet with kneeling figures; conservative for its date. – Above it a HELMET of c.1530. – PLATE. Paten on foot and Flagon presented in 1720; Gothic Chalice and Paten, 1849.

HOUSE opposite the church, of c.1700, partly with the old window casements and leading.

HOUSE, ½ m. NE, on the A road. Gothick, of three bays and two storeys, with polygonal angle shafts, battlements, and a porch with finials.

BODHAM
1030

ALL SAINTS. W doorway Dec, and re-set in it in a clumsy way the tracery of a Dec window. S doorway Dec, chancel arch early C14 or Dec. Mostly minor Perp. – PLATE. Flagon, London, 1774; Chalice, London, 1777; Paten, 1778.

BOOTON
1020

ST MICHAEL AND ALL ANGELS. Built to the design of the rector, the Rev. *Whitwell Elwin*, who died in 1900, aged 83, having been rector for fifty years. The church was begun c.1875 and completed in 1891. It is a lavish building, designed with knowledge of E.E. detail but a happy disregard for principles of E.E. composition.* The diagonal placing of the two W towers is a conceit one would expect to find in 1820 rather than 1890. The church is of knapped flint and stone. The towers have two tiers of exaggeratedly elongated blank arcading. The tracery of the nave and chancel windows is Geometrical. There is an excess of pinnacles, including an odd three-tier one on the W gable, an equally odd rotunda-like pinnacle on the E wall, and a sanctus turret. Inside, the most surprising feature is the enormous window in the form of a spherical triangle above the chancel arch. The equipment of the chancel is very rich, but depressingly antiquated for the time when Morris and his disciples were busy in many places. – SCULPTURE. A beautiful, unfortunately headless, seated C14 figure in the N porch. Found in a wall of the old church. – PLATE. Norwich-made Chalice of 1567 (at the Norwich Museum).

* Lutyens said of it: 'Very naughty, but built in the right spirit.,

RECTORY. Symmetrical façade, Jacobean, brick and stone, also
by *W. Elwin*.

SCHOOL. 1896. By the same.

BOOTON HALL. Red brick, Georgian.

BRADESTON *see* BRAYDESTON

BRADFIELD

2030

ST GILES. Exceptionally fine Dec chancel, remembered by its
E wall with a five-light window (cusped intersected tracery interrupted at the top to fit in a broad pointed quatrefoil; plenty
of minor ogee arches) and polygonal angle buttresses with
flushwork panelling and prominent stone pinnacles. The
church originally had aisles. These seem to have been pulled
down *c.*1785. The arcades still in existence have octagonal
piers and double-chamfered arches and seem Perp (but Cautley dates them *c.*1340). Single-framed, scissor-braced, i.e.
early, roof. Tall Perp W tower without parapet. Sound-holes
with tracery. – FONT. Octagonal stem with eight attached
shafts. Bowl with alternating panels of two ogee arches and of
a four-petalled tracery form. – SOUTH DOOR. Plate for the
knocker of the C13. – PAINTING. Above the chancel arch
Christ on a rainbow displaying his wounds. – PLATE. Chalice,
London, 1638.

BRAMPTON

2020

ST PETER. Round tower with octagonal C16 brick top. A S aisle
arcade must have been demolished, so that now only the
blocked arch remains that led from it into a S chapel, also demolished. – FONT. Octagonal, with shields in quatrefoils. –
SOUTH DOOR. Traceried. – PLATE. Chalice and Paten, Norwich-made, 1567. – BRASSES. Robert Brampton † 1468 and
wife, in shrouds, 15 in. figures (chancel N). – John Brampton
† 1535 and two wives, 22 in. figures.

BRANDISTON

ST NICHOLAS. Norman round tower with later octagonal top. [1020]
Its date is probably that of the rebuilding of the church on a
much larger scale, so that the site of the nave and chancel became that of the N aisle and a new nave was erected S of it. The
chancel which belonged to this nave has been pulled down.
The date of erection appears to be the mid C14, see the W window, with its flowing tracery, the arcade of three bays (origin-

ally four bays) with quatrefoil piers and double-chamfered
arches, the s doorway, and the N aisle E and one N window.
However, the date may after all be later than it appears; for on
13b the s side are three large and prominent windows with identical rere-mouldings. The middle one is Dec, like the windows
so far mentioned, but the other two are entirely Perp. Might
this then be a case of overlap, of the Dec going on right to 1375
and after? – STAINED GLASS. Bits in a s window. – PLATE.
Chalice, Norwich, 1567.

BRANDISTON HALL. Built in 1647 and much enlarged in 1875
(Kelly). What seems original is the shaped gable-ends of the s
range, running W–E. The enrichments of the s front itself
however, and the N part of the W range, must be Victorian.
Good STAINED GLASS roundels of the Labours of the Months,
School of Norwich, late C15. They come from Marsham, and
originally probably from a Norwich house.

BRAYDESTON
3000

ST MICHAEL. Remains of a Norman window (or a small early
lancet?) in the N wall. Chancel C13 with one lancet window in
the N wall, and the piscina. Next to this a rare stone shelf on
an arched bracket across the SE corner. There was a s aisle
originally, and this also had a C13 arcade. The remains of the
piers show it. The W tower, being unbuttressed, may be in its
structure as old too, or older, but it is so over-restored that
nothing can be said. Dec chancel E window with reticulated
tracery. Perp nave windows and N porch (shields in the spandrels of the entrance arch). – FONT. Coarse octagonal bowl
with elementary tracery patterns. – SCREEN. The small carving of the dado is original and good. – HOURGLASS STAND, a
little more elaborate than usual. – PLATE. Norwich-made
Chalice of 1567–8 and Paten of 1633. – MONUMENT. Spencer
T. Foot † 1847, with a standing mourning woman by an
altar; still entirely pre-Victorian. By *Gaffin*.

BRININGHAM
0030

ST MAURICE. The nave must be earlier than the tower, see the
W wall. Yet the bell-openings of the tower and the W window
represent the same style, of c.1300. Dec the chancel with its
priest's doorway, its flowing tracery in the E window, the ogee-
headed niches to its l. and r. inside, the piscina, and the chancel
arch. Dec also the nave s doorway and the one surprisingly

large four-light window on the s side. Inside this window an
odd re-use of two Norman nook-shafts with leaf capitals. What
was their original purpose? Most of the windows of the church
are Perp. – COMMUNION RAIL. Probably of *c*.1700. With
turned balusters, excessively fat at the foot. – MONUMENT. To
the E of the church, in the churchyard, Victorian pyramid to
commemorate the Brereton family.

(BRININGHAM HALL. 1838, according to Mr Cozens-Hardy.)

BRINTON

0030

ST ANDREW. Very renewed in 1873. W tower Perp, s windows
straight-headed Perp. The E window of the C17 or later, a
closure after the chancel had collapsed. On the N wall of the N
transept small STATUE in niche. The interior of the church is
more satisfactory than the exterior. Tower arch on head corbels (one opens his mouth with both hands). Perp N arcade.
The piers with four major and four minor polygonal shafts.
Double-hollow-chamfered arches. Good roof with an alternating rhythm. Wall-posts, longitudinal arched braces. Arched
braces to the ridge, every second pair standing on the apexes
of the longitudinal braces. Demi-figures of angels. – PLATE.
Chalice and Paten, Norwich, 1567.*

Opposite the church a good early C19 house of yellow brick, five
by four bays, with a porch on elongated Doric columns. Low
hipped roof. The date is supposedly 1822.

BRISTON

0030

ALL SAINTS. A round tower fell in 1795. Fine Dec chancel.
The E window of five lights has reticulated tracery. On the s
side one window high up and straight-headed because of the
Sedilia beneath. They have ogee arches and delicate quatrefoil shafts with a fillet towards the chancel. The Piscina is
double and has a shelf. The chancel arch is Dec too. Long
nave. In the s wall a short length of C13 dog-tooth has been
re-used. Several Perp windows. On the N side remains of a
former aisle with octagonal piers and double-chamfered arches.
– COMMUNION RAIL. With fat turned balusters, probably of
the late C17. – PLATE. Norwich-made Chalice and Paten on
foot, 1567; Paten, London, 1784(?). – CURIOSUM. A CELLO
made of metal by a local blacksmith about 1700.

* Kelly and Bryant print a long story about Saxon, Norman, and E.E. *See*
masonry which it is impossible now to verify.
p.
389

CONGREGATIONAL CHURCH, The Lane, NW of the church. Built in 1775. Brick with brick quoins. Four bays long with the doorways formerly in the first and the fourth. A two-bay house, no doubt the manse, attached on the r. hipped roof.

BROOMHOLM see BACTON

3020

BRUMSTEAD

ST PETER. Perp w tower. Early C14 nave. The chancel was cut short and rebuilt in 1827. Finely moulded arch of the s doorway. – FONT. Octagonal; panelled stem, bowl with quatrefoils. – PLATE. Chalice and Paten, Norwich, 1567–8; Flagon, London, 1728.

3000

BRUNDALL

ST LAWRENCE. Small. Nave and chancel and a double bellcote which looks original. The two arched openings are single-chamfered. As the windows and the s doorway of the church look late C13, that will be the date of the bellcote as well. N aisle added in 1900. – FONT. C13. The only lead font in Norfolk. Circular. The decoration consists of two motifs repeated: the Crucifixus and a knot of fleurs-de-lis widening at the foot so as to allow for a small fleur-de-lis to be set in. – STAINED GLASS. One Netherlandish C16 roundel of St Lawrence. In the w window glass by *Kempe*, 1903. – PLATE. Stem of an Elizabethan Chalice with a new bowl.

Brundall has many Norwich villas and smaller houses. A recent housing development, called St Laurence Avenue, to the N of the church and at r. angles to the main road, is designed by *Anthony Haydon*, a nice job of one- and two-storeyed cottages.

3000

BUCKENHAM

ST NICHOLAS. The w tower is octagonal from the foot and has all round the bell-stage tall blank lancet arcading by means of a continuous roll moulding with smaller lancets as bell-openings. Yet there is a Norman w doorway in this tower, and if it is re-set, it was re-set before 1813 (*see* an illustration), which is improbable. So the C13 work is perhaps a re-modelling only (cf. Toft Monks, vol. 2). The doorway has one order of shafts with scalloped capitals and zigzag in the arch. There is also a s doorway with a Norman zigzag, but that is clearly a re-used piece. The s doorway is a fine piece of E.E. design, with one order of shafts, a keeled roll, and some dog-tooth ornament.

Dec chancel, see the E window of five lights with ogee detail,
the Piscina, and the chancel arch. Dec nave N windows, plus
one Perp, of three lights. – FONT. Perp. Against the stem four
statuettes and four seated figures, against the bowl eight seated
figures in ogee-arched panels. Well preserved. – STAINED
GLASS. The chancel has a date 1823–4, referring to some restoration. The glass in the E window is of that date. – PLATE.
Chalice, Paten, and Flagon, made at Newcastle in 1744. –
MONUMENT. Anne Newbury † 1707. Tablet still entirely in
the C17 style.

BURGH-NEXT-AYLSHAM   2020

ST MARY. The church, quite unexpectedly, has one of the most
ambitious E.E. chancels of any Norfolk parish church. It is
wide and surrounded inside by blank arcading with stiff-leaf
capitals, and the lancet windows above are again framed by
blank arcading. The two easternmost bays are an extension of
1876–8 (*R. M. Phipson* with suggestions from *Scott*). W of that
there are, outside on the S side, three lancets, a buttress, and
another three lancets. Inside, however, the row is perfectly
even. Moreover, on the N side opens a chapel with an even   22a
more lavish arch, carried on each side by three shafts with
shaft-rings set in depth. The capitals on the E have pecking
birds in addition to stiff-leaf. The date of the chancel is probably *c.*1220–30. Perp W tower, traceried sound-holes, flushwork panelling on base and battlements. C19 nave. – FONT.
Octagonal, Perp. Stem with four statuettes and four shields,
bowl with demi-figures of angels against the underside and
panels with the Seven Sacraments. – PLATE. Norwich-made
Chalice of 1567 and Paten of 1570–1.

BURGH PARVA
½ m. N of Melton Constable station   0030

ST MARY. In ruins. Unbuttressed W tower, the W window Perp,
the bell-openings with cusped Y-tracery. The tower arch is
reinforced with brick. The S wall of the nave overgrown with
ivy. Shapeless doorway.
(BURGH PARVA HALL. Of *c.*1600 plus an early C19 N wing of
white brick and further additions of 1881. B. Cozens-Hardy)

BURGH ST MARGARET   4010

ST MARGARET. All but rebuilt. Unbuttressed W tower. Norman
S doorway with one order of shafts. The bases like reversed

capitals, the capitals of single scallops. Coarse zigzag and billet in the arch. The N doorway also with a billet frieze, perhaps re-used. – PLATE. Chalice and Paten Cover, made at Norwich, 1567–8. – BRASS to John Burton † 1608; a kneeling figure.

WESLEYAN CHAPEL. 1841. Very neat brickwork, grey bricks, arched windows.

WINDMILL. Derelict tower mill, ¼ m. NW.

BURLINGHAM ST ANDREW
3010

ST ANDREW. Above the S porch entrance a hood-mould, clearly re-set and probably Norman. Dec nave and chancel, in spite of Perp windows, see the N doorway and the chancel E window. Perp N arcade very rough. Four bays, octagonal piers, four-centred arches. Another opening, equally rough, into the N chapel. Fine nave roof with hammerbeams. Longitudinal arched braces between them. Decorated wall-plates. Angels with spread wings against the hammerbeams. – FONT. Octagonal, with elementary decoration. – SCREENS. Of the rood screen eleven painted Saints survive; 1536, the latest dated screen in Norfolk (cf. Horsham St Faith). – The tower screen was salvaged from Burlingham St Peter. It has one-light divisions with crocketed ogee arches and panel tracery over. In the spandrels of the doorway openwork figures of angels holding shields with the crossed keys of St Peter. – *39b* PLATE. Chalice, 1567–8; Flagon, London-made, 1727. – Also the Plate of 1715 from Burlingham St Peter. – MONUMENT. (Brass inscription to Elizabeth Framlingham † 1559; palimpsest of part of a lady of *c.*1375.) – Gregory Mileham † 1615. With two standing putti l. and r., one with an extinguished torch, the other with a spade. The composition is unusual for a date so early in the C17.

BURLINGHAM ST EDMUND
3000

ST EDMUND. Norman S and N doorways. The former has one order of shafts, a rope necking, capitals with volutes, zigzag in the arch, and a head above the apex, the latter one order of shafts with decorated scallop capitals and an arch intended to have beakheads (a rarity in Norfolk), but in the end left with the stones uncarved. In the nave one Norman window can still be seen. Nave and chancel are thatched. Their windows point to *c*.1300 (Y-tracery, intersected tracery). The nave roof is single-framed with upper scissor-bracing and is perhaps original. The w tower is Perp, its bell-openings are C20. – PULPIT. An exceptionally pretty Perp piece, with Jacobean back-panel and tester. The Perp part has narrow panels, horizontally subdivided, and a good deal of small-scale ornamental painting. – The painting is the same on the dado of the SCREEN. The upper parts are in broad one-light divisions with ogee arches and panel tracery above. – COMMUNION RAIL. C17 (cf. Lingwood). – BENCHES. A number with poppyheads. On one a king's and a bishop's head. There are also pierced traceried backs. On arms the Elephant and Castle, a seated man, a bird on a dog, etc. – HOURGLASS STAND. – PAINTINGS. On the s wall of the chancel large scene of the Murder of St Thomas Becket, *c*.1400. – On the nave N wall faded St Christopher, *c*.1350. – PLATE. Chalice, Norwich, 1567–8; Flagon, London, 1727. – BRASS. Chalice brass, probably to William Curteys † 1540 (chancel floor).

OLD HALL FARMHOUSE, ¼ m. s. The house has a fine Elizabethan porch, red brick, three storeys in height and with polygonal angle shafts with round decorated brick finials. The entrance has a four-centred arch and a pediment over. The pediment above the first-floor windows is enriched by two rustic figures of mermaids holding a cartouche with a head. On the N gable of the house remains of round finials too.

BURLINGHAM ST PETER
¼ m. E of Burlingham St Andrew

3010

ST PETER. In ruins. The tower has collapsed. Nave and chancel are still roofed.

BURNLEY HALL *see* EAST SOMERTON

BUXTON

2020

ST ANDREW. w tower 1881. Nave with tall Perp windows. Chancel *c*.1300. On the s side a low-side window in the form of a quatrefoil. Sedilia and Piscina still without ogee arches. The w respond is a head-corbel. Tall C14 arcades of three bays. Octagonal piers, double-chamfered arches. Quatrefoil clerestory windows. – SCREEN. Wide ogee-headed single openings. Much is C19. – STAINED GLASS. s aisle E window *c*.1859–60 by *T. Willement*. – PLATE. Norwich-made Chalice of 1567; Paten of 1719. – BRASS. Robert Northen, vicar, † 1508, a chalice (13½ in.; chancel s).

BYLAUGH

ST MARY. Close to the river Wensum, hidden in trees. Round tower with octagonal early C14 top. Small Perp nave. Transept and chancel 1809–10, with polygonal angle turrets and the typical revived intersected tracery. – FONT. Octagonal, with shields. – Three-decker PULPIT, BOX PEWS, and PEWS no doubt of 1810. The pews leave an octagonal space in the crossing. In the transepts are fireplaces. – REREDOS with Commandments, Lord's Prayer, and Creed. – COMMUNION RAIL of cast iron. – PLATE. Chalice, Norwich, 1567; Paten, London, 1831. – MONUMENTS. (Brass to Sir John Cursun † 1471 and wife; 3 ft 6 in. figures; aisle E.) – John Bendish † 1707, charming cartouche. – Sir John Lombe † 1817. Simple Gothic tripartite composition, odd and with no specific compositional compulsion behind. Without figures. By the younger *John Bacon*.

BYLAUGH HALL. A conspicuous ruin. The house was built by *Charles Barry Jun. & R. Banks* and illustrated in 1852. It is Elizabethan in style and derives from Wollaton on the one hand, from the elder Barry's Highclere on the other.

OLD HALL FARMHOUSE. C17. With shaped gables of the same shape as at Bawdeswell.

CAISTER

HOLY TRINITY, East Caister. The nave belongs to the early C13, as is proved by one narrow lancet in the N wall. The s aisle was added about 1300, see the windows, including the quatrefoil w window. The arcade on the other hand (four bays, octagonal piers, double-hollow-chamfered arches) is Perp rather than earlier. Chancel with Dec Sedilia and Piscina, but Perp E window. – FONT. Quite remarkably big. Stem with eight attached shafts. Bowl with alternation of quatrefoils containing shields with angels and quatrefoils pushed down in their square fields by two mouchettes joining up above them. Castellated rim. The font comes from Eye, Suffolk. – PAINTING. In the tower Commandment Board with, l. and r., the figures of Moses and Aaron. – PLATE. Chalice with Elizabethan foot and bowl inscribed 1617; Paten of the mid C17; both made in Norwich. – MONUMENTS. William Crowe † 1668. Good bust on a plinth between two black columns. – Roger Crowe † 1727. Inscription in a purely architectural

setting. The monument stands across the NE corner of the ^{See}
chancel, an unusual position.   p.
                                                            389

ST EDMUND, West Caister. Only the tower stands, just behind³⁸⁹
the small present church, and of the tower only one and a half^{See}
sides.   p.
                                                            389

CAISTER CASTLE. Built for Sir John Fastolf in 1432–5 and one^{47b}
of the most impressive of the C15 castles of England. It is a
regular rectangle in plan with angle towers much like Kirby
Muxloe in Leicestershire, which is, however, fifty years later.
The NE third was originally divided from the rest by a moat
and seems older than the C15. It has arrow-slits, whereas the
SW part has gunports. The castle is of pink to yellow brick
and was surrounded by a moat. Kirby Muxloe also has gunports and also is of brick. At Caister, the NE court had NE,
NW, and SE ranges. The main buildings in the SW court are
less regular. At the W corner is a circular tower of 98 ft with a
higher stair-turret. Both had machicolations at the top. Near
the bottom is an oriel window. To the SW and NW the wall
stands up high and is crowned by machicoulis. In the SW wall
is a gatehouse, but the main gatehouse seems to have faced
NE and to have been connected by a bridge to the older NE
court. The SW gatehouse led to an outer court, left, it seems,
unfinished. The present Caister Hall is L-shaped and in the S
corner. It presupposes a corresponding building in the W
corner and also a moat. Caister Hall has in the angle a round
tower. Externally the house presents itself otherwise as a
minor example of the Georgian style. Underneath the SW
wing of the house ran the original Barge Canal, approaching
the castle from the SW. The arches are preserved. At the
outer, i.e. S, corner of the house and its wing is yet another
round tower to protect the approach by barge.* From 1459
to 1599, with a short break, the Pastons lived at Caister
Castle.

ROMAN TOWN. The site of the rectangular walled Roman
harbour town lies mainly on the N side of the Caister–Acle
road. It is over 30 acres in extent, and was most recently
excavated in 1951–4 and again in 1961. A town wall 10 ft thick
and faced with flints was shown to have replaced a ramparted
wooden palisade c. A.D. 125. At the S gate a cobbled road
crossed over the double V-cut ditch by a wooden bridge and
led SW, presumably to the wharves. At the end of the C2 a

* Dr Simpson has drawn interesting parallels between Caister and the
Wasserburgen or *Wasserschlösser* of Westphalia, e.g. Kempen.

seamen's hostel was built W of the main street, including a courtyard and a T-shaped structure, perhaps the laundry. The S wing had an apsidal end and contained a number of timber-divided cubicles. Parts of the building continued in use until the late C4. Romano-Saxon pottery in use *c.* A.D. 300 suggests trade or *foederati*. About 150 burials of the later Saxon period (*c.* 650–850) have been found outside the walls, some dozen being covered with ship's timbers – poor men's boat burials – while a number of contemporary oval or round huts were erected inside the still substantial walls. This village may have been evacuated during the period of the first Danish settlement (A.D. 879). The Ministry of Works has consolidated some of the structural remains.

CALTHORPE

1030

ST MARGARET. E.E. chancel; but the E window is of 1822. Perp nave windows. What is the date of the unbuttressed W tower, faced with knapped flint? The tower arch is low and has many mouldings dying into the imposts. Arch-braced nave roof. – FONT. Octagonal. At the corners of the stem four lions; against the underside of the bowl demi-figures of angels; against the bowl tracery. – PULPIT. Jacobean, with flat carving. – BENCHES. Some with poppy-heads. The blocks open diagonally at the back to allow space for the font. – COMMUNION RAIL. C17. – PLATE. Chalice, Norwich, 1567–8; Paten much altered.

CANTLEY

3000

ST MARGARET. Above the priest's doorway a re-set piece of Norman zigzag. Unbuttressed W tower of undefined date. The bell-openings probably *c.*1300 (Y-tracery). Chancel and N vestry have windows with Y-tracery too. C14 S doorway with finely traceried spandrels containing shields. Perp nave windows and one chancel window, with stepped horizontals between the lights and the head tracery. – PLATE. Two-handled Cup, made in London, 1801. – MONUMENTS. Simon Kidbull † 1735. Architectural tablet without figures or specific illustrative motifs. – Jonathan Layton † 1801. Obelisk with a wheatsheaf in front. At the foot roundel with a bullock.

CARROW ABBEY *see* NORWICH, p. 286

CATFIELD

3020

ALL SAINTS. W tower early C14 (Y-tracery). The rest mostly
Early Perp with Dec reminiscences. Large nave and chancel
windows of the same alternatingly Perp and semi-Dec patterns.
S porch two-storeyed. The staircase to the upper storey starts
inside the aisle. N doorway with tracery in the spandrels. S
doorway with a hood-mould decorated with fleurons. The
same pretty motif is applied to alternating capitals of the
arcades inside. Five bays, octagonal piers, double-hollow-
chamfered arches. In the chancel blank giant arcading taking
in the windows. – FONT. Flatly modelled tracery and enriched
quatrefoil patterns. – SCREENS. Rood screen with two-light
divisions. On the dado sixteen painted Saints; defaced. –
Tower screen with a date 1605; simple. – HOURGLASS STAND,
of iron, by the pulpit. – BANNER STAFF LOCKER, nave, W
wall. – PAINTINGS. Wall paintings above the arcades. On the
N side nothing recognizable, on the S side little. In a S spandrel
the stoning of St Stephen. – PLATE. Paten, 1715; Chalice,
London-made, 1820.

CATFIELD HALL. Georgian. Of five bays and two storeys. Doorway with broken pediment on fluted pilasters. Low retaining
walls l. and r.

CATTON *see* p. 287

CAWSTON

1020

ST AGNES. A grand Perp church, due to the munificence of
Michael de la Pole, Earl of Suffolk, † 1414, and his widow. Of
an earlier date only the chancel, whose E window of five lights
has intersected tracery unfinished at the top to leave space for
a pointed quatrefoil broader than it is high – a typical conceit
of *c*.1300. The tracery of one S window (Y) and the details of
the priest's doorway fit that date. The S transept also is pre-
Perp, see its tall S window with flowing tracery, and the E
windows, both straight-headed yet also clearly Dec. Of the
de la Pole work the most impressive is the W tower, 119½ ft
high and strangely forbidding in comparison with the neighbouring and contemporary Salle. Of elephant-grey, very even
stone. Tall and bare to the N and S. Totally devoid of a top
finish by battlements or pinnacles or indeed a suitable parapet.

Two decorated base-courses. They run all round including the buttresses, and even those now inside the nave – a proof that the tower was built or at least begun before the nave. Doorway with niches l. and r. In the spandrels a Wild Man with a club and a Dragon. A frieze of shields over. Tall transomed W window. A fleuron frieze runs round about a quarter up the height of the window, but turns down and up again to take the window in. Tall, thin, two-light sound-holes; elongated, two-light bell-openings. Towards the nave tall arch with a traceried W gallery on arched braces, again with tracery in the spandrels. On it the inscription:

> God spede the plow
> And send us all corne enow
> our purpose for to mak
> at crow of cok of ye plowlete of Sygate
> Be mery and glade
> Wat Goodale yis work mad.

The S aisle has a thinly decorated parapet. Aisle and clerestory windows of course Perp. S porch two-storeyed. Just as at Salle there is a niche above the entrance flanked by two one-light windows. Also as at Salle the tierceron-vault inside with bosses.

Six-bay nave arcade of octagonal piers and double-chamfered arches. The first bay is wider, to reach the tower. While there is disappointingly little of interest in this arcade design, the roof saves the situation. It is one of the most wonderful in Norfolk, a hammerbeam roof, as richly appointed as any. Wall-posts on stone brackets. Long arched braces. Wall-plate with angels with spread wings. Hammerbeams with angels, again with spread wings. Tracery below and above them. Plenty of bosses. Plenty of bosses also in the S transept roof. Simpler aisle roofs. It will be noted that towards the E end of the nave the last three figures are not angels. The suggestion has been made that two of them are the Virgin and St John from the former rood. That seems untrue. One could be a Virgin of the Annunciation, another a martyr with a palm-frond (or the Angel of the Annunciation?). N chancel chapel of two bays. The piers have a moulding more characteristic of the C15 than those of the nave (big polygonal projections to chancel and chapel and slighter semicircular projections to the arches). Of small interior details the charming piscina in the S transept ought to be noticed. It has an ogee gable and, in the spandrels, again a Wild Man and a Dragon.

FURNISHINGS. FONT. Perp, octagonal, on one step decorated with quatrefoil etc. panels. Stem closely decorated with small quatrefoils or cusped fields carrying shields. The bowl is simply panelled. – PULPIT. Perp. – SCREEN. Tall, of one-light divisions. With doors, a rarity in East Anglia. Cusped, ogeeheaded arches. Against the dado twenty painted Saints, not defaced, but not good either. One of the Saints is Master John Schorne, never canonized. Wills make a date *c.*1505 likely. – STALLS. Three with MISERICORDS: two caryatid youths, a man's face, a stag in foliage. – BENCHES. Only two with traceried backs and animals on the arms; the rest just with poppy-heads. – COMMUNION RAIL. C17. – PAINTING. Unrecognizable; above the chancel arch. – Formerly good large seated C14 figure in the S transept, suggested to be St Agnes. A small figure to her r. – STAINED GLASS. A jumble of parts of figures etc. in a S aisle window. – PLATE. Chalice, probably Norwich, 1567; Paten, London, 1628; Paten, London, 1724. Also a beautiful drum-shaped Chalice Case of leather, made in the C14.

Many nice minor red brick houses, e.g. one at the w end of the village with remains of a brick pilaster.

WOODROW INN, off the Aylsham road, s of the cross-roads, 1 m. E. In the trees, 100 yds S, the DUEL STONE, a coarse urn on a pedestal, set up to commemorate a duel fought by Sir Henry Hobart and Oliver Le Neve in 1698.

(CAWSTON MANOR, 1½ m. E. 1896 by *Sir Ernest George*.)

CLEY-NEXT-THE-SEA

ST MARGARET. At Newgate, to the S of the present town. Cley church is a most striking and improbable-looking building, splendid from the S, but splendid in large parts rather than as a whole. The parts are the S transept, the S porch, and the clerestory. The N view is a grave disappointment, and *S. S. Teulon*, not usually the most sensitive architect, was right in 1849 to suggest covering it with a tall spire with spireletpinnacles. The fact that the S transept is in ruins,* on the other hand, helps the effect, by showing up the filigree of the tracery.

The clerestory is perhaps the most delightful feature at Cley, not very high nor placed very high up, but an alternation of big cinquefoiled and, moreover, cusped circles with smaller

---

* It was ruinous already about 1600.

two-light windows. The openings crowd together, which makes them look all the more vivacious. Pinnacles with supporters and crosses at the W and E ends. The clerestory had an E window too, above the chancel, but that is blocked. The clerestory, and the arcades which carry it, as we shall see, are Dec.

The S transept is of the same time. It has big pinnacles to the S and – a most unusual thing – crockets on the gable. The S window below is large and has equally unusual tracery. The four lights carry two cusped quatrefoiled circles, and above them is a big, almost square-sided spherical quadrangle. The E window is straight-headed, the W window has reticulated tracery.

The S porch is as splendid, but Perp. It is ashlar-faced and two-storeyed. Base-frieze with shields. Niches in the buttresses. Entrance with shields up the jambs and the arch. In the spandrels shields in front of panelling. Two upper three-light windows with stepped transoms. A niche between them with a solid three-tier canopy. The filigree battlements with prominent reticulation units are as fantastic as if the donors had been the Reyes Católicos. A turret in the NW angle. The porch is vaulted inside with one pair of tiercerons in the N–S, but three pairs in the E–W direction.* With the S doorway we are back from the sumptuous Perp in the sumptuous Dec. Cusped and subcusped ogee arch and hood-mould on beautiful lions' heads. The W doorway (inside a small porch) is even more lavish. Cusped and subcusped with big leaf cusps. A touch of ogee at the apex. Big crocketed hood-mould on head-stops.

The Perp contributions other than the S porch are less outstanding (W window of six lights with embattled transom, four-light S aisle windows and parapet panelled in flushwork, transverse arches across the aisles in their last bays, chancel E window, small N porch), and the other Dec contributions need also no more than a postscript: the low chancel with cusped Y-tracery, the N transept, also in ruins, originally probably with the straight-headed windows now re-set at the E end of the N aisle (ogee-headed lights), and the NW tower. The tower has a plain double-chamfered arch towards the N aisle, small lancet windows, and bell-openings with cusped Y-tracery, i.e. was probably begun earlier than anything else.‡ The Dec

---

* Among the bosses one shows a woman chasing a fox with her distaff.
‡ Equally early the traces of a group of lancet windows in the chancel E wall (C. L. S. Linnell).

arcades inside are of five bays. The octagonal piers seem a little drab after the fireworks in the open. Arches with convex and concave curves. Whole little figures as hood-mould stops. Above the arcade in the spandrels wonderful tabernacles for images. They rest on brackets richly appointed, and on the S side more so than on the N. On the N they are heads or leaves carrying cones with blank tracery. On the S there are an angel playing the cymbals, another angel, a lion, big leaves, St George in close combat with the Dragon. The canopies are beneath the two-light not the circular clerestory windows. Caryatids and leaf corbels even for the aisle roofs. One little figure turns his back and holds his hand on his buttocks, no doubt a rude gesture.

FURNISHINGS. FONT. Against the stem flat defaced statuettes, against the bowl the Seven Sacraments. – STALLS. Six with MISERICORDS. All have coats of arms, including that of the Grocers' Company which was given only in 1532. Also the initials J.G. for John Greneway, an early C16 merchant of Cley. – PULPIT. Colonnettes at the angles and the usual short blank arches in unusually heavy relief. Dated 1611. – BENCHES. With poppy-heads or figures in their stead. Figures, seated and standing, and animals on the arms. – SCULPTURE. Two terracotta panels with seraphim, from a house at Cley (cf. below). – STAINED GLASS. Bits in one chancel N window and the S aisle windows. – BRASSES. In the N aisle John Yslyngton, priest, c.1520 (16½ in.), and a Civilian of c.1460 (19½ in.); in the S aisle a Civilian of c.1460 (21½ in.), John Symondes † 1505 and his wife, in shrouds with the inscription 'Now thus' (3 ft 2½ in.), and Robert Tayllar † 1578, a palimpsest brass, with, at the back, C14 Flemish canopy work. – HEADSTONES in the churchyard. A large number with decoration,[45b] worth sampling.

THE TOWN. A very small, very pretty town of small houses built of flint with red-brick dressings. It does not lie where the medieval Cley had been. This lay S of the church by the river and was, like Wiveton across, a busy little port. It was ruined by embanking, which prevented the tides from reaching the neighbourhood of the church.

On the way from the church to the quay one passes one group of nice houses S of the George Hotel, another in the main street running W–E. Here, on the S side a house with a C15 stone doorway, on the N side a seven-bay house of yellow brick and two storeys with a tripartite doorway (c.1800?), then a recessed red-brick house of two storeys dating from *c.*1700. The top windows have frills along the lintel. A small passage with an apsed head leads through to the l. On the s side again a house with just such a terracotta panel with a seraph as those in the church. Finally at the NE end a largish house by *Guy Dawber* (cf. Wiveton). Entrance in a round tower.

BARROWS. For barrows on the E boundary of the parish *see* Salthouse.

4010   CLIPPESBY

ST PETER. Round tower. Octagonal top of 1875. Norman N doorway with one order of colonnettes, the bases cushion-shaped, the capitals renewed. In the arch zigzag, billet, and other decoration. The s doorway and s porch also incorporate bits from a Norman doorway. In the N wall of the nave two narrow lancet windows and a third blocked. The chancel Piscina could be of the date of the lancets, i.e. of *c.*1200. Two shafts, arch with several fine rolls. – FONT. Octagonal, panelled stem, demi-figures of angels against the underside of the bowl. – PLATE. Chalice and Paten 1716. – BRASS to John Clippesby † 1594 and wife and children, 2 ft 2 in. figures (s aisle E).

WINDMILL. Stump of a tower-mill, $1\frac{1}{8}$ m. SW.

9040   COCKTHORPE

ALL SAINTS. Small, with an unbuttressed W tower of *c.*1300 and a short nave with s aisle of two bays with octagonal pier and double-chamfered arches and a clerestory. The angle Piscina in the nave is of *c.*1300. The arcade could be of the same date, if one assumes that the bases were altered. Good roof with wall-posts connected by longitudinal arched braces, a wall-plate originally all enriched by quatrefoils, and arched braces up to the ridge. – FONT. Octagonal, Perp, with shields exhibiting the Symbol of the Trinity, the Instruments of the Passion, the crossed keys and crossed swords, two different crowns, and three shells. – BENCHES. Some few minor ones. – PLATE. Chalice and Paten, London, 1820. – MONUMENTS. Sir James Calthorpe † 1615. Very big Jacobean tomb-chest with, against it, only two shields in cusped lozenge fields remaining. – Tablet to the same Sir James Calthorpe and his wife † 1639. The tablet must be of approximately the latter date. The Calthorpe mansion has disappeared.

COLBY

2030

ST GILES. Tall unbuttressed w tower, early below, but much raised. Sumptuous s porch of two storeys. Flushwork base. Flushwork panelling l. and r. of the entrance. Flushwork and shields above the entrance. Above a niche between two windows. Early C14 Sedilia and Piscina, with ogee arches. s windows Perp, N side brick with arched windows; 1749. – FONT. Octagonal; panelled stem, bowl with the Signs of the four Evangelists, a kneeling Saint with an axe and a dog, and a panel with two kneeling donors. – REREDOS. Late C17 with pilasters, a centre made for the Commandments, and the painted figures of Moses and Aaron l. and r. – BENCHES. A few ends with poppy-heads.* – HOURGLASS STAND and hourglass. – PLATE. Pre-Reformation Paten of c.1520. Face of Christ in a circle against a cruciform halo. – Chalice inscribed 1568. – In the churchyard, w of the porch, base and short stump of a CROSS.

COLBY HALL FARMHOUSE. Of five bays and two storeys with shaped gable-ends and good outbuildings.

COLTISHALL

2010

ST JOHN BAPTIST. In the N wall two circular Anglo-Saxon windows. The double-splay is characteristic. The position of the windows is curiously high. Chancel of c.1300, see the one See p. 389 lancet preserved in its original state because now connecting with the vestry. The other chancel windows all over-restored. Dec s arcade with quatrefoil piers. The foils have fillets, and there are thin fillet shafts in the diagonals. Tall Perp w tower, ornately decorated. Base frieze with crowned Is (for John), flushwork panelling l. and r. of the doorway, frieze with shields and crowned Is above it. Window with niches l. and r. Traceried sound-holes. However, the bell-openings look decidedly Dec. Perp N porch with niche above the entrance. – FONT. Square, Norman, of Purbeck marble, with four shallow blank arches on each side. – SCREEN. One-light divisions. Ogee arches crocketed and with tracery above them. Much renewed. – WEST GALLERY. Late C17, with twisted balusters. – STAINED GLASS. In the weird big Victorian circular window on the N side a Netherlandish roundel. – MONUMENTS. Henry See p. 389 Palmer † 1714. Two pilasters, inscription plate with drapery looped off it. – John Hapman † 1719. With two putti, seated,

* More stored on the upper storey of the porch.

l. and r. of the inscription plate. – Henry Smith † 1743. Remarkably classical tablet; pilasters and a pediment, both richly decorated, but only where it is structurally permissible.

THE VILLAGE. Coltishall is surprisingly rich in good C18 brick houses and ought to be properly perambulated. A first group with nothing special to be singled out is between the bridge and the War Memorial at the W and NW of the village. Then on the way to the church the OLD HOUSE, five bays, two storeys, with giant pilasters and a parapet with sunk panels, i.e. of c.1710–20 (cf. Aylsham). After that another five-bay house with dormers with steep gables alternatingly triangular and semicircular, i.e. of c.1690 at the latest. Then, well past the church to the E and towards the river, THE LIMES, the finest house in the village. It has a forecourt flanked by outbuildings. The façade itself is of seven bays with a recessed three-bay centre, brick quoins, and a hipped roof. Broad doorway with Doric pilasters and a segmental pediment. Minor staircase with dumb-bell balusters. The house is dated 16(9)2. It is a brother of Aylsham Old Hall. Several houses with shaped gables, then at the corner of the lane to Market Street HAZELWOOD with a five-bay front with two shaped gables. Both are dated, but both with later dates than the house (1766 and 1780). A little to the N another five-bay house with a shaped gable. Finally at the E end COLTISHALL HALL, of seven bays, with lower two-bay wings. The middle bay projects and has quoins, as have the angles. Rusticated door surround. Probably c.1700.

ROYAL AIR FORCE ESTATE, 2½ m. NW. A whole neighbourhood of streets of cottages.

CORPUSTY

1030

ST PETER. Above the village, with no houses near by, and looking across the valley to the sister church of Saxthorpe. Perp W tower, the N and S windows of the church also Perp, and probably before 1400. – SCREEN. Largely C19. – COMMUNION RAIL. C17.

CROMER

2040

16b   ST PETER AND ST PAUL. Externally a very impressive church,
3a   the visual centre of what was once a prosperous little town. The tower is with its 160 ft by far the tallest of any Norfolk parish church. It is moreover extremely lavishly detailed. Big W porch, of squared knapped flint. Niches l. and r. of the entrance. Decorated battlements. Tierceron-star-vault inside.

The inner doorway most elaborate, with one moulding of quatrefoils of alternating details and one with very cusped fields containing alternatingly shields and angels. The lowest stage of the buttresses is also decorated. Five-light w window. Intricately traceried sound-holes. Two tall two-light bell-openings in each side. Battlements of frilly, bulbous forms and pinnacles. The aisle windows are tall and transomed with tracery below the transoms. There are seven of these on the s and seven on the N side. Buttresses with niches, the upper ones with little pedestals for statues. The clerestory is less conspicuous. A fleuron frieze terminates its wall. The chancel was pulled down in the late c17 and rebuilt with only two short bays by *Sir Arthur Blomfield* in 1887–9. On the N side still the remains of the collapsed rood-turret. Two-storeyed s and N porches, the former vaulted with a tierceron-star, the latter only with springers for such a vault. Both porches have tall flushwork panelling on the side walls. Both porches have flushwork-panelled stair-turrets rising higher than the roof of the porch. The s porch has a doorway with one moulding of quatrefoils, the N porch one with little niches for statues.

The interior, after so much display, is a little disappointing, though its loftiness is exceptional. Enormously tall tower arch. Very tall arcades, the piers lozenge-shaped with long shallow wave-mouldings in the diagonals and thin shafts in the four main directions. Many-moulded arches. Very tall also the chancel arch.

The FURNISHINGS are somewhat meagre. – SOUTH DOOR traceried. – STAINED GLASS. In the s aisle *Morris* glass of *c.*1874, large figures against foliage backgrounds. – PLATE. Paten of *c.*1500. Sexfoiled depression with the Hand of God in a decorated circle. – Chalice, made in Norwich, 1567; two Cups, gilded inside, unmarked. – Paten, London, 1810. – MONUMENTS. Brass to Margaret Cornforth † 1518, 17½ in. long (chancel, w wall). – J. H. Earle † 1858. Obelisk on base; in the churchyard.

THE TOWN. Of the old town cottages remain round the church,[3a] enhancing its scale by their humility. But there is nothing one can single out. Then, early in the c19, some seaside development set in; Mr Ketton-Cremer quotes from Jane Austen's *Emma*: 'Perry was a week at Cromer once, and he holds it to be the best of all the sea-bathing places.' This development is witnessed by BRUNSWICK HOUSE (the name dates it),*

* The Prince of Wales married a princess of Brunswick in 1795.

Brunswick Terrace, East Cliff, with two bow windows, and by
the pretty Gothick oriel window at the corner of HIGH
STREET next to the Hotel de Paris.
The principal development belongs to the 1890s and is in the
red-brick style of Norman Shaw or rather Sir Ernest George,
tall houses with bay windows, gables and dormers, and
occasionally domed angle turrets. The stylistic elements are
enriched by some derived from the châteaux of the Loire. The
principal architect was *Skipper* of Norwich. His are the GRAND
HOTEL, dated 1891, the HOTEL DE PARIS of 1895–6 with
Chambord centre and wings projecting at an angle, and the
HOTEL METROPOLE, dated 1893. The ESPLANADE and the
PIER incidentally were built in 1894 and 1899 respectively.
The TOWN HALL (in Prince of Wales Road) is a little older –
of 1890 – and also by *Skipper*. It is a modest building. A little
later and of a more personal character is the CLIFTONVILLE
HOTEL, by *A. F. Scott & Son* of Norwich.
Finally CROMER HALL, to the s of the town, in its own grounds.
It is of shortly after 1829 by *Donthorne*, and on a remarkably
lavish scale – all flint and all Gothic. It had a nearly symmetrical façade first, but the addition of the porch made it asymmetrical and more picturesque.* It has battlements and
turrets.

CROSTWICK
2010

ST PETER. Perp w tower. Handsomely decorated battlements
with pierced parts, i.e. not with flushwork, as was the common
thing. C16 N brick porch with a brick niche above the entrance. Brick s doorway. Half-collapsed brick stair-turret.
Nave and chancel have Perp windows. Single-framed chancel
roof. – BENCH. Just one old one with poppy-heads. – PLATE.
Chalice, a secular cup, London, 1770; Chalice, London, 1811.

CROSTWIGHT
1030

ALL SAINTS. Big w tower, the upper part taken down in 1910.
Nave and chancel. All windows renewed. What can be trusted
looks early C14: Y-tracery in chancel, nave, and also w tower.
The arch from the tower to the nave is no more than a doorway. It has two continuous chamfers, which again points to
the early C14. – FONT. C13, octagonal, of Purbeck marble,
with the familiar two shallow pointed arches on each side. –

* Alterations and additions are recorded for 1875. The architect was *D.
Brandon*. Donthorne had built the house in 1827, but it was destroyed or
damaged by fire in 1829.

SCREEN. Mainly the dado original. – PAINTINGS. C14. Tree with the Deadly Sins. – Also a scene with angels. – St Christopher. Further E Scenes from the Passion, the Crucifixion easily recognizable, Christ before Pilate also just recognizable, the rest hardly to be deciphered. – PLATE. Very striking Flagon, Norwich-made, c.1570; Chalice and Paten Cover, 1716. – MONUMENT. James Shepheard † 1810. With an urn in front of an obelisk.

CROSTWIGHT HALL. Ruin of a C16 house with a two-storeyed porch and wings on the l. and r. The entrance to the porch is Perp, i.e. pre-Reformation in appearance.

CROXTON
1 m. ESE of Kettlestone

9030

ST JOHN BAPTIST. In ruins and all smothered in brambles.

RECTORY. Of about 1700. Chequer brick front, shaped gable-ends. Seven bays, two storeys, a three-bay centre, brick quoins.

WINDMILL. The stump of a brick tower-mill.

DILHAM

3020

ST NICHOLAS. Of the round tower only the fragmentary base remains. The rest 1931 (*C. G. Hare*). Nave and chancel in one. Straight-topped fancy Perp windows. E window high up. No aisles, but blank arcading inside. The piers have no capitals. Old materials re-used in the roof. – FONT. Panelled stem. Bowl with an unusual panel motif. – PLATE. Norwich-made Chalice of 1567; Paten without marks. – MONUMENT. The heavy Obelisk in the churchyard to the SE commemorates William Norfor † 1851.

DILHAM HALL, ½ m. E. Close to the house, smothered in ivy at the time of writing, the remains of a pentagonal tower of Dilham Castle. Also a stretch of wall. The tower is surrounded by architectural fragments not connected with the castle: the three crocketed ogee gables e.g. are said to come from Dilham church.

WINDMILL. Derelict tower-mill, 1½ m. SE.

DRAYTON

1010

ST MARGARET. Over-restored. The chancel rebuilt in 1866, but the original Piscina kept. The W tower is unbuttressed and may be E.E. How much of the lancets can be trusted is doubtful. – FONT. On two halved Norman colonnettes and a centre support. – PLATE. Norwich-made Chalice, probably of 1567.

CROSS. On the Green, s of the church. Just the base and a length of the originally reeded shaft.

THE LODGE. In the garden of the Nurses' Home on the Norwich
. road. An oblong structure of pinky grey brick with four round corner towers. Probably a plaisance of the C16 connected with a house of the Pastons at Drayton.

EARLHAM *see* p. 288

EARLHAM *see* p. 288

9030
EAST BARSHAM

ALL SAINTS. A sadly mutilated building. Of the N tower, a C17 structure, only the ground-stage is preserved, which served and serves as a porch. The chancel and transept are altogether demolished, and only foundations tell of their size. What remains still contains a plain Norman s doorway, a N doorway with a round, moulded arch of *c.*1200, and Perp windows. – PULPIT. C17, very simple. – BENCHES. Simple, with poppy-heads. – STAINED GLASS. In a N window original angels and canopies. – SCULPTURE. Small group of St Anne teaching the Virgin to read. Alabaster; from an altar, as they were usual. – PLATE. Chalice 1631; Paten probably 1631; Flagon 1714; Almsdish 1728. – MONUMENT. Mrs Calthorpe † 1640, signed by *John and Matthias Christmas*. Large hanging monument. She rises out of a coffin, still in her shroud. The conceit was fashionable just at that moment. Against the coffin the inscription 'Come Lord Jesu come quickly'. Behind and above her two Virtues in niches. On the quadrant fragments of the pediment more virtues. Between them an angel blowing the last trump. In the frieze and at the foot skulls. The monument is almost identical with one at Steane (Northants) by the same carvers.

50a MANOR HOUSE. East Barsham is the picture-book ideal of an Early Tudor house. It seems still too good to be true when one first sets eyes on it from the road which runs above it to the s. Its mellow brick, its twisted and adorned chimneys and finials, however many of them may be the work of a restorer, are irresistible. A restoration was undertaken for Mr Colman of Norwich from 1919 onwards and the ruined part of the house made habitable again in 1938 for Count Habsburg-Lothringen. The work of both periods was conscientious and judicious. Of the house as it now is, the E part is original to and including the porch. Of the w part only the façade and the chimneys culminating in a splendid group of circular

shafts are as they were built. In addition the gatehouse is
original too. The house is undated and not precisely datable. It
was built by Sir Henry Fermor about 1520–30. The royal arms
over the porch, carved out of the brick *in situ*, have the griffin
and the greyhound, those over the gatehouse the griffin and the
lion. The change from the one to the other took place in 1527.
So the gatehouse seems to come after the house, but by its
architectural style only slightly after.

The house is approached by this gatehouse, which is two-
storeyed and has at the angles polygonal buttresses with round
finials. The archway has Perp stone jambs and a moulded brick
arch, continuing the same mouldings. Above the arch the royal
arms, again of carved brick, and, above them, a three-light
window with depressed-arched lights and blank panelling l.
and r. The angle buttresses on the upper level are closely
panelled, almost as though reeded. Panelled battlements and
fat finials. The interior of the archway is not now vaulted.
Towards the house the archway is completely moulded and
has a crocketed ogee gable in a rectangular fleuron-frame. The
gatehouse was always a separate structure, as is proved by the
projecting staircase and chimneybreast. Probably there were
only walls and less permanent lower buildings on the l. and r.

The house itself has a long embattled façade punctuated by
eight polygonal buttresses of varying girth. They carry (or
carried) finials. Only the SE finial is completely original. Ample
horizontal friezes of moulded brick forming panels with arms,
tracery, and heads. There is no Italian motif in all this as they
were used in the same years at Layer Marney and Sutton
Place. The porch is in an approximately, but only approximately, central position. It has a two-centred stone arch as its
entrance which looks decidedly earlier than 1520. The large
coat of arms is again of carved brick. The buttresses to the l.
and r. are panelled with a flint and stone chequer. The upper
window also could well be re-used. To the l. of the porch extends the Hall. Its front has one recessed bay and then the
broad projection of the bay window. Six lights with a transom
and four-centred arches to the lights above and below the
transom. The Hall was always one-storeyed, though the
windows above it are new restoration work. The bay to the l.
of the bay window is entirely of 1938, but the angle buttress is
original. In it runs the shoot of an upper lavatory. The w wall
and the w half of the N wall are mostly restoration, but – as has
already been said – the prodigious group of ten chimneyshafts

with different patterns of decoration – fleurs-de-lis, reticulation, diapers etc. – is genuine work of *c.*1525. To the r. of the porch is no recessed bay. The wall runs flat here, but the middle of it is raised in a three-storeyed tower. It is likely that the hall bay had another such erection. The E wall and the E half of the N wall are of the date of the house, but disturbed.

Inside, the Hall bay has the original four-centred, shafted entrance arch and the original huge fireplace.

In the rooms to the r. of the porch there is plenty of un-explored evidence, divers doorways with four-centred heads, in the room next to the porch a lavish Jacobean chimneypiece brought in, in the room to the E of this, that is the room under the tower, a brick rib-vault with an odd lierne pattern and a brick vault on the upper floor too. Were they merely a structural device?

EAST CAISTER *see* CAISTER

³⁰²⁰
EAST RUSTON

ST MARY, $1\frac{1}{2}$ m. NE of the village. W tower, formerly with a spire. The tower opens to the nave only with a small doorway. The N side of the church C18 brick; on the S side Dec and Perp windows. S arcade C14, of five bays with octagonal piers and double-chamfered arches. – FONT. Octagonal, much re-cut. Demons on the foot. On the bowl the Signs of the four Evangelists and four bearded heads. – SCREEN. The top damaged. With eight painted Saints on the dado. Much charming ornamental painting. The most curious thing is the apparently original arrangement of two inner posts, set inside the entrance close to the posts of the entrance and carrying two lions. – PLATE. Chalice and Paten, Norwich, 1567–8; Paten, London, 1810.

WINDMILL, $\frac{1}{2}$ m. NW of the church. Tower-mill with cap and damaged sails.

⁴⁰¹⁰
EAST SOMERTON
$\frac{1}{2}$ m. E of West Somerton

_{4a}ST MARY. In ruins, in a wood belonging to Burnley Hall. The ruin stands most romantically amid the beech trees and other trees, with an oak growing inside the nave. The W tower of knapped flint is more decayed than the rest. The nave had tall transomed Perp windows. The chancel has disappeared, and only the chancel arch survives.

BURNLEY HALL. An extremely handsome house of about 1700.

Seven bays, two storeys, of red brick, with a recessed three-bay centre, brick quoins, and a hipped roof. The doorway with its broken pediment is a Later Georgian alteration. The side porch with Greek Doric columns may well have been built when the other doorway ceased to be used.

EATON see p. 289

ECCLES
1 m. NE of Hempstead

CHURCH. The village has long disappeared in the sea, and of the church whose tower old people still remember there is now no more than two heaps of flint on the beach the size of two beginners' sandcastles.

EDGEFIELD

OLD CHURCH, ⅜ m. NW. Octagonal W tower of the C14, a 'modern' version of the round towers of East Anglia. The rest has virtually disappeared.

ST PETER AND ST PAUL. 1883. Said to be by *Sedding*, but with much use of the materials of the old church and very close to it in style. Sedding's contributions would be the NE tower of pebble, the broad band of stone and flint chequer, the E end, and the clerestory. The W window of four lights has reticulated tracery.* On the S side one segment-headed Dec window. Three-bay arcades, that to the N Dec with octagonal piers and double-chamfered arches, that to the S Perp with piers of a four-shafts-four-hollows section. – FONT. Octagonal, C13, of Purbeck marble, with the two familiar flat pointed arches. – SCREEN. In the S aisle, with paintings of donors. Dated 1526. – PLATE. Chalice, Norwich, inscribed 1568; Paten, Norwich, 1691 (?); Almsdish, London, 1829.

RICHE'S FARMHOUSE, ½ m. N; i.e. N of the council houses. Porch with polygonal finials. Two storeys and a third in the gable. Pediments to the doorway and all windows. Probably early C17.

BARROW. On the Heath a bowl barrow.

EDINGTHORPE

ALL SAINTS. Round tower, noticeably tapering. Octagonal top. One of the bell-openings is straight-headed. Thatched nave. Divers Dec windows, but the N doorway Transitional, of c.1190. The chancel seems to be of the C19, but the small E

* It was originally the E window.

window with reticulated tracery is original. Inside, the most attractive feature is a little niche in the N wall above the doorway to the rood-loft stair. It stands on a bracket with little heads, and is painted inside and surrounded by a painted frame of fleurons. – FONT. Panelled stem, quatrefoiled bowl. – READER'S DESK. Dated 1587. Of panels rather roughly put together. – PULPIT. Dated 1632 in a panel on the side. – SCREEN. The upper part clearly C14. Shafts instead of mullions. Pointed arches with mouchettes. Ogee-headed entrance with two large circles in the spandrels, containing intricate rose tracery. On the dado only six painted Saints. The tracery painted white on the dark-coloured grounds as if it were flushwork. The style of painting also would fit a date before 1400. – BENCHES. Very rustic, with flat, cut-out poppyheads. – PAINTINGS. Of c.1400. Good St Christopher. To the E fragment of the Seven Works of Mercy on branches of a tree. – SOUTH DOOR. The knocker probably of the C14. – PLATE. Chalice, Norwich, 1567; Paten, London, 1700.

HALL FARM, ½ m. SW. Flint and stone dressings. Elizabethan or Jacobean. With two gables and a recessed centre. Pedimented windows of six or four lights with a transom. The former staircase windows under the l. gable are blocked. They would have broken the present symmetry.

ERPINGHAM

ST MARY. Big Perp W tower. Base frieze including two tiny figures by the doorway. Battlements with initials. They read ERPINGHAM, the letters being separated by crowned Ms and shields with the Instruments of the Passion. Dec the S aisle W window (reticulated tracery) and the chancel, though most of the chancel windows are Perp, of the same design (with stepped horizontals at the top of the three lights) as in the S aisle. S arcade of four bays with octagonal piers and double-chamfered arches. – FONT. Octagonal, with statuettes against the stem, ribbing against the underside, and eight drastically re-cut seated figures against the bowl. Christ on the rainbow e.g. has become a woman. – WEST DOOR. With tracery. – SCULPTURE. Four damaged statues (chancel), probably the former tower pinnacles. – STAINED GLASS. Many good Flemish panels of the C15 and C16 fill the E window. They come from Blickling Hall. One figure in the S aisle E window. – PLATE. Chalice and Paten Cover, Norwich-made, 1567. – BRASS. Sir John de Erpingham, c.1415. The figure is 4 ft 7 in. long (S aisle, E end).

FAKENHAM 9030

ST PETER AND ST PAUL. With its commanding w tower, the beacon of the little town. The oldest piece is the partly E.E. N doorway. The colonnettes have stiff-leaf capitals; the hood-mould has some dog-tooth. The s doorway is bigger, simpler, and probably a little later. Dec s and N windows, much renewed, big Dec E window of five lights with flowing tracery. Of the same date the chancel arch and the Sedilia and Piscina. The latter have crocketed ogee arches and a cornice of fleurons. A fleuron also in each spandrel. The arcades of six bays are later, though they seem to be still C 14. Octagonal piers, double-hollow-chamfered arches. The w tower is remarkably big and quite lavishly decorated. Flushwork frieze at the base, frieze of shields in cusped panels above it. w doorway with niches l. and r. Shields and tracery in the spandrels. Frieze of crowned Ds. Six-light w window with embattled transom. Panelled buttresses. Below the clock-stage sound-holes with a grid of panel units. Transomed three-light bell-openings. Tall arch towards the nave and vault with a central lozenge for the bell-ropes. – FONT. Perp, octagonal. Stem with crowned letters, apparently Ds, bowl with the Signs of the four Evangelists and shields with the Symbol of the Trinity, the Instruments of the Passion, and arms. – SCREEN. Of two-light divisions. Dec, but mostly C 19. With shafts with shaft-rings instead of mullions, ogee arches, and tracery including mouchette wheels. – PLATE. Cup 1567; Paten c.1660; Paten on foot 1697; Flagon 1745. – BRASSES. Priest, early C 15 (31 in.; chancel). – Husband and two wives, c.1470 (c.16 in.; chancel). – Four double hearts, c.1470 (floor, nave). – Audrie Narborow, c.1510 (chancel).

Apart from the church, there is not much to be seen at Fakenham. The MARKET PLACE and THE SQUARE form an irregular group in the centre, a little confusing for the motorist, but nice to wander through. In the Market Place, facing each other, the RED LION, red brick, C18, and the CROWN HOTEL, whitewashed, with rusticated quoins, early C 19, and apparently lacking its r. hand termination. In The Square a few creditable Georgian houses – and that is all. See p. 390

FELBRIGG 2030

ST MARGARET. The village to which the church originally belonged has disappeared, and the building is now alone in the

Felbrigg church, brass to Sir Simon Felbrigg and wife † 1416.

grounds of the Hall. W tower with flushwork panelling on the base, a doorway with shields and tracery in the spandrels, and sound-holes with tracery. The lion and the fetterlock (of Sir Simon Felbrigg) appear on the tower and also on the nave buttresses. Tall Perp windows. Good Perp chancel E window of five lights. Good Perp Sedilia and Piscina with little vaults, and in the spandrels shields on cusped quatrefoils. Opposite, in the chancel N wall, a quatrefoil niche, originally, it seems, the opening into the vestry, which stood to the N of the chancel. But what was its purpose? Merely a squint? Or is it not *in situ*? The S porch has flushwork panelling, and there is also some flushwork panelling above the N porch. Inside the tower a small fireplace, presumably for the baking of the wafers. The nave roof has arched braces and a number of genuine bosses. – FONT. Octagonal, C14, with eight shafts attached to the stem, and against the bowl on each side two ogee arches (cf. Runton). – BOX PEWS. – PLATE. Very fine Paten of *c*.1500 with the engraved figure of St Margaret set in 39a a sexfoiled depression; Chalice, 1567, made in Norwich. – MONUMENTS. A most impressive series of brasses, starting with those of Simon de Felbrigg † 1351 and his wife and Roger † 1380 and his wife (in front of the sedilia). The four figures have a joint inscription in Norman French, a singularly late case of the language being used in England. They were probably made shortly after Roger's death. The figures are 3 ft long. – Sir Simon and his first wife, who died in 1416 and was cousin to Anne of Bohemia, Richard II's Queen (nave). Outstandingly good figures, 5 ft 4 in. long, under ogee canopies and between thin buttresses. – A Lady, $13\frac{1}{2}$ in. figure, *c*.1480 (nave). – Thomas Windham † 1599, 3 ft 2 in. (nave). – Jane Coningsby, his sister, † 1608, 3 ft 1 in. (chancel). Both these brasses were sent from London. – Stone tablets, more than can here be enumerated. Thomas Windham, made in 1669 by *Martin Morley* of Norwich, who received £45 for it. Rustic work. – William Windham † 1686. £50 was paid for this to *Grinling Gibbons*. White. Inscription flanked by hanging garlands of flowers. On the top two putti l. and r. of an urn. Two cherubs' heads at the foot. – Ash Windham † 1749. Black obelisk with inscription partly in black-letter. At the foot of the monument a shield with foliage. – William Windham, 1813 by *Nollekens*. Standing monument with an excellent bust on a plain sarcophagus.

FELBRIGG HALL. Felbrigg Hall is mentioned in the Paston

letters when it changed hands and came from the Felbrigges
to the Wymondhams, later Windhams and Wyndhams. The
house was built for Thomas Windham about 1620, and enlarged in 1674–87 and again in 1750. The original part of the
51b   house is the SOUTH RANGE. It is of brick with stone dressings
and not large; but it has the lively projections and recessions
of the Jacobean style. There are seven bays, the middle one
with a square porch projection, the angle ones with canted bay
windows. The house is only two storeys high, with large
mullioned and transomed windows. They have two transoms
on the ground floor, one on the first floor. The front ends in a
tall parapet, and on the porch and bays balustrading with the
words GLORIA DEO IN EXCELSIS in cut-out 'Grotesque'
letters. There are not many houses that have this motif. It
seems to have originated in France (La Ferté–Bernard, 1535–
44) and appears in England at Castle Ashby, Temple Newsam,
and Skipton Castle. On the balustrade small supporter figures.
The chimneystacks are of three polygonal shafts each with star
tops. The house of c.1620 was only one room deep. It has a
shaped gable to the w, and the back exit to the N is preserved,
now of course inside the building. The HALL is in the traditional position. Its plaster ceiling with pendants seems to date
from c.1830, as do also the door surrounds with their heavy
strapwork and probably even the yet heavier overmantel. In
the Hall windows STAINED GLASS, partly from St Peter Mancroft at Norwich, partly Swiss of the C16.

To this range a WEST WING was added to the design of
William Samwell, a gentleman architect and lord of the
manor of Watton in Norfolk. Little survives or is known of his
buildings. He died in 1676. The w range at Felbrigg is a sedate,
but engaging piece of design, eight bays wide and two storeys
high, with a hipped roof with dormers and just two pediments
to accentuate individual windows – or rather a doorway and a
window. The two middle bays project slightly. The whole
front and this projection have brick quoins. In Samwell's
design, preserved at the house, a niche with a statue was provided as a (rather inadequate) central effect. The windows were
of the cross-type but are now sashed. They are long and
slender and, with the one exception already mentioned, quite
unmoulded and undecorated. Inside, the DRAWING ROOM
56b   has a splendid plaster ceiling carrying the date 1687. The
stucco, with its deeply undercut flowers and leaves in frames
and panels, is very similar to that of the Drawing Room at

Melton Constable, which is also dated 1687.* It was no doubt done by the same group of workmen. To the s of the drawing room was the grand staircase which appears in Samwell's plan. Of this only one corner of the stucco ceiling survives on the upper floor. It is in the same style as the plasterwork of the drawing room, and there is also a cornice in one upper bedroom which goes with the drawing room and staircase. The cabinet, at the NW corner, is more intriguing. It seems to belong entirely to the same group, but it is clear externally that the bay window is mid-Georgian. This was in fact added about 1750, when *James Paine* worked for William Windham, the father of the politician of the same name. The stucco in the bay is a remarkable piece of adaptation to the style of the 1680s.

James Paine removed Samwell's staircase and redecorated the space which it had filled. The room thus gained became the DINING ROOM. It has beautiful stucco by *Rose*, specially in the wall panels, and a fireplace similar to those by Kent at Holkham. The new STAIRCASE has more modest plaster decoration. The balustrade is of wrought iron and the ceiling was originally tunnel-vaulted. *Humphry* and *J. A. Repton* altered this in 1806. Paine's LIBRARY in the s range on the upper floor above the Hall is mildly Gothick.

Paine may also be responsible for the SERVICE RANGE to the E of the s façade. Its own s façade however was altered, by the addition of pavilions with shaped gables, at the time when the stables were built. The range has a cupola and to the s a pediment with a circular window. Other outbuildings include the ORANGERY, built in 1704–5 in beautifully precise brickwork. It is seven bays long and has a hipped roof. In the kitchen garden is an octagonal DOVECOTE, which also seems to be of C18 brick.

The STABLES were rebuilt by *Donthorne* in 1825. They are large, of brick, castellated, and make use of the handsome motif of the screen wall with traceried window openings on the pattern of Wilkins's King's College, Cambridge.

CROMER LODGES. Neo-Jacobean, 1841, signed by the *Bucklers*.
WINDMILL, 1¼ m. E of the church (at Roughton). Tower-mill, now without sails and cap.

FELMINGHAM 2020

ST ANDREW. Very big and powerful w tower, left without a parapet. Flushwork panelling on the base, flushwork

* And the Drawing Room at Hintlesham in Suffolk.

decoration on the buttresses, flushwork panelling l. and r. of the entrance. This has spandrels with shields on tracery. Tall w window. Traceried sound-holes. Very tall arch towards the nave. The body of the church was rebuilt in brick in 1742, but the Perp s doorway (with heads and shields up one order of moulding) and the Dec windows (reticulated tracery and an odd variant of it with two sexfoiled circles instead of two reticulation units) were kept. – FONT. C14 stem, but C13 bowl of the familiar Purbeck type with two shallow arches against each of eight sides. – STAINED GLASS. Bits in the NE window. – PLATE. Nicely engraved Chalice of 1567, Norwich-made; Paten, undated. – BRASS. Robert Moone † 1591. Palimpsest of a mid-C15 brass of a priest.

₁₀₁₀   FELTHORPE

ST MARGARET. Small w tower with Dec window and C17 (?) brick parapet with obelisk pinnacles. Nave, N aisle, and chancel with a variety of windows, C14 to C15. The s aisle was added in 1878. Four-bay arcades with octagonal piers and double-chamfered arches. – STAINED GLASS. Much of the 1880s by *H. Hughes* and *Hughes & Ward*, to the detriment of the church.

(FELTHORPE HALL. White brick; built soon after 1825. Additions after 1935. B. Cozens-Hardy)

₀₀₃₀   FIELD DALLING

ST ANDREW. Dec w tower and chancel, Perp nave and N aisle. The tower is not in line with the nave. It has Dec bell-openings, but a Perp w window and tower arch. The chancel E window is Dec, of five lights with reticulated tracery. s window with segmental arch. On the N side traces of a Perp chapel. The nave s windows big, of four lights, the N aisle with smaller Perp windows (but an earlier doorway, as is found so frequently). Four-bay arcade. Elongated octagonal piers with the diagonals long and concave. Shafts against the principal sides. Arch-braced nave and aisle roofs, chancel roof with hammerbeams. – FONT. Octagonal, Perp, drastically re-cut. Instruments of the Passion and emblem of the Trinity, St Andrew's Cross, crossed swords, monogram of Jesus, etc. Fleurons against the underside. – FONT COVER. Jacobean, radially set, fin-like volutes. – BENCHES. Many, with poppy-heads. – Some BOX PEWS. – STAINED GLASS. Original small figures in the s

windows and one N window. – PLATE. Chalice, Norwich, 1567;
Paten, London, 1591.

TUDOR HOUSE, SE of the church. A curious house, no more
than a three-bay cottage, yet with a gabled Elizabethan or
Jacobean porch and pedimented windows.

FILBY

4010

ALL SAINTS. Mostly Dec, but all window tracery Victorian.
The S and N doorways are authentic, and the clerestory with
alternating quatrefoils in circles and blank quatrefoils can also
be believed. The arcades inside, however (five bays, octagonal
piers), though the mouldings of the arches are Dec, have bases
which look decidedly Perp. Perp also the W tower, with flushwork panelling on the base and triple-stepped battlements.
Tall Perp two-light bell-openings. Figures instead of pinnacles. – FONT. Octagonal, of Purbeck marble, with two
shallow blank arches on each side, drastically re-cut. – PULPIT.
Perp, with blank tracery. – SCREEN. On the dado eight painted
Saints, of quite good quality. Well carved vine trail along the
top rail. – BENCHES. Some ends with poppy-heads, loose in
the porch. – NORTH DOOR. With cross-shaped foliated ironwork round the knocker; C14. – STAINED GLASS. Twelve
panels in the C13 style, said to be Parisian of c.1850. – PLATE.
Chalice, Norwich, inscribed 1636; Paten Cover, plain. –
MONUMENTS. Gibson Lucas † 1790. A small-headed genius
seated on a sarcophagus and touching an urn. Unsigned. –
Charles Lucas † 1831. Stele with a genius holding an extinguished torch. On the ground a capital of a broken column
and an urn inscribed Ossa. An excellent piece, by *Joseph Her-
mann* of Dresden, who was a pupil of Thorwaldsen and spent
the years 1820–31 in Róme.

FILBY HOUSE. Early Georgian, of seven bays and two storeys.
Segment-headed windows. The doorway with fluted pilasters
and a metope frieze. The window above it is altered.

See
p.
390

FISHLEY

3010

½ m. SE of Upton

ST MARY. Round tower, probably Norman, with unmoulded
tower arch. Later brick top. Norman S doorway with one order
of colonnettes with scalloped capitals. Billet frieze on the hood-
mould. All much restored (1861). The rest of the church probably essentially of the late C13, though also much restored.

Nave and chancel in one. In the w wall of the nave (towards the tower) a small opening in the shape of a pointed quatrefoil. In the E wall of the nave a rounded quatrefoil window. The N side otherwise with small lancets. Did perhaps a N aisle exist? – ORGAN CASE. Of 1781.

0020

FOULSHAM

HOLY INNOCENTS. The beginning is the first three bays of the N arcade. They are of the C13 and have circular piers with circular capitals and abaci and double-chamfered arches. The s arcade (octagonal piers) is Perp, and so is the E part of the N arcade (polygonal projections). The Perp work in the church is assigned to the late C15 (arms of Lord Morley) and comprises the aisle windows and clerestory with twice as many windows as there are bays * and the ambitious w tower. Flushwork base, doorway with some flushwork panelling, the base course cutting through the doorway shafts, shields in the spandrels, a four-light window, sound-holes with a grid of panelling units, three-light bell-openings, and double-stepped battlements with shields and Ms (for Mary). The chancel arch is Dec, and some chancel N and S windows confirm this. The E window is Victorian. So are to all intents and purposes the Sedilia. The detail of the church is not wholly trustworthy, as a lot of repairing became necessary after the town fire of 1770 (the nave ceiling probably belongs to the repairs) and after a gale of 1895. – FONT. Octagonal, Perp, with a panelled stem and a bowl with flowers in quatrefoils. Rolls run along the ridges and form pendants on the underside of the bowl. – STAINED GLASS. Original C14 glass in the tracery heads in the chancel windows. – E window by *C. A. Gibbs.* – PLATE. Chalice, originally Elizabethan? – MONUMENTS. In the churchyard, NW of the tower, a tomb-chest the panels of which seem to be made up of panels of architectural decoration. Two quatrefoils each with three crowned letters over. – Sir Thomas Hunt † 1616. Alabaster tablet. Three depressed arches and kneeling under them Sir Thomas and his three wives.

Right by the church a group of attractive Georgian brick houses built after the fire of 1770. Two face each other with their porches with fluted Doric columns. N of the church CHURCH FARMHOUSE, with a minor Georgian three-bay front to the road and a big shaped C17 gable to the E.

---

* Ten plus four in the chancel.

OLD HALL FARMHOUSE, ⅜ m. ESE. C16. The E and W gables
have round, decorated chimneyshafts and stone finials. (Inscribed date 1556. B. Cozens-Hardy)

FOXLEY

0200

ST THOMAS. Late C13 chancel, the E window with intersected
tracery. Tall Dec W tower. Flushwork panelling applied to the
battlements. Pretty entrance to the S porch. In the l. spandrel
the lopped tree. – FONT. Octagonal, simple, with quatrefoils. –
SCREEN. Single-light divisions, the arches prettily cusped and
subcusped, in two layers in depth. Of the paintings on the dado
four are left. – Two-decker PULPIT and BOX PEWS. Also
C17 BENCHES with poppy-heads. – COMMUNION RAIL. C17.
– PLATE. Paten of the early C15. With a sexfoil and a hand of
God in a circle. – Norwich-made Chalice, 1567.

FREETHORPE

4000

ALL SAINTS. Round tower, incomplete, with a conical roof.
Nave, N aisle, and chancel E.E. The arcade is of two bays and
has the usual octagonal pier and double-chamfered arches, but
the mouldings make a date in the C13 certain. The W windows
of the nave – the only trustworthy ones – are lancets. In the
chancel a good big lancet window, inside with prominent
shafts, outside with charming little stiff-leaf curls l. and r. –
FONT. Octagonal, the stem with sides carved in a reeded
fashion. – PLATE. Chalice, made in Norwich, 1567–8. –
MONUMENT. Edward Walpole (of Savile Row in the County
of Middlesex) † 1844, with a life-size free-standing bust at the
top.

FRETTENHAM

2010

ST SWITHIN. The church stands on its own, Dec with a chancel
of 1869 (by *Phipson*). W tower with traceried sound-holes.
Parapet dated 1672. Arcades of three bays. The piers quatrefoil with slim filleted shafts in the diagonals. The arches have
two small wave mouldings. Clerestory with quatrefoil openings. Chancel arch going with the arcades. The S porch is Dec
too. – FONT. Octagonal, C13, of Purbeck marble, with the
usual two shallow arches on each side. – BENCHES. In the N
aisle, with poppy-heads. – STAINED GLASS. An angel in a
chancel S window. – PLATE. Chalice, Norwich, 1567. –

BRASSES. Alys Brunham, *c*.1420, $25\frac{1}{2}$ in. figure (chancel s wall). – Another Lady, *c*.1460, 19 in. (chancel floor).
WINDMILL. A derelict tower-mill without cap or sails.

FULMODESTONE
$1\frac{3}{4}$ m. ESE of Kettlestone

9030

ST MARY. Disused and roofless. w tower with Y-tracery in the bell-openings and specially pretty sound-holes with cusping and other decoration. Nave and chancel in one. The E window of three lights with intersected tracery. Is it original? In the nave on the s side lancet window.
CHRIST CHURCH. Built in 1882 to the design of *William Basset Smith* of London. No tower. In the Dec style, brick-faced inside. – PLATE. Cup and Paten, 1827.

GIMINGHAM

2030

ALL SAINTS. Small. Dec chancel (windows with reticulated tracery, nicely shafted inside), Perp nave, w tower, and prettily decorated s porch. Two storeys. Quatrefoils with shields on the battlements to N and S, to the entrance a flushwork chequer pattern. Above the entrance a three-light window with another quatrefoil frieze below. – FONT. Traceried stem, on the bowl four pairs of blank arches and four cusped pointed quatrefoils. – BENCHES. Two ends are re-used in the prayer-desk. They have poppy-heads and little animals. – PLATE. Chalice and Paten Cover on foot, Norwich-made, 1567.
JOHN OF GAUNT'S HALL, $\frac{5}{8}$ m. SW. A small, oblong Jacobean house with a symmetrical front of only three bays. Mullioned and transomed windows of five to three lights. Stepped gable-end. Fireplaces also in the end-walls. Staircase in the NW angle. Oven close to the SE corner.

GLANDFORD

0040

ST MARTIN. Sir Alfred Jodrell of Bayfield Hall (*see* p. 85) built the village and the church, the latter with the use of materials from its decayed predecessor, which was already in ruins in the early C18. The church was designed by *Hicks & Charlewood* and built in 1899–1906, a memorial to Sir Alfred's mother, whose MONUMENT, a white angel of the type familiar from the Père Lachaise or the Cimitero of Staglieno, is in the church. It is in fact the work of *Pietro Bazzanti* of Florence.

The church is a restoration of the medieval church, which had a Perp arcade with octagonal piers and double-chamfered arches. The chancel is generously appointed: hammerbeam roof, wooden panelling, screens with much tracery. – STAINED GLASS by *Kempe* (E and N aisle E) and *Bryans*. – The FONT is a copy in marble of the Seven Sacraments font of Walsoken. – PLATE. Chalice and Paten, inscribed 1568; Salver, made in Birmingham, 1774.

THE VILLAGE. A model village of flint and red-brick houses and cottages, mostly with shaped gables.

GORLESTON

5000

ST ANDREW, Church Lane. Big W tower of the late C13 and later. Lancet windows below and a low tower arch with broad semi-octagonal responds and a triple-chamfered arch. Perp bell-openings. Double-stepped battlements with flushwork panelling. Prominent S stair-turret. Of the early C14 the N and S doorways and the N aisle W window. The rest externally all Victorian, especially the E view with the three separate roofs. No structural division inside between nave and chancel. Seven-bay arcades with octagonal piers, too low to be effective, and double-chamfered arches. The S arcade is of the early C14, and this is confirmed by the S chapel Piscina. The tower cuts into the S arcade, which indicates that further buttressing was provided when the Perp heightening took place. The N arcade is Perp. Pretty E respond with a foliage capital. Yet the N chapel has a Dec Easter Sepulchre with a cusped and sub-cusped ogee arch, crockets, and flanking buttresses, and a Dec Piscina. – FONT. Very defaced, with statuettes against the stem and the Seven Sacraments against the bowl. – STAINED GLASS. Some glass by *Ward & Hughes* in the S aisle; terrible. – PLATE. Silver-gilt Chalice, 1567; Cover, 1567; Cup, 1811. – MONUMENTS. Excellent brass to a Knight, c.1320, the figure 4 ft 8 in. long and cross-legged, not a frequent feature in brasses (N chapel, N wall). – Several tablets with urns and obelisks.

ST MARY, Southtown Road. *See* Great Yarmouth, p. 147.

ST PETER THE APOSTLE (R.C.). *See* p. 390.

The development of Gorleston has been closely linked to that of Yarmouth, and some of the houses here referred to are administratively at Southtown, Yarmouth, and not at Gorleston. This applies to Messrs Coleman's offices and warehouses in SOUTHTOWN ROAD, which were built as an ARSENAL by

James Wyatt in 1806. There were originally two facing blocks
of living quarters and a storehouse at the back. The block on
the r. is in its original state. Two storeys, red brick, pedimental
gable-ends. The block at the back is seven windows wide and
has blank arches on the ground floor. The other noteworthy
houses in this neighbourhood are villas. The nicest is No. 5
PIERPLAIN, called THE GROVE, early C19, of three bays,
with giant pilasters carrying a pediment that runs all along the
façade. Ground-floor windows and doorway arched. In the
HIGH STREET, i.e. further N, No. 102 with a shaped gable
and yet as late a date as 1720, and then the SEA CADET UNIT,
another early C19 villa, of grey brick, seven bays of which
three form part of a central bow window. In this the entrance
with recessed Greek Doric columns.

Finally, at the end of High Road turn w either down Burnet
Lane or BEILLES ROAD. Here, behind Nos 79–81 (or behind
49 Burnet Lane), the few insignificant remains of the important house of AUSTIN FRIARS, founded in 1311. Further
on OTTEY'S FARMHOUSE, with two Dutch end-gables (i.e.
shaped gables with proper pediments on top). Blocked oval
windows. The date is no doubt the later C17.

Of Gorleston as a seaside resort only the PAVILION, 1898
by *J. W. Cockrill*, is worth noting. Red brick and Venetian
tracery and four copper domes.

GORLESTON LIGHTHOUSE. Erected *c.*1877.

GREAT HAUTBOIS *see* HAUTBOIS

GREAT ORMESBY *see* ORMESBY ST MARGARET

3000
GREAT PLUMSTEAD

ST MARY. w tower of 1711. Brick, with arched bell-openings
and battlements prettily faced with brick and flint in a chequer
pattern. The chancel all Victorian, but the E wall with a renewed Perp window and to its l. and r. close to the corners two
lancets, i.e. a sign of an E.E. chancel. The arrangement is the
same as at Acle, and one is left wondering whether there were
three or five windows in the wall.

9030
GREAT SNORING

ST MARY. The first phase in the architectural history of the
church is the C13, to which belong the s doorway with one
order of shafts and the four-bay s arcade with circular piers

carrying circular capitals and abaci and double-hollow-chamfered arches. In the s aisle a contemporary angle Piscina with a leaf capital. The second phase, the end of the C13, is represented by the priest's doorway and the fine chancel E window. This is of five lights with intersected tracery interrupted at the top to allow for the insertion of a quatrefoiled circle. Phase number three is Dec. To this belong the stepped Sedilia and Piscina with an ogee arch, a crocketed gable, and simple little quadripartite rib-vaults inside. The shafts come to a sharp edge towards the front, i.e. appear to be set diagonally. The s aisle E window is also probably Dec. Finally the Perp contributions, i.e. the W tower, the nave windows (those on the N side with embattled transoms), and the chancel side windows and chancel arch. It ought to be assumed that the rare feature of a frieze of shields on cusped fields behind the altar is also a Perp addition. – FONT. Of Purbeck (Tournai?) marble. Square, with tapering sides, on five supports. C13 (?). – SCREEN. Tall, with one-light divisions and ogee arches. – BENCHES. With poppy-heads. – SOUTH DOOR. Traceried and with a frame of quatrefoils. – SCULPTURE. Large terracotta tile with the figure of an angel (N wall). – PAINTING. 'Christ ^{See} healing', perhaps Dutch late C17. – STAINED GLASS. In the ^{p.}₃₉₀ chancel original bits. – PLATE. Elizabethan Chalice, Norwich-made; Paten, London, 1827. – MONUMENTS. Fine, but much damaged early C15 brasses of a Knight and Lady, the figures c. 3 ft 4 in. long (chancel, N side). – Several minor tablets, e.g. Robert West † 1610, alabaster.

RECTORY. A substantial part of a manor house built about 1525 for Sir Ralph Shelton. The house is of brick and belongs to the group of East Barsham and Thorpland and, outside Norfolk, Sutton Place and Layer Marney. What survives is a plain front, now plastered, which is flanked by polygonal turrets and, at an obtuse angle to it, a much more ornate shorter front. The latter has original windows of three and four lights, on the ground floor with basket arches and fine continuous mouldings, on the first floor with more normal uncusped four-centred arches. One distinguishing feature of the house is the two friezes of moulded bricks (or rather terracotta) above the ground floor and the upper floor, the former of Gothic panels and a running frieze of M IHS M IHS below, the latter of Renaissance motifs, i.e. little balusters and little profile heads. The frieze continues or continued along the longer side as well. The turrets in their upper parts are panelled on a much bolder scale, again still entirely Gothic in style. The chimneyshaft are much renewed.

Nice village street down the hill.

GREAT WALSINGHAM

St Peter. A singularly beautiful church, because its architecture is all one and its interior furnishing is also happily preserved. The felicitous effect is gained against heavy odds; for the church lacks its chancel. The prevailing style of the building is Dec, and the *Leitmotiv* is the reticulation unit filled with small flowing tracery. This occurs in the tower w window and in the N aisle and S aisle windows, including their E windows. The clerestory windows are quatrefoils in circles. The w tower is tall. The bell-openings are Dec too, and on the top is a curious little pyramid roof, of course of later date. The present E wall has two prettily fringed domestic-looking two-light windows, one on top of the other. The jambs of one s window (and the chancel arch inside) prove that the chancel was Dec too. Big N and s porches, the only Perp additions. The s porch has flushwork decoration and a niche l. and r. of the entrance. Arcades of four bays. Quatrefoil piers with the foils somewhat squashed and provided with fillets. In the diagonals slim shafts, also with fillets. The capitals are polygonal. The arches have two sunk quadrants dying into short vertical pieces at the start. The tower arch and the chancel arch go with them. The floor is tiled, which always helps to make a church interior attractive. Good roof with arched braces to small, high collar-beams. A corresponding roof in the N aisle. But the supreme delight of the church is the BENCHES, a complete set, in nave and aisles, and in the aisles even still attached to former wall panelling. They have pierced backs with a variety of tracery motifs; the front row has linenfold panelling, and the ends have poppy-heads with vine, oak, and other leaves and even a figure and, on the arms, little animals, but also the figures of the Apostles, and angels with shields containing no doubt the initials of donors. – FONT. Big, octagonal. Bowl with two simple panels on each side. – PULPIT. The pulpit may incorporate Perp panels. The date 1613 painted on cannot apply to them. – COMMUNION RAIL. C17, with thin, tall, column-like balusters. – STAINED GLASS. Many original fragments in the heads of the N and s aisle windows. – PLATE. Chalice made in Norwich in 1567–8; Paten also Norwich-made, inscribed 1679.

BERRY HALL, in the centre of the village, i.e. at the triangle to the N of the church. With a porch which has a four-centred brick doorhead and a stepped gable. The other porch is an addition. Inside, the Hall has moulded beams and a moulded lintel above the fireplace. The Hall and the exterior, save for the stepped gables, chimneystacks, etc., is Early Tudor. Georgian staircase. Drawing room with Jacobean panelling and chimneypiece.

Opposite the entrance to Berry Hall, the so-called MANOR HOUSE, a cottage with an oversailing timber-framed upper storey. To the NW of the triangle WESTGATE HOUSE, and in a field S of, and close to, this the foundations of the CHURCH OF ALL SAINTS.

Finally, ½ m. E of the church, in the HINDRINGHAM ROAD, a house with ashlar quoins (opposite a garage) which has in its wall many medieval fragments, including a figure of an angel in the spandrel of a steep crocketed gable.

GREAT WITCHINGHAM   *0010*

ST MARY. Late C13 chancel; the E window with its cusped intersected tracery is unmistakable. Tall Dec W tower, see the arch towards the nave and the bell-openings. Niches l. and r. of the W window. Dec four-bay arcades, with octagonal piers and double-chamfered arches. The bases differ. Dec also the S windows, if they are original. Perp S porch with a nice façade. Entrance arch with the Annunciation in the spandrels. Flushwork frieze at the base and above the entrance, with crowned Ms (for Mary). A niche in the gable. Eight closely set clerestory windows, Late Perp, with flint and brick patterns. Fine nave roof with wall-posts on stone gables, longitudinal arched braces, and arched braces up to the ridge. Figures of angels against the ridge. Perp aisle roofs too. – FONT. Octagonal. Saints against the stem. Against the bowl the Seven Sacraments and the Assumption of the Virgin. – BENCHES. With poppy-heads; some with pierced tracery in the backs. – PLATE. Chalice and Paten-Cover, Norwich, c.1660.

GREAT WITCHINGHAM HALL, 1⅛ m. SE. The front is of 1872, a spectacular piece of Victorian–Elizabethan. However, some Tudor brickwork betrays the true date of the house, and this is more clearly visible at the back. Here the porch and two adjoining bays remain fairly undisturbed. All three units have stepped gables, mullioned and transomed windows, and pediments above the windows. The S wing was built in 1812.

Inside the house a good fireplace of 1609 (from Bacon's House, Colegate, Norwich), with female figures against the overmantel.

EADE'S MILL, 1⅛ m. NW. Nice brick group of the mill and the five-bay miller's house with brick quoins.

GREAT YARMOUTH

INTRODUCTION

Herrings have made Yarmouth what it was from the time St Nicholas was built to the time when Defoe wrote of the Yarmouth fishermen's 'prodigious catches' and beyond. Seaside pleasures came only in the course of the C18. A bathing house on the beach is mentioned in 1759, a ballroom was added in 1788, and hotels began to appear in the early C19. But the main building activity is Victorian. Socially, Great Yarmouth had its golden days about 1850. Today the seaside pleasures are more popular than fashionable. This being the history of the town, there are three Yarmouths, the medieval town with its developments into the C18, the seaside resort of the C19, and the seaside resort of today. One thing medieval Yarmouth and C20 Yarmouth have in common is the long, narrow plan stretching N–S with very little E–W development. This is of course due to the position of the town between the river Yare and the sea. Today Yarmouth goes on for about 4 m. In the Middle Ages the whole circuit of the walls was only 2280 yards, but the shape was similar. Medieval and C16 and C17 Yarmouth had only three main N–S roads, even if, in their courses, they went on changing their names. The plan can well be compared, on its own intimate scale, with that of Manhattan.

Medieval Yarmouth had nothing to do with the sea. Its face was turned to the river, not the sea. There were no walls to the river, though in all other directions. The TOWN WALLS were begun after 1260 and completed in the C14. They were over 23 ft high and had sixteen towers and ten gates. Their design was the usual one, with blank arches to the inside carrying the wall-walk. There were cross-shaped loopholes under the arches as well as above. On the whole the walls are remarkably well preserved, and can be followed, with gaps of course, from the W–E stretch N of Mariners' Road, then running N along Blackfriars Road and St Peter's Place to S of the Hospital School in the Market Place, and then turning W again to Town Wall Road and the final NW tower at the N end of Rampart Road. Reference to the walls will be found in the text later on.

Inside these walls the medieval and the C16 and C17 town lived its busy life. The importance of the town can be judged from the existence of houses of the Franciscans, the Dominicans, and the Carmelites, apart from a small Benedictine priory. The most distinctive feature of medieval Yarmouth was preserved remarkably completely to the Second World War: THE ROWS, narrow passageways of between 2 ft 6 in. and 6 ft in width, which connected the three main N–S streets. To revert to the comparison with Manhattan, they were the streets, the N–S streets the avenues. The Rows were, according to the late St J. O'Neill, substantially of the late C16,* though much may have gone back to the earlier C16 and yet earlier predecessors. The war did much damage to The Rows, and it would obviously be neither desirable nor possible to reconstruct them. So it is the three main N–S thoroughfares which now contain the houses worth admiring in Inner Yarmouth, and they are, with the exception of very few, of the years between the late C17 and the early C19.

CHURCHES

ST NICHOLAS. Yarmouth prides itself on having the largest parish church of England. The area of St Nicholas is about 23,000 sq. ft. The history of the building is long and has its ups and downs. The first church was built in the early C12 and completed in 1119. It was attached to a Benedictine priory on which see p. 148. Of the C12 church no more remains than the lower parts of the outside of the crossing tower. The nave arcades were made in the late C12 and narrow aisles built. The tower was heightened at about the same time. The W front is of the C13, and so are parts of the S transept, the crossing arches and the chancel aisles. A dedication in 1286 is recorded. The S porch was or is Dec, and some windows were or are Perp. The church became ruinous in the C17 and C18, and restorations took place in 1847 (*Hakewill*) and 1862 etc. (*Seddon*). In 1862 etc. the tower pinnacles were put on, the S aisle was rebuilt, and the E end was lengthened. In 1942, in the Second World War, the church was gutted by fire and much of the interior stonework calcined. Rebuilding took place in 1957–60 under Mr *Stephen Dykes Bower*.

EXTERIOR. We start at the WEST FRONT. This is of two phases in the C13, the centre earlier and narrow, the side pieces, representing the aisles, a good deal wider. The lower

* In 1598 Nash speaks of seven-score of them.

stage is flint-faced, the upper ashlar-faced. In the centre part
is a doorway with four orders of shafts carrying moulded
capitals. The arch mouldings are simple steps slightly rounded.
Above, a group of three lancets, stepped, and with dog-tooth
on the hood-moulds. Small trefoil window in the gable. The
gable front on thin corbels. Two plain octagonal pinnacles.
The side pieces have each a stepped group of three two-light
windows. The s piece is more ornate, with blank lancets
between the windows, a blank round arch above the whole
group with decorative quatrefoil circles and pointed trefoils
and at the top in the gable a pointed sexfoil in a circle. The N
piece has simply Y-tracery in the windows. The outer pinnacles are panelled, but were rebuilt c.1862.

In front of the w front the grass-covered foundation of the
Bachelors' Aisle, a w transept begun in 1330 but never continued. It had a deep w doorway. To the SE of the w front
some foundations supposed to be of the charnel-house.

The rest of the exterior is in most of its features C19 or C20,
except the TOWER. The lowest stage of this has much restored blank Norman arcading, the next Norman windows.
Above that work of c.1200: three single lancet windows on
each side. Victorian parapet and pinnacles.

Now for a walk round the church. The s aisle windows are
all of c.1862. The s porch is Dec, but in its present form also
clearly Victorian, though after 1862. The porch may,
however, always have been Dec. It certainly has its three-light
windows in early C19 engravings. The present tracery is
flowing. Inside the porch two quadripartite rib-vaults with
genuine-looking bosses. The inner s doorway is E.E., but
apparently all Victorian. The s transept has to the w a genuine
E.E. doorway. Three orders with stiff-leaf capitals. Arch with
fine, keeled mouldings. The rest of the s transept features and
all features of the E parts are C19 or C20, except for a pair of
low, plain tomb recesses in the s chancel aisle. In the N
transept to the N and w blocked windows which look rather
earlier than Victorian. To the N a small later C13 doorway. In
the N aisle an original doorway too, E.E., of two orders of
colonnettes with moulded capitals. Arch mouldings with fillets.

INTERIOR. The general effect is spacious and impressive,
but puzzling. The interior is evidently Gothic, of c.1190 to the
late C13, but features face the observant visitor at once which
cannot convince historically. When one realizes the actual
happenings, puzzlement grows into acute disappointment.

The story is this. The church was, as we have seen, gutted in 1942. Of course it could have been reconstructed as it was at the time, largely original and partly Victorian. Nothing would have been wrong with that. What Mr *Dykes Bower* did instead is not to copy but to make up his own Transitional and Gothic. What an opportunity was lost thereby! What thrilling things might have been done inside! A modern interior, airy, noble, of fine materials could have arisen to affirm the vitality of C20 church architecture inside the C13 walls. How defeatist does the imitation-Gothic interior appear, once this has been realized.

We must now look at it in detail. The nave, dating from *c.* 1190, is narrow, as narrow as the measurements of the earlier crossing-tower dictated. The aisles are the widest in England, 39 ft wide, i.e. considerably more than the nave. The arcades were till 1942 of eight Transitional bays. Mr Dykes Bower reduced them to four very wide ones to pull the interior together, but he chose to give them Transitional capitals. The nave has a boarded, canted ceiling, the aisles have flat ceilings. In the W wall of the nave are blank shallow niches l. and r. of the doorway, in the aisles blocked W doorways showing how narrow the aisles of *c.*1190 were. Amply shafted W windows, those of the S aisle again with blank lancets between them. The W arch of the crossing is C13. It has strong triple shafts. The E, N, and S arches were remodelled in the late C14, it looks. The N and S arches have halfway up three quatrefoiled bands across their shafts. Flat ceiling. The wide arches from the aisles to the transepts differ. The S transept arch is round, the other pointed. The triple shafts are again, it looks, original. The chancel opens into its side chapels by two arches on each side. This is the original arrangement, but the detail is not. The division of the chapels by a row of slender octagonal piers along from W to E is entirely Mr Dykes Bower's. There was no such sub-division before. The chancel has a steeply canted boarded ceiling, the chapel and transept ceilings are flat. The REREDOS does not stand against the E wall, but somewhat to its W so that an E vestry is formed (now a store-room). Access to it is by two pretty small Perp doorways with a quatrefoil band up the jambs and along the arch. In the main vestry the re-erected Perp PULPITUM which once separated the parochial from the monastic part of the church. It has three depressed two-centred arches and much blank tracery in the spandrels.

FURNISHINGS. FONT. From Highway in Wiltshire. Norman; small, circular. With scalloping below the upper rim and elementary leaves above the lower rim. – FONT COVER. The tester of the pulpit. – PULPIT. From St George's church. Of *c.*1715–20. Panelled, but with small-scale leaf decoration on the top and bottom mouldings and the angle-shafts. Part of the staircase railing placed round the LECTERN. – PEWS. Also from St George's; simple. – ORGAN CASE. Designed by Mr *Dykes Bower*. Gaily painted. – STAINED GLASS. E windows and S transept S window by *Brian Thomas*, 1959–60. Religious subjects. Deep colours and no transparent glass. – PLATE. Four large Chalices, London, 1548; Credence Paten, London, 1776; Paten, London, 1796; Spoon, Edinburgh, 1798–9. – MONUMENTS. Two Perp recesses with crocketed arches and side buttress shafts, in the S aisle said to be to the Fastolfs, in the N aisle to a prior of Yarmouth. Both rebuilt in 1959. – Spacious CHURCHYARD with trees and many gravestones.

ST ANDREW, North Quay. 1857–60 by *J. H. Hakewill* (or *C. E. Giles*), a depressing design in the lancet style. No tower, but a semicircular apse. Interior with exposed brick facing.

17 ST GEORGE, St George's Plain. 1714–16 by *John Price* of Wandsworth. Though he went to Wren's churches for inspiration, he produced a naive, unlearned design more lovable than admirable. Brick with stone dressings. W tower with pedimented doorway, an arched window over, and doorway and window framed by giant Tuscan pilasters with a broken pediment. Pilasters at the bell-stage. Wooden lantern in two stages, the lower with diagonally placed, coupled, very elongated columns. The body of the church has windows in two tiers. The connexion between the tower and the nave is gained by the awkward device of two quadrant bays. The nave has five giant pilasters each carrying its own bit of entablature. Another two quadrant bays then recede to the chancel E end, which has two giant Corinthian pilasters and again a broken pediment. Inside, the galleries are preserved. They rest on square wooden pillars and are connected with the ceiling by wooden Tuscan columns with rather fussy abaci. The nave has a shallow tunnel-vault with penetrations for the aisles The aisles have transverse tunnel-vaults below and groinvaults above. The transition to the chancel is emphasized by way of Corinthian columns on the gallery. – BENCHES. All

original. – For other furnishings, *see* St Nicholas. – PLATE. Spoon, London-made, 1732.

ST JAMES, Queen's Road. By *J. P. Seddon*, 1870–8. Flint and red brick. No tower. Geometrical tracery with original touches. Inside facing yellow, red, and blue brick. Tunnel-vaulted wooden ceiling. Arcades with round piers with very thick stiff-leaf capitals.

ST JOHN, York Road. By *J. H. Hakewill*, 1857, with later s aisle. A very odd, not very attractive group, with the transepts, the s transept turret, the three roofs of the chancel and the chancel chapels, and a chapterhouse-looking annexe to the SE. Flint, stone (e.g. for the terrible plate-tracery windows), and brick. Very low arcades with columns. – PLATE. Paten, Dublin, 1725(?).

ST MARY, Southtown Road. 1831–2 by *J. J. Scoles*. Yellow brick, in the lancet style, without a tower.

ST MARY (R.C.), Regent Road. 1848–50 by *J. J. Scoles*, a serious effort in the traditional Norfolk style. N tower, with flushwork decoration and a stair-turret with spirelet (the only inaccurate feature). Nave and aisles with arcades of octagonal piers. The Presbytery adjoining, and no doubt by the same architect and of the same time.

ST PETER, St Peter's Road. By *J. J. Scoles*, 1831–3. Large and uncommonly dull. Yellow brick, with a big W tower and nave and aisles and clerestory. Tall piers without capitals. – STAINED GLASS. Chancel N and s by *Kempe*, 1899.

CENTRAL HALL, Dene Side. Built as a Congregational church in 1850. Grey brick. Emphatically in the *Rundbogen* style. Two poor towers flank the entrance. It faces St George, and looks doubly starved of invention by the side of John Price's effort.

METHODIST TEMPLE, Priory Plain. 1875, and typical of that date. Very large façade with attached coupled giant pilasters and a steep all-over pediment. A gross design so near Church Plain.

FRIENDS' MEETING HOUSE, Howard Street North. In its s side, facing on Row 63, the l. jamb and part of the arch of a medieval doorway belonging to the Yarmouth cell of the Augustinian priory of Gorleston.

PUBLIC BUILDINGS

TOWN HALL. 1882–3 by *J. B. Pearce*. Red brick, in the so-called Queen Anne style, i.e. picturesquely asymmetrical, with a tower and with dainty detail including window pediments and garlands. – REGALIA. Small Maces, 1562 etc.; Sword, silver-gilt, *temp.* Charles II; two large Maces, 1690; Chain of gold, 1734, over 23 ft long; Oar, silver-gilt, 1745.

TOLHOUSE, Tolhouse Street. Not built as a public building, but probably as a private house. Much restored in the C19 and severely damaged in the Second World War. Since again restored. An outer staircase leads up to the upper hall. The hall windows have late C13 tracery. The cusped windows of the forebuilding and the doorway from this into the hall also fit such a date. Inside another E.E. doorway. Both have dogtooth enrichment. Along the side C17 mullioned and transomed windows.

CUSTOMS HOUSE. *See* South Quay, p. 151.

SCHOOL OF ARTS AND CRAFTS, Nelson Road Central. 1912 by the borough surveyor, *J. W. Cockrill*. A remarkably sensible design. A block of three by four bays with large unmoulded windows separated mainly by a kind of buttress piers.

PRIORY SCHOOL, Priory Road. The school buildings are by *Hakewill*, of 1853, but they are composed around, and in only too close harmony with, the surviving fragment of a small Benedictine priory, founded from Norwich in 1101. This fragment is supposed to be the refectory. It has large N and S windows with Dec tracery not to be trusted and doorways to N as well as S. To the N the only doorway is in line with one to the S, and immediately W of the passage connecting them, no doubt a screens passage proper, are five arches with the middle one bigger. They may have given access to the offices and kitchen, in which case the whole arrangement is that of a manor house rather than a monastic refectory. There is also a doorway from the presumed high table end to the S, more ornate than the others. The detail seems all of the late C13 to early C14. The monastic quarters lay round a courtyard to the S of the hall.

59 ST NICHOLAS HOSPITAL, Queen's Road. Built as the Naval Hospital in 1809–11, and designed by *Edward Holl*. A very large composition of four independent blocks of grey brick, connected by lower links at the corners. Each block is twentynine bays long with a projecting arcade on the ground floor and a three-bay pediment. Below this on the ground floor an accent by a portico of coupled Tuscan columns. The far wing has a lantern turret. The group is approached from the N by a gatehouse formed as a tripartite triumphal arch with giant Tuscan pilasters. To its NW a semi-detached house for

officers. This is (or was) of five bays. The whole composition, though utilitarian, is remarkably monumental and ought to be better known.

NORTHGATE HOSPITAL, Caister Road. Built as the workhouse in 1838 to the design of *John Brown*. Red brick and still classical in its proportions and details, i.e. not yet Tudor, as workhouses turned about that time.

SOUTHTOWN STATION. 1859, for the Eastern Counties Railway. A neat, very satisfactory design. Yellow brick and still essentially Georgian.

POWER STATION, South Denes. Brick, of the type which became usual in England from the 1930s onwards. By *C. A. Smeed*, 1954–7.

PERAMBULATION

Yarmouth has two natural centres, the Market Place and Hall Quay, and it seems more instructive to start at the latter, i.e. at the place where the BRIDGE connects the long tongues of land on which the town lies with the mainland.

HALL QUAY is where the town hall, the post office, and the principal banks are. Of these the most interesting is BARCLAYS BANK, built as Gurney's Bank in 1854 to *Anthony Salvin*'s design, a modest palazzo, if that contradiction be permitted. Only five bays. Brick and stone dressings, with a rusticated ground floor. To the S of it a gabled house in a rather Dutch style, also by *Salvin*. To the S of this LLOYDS BANK, qualifying for inclusion in this survey only by two excellent wooden chimneypieces not *in situ*. They are both dated 1598, and have a very personal character, with their termini caryatids with masks below where the half-bodies end. The ornament, partly arabesque and partly rather gristly of the Dietterlin kind, is equally characteristic. To the l. of Barclays Bank the DUKE'S HEAD HOTEL, early C17 (date-stone 1609) but re-windowed in the Early Georgian decades, has inside, and this time *in situ*, a panelled room with another good chimneypiece. Finally the CONSERVATIVE CLUB on the N side, inconspicuous mid-C19 from outside but with a handsome early C18 staircase (two turned and one twisted baluster to each step).

From Hall Quay to the W, across the bridge, lies Southtown, and here, in SOUTHTOWN ROAD, one can watch the usual pattern of the early C19 arterial road: minor Late Georgian and Early Victorian houses, in pairs or terraces or singly. An example is No. 97. A speciality here, however, is that the outer growth of

Yarmouth is met by the outer growth of Gorleston. For this
see p. 137.

Back to Hall Quay, and now to the N, where there are in GEORGE
STREET only minor things, except for the very pretty shopfront of Nos 55–7 with Roman Doric columns. To the s in
REGENT STREET only one remarkable house, FASTOLFF
HOUSE, in the lushest Arts and Crafts taste with plenty of
panels and friezes with the typical flat plant forms spreading
out. The house is of 1912, by *Cockrill*. Off Regent Street, in
HOWARD STREET SOUTH, No. 79 has another attractive
shop-front, this time with Ionic pilasters and Gothic glazing-
bars.

But the most rewarding of all Yarmouth walks is that s from Hall
Quay down SOUTH QUAY. Here you have the steamers on
your r., and on your l. a sequence of houses not easily matched.
Defoe calls it the finest quay in England and not inferior to
Marseilles (a strange comparison), and he calls the houses little
palaces. The houses follow each other like this. Nos 1–2 seems
to be of *c.*1700 (eight bays; bays one and eight very narrow),
but has an excellent Jacobean plaster ceiling with ribs forming
concave-sided stars on the ground floor and a simpler one with
square panels and small pendants on the first floor. There is
also one wooden mullioned and transomed window left. No. 3
is of grey brick with an iron balcony. No. 4 looks of the same
early C19 style, but is bigger. It is of six bays; iron balconies
again, and a Roman Doric porch. Inside, however, half the
first-floor front is taken by a splendid Late Elizabethan room
with panelling, a wooden chimneypiece, and a splendid and
55   unusual plaster ceiling. The ribs are very high in relief, and at
certain joints twist round each other. On the ground floor also
a panelled room with a wooden chimneypiece. The house was
in fact built in 1596. No. 5 is of four bays and has a doorcase
with exuberantly carved spandrels. The house was originally
of red brick and had brick quoins. The date must be the early
C18. Nos 7 and 8 seems Late Georgian. It has two canted bay
windows and a shallow forward-curving porch between. Nos
11 and 12 are a pair of three-bay houses, three-storeyed with
balconies. Then an opening (a former Row) allows access to
the scanty ruins of the GREYFRIARS, the Franciscan establishment of Yarmouth, founded in 1226, but not mentioned with
its house till 1271. Site enlargements late C13. What remains
is the southern two-thirds of the w wall of the cloister (with
tierceron-star-vaults and bosses), a two-bay chamber to its w,

also with tierceron-star-vaults, and some bits of walling s of Row 92 and N of Row 96. In the former two C15 windows. The church was to the N, across Queen Street. It was 177 ft long. The cloister and the room in the W range seem to belong to the C14. The site went as far W as South Quay and as far E as Middlegate Street.

After examining this somewhat disappointing fragment, we return to South Quay, where No. 16 is again early C19, of grey brick, and has a colonnade of elongated Doric columns in front of the ground floor. No. 17 is narrow, with a three-storeyed bow, but No. 20 is the most swagger house in the Quay. It was built about 1720 by John Andrews, called 'the greatest herring merchant in Europe', and is now the CUSTOMS HOUSE. It is six bays wide and three storeys high and has further two-storey, one-bay attachments on the l. and r. It is of red brick with stone trim and has segment-headed windows, those on the ground floor being remarkably long. The big porch with its elongated Greek Doric columns is of course an early C19 addition. The staircase has two twisted and one turned baluster to each tread. No. 24, a nice early C19 house of five bays with iron balconies, is the last of note in South Quay for quite a stretch. What follows is all COUNCIL HOUSING of the 1950s, also stretching back right across to where Middlegate Street used to be. The architecture is friendly, if in its details a little mannered, and the layout is excellent, with the former Rows being replaced by plenty of pedestrian passages from W to E. The design is by the Borough Engineer's Department (H. F. Dyson, borough engineer).

At the beginning of this renewed quarter the GALLON CAN INN. Here, a little recessed and not originally belonging to the Quay but to one of the Rows, the so-called OLD MERCHANT'S HOUSE, now a museum. This is of the C17, brick, with wooden mullioned windows and on the ground floor and first floor ceilings with thick ribs. The W front and the staircase are Georgian.

The only further house of note in South Quay is Nos 74–5. It is neglected at the time of writing, but ought to be preserved. It must once have been one of the most worthwhile houses of Yarmouth, and also seems to belong to c.1720. It is of seven bays and three storeys, faced with squared knapped flint and originally, it seems, with brick dressings. It has a two-storeyed porch with the ground floor open on Tuscan columns and the upper floor with Corinthian pilasters and the typical frieze running up to a point in the middle; segmental pediment, and, above the porch in the main cornice of the house, another one-bay pediment. The house is decidedly provincial, but has great charm.

Past this house one reaches MARINERS ROAD, and here the TOWN WALL begins to appear (*see* above, p. 142). This was begun when Henry III had granted a licence in 1260. Work went on into the C14. The wall stands in places to the height of 23 ft. The first remaining tower is at the corner of BLACK-FRIARS ROAD, so called after the Dominican house of Yarmouth, which was situated here. The wall can be followed to the N along Blackfriars Road. It has another tower, flat at the base, and then for a stretch even its battlements.

When St Peter's church is reached the quest for the walls must temporarily be abandoned. The perambulation now goes on to the N but along a line a little further W. The street is KING STREET, the principal shopping street of the town. The most interesting houses are near its S end. Many appear to be late C17 to early C18. I would recommend the following. On the W side the WHITE LION, at the corner of Nottingham Way, Elizabethan or Jacobean, though externally much remodelled. (Early C17 staircase etc. MHLG) Opposite No. 51, the LABOUR CLUB, a fine Early Georgian house of five bays and two and a half storeys. Doorway with rusticated surround; brick quoins. The middle window is arched on the first, segment-headed on the half storey. Then, facing St George's Plain, No. 141, three bays, the centre with a handsome Late Georgian shallow bow on Tuscan columns. After that still bow windows and bay windows, up to No. 148, and then no more. The commercial present of the street has swallowed its residential past.

The MARKET PLACE, at the N end of King Street, is large and not strictly rectangular. That is one of its attractions. The other is that it merges imperceptibly into Church Plain, which has trees, while the Market Place of course has not, and then, round the bend by St Nicholas church, into White Horse Plain and so Northgate Street. It is a good sequence, whether experienced from the S or the N. Of individual houses nothing at all need be singled out in the Market Place, but a special note is due to MARKET ROW, continued to the W by BROAD ROW to George Street and Hall Quay. These two are shopping streets for pedestrians only, the former as narrow as the narrowest in Venice, the latter somewhat wider. In Broad Row No. 5 (Messrs Platten's), unnoticeable from the front, is an

Elizabethan or Jacobean house. It has a tall polygonal stair-turret at the back. On the opposite side of Market Street, in the yard of the Hospital School, the TOWN WALL appears again prominently with its tall blank arches.

CHURCH PLAIN has two of the most admirable buildings in Yarmouth, the Fishermen's Hospital and the Vicarage. The FISHERMEN'S HOSPITAL was founded by the Corporation in 1702. It has a central yard surrounded by three ranges and returning in two projections on the fourth, i.e. the entrance side. The building is one-storeyed with dormers in the roof, and has in the centre at the back a lantern and below it a steep pediment on Doric pilasters. In the pediment relief of a sailing ship. The return wings, l. and r. of the entrance, end in Dutch gables, i.e. shaped gables with proper pediments at the top. On the wall are oval inscription boards with lush carving above. In the middle of the yard Statue of Charity. Between the Fishermen's Hospital and the Vicarage SEWELL HOUSE, with a timber-framed gable (the only piece of timber-framing at Yarmouth worth a mention) and the date 1641. The VICARAGE was built, also by the Corporation, in 1718 and altered in 1781. The old part is of eight bays and two and a half storeys with a parapet. The windows are slim, and the doorway is uncommonly slim. It has a shell-hood. The later date of the house probably refers to the extension into the churchyard, with its canted bay window. There is also a Victorian bay window. Pretty staircase with slender turned balusters. Opposite, in the part appropriately called BREWERY PLAIN and not Church Plain, though entirely part of the same space, LACON'S BREWERY. The oldest surviving buildings are no older than 1868. N of this the architectural interest tapers off. In WHITE HORSE PLAIN still some nice Georgian houses, e.g. Nos. 14–15 with a pair of doorways side by side. In NORTHGATE STREET also some houses deserve a passing glance, e.g. Nos 221–222. To the r. TOWN WALL ROAD allows another glimpse at the walls. The tower is the NE tower. Opposite at the W end of RAMPART ROAD the NW tower, i.e. the end tower, is exposed, and with this ends the perambulation of pre-C19 Yarmouth.

The seaside development is an entirely independent story. The S part of the tongue on which Yarmouth lies was largely in the hands of the Admiralty. The former Naval Hospital has already been described. Further S, in 1817, the NELSON COLUMN was erected. The site at the time was nowhere. It was

designed by *William Wilkins* and is 144 ft high. The Nelson
Column in Trafalgar Square is 145 ft high, and came much
later. The predecessors of the Yarmouth column are of course
the Monument in London and, close in time, the column in
the Place Vendôme in Paris of 1806, that to Nelson in Dublin
of 1808, and that to Lord Hill at Shrewsbury of 1816. The
idea was taken over from Antiquity. The column stands on a
noble plinth. It is a fine specimen of the Greek Doric order
and carries a drum on which Victories with held-out wreath
support a gilt statue of Britannia, turning w not e – proof, that
is, of the fact that even in the early c19 Yarmouth was
orientated to the river and not the sea. The figures are all of
Coade stone. The monument finds itself now in the most in-
congruous surroundings of the factory sheds of recent
factories.

Nor did seaside Yarmouth start to develop from this landmark,
or ever take it in. To its N are developments of small houses of
between the wars. Then follows the distant Naval Hospital,
and only after that does c19 Yarmouth begin. Its centre is the
area from King's Road to the Coastguard quarters. Here lies
the JETTY, which was first built in 1560 and rebuilt in 1701
and after 1805. It was lengthened in 1846 and again in 1870.
Here also is the BATH HOTEL, said to date from 1835, plain
yellow brick with canted bay window, and one or another
house that may be of the thirties, e.g. one at the corner of
Devonshire Road. But the great advance dates from the mid-
century. The architecture is based on that of Brighton and the
other Regency resorts, but is no longer as restrained and well-
mannered. There are many pitfalls that could be enumerated.
Anybody at all sensitive to detail (and indeed proportions) will
see them at once. Examples are the ROYAL HOTEL, first built
early in the c19, but gradually added to and altered, the whole
front of KIMBERLEY TERRACE (with the Carlton Hotel),
begun in 1842 (architect: *Thomas Marsh Nelson*, but of the
centre house *John Brown*), and also ALBERT SQUARE and
CAMPERDOWN ROAD of *c.*1844 (with the monumental
mews archway behind in WELLINGTON ROAD). The change
of style also involved a change from the Classical to the
Italianate, and a nice example of this is the MASONIC LODGE,
built as the ASSEMBLY AND READING ROOMS in 1863 (by
H. H. Collins of London). It has a handsome five-bay arcade
on Tuscan columns. Opposite, the Wellington Pier and the
WINTER GARDENS, equally handsome in its Crystal-Palace

way. It is a glass structure, stepped up in its parts and ending in a pyramid roof. It was built in 1878–81 at Torquay (architects *Watson & Harvey*) and re-erected at Yarmouth in 1903. The WELLINGTON PIER dates from 1853, the BRITANNIA PIER from 1857 (rebuilt 1901–2; the present Pavilion of 1958). The only buildings between Jetty and Britannia Pier which ought to be taken in are the SAILORS' HOME, a rather dreary block of yellow and red brick, built in 1858 by *Morant*, and the COASTGUARD STATION of 1859–61, three ranges round a courtyard, yellow brick, with the typical elongated arched two-light windows of the mid-century Italianate. N of the Britannia Pier, in MARINE PARADE NORTH building began much later. NORFOLK SQUARE was the first square to be laid out, and this was begun in 1875. On the whole the style is that of the 1890s and after.

GRESHAM
1030

ALL SAINTS. Round tower with early C14 bell-openings. Two-storeyed Perp s porch faced with knapped flint. On the upper floor a niche between two one-light windows. Early C14 chancel, the E window with flowing tracery. Perp nave windows. – FONT. On the bowl the Seven Sacraments. – PLATE. Chalice, London, 1815; Flagon undated, C19.

GRESHAM CASTLE, ¾ m. s. Apparently of the same shape as the neighbouring Baconsthorpe Castle: quadrangular with a moat. Nothing now stands up to any substantial height, and everything is swamped with trees, bushes, and nettles. A licence to crenellate was granted in 1319 to Sir Edmund Bacon.

GUESTWICK
0020

ST PETER. Unbuttressed tower, now to the N of the chancel. However, originally it stood in the context of an entirely different church. It was a building of nave, central space, and chancel, and the tower crowned the central space. The arches towards the former nave and former chancel are still visible. The date must be the late C11, that is the time of the so-called Saxo-Norman overlap; for the windows are Norman and the imposts are Norman, but the W side of the E, i.e. chancel, arch is accompanied from floor to apex by three continuous half-rolls, an unmistakably Saxon motif. The rest is all Perp, nave and aisles, clerestory and chancel. Four-bay arcades, octagonal piers, double-chamfered arches. The nave W window can hardly be trusted. – COMMUNION RAIL. C18. – STAINED

GLASS. In two S aisle windows a jumble of old glass including whole C15 figures. – PLATE. Norwich-made Chalice and Paten, c.1590. – MONUMENTS. Brasses to (John Robertson † 1504, a chalice brass), Richard at Hylle † 1505 (13 in. figure; nave E), and Jacob at Hylle (13 in. figure; N aisle E). – William Bulwer † 1753. Tablet with three sensitively carved putto heads at the foot.

CONGREGATIONAL CHAPEL, N of the church, in a field. Founded in 1652 – a very early date – but partly rebuilt in 1840. What was done is not quite clear, but it seems that the windows owe their shape to the later date and that the polygonal angle turrets are also not original. The porch is of 1840, and so is the interior in all its features.

GUIST

ST ANDREW. Unbuttressed W tower with Perp top. The body of the church externally all renewed. The N aisle after 1861, the chancel entirely rebuilt in 1886. – PLATE. Norwich-made Chalice and Paten inscribed 1660 and 1661; Paten 1709. – MONUMENTS. Robert Wiggett † 1697 and his wife † 1722, and Richard Wiggett † 1749, the former with a column in front of a back-plate with curved sides, the latter with a Rococo cartouche against an obelisk. Both monuments seem to date from the mid C18.

SENNOWE HALL. Mostly by *Skipper*, 1908, but a core of the C18. Brick, brown stone, and red stone. The façade is seventeen bays wide. Its centre has giant columns. Windows with segmental heads and also with segmental heads as well as segmental sills.

GUNTHORPE

ST MARY. Perp W tower and nave (but with doorways of c.1300), chancel of 1863–4 (but with a Dec E window with reticulated tracery). – FONT. Octagonal. Bowl with four seated figures and the signs of the Evangelists. – PLATE. Chalice and Paten (Norwich), 1567; Flagon (London), 1709.

SCHOOL. In splendid isolation by the church. 1869 by *Preedy*.

GUNTHORPE HALL. *Sir John Soane* built it, but neither his portico nor his arched front windows were allowed to remain. Only one room on the first floor with an apsed end may be his. The façade received its two bay windows with their segment-headed windows and hood-moulds about 1880, and the portal and tower about 1900.

GUNTON

GUNTON PARK. The house was built in two periods. First, after 1742, *Matthew Brettingham* built a classical house of seven by five bays facing E and S, then, about 1785, *James Wyatt* embellished it outside and added a range. The earlier house was almost entirely gutted by a fire in 1882 and never reconstructed. It is of grey brick with all detail also in brick and has quoins of even length, windows with Gibbs surrounds, and three-bay pediments to both principal sides. One room remains with its original decoration and a fine mid-C18 chimneypiece. Wyatt added to the S an eight-bay colonnade of Tuscan columns flanked by two one-bay conservatories. He also added to the N of the E range a three-storeyed bow with delightful iron verandas reminiscent of the seaside, and a five-bay, three-storeyed range with elongated fluted pilasters and a lower service wing.

St ANDREW. Only a couple of hundred feet from the E front of[18a] the house. Designed by *Robert Adam* in 1769. Grey brick with a fine four-column portico of Tuscan columns, along the sides two columns deep. The sides of the church have four niches on the ground floor and four upper windows. The whole is much like a garden temple. Delicate interior in which the REREDOS with dark brown and gold attached fluted Corinthian columns is echoed by the WEST GALLERY on fluted Corinthian pilasters. Fine plaster frieze. – PLATE. Chalice and Paten, Norwich, *c.*1670; Chalice, Cover, and Jug, 1774 by *Matthew Boulton* and *James Fothergill* of Birmingham; Almsdish, London, 1824.

STABLES. Entrance with coupled Tuscan columns carrying a pediment.

OBSERVATORY TOWER, 1 m. NE. A curious structure of grey brick; looks Early Victorian. Archway with one-storey wings curving forward to the outside as well as on the inside. Upper storey with twin arched windows, top storey glazed with detached angle columns and spirelet.

HANWORTH LODGE, ½ m. SW. Archway with coupled Tuscan columns and pediment.

HACKFORD *see* REEPHAM

HAINFORD

OLD CHURCH, ⅝ m. from the new church. In ruins. Unbuttressed W tower and, added in its E side, a Victorian chapel.

ALL SAINTS. 1838–40 by *John Brown*. Nave and chancel, transepts and bellcote. Flint with generous red-brick dressings. Lancet windows, including stepped groups of three in the w and E walls.

4000   HALVERGATE

ST PETER AND ST PAUL. Behind a screen of lime trees. Big w tower with flushwork panelling on the base, traceried sound-holes, two-stepped battlements, and formerly standing figures as pinnacles. They now stand by the porch and prove to be rustic C19 work with a Baroque overhang, folk-art of a kind one expects to find in Bohemia or Brazil rather than England. Nave and chancel seem to be of the early C14, see the paired lancets and the one Dec window in the nave on the N side (both correct according to Ladbrooke) and the good s doorway with flanking buttress shafts, a finely crocketed ogee gable, and a finial. The delicate arch mouldings all die into the imposts. – BANNER STAFF LOCKER, nave s side. – STAINED GLASS. A tiny St Christopher, complete, and early C14, in the head of a N window. – PLATE. Norwich-made Chalice, 1567–8. – BRASS. Framed in a chancel N window a palimpsest brass. On one side the head and shoulders of Frater William Jernemouth, a Franciscan of Yarmouth of *c*.1440, on the other bust of the wife of Robert Swane, *c*.1540.

HALVERGATE HOUSE, to the ESE. Early C19, of grey brick with a low hipped roof. Three by four bays, the windows set in panels with raised frames. One-bay pediment. Doorway with two angle pillars and two unfluted Ionic columns. Of the same time and type, and also of grey brick, THE ROOKERY, NE of the church. Three by five bays. Porch on Tuscan columns.

Halverstone has a WINDMILL, now without sails, ½ m. to the SSW, and also a number of DRAINAGE MILLS, with and without sails. They lie a good deal E in the marshes.

1030   HANWORTH

ST BARTHOLOMEW. Chancel Dec with one blocked quatrefoil clerestory window. Perp w tower with traceried sound-holes. Perp N side, humble Perp s aisle. The arcade of very coarse Late Perp details. Clerestory with double the number of windows as the arcade arches below. Arch-braced roofs in nave and aisle. – PLATE. Paten of *c*.1500. Foiled depression with the face of Christ in a decorated circle. – Chalice and Paten without marks.

HANWORTH HALL. A plain but very fine house of the early
C18. Nine bays, two storeys, red brick with a three-bay pediment and a hipped roof. Doorway with pairs of brick pilasters,
the outer a little recessed, and with a big bulgy frieze. The
same typical motif in the noble and simple stone fireplace in
the entrance hall and the doorcases. Staircase with strong
twisted balusters, thin bottom part of bulbous shape.

POST OFFICE, 1¼ m. SE. This must once have been a lodge to
the Hall. Pebble and yellow brick, canted two-storeyed centre,
one-storeyed wings.

HAPPISBURGH
3030

The village lies happily between the church tower and the red
and white LIGHTHOUSE, built in 1791.

ST MARY. Above the sea. Standing in the churchyard one hears
the rollers come in. Very tall W tower, 110 ft high. The colour
appears to be beige, so much plaster is used between the flints.
W doorway with suspended shields up one order of jambs and
arch. Shields on tracery in the spandrels. Five-light window
with transom (renewed). Sound-holes with specially busy and
pretty tracery (four squares each with the motif of the four-
petalled flower). Three-light bell-openings. Flushwork panels
on the battlements. Flushwork panels also on the battlements
of S aisle, S porch, and clerestory. The clerestory has an E
window, which is not a frequent feature. All this is Perp, and
all is renewed. The N aisle windows are identical with the S
aisle windows. At the W end of the S aisle was an extension.
This is unexplained. The chancel is earlier than the nave. Its
style was Dec, but all windows are renewed, and the E window
is Perp; yet the Piscina indicates the true date of the chancel.
On the S formerly a two-bay chapel with octagonal pier. This
must have been built before the aisle arcade or the chancel arch
was made. The present arcades are Perp, but at the E end of
the N arcade is a respond showing that a lower N arcade, also
with octagonal piers, had existed. Much material was no doubt
re-used in the Perp heightening. Five bays, octagonal piers,
double-chamfered arches. In the S aisle a charming niche with
a little vault. Fine Perp S porch of two storeys. Entrance arch
with traceried spandrels containing shields. Wooden roof with
diagonal and ridge-ribs and a central boss. The ribs are of
course really arched braces. On the upper floor a niche between
two one-light windows.

FURNISHINGS. FONT. Of an ambitious Suffolk type. Octagonal, with four lions and four Wild Men against the stem,
and against the bowl on the underside demi-figures of angels,
above the signs of the four Evangelists and four angels with
musical instruments. The font stands on three steps, the top
one decorated with little lions at the corners and with quatrefoils. – SCREEN. Two-light divisions, crocketed ogee arches
with panel tracery over. The screen was vaulted. – STALLS.
Ends with poppy-heads. – PLATE. Paten, hall-marked 1506.
In a foiled depression the head of Christ, set in on a separate
plate. Very good, but much repaired; Chalice, 1817. – CROSS
on the altar, wood faced with mother-of-pearl. Probably
Spanish and C17.

E of the church, facing the Walcott road, a row of thatched
cottages containing some medieval fragments, including a
Piscina and two brick-arched doorways, side by side.

A little further E the capital house of Happisburgh, HAPPIS-
BURGH MANOR, *Detmar Blow*'s first important work and perhaps his best, much in the Prior–Early-Lutyens style. The
house is dated 1900. It consists of an oblong core containing
the principal room and four wings projecting diagonally. To
the sea, i.e. the N, terrace with two summer houses. The
materials used are much like those which fascinated Lutyens
(*see* Overstrand Hall): flint, pebble, brick, thin tiles. Steep
central gable on the N as well as the S with angular fancy
ornamentation.

HASSINGHAM

ST MARY. Round tower with Perp W window. Octagonal top
with big lancet windows. Perp battlements with flushwork
panelling. S doorway Late Norman with zigzag in the arch,
billets in the hood-mould. Perp tower arch and chancel arch,
the former with four-centred, the latter with two-centred
head. Arch-braced nave roof. – STAINED GLASS. E window
with much bought-in foreign C16 and C17 glass. – BANNER
STAFF LOCKER. N wall. – PLATE. Chalice, Norwich, 1569;
Chalice of medieval design, Paten, and Flagon, all given in
1832.

HAUTBOIS

OLD CHURCH, ¼ m. NW of Holy Trinity. In ruins, or rather
roofless, though the chancel does still have its roof. Thin
round tower with round-arched bell-openings. Some carstone
is used. S arcade of two bays with octagonal piers.

HOLY TRINITY. 1864. Minimum E.E., of nave and chancel. Surprisingly by *Thomas Jekyll*, later architect to Whistler's Peacock Room and a believer in Japanese art. – PLATE. Chalice, Norwich, 1567.

LITTLE HAUTBOIS HALL. Elizabethan, a flat brick front with mullioned and transomed windows and dormers with pinnacles. The main gables also have pinnacles. At the back, reset, the former porch entrance, a broad four-centred brick arch. Polygonal chimneys. The lower addition on the w side is original work too. The date 1607 appears on a garden wall.

HAVERINGLAND   *1020*

ST PETER. In a desolate position, more or less on an abandoned airfield. Norman round tower. The rest of 1845.

QUAKER FARM, 1 m. ESE. Of *c.*1700. With shaped gable-ends but a five-bay front of two storeys with wooden cross-windows. Red brick with vertical bands of vitrified, i.e. dark blue, brick.

HELLESDON *see* p. 290

HEMBLINGTON   *3010*

ALL SAINTS. Round tower with a rather battered top. Nave and chancel early C14. One Dec window in the nave and one with Y-tracery in the chancel seem reliable. Roof rebuilt in 1910. – FONT. On two steps. Octagonal. Eight statuettes against the stem, ribbing on the underside of the bowl. The Trinity and seated figures against the bowl. – PULPIT. Plain, C18, with back panel and tester. – BENCHES. Ends with poppy-heads; also pierced, traceried backs and some figures on arms. – PAINTING. Discovered in 1937. Large St Christopher and l. and r., partly on the green grass seen from above and partly in little houses, scenes from the Life and Martyrdom of St Christopher. – PLATE. Chalice with Elizabethan stem; London-made Flagon of 1727 and Paten of 1768.

HEMBLINGTON HALL. Built about 1700. Five bays and two storeys. Brick with brick quoins. Dormers with segmental pediments. Doorway of brick with rusticated pilasters, against a rusticated ground, carrying a pediment.

HEMPSTEAD   *4020*
1 m. E of Lessingham

ST ANDREW. Late C16 chancel. The E window (three stepped lancet lights under one arch) would fit the date, if it is original. Perp w tower. The w window with an embattled transom.

Two-storeyed Perp s porch. Decorated battlements. Upper windows to the s blocked with a niche between. The nave has the three N and three s windows customary in Norfolk. They represent a widening; for the w windows show that the church formerly had aisles and yet was not wider. Nave and chancel are thatched. – FONT. Perp, octagonal. Four lions against the base, four shields and four flowers against the bowl. – SCREEN. Good. With two-light divisions, ogee arches with tracery under and over. The top tracery is of an unusual pattern. Against the dado painted Saints, damaged, but clearly late C14 in style. – PULPIT. Jacobean. On four legs with a cross-stretcher. They may, however, not belong. – READER'S DESK. With Jacobean woodwork. – BENCHES. Two with poppy-heads. – SOUTH DOOR. With tracery. – PLATE. Silver-gilt Chalice, Norwich, 1567–8; silver-gilt Paten, 1567–8, without marks; Flagon by *Richard Bayley*, London, 1727.

HEMPSTEAD
2 m. SE of Holt

1030

ALL SAINTS. NW tower, largely rebuilt in brick in 1744. In the w wall a two-light window with Geometrical tracery. This must have belonged to an E.E. aisle which was later removed. Early C14 (or late C13?) s doorway. Windows renewed in the C17 (?). The apse is of 1925. – BENCH. One original bench, incomplete. – ORGAN CASE. Gothic, early C19. – PLATE. Norwich-made Chalice, 1567.

HEMSBY

4010

ST MARY. Early C14 chancel (Y-tracery, uncusped and cusped), but with a Perp E window with the heads of the lights triangular instead of arched. Dec w tower with flushwork panelling on base and battlements. The arch towards the nave, however, is Early Perp. Perp nave with three windows each side, but earlier doorways. No chancel arch. Of the nave roof only the bosses are original. Two-storeyed s porch with a niche above the upper window and a tierceron-star-vault with bosses inside. The bosses illustrate the Life of the Virgin and include a Nativity. – PLATE. Chalice, Norwich, 1567–8. – MONUMENT. Pretty tablet to Robert Tilyard † 1786, signed by *John Athow* of Norwich.

THE HOLLIES, SW of the church. Good Georgian house of five bays and two storeys, with a one-bay pediment and a Greek Doric porch.

HEVINGHAM

ST BOTOLPH. Outside the village, quite big. Heavily restored in
1881–94. w tower with bell-openings with cusped Y-tracery, a
Perp window and a parapet with flushwork panelling, big two-
storeyed s porch with a large transomed three-light window,
mostly blank. Dec nave with large two-light windows; s transept Dec, see the reticulated tracery of the s window. s doorway
with spandrels inlaid with dark stone to form a tracery pattern.
Chancel all re-done, but must have been of *c.*1300, on the
evidence of the angle piscina. – FONT. Only the stem is
original. Hexagonal with statuettes in niches. – STALLS. Very
remarkable. They come from the former schoolroom in the
upper chamber of the s porch. Probably of the C14. Broad
surfaces to place the books on. Blank-traceried fronts with
ogee arches and carved spandrels. – STAINED GLASS. Some
C16–17 pieces in a s window. – PLATE. Chalice, probably
Norwich, inscribed 1686; Paten, London, 1796. – MONU-
MENT. Small lead plaque to John Barrett † 1765 (s transept).
POUND FARMHOUSE. With shaped gable (concave-convex)
dated 1675. The front re-windowed, but probably regular from
the start.

HEYDON

ST PETER AND ST PAUL. Tall w tower of knapped flint. Ten
marks were left to its building in 1469. Tall tower arch, w
doorway and w window. Sound-holes square cusped, with
shields. Two-storeyed Perp s porch with tierceron-vault with
bosses. Aisles and chancel all tall Perp windows. The clerestory
originally alternated between encircled quatrefoils and normal
two-light windows (cf. Cley etc.). The arrangement is preserved only near the E end. The attached Bulwer Mausoleum
dates from 1864. The only Dec contributions externally visible
are the aisle w windows (N aisle renewed). But the arcades inside are also C14, if probably some time in the second half.
Four bays, quatrefoil piers with thin filleted shafts in the
diagonals. Polygonal capitals. Double-chamfered arches.
Arch-braced roofs. – FONT. Plain, big, of cup-shape, impressive. C13. – PULPIT. Perp, on a re-used stone with
fleurons. The back panel probably Flemish C18. – SCREEN.
One-light divisions. Dado with painted decoration and an inscription referring to the donation in 1480. – FAMILY PEWS,
one put up in 1698, the other earlier. – WEST DOOR. With
tracery and a framing band of quatrefoils. – Two HELMS (N

aisle E). – STAINED GLASS. Some original glass in the head of
a chancel s window. – PLATE. Chalice, London, Elizabethan. –
MONUMENT. Erasmus Earle, 1690. Enormous black slab on a
plain tomb-chest. The fine IRON RAILINGS look earlier C17.

50b HEYDON HALL. A beautiful sight from the S, at the end of an
avenue, across the lawn. The centre is the house of 1581–4
built for Henry Dynne, one of the Auditors of the Exchequer,
and it is a pity it was enlarged to the W and E. The centre is a
compact block with a façade only five bays wide to a height of
three storeys. The material is brick, the dressings are cemented.
Angle shafts with finials. Two rectangular bay windows and
a porch of the same shape with angle shafts. Straight gables
with finials. All windows have mullions and transoms, but
they differ in size. The largest are on the ground floor, the
lowest on the second floor. Doorway with a four-centred arch
and heraldry panels above, still essentially Gothic. The roof-
line is dominated by two rows of fine polygonal chimneys
rising above the two bay windows and all facing S. Thin
wooden lantern. To the N all detail is Victorian except the
doorway, which has two decorative bands across the flanking
pilasters. In the Hall a big fireplace of the C17; the rest all
later. In other rooms fireplaces of c.1740 and the late C18. The
addition to the E of the house dates from 1797. It has been
partly pulled down recently. The architecture of the Service
Court on the E side is perfectly straightforward, but the façade
has in the C19 been Elizabethanized. This process included
the making of a tower with a very tall window. A further piece
between the work of 1581–4 and that of 1797 was inserted in
the C19. The W additions are of the C19 too.

E of the Service Court a small C19 building with shaped
gables and a very picturesque wooden bell-turret also in the
Jacobean style. An ICE HOUSE to the N, a LOOKOUT TOWER
to the SE.

VILLAGE GREEN and STREET, S of the church. Unusually
pretty, though only one individually remarkable house. This,
supposed to be the former Bakehouse of the Hall, has a stepped
gable and a central porch, i.e. looks as if converted to a
superior domestic use about 1800.

CROPTON HALL, $\frac{3}{4}$ m. NW. With a big shaped gable. W front of
c.1700, five bays, two storeys, doorway with segmental pediment on Doric brick pilasters. Windows with wooden mullion
and transom crosses. The shaped gable might well be contemporary.

HICKLING
4020

ST MARY. Tall w tower. Wavy base frieze. Doorway with suspended shields all up one moulding of jambs and arch. Spandrels with foliage. The w window has again a moulding with suspended shields. Quatrefoil frieze below the window. Niche above it. Traceried sound-holes. Two-light bell-openings with Dec tracery. Two-storeyed s porch. In the spandrels of the entrance tracery and shields. The buttresses with flushwork panelling. The upper storey altered. The aisle windows all Dec, but all renewed, the chancel E window also. Dec arcades of five bays with octagonal piers and double-chamfered arches. The chancel arch is of the same details. – FONT. Octagonal; stem with four traceried panels and four with leaf. The same arrangement on the bowl. – PLATE. Chalice and Paten, Norwich, 1568–9. – MONUMENTS. Coffin-lid with exceptionally lavishly foliated cross and inscription in Lombardic letters, c.1250–75. – Mid or later C16 tomb-chest with shields. – In the churchyard urn on a big square base; to John Bygrave, † 1818.

PRIORY. The Augustinian priory was founded in 1185. Of the buildings the following survive at Priory Farm: the undercroft of the w range of the cloister precinct, vaulted, as the springers show, and a room to its N which was probably the Parlour. This was vaulted also. The capital and springer in one corner point to a C13 date. The cloister can be recognized to the E and a large fragment of masonry which must have belonged to the E range. Of the church only excavations could establish the plan.

HICKLING HALL. Built about 1700. Red brick with a diaper of vitrified dark blue headers. Seven bays with a recessed three-bay centre; two storeys and a hipped roof. Doorway with an open segmental pediment. Pulvinated frieze.

WINDMILL. Tall tower-mill, without sails, ⅛ m. SW.

HINDOLVESTON
0020

ST GEORGE. 1914 by *H. J. Green* (GR). Parts of the old church were re-used, e.g. the octagonal arcade piers and semicircular responds, a shaft of c.1300, probably from an angle Piscina, a rib-vaulted little niche with angels l. and r. Also from the old church some furnishings. – FONT. Octagonal. Crowned letters against the stem, against the bowl the signs of the Evangelists, of the Trinity, and of the Passion; also Crucifixion. – BENCH

ENDS. A few with poppy-heads. – BRASS. Edmund Hunt
† 1558 and family. Groups of kneeling figures. The inscription
still in black-letter.

OLD CHURCH. In ruins. The w wall of the tower survives with
a three-light Perp bell-opening. The rest is only lumps of
masonry.

CHURCH FARMHOUSE, by the old church. Slightly recessed
centre with the chimneybreast of the former hall. On the
opposite side of the house the two-storeyed porch. The r. projection has a wavy shaped gable, the l. a stepped gable and a
date 1722. This part of the front may be altered. In the other
projection one window on each floor with a pediment over.
The date is probably the early C17.

WINDMILL. Stump of a brick tower-mill, s of the Red Lion.

HOPE HOUSE, at the start of the Melton road. Fine Georgian
seven-bay front with a projecting, pedimented one-bay centre.
Blue brick with red brick dressings.

9030

HINDRINGHAM

ST MARTIN. Much Dec work, namely the tall, slender w tower
(bell-openings with pretty tracery inside reticulation units,
but Perp the w window and the arch towards the nave), the
doorways, the five-bay arcades (octagonal piers, double-chamfered arches, capitals not identical), the chancel arch, and the
two-bay N chapel arcade. Perp aisle and clerestory windows. –
FONT. Perp, octagonal, on two steps, the upper with quatrefoils etc. Against the stem crowned letters, against the bowl
the signs of the Evangelists, the emblem of the Trinity, the
Instruments of the Passion, the Crucifixion, and the arms of
England quartering France. – CHEST. This is the great pride
of Hindringham. It may well be the earliest chest preserved in
England. It is certainly Norman. The front consists of two
broad upright boards with rosettes and three horizontal boards
framed in, with one row of tall intersected arches. – STAINED
GLASS. Some original glass in the s aisle E window. – PLATE.
Chalice, Norwich, 1567–8; Paten, London, 1724.

HINDRINGHAM HALL. With a complete moat. C16. Front with
a porch with stepped gable and a slightly projecting l. wing
with a bigger stepped gable. The r. wing has a straight gable
and is said to be earlier. (Interior largely in its original state.
Mr Cozens-Hardy draws attention to the fact that the house
is called 'now being edified' in 1562.)

GODFREYS HALL. Just SE of the house, by some cottages, the lonely porch of a C16 mansion. Round-headed doorway. Three-light mullioned and transomed windows with pediment.

WORKHOUSE, 1¼ m. SE. 1837 by *William Thorold*. Red brick, with the usual octagonal centre and wings. The details still classical.

HOLT

ST ANDREW. To the E of the Market Place, with no part to play in the image of the town. The views are to the E and S still decidedly rural. The church itself is alas over-restored (*Butterfield*, 1864) and not of much interest. The W tower had a spire. Chancel N and S humble early C14.* The E window is Perp. Aisle and clerestory windows Perp. Interior with arcades of the early C14. Low octagonal piers, arches with one chamfer and one hollow chamfer. The chancel arch is the same. In the S aisle angle Piscina, again early C14. The chancel Sedilia and double Piscina are Dec. – FONT. Cup-shaped with stylized fleurs-de-lis connected by curves; probably C13. – STAINED GLASS. The Canterbury Pilgrims, N aisle E window, 1933 by *F. H. Spear*.‡ – PLATE. All made in London: Almsdish, 1717; Chalice by *Thomas Farrer*, 1722; Flagon, Paten, and Almsdish, 1724, the Flagon given by the Prince of Wales, the Almsdish by Robert Walpole; Lavabo Dish, 1837; Cup, 1837. – MONUMENTS. A number of tablets, especially Edmund Newdigate † 1784. Urn in front of an obelisk.

METHODIST CHURCH, at the W end of the High Street and hitting one in the face as one approaches it. Yellow brick with red brick and flint. Polygonal apse and asymmetrically placed N turret with spire. Built in 1862 to the design of *Thomas Jekyll*.

GRESHAM'S SCHOOL. Founded by Sir Thomas Gresham in 1555. The school remained quite small until it was made a Public School in 1900. Its former building stands on the site of Gresham's former manor house at the E end of the Market Place and is no bigger than a small-town school would be. It was erected in 1858 and designed by *Suter*, architect to the Fishmongers. It is a handsome symmetrical Tudor brick building. The school moved out to the Cromer Road in 1900, and BIG SCHOOL and the boarding house HOWSONS were built in 1900–3. The architect was *Howard Chatfeild Clarke*.

* But the masonry may be much older; for a 'little rownde window' in the N wall is mentioned in 1575, and that sounds Saxon.

‡ The glass in the E window is by *Bryans* (C. L. S. Linnell).

Big School is of brick, in the Tudor style, and includes the Hall, with a hammerbeam roof. Howsons is also Tudor. The CHAPEL is to the NE of Big School. It was designed by *Maxwell Ayrton* and built in 1912–16. It is in a free Gothic style with a façade twin-buttressed in an original way, two angle turrets, and a very big roof. Of school houses WOODLANDS, to the W of Howsons, is early C19, of yellow brick, with later additions. FARFIELD, to the SE of the chapel, is Neo-Georgian, dates from 1911, and was designed by *Chatfeild Clarke*. Across the road, immediately S of Big School, is the LIBRARY, by *Alan E. Munby*, 1931, in a Classical-Re-Revival. Nearer the town, on the S side of the road and NE of the parish church, NEW KENWYN, of 1957–8 by *Grenfell Baines*, pretty, of pale brick, with a square cupola set diagonally, and CAMPIONS, W of New Kenwyn, of 1956–7 by *H. C. Boardman*.

THE TOWN. The HIGH STREET runs E–W from the Market Place to the Methodist Church. It is a friendly street, but has no architectural interest. There is the occasional pretty shopfront and the occasional more ambitious Georgian house, such as the MANOR HOUSE (five bays, two storeys, red brick, doorway with broken pediment on Roman Doric columns). Near the E end to the N is HANWORTH HOUSE in BULL STREET also red, also Georgian, also five bays, but two and a half storeys. At the N end is HILL HOUSE, N of the Methodist Church, again red, again five bays and two storeys, but with brick quoins and also brick quoins to the one-bay centre. In front an C18 MILESTONE which, apart from the distances to towns, also records squirearchically those to Blickling, Holkham, Houghton, Raynham, Wolterton, and Felbrigg.

But what is far and away the most interesting building in Holt is seen by few and can only be seen if one looks for it, HOME PLACE (originally Kelling Place, now a Convalescent Home), on the Cromer Road, E of the Kelling Sanatorium. It was built in 1903–5 by *E. S. Prior* for the Rev. Percy R. Lloyd and first called Voewood. The building was superintended by *Randall Wells*. No contractor was employed. The house is a most lavish and at the same time most violently idiosyncratic house and cost £60,000 to build. The walls are of mass concrete faced with pebble and occasional bonded-in brown stones. There are also very thin tile-like bricks. Prior's passion for local materials amounted to fanaticism. The entrance side is a good introduction to his idiom. The centre is a canted bay in which the doorway is set. It is an arch on heavy, cyclopean columns. The basement windows and doors are recessed behind heavy arches. The windows on the two main floors are connected vertically by St Andrew's crosses of brown stone, and the principal-floor windows are moreover set between two broad bands of brown stone. Parapet of brick slates; tall, round decorated chimneyshafts. The garden façade is far more [61] elaborate. It is at r. angles to the entrance and has two wings projecting diagonally (as in Prior's earlier The Barn, Exmouth, and in Lutyens's Papillon Hall). This main front defeats description. Colonnades with cyclopean brown columns in the wings. Their ends are canted and have gables and chimneys set asymmetrically. The recessed centre has two gables as well as parapets curving upward. A fine formal garden extends down from the front, with low pebble and brick walls. The back is no less interesting. It is symmetrical, as are the entrance and garden sides. Behind it stables and outbuildings, again symmetrical. The coach-house (or garage) entrances have gaping three-quarter circles as arches. The whole is full of mannerisms, yet it is inventive and daring, and the inventions sometimes remind one almost of Gaudí.

HONING

3020

ST PETER AND ST PAUL. Tall Perp w tower with flushwork panelling on base and battlements. Very tall three-light window with transom and tracery under. The chancel cut short so that the Perp chancel arch is close to the E window. This dates probably from 1795, when the chancel was remodelled. It has the intersected tracery so beloved of the Gothick decades. The same also in the N and s windows, behind which the arcades were left standing. The arrangement as it now is remains puzzling. The arcade piers are of so coarse a shape that they cannot be original Perp work. But several of their bases are. The arches also seem Perp. They are four-centred. They make the aisles absurdly narrow. Yet the wall of 1795 cannot have been taken back, because the s porch is original and determines at least the s wall. It is not likely that they would have re-erected the porch stone by stone in 1795. – FONT. Perp. Panelled stem. Underside of the bowl with heads. But the bowl itself the typical Purbeck marble bowl of the C13, with two shallow pointed arches to each side. – PLATE. Chalice, Norwich-made, but quite different from the usual Norwich products, C16?; undated Paten. – MONUMENTS. (Brass to Nicholas Parker † 1496; 21 in. figure; E end, floor.) –

Tablet to Thomas Cubitt † 1829. An identical companion for another Cubitt who died in 1865.

HONING HALL. Built in 1748. Alterations contemplated and a few made about 1790 by *Soane*, and also by *Repton* in 1792. Repton landscaped the grounds. The exterior of the house is of 1748. Five by five bays, red brick, of two and a half storeys. Three-bay pediment to the s. Coat of arms and garlands in the pediment. Doorway with pediment on Ionic columns. To the W a bow window, probably a slightly later alteration. The horizontal band between the storeys an addition made at the suggestion of Repton. Inside the entrance hall with its fireplace and the doors are of 1748. In the drawing room simple fireplace apparently by *Soane*. The iron railing of the principal staircase also of the late C18. The other staircase has balusters of 1748.

HORNING
3010

ST BENEDICT. C13 the priest's doorway with its dog-tooth decoration and the arcade to the former N aisle, though the capitals have been badly mauled (four bays). C14 the W tower (flushwork chequer along the base, traceried sound-holes, figures instead of pinnacles). C14 also the s aisle W window and the s arcade (octagonal piers, arches with two slight chamfers). One chancel window Dec, the others Perp, and Perp the Piscina. – FONT. Octagonal, with simple tracery. – BENCHES. With poppy-heads and reliefs against the ends, e.g. the devil pushing a human being into the mouth of hell, a combat of a man with a dragon, and also ornamental reliefs. – PLATE. Chalice and Paten Cover, made in Norwich, 1567.

HORNING HALL. The barn is the chapel of the former ST JAMES'S HOSPITAL, a hospice along the road from Horning to St Benet's Abbey (*see* Ludham, p. 191). The old road went along a causeway which in parts still exists. The chapel has little detail left to date it. The window surrounds, however, exclude a date before the C14.

HORSEY
4020

ALL SAINTS. Round tower, thin octagonal top with battlements. Nave and chancel in one, thatched. – FONT. Octagonal, Perp. – SCREEN with one-light divisions. Ogee arches and panel tracery above them. – BENCHES. A number of ends with poppy-heads. – AUMBRY. In the chancel, three separate little cupboards. – STAINED GLASS. To commemorate Miss

Catherine Ursula Rising, † 1890. To one's surprise the glass represents the lady herself painting a picture, not St Luke, the patron saint of painters. – PLATE. Chalice, London-made, inscribed 1666.

WINDMILLS. An excellently preserved drainage mill, still with cap and sails, ½ m. s. (Stubb Mill, ½ m. w of this.)

HORSFORD

ALL SAINTS. w tower of *c.*1456 (Blomefield) with traceried sound-holes, bell-openings definitely of a Dec design, and flushwork panelling on the battlements. N aisle of 1869, and the rest so restored that it looks Victorian too. The chancel lancet windows could be correct. – FONT. Square, Norman, of Purbeck marble, each side with four shallow blank arches. – SCREEN. With one-light divisions, and pointed arches with tracery in two tiers in depth. – STAINED GLASS. Memorial to three consumptive sisters who died in 1891–3. By *The Royal Bavarian Institute for Stained Glass F. X. Zettler Munich.* – PLATE. Norwich-made Chalice of 1566 and Paten without date. – MONUMENT. Mrs Jane Day † 1777. Signed by *J. Wilton.* Of high quality, though quite simple, with an urn on a plinth with a wreath. Vases l. and r. The inscription includes lines from Milton and Young.

HORSFORD HALL, opposite the church. Simple Georgian five-bay house with a doorway with pilasters and fanlight.

DOG INN. Early C17. With stepped gables and one pedimented window.

WINDMILL, at St Helena, 1 m. NNW. Derelict tower-mill without cap and sails.

CASTLE HILL, ½ m. NE. A substantial motte-and-bailey castle. The motte is to the N, the bailey on the other three sides. The motte is not artificially raised. Aerial photographs have shown that there was a large rectangular building on the motte, and a barbican of some sort between motte and bailey.

HORSHAM ST FAITH

ST MARY AND ST ANDREW. A large parish church, s of the Priory. w tower Dec, but with a Perp arch to the nave. Perp all the rest, except the E wall of the chancel, which was left intact with its three stepped E.E. lancet windows. The wall itself has a handsome flint and stone chequer pattern. The N lancet in the chancel is evidently not *in situ* or in its proper context. It was probably originally part of a two-light window. Perp s porch, two-storeyed. Above the entrance a niche between two small windows. Parapet with shields in a wavy frieze. Tierceron-star-vault inside with a central boss representing the Crucifixion of St Andrew. Interior with six-bay arcades of the C19. Slender piers with four shafts and, in the diagonals, four wave mouldings. Against the s aisle wall giant blank arcading comprising the windows. In the chancel one head-bracket preserved; for the lenten veil. – FONT. Octagonal. At the foot four lambs' heads. Panelled stem. The bowl is totally re-cut. – FONT COVER. A fine Jacobean piece. On the lid stands an openwork obelisk in the middle and round the rim four tall Tuscan columns, carrying an entablature. Ogee volutes above and a top obelisk also openwork. – SCREEN. The dado with twelve paintings of Saints and an inscription with the date 1528. The upper part in one-light divisions with cusped ogee arches and very charming, small-scale, two-tier cusping, i.e. in two tiers in depth. – PULPIT. With bad painted panels and also a painted donor, kneeling, and the date 1480.* – BENCHES. In the N aisle, with poppy-heads. – PLATE. Chalice and Paten, Norwich, inscribed 1663.

See p. 390

PRIORY OF ST FAITH, at ABBEY FARM, N of the church. The Benedictine priory was founded as a cell of Conques about 1105. The remains are interesting enough to deserve study. A square walled garden represents the cloister. This lay to the N, not the s of the church. In the E wall there is still enough left to show that the entry to the chapter house was a most sumptuous Later Norman piece. To the N, i.e. the refectory, there is also a (simpler) Norman doorway. The farmhouse covers the ground of the N range. There is a W doorway of the refectory in the house, and there are also two Perp two-light windows to the s. The range is buttressed to the s as well as to the N, which is puzzling. Indeed the site is puzzling altogether, and ought to be properly investigated. Did e.g. the church lie immediately N of the parish church, i.e. did it adjoin the s wall of the cloister? ‡

MISSION ROOM, s of the church. The doorway has a round arch which comes from the Priory. It has the typical Late

---

* Mr Croft-Murray points out that one of the panels must be of *c.*1528.

‡ Tristram reports a PAINTING of the Crucifixion on the end wall of the former refectory. I could not find it. It is supposed to be of the mid C13 and similar in style to the Amesbury Psalter.

Norman enrichment of what is no longer zigzag and can but
be described as half-dog-tooth. The arch has also a roll moulding with fillet and stiff-leaf stops, i.e. dates from c.1200. Of
the same date and with the same half-dog-tooth ornament,
preserved inside the Mission Room, a smaller doorway and the
sedilia arches of the priory church.

HOUSES, to the SW of the church. A late C17 row of rustic gaiety.
Brick, of two storeys, with odd broad raised brick surrounds
to the upper windows, small aprons below, and also raised
oval brick panels. The W gable is stepped.

MILE FARMHOUSE, ⅝ m. NE. The BARN has an inexplicably
ornate gable with a big blank arched niche, four small windows,
and a smaller niche on top – a very pretty composition. The
house has also a (blocked) oval brick window. All this is probably of the same time as the houses by the church.

CREMATORIUM. 1936 by *J. P. Chaplin*. The chapel is large, of
red and mauve brick with a central tower and in an odd mixed
style, with Gothic and free round-arched elements, inspired it
seems by Sir Edward Maufe.

HORSTEAD

ALL SAINTS. Slender W tower, perhaps C13 and buttressed
later. W lancet with transom. Below it a niche. The rest of
the church of 1879 by *R. M. Phipson*. The S doorway however is genuine early C14 work. Fleurons in the hood-mould.
– SOUTH DOOR. With tracery. – STAINED GLASS. In a S aisle
window *Morris* glass, designed by *Burne-Jones*. Date of com-
memoration 1893. – S aisle by *Kempe*, c.1900. – E by *Kempe &
Tower*, c.1912. – PLATE. Chalice and Paten, Norwich, 1627;
Almsdish, London, 1826. – MONUMENTS. George Warren
† 1728, by *James Barrett*, a column in front of a black obelisk.
– John Langley Watts † 1774. Neo-classical, yet as asymmetrical as any daring Rococo vignette.

MILL. A delightful sight, even if not a self-conscious work of   2b
architecture. Weatherboarded. The ground floor on arches, the
top six little gables. The miller's house stands across the road.
Early C19, yellow brick, three bays, doorway with Doric
pilasters.

(Mr Cozens-Hardy also mentions HORSTEAD HOUSE of
c.1620, HORSTEAD HALL of 1835, and HEGGATT HALL
with an Elizabethan porch and stepped gable.)

HOUGHTON ST GILES

ST GILES. Rebuilt in 1879, but apparently with extensive re-use
of old materials. The exterior is dull, as one would expect,
with the low W tower carrying a little pyramid cap and the long
nave and chancel under one tiled roof. But the mixture of
windows cannot but be original. The E window with its flowing
tracery e.g. looks entirely confidence-inspiring. – SCREEN.
Very delicate cusping and subcusping at the top. Dado with
paintings of twelve Saints. The back of the dado with ornamental paintings. – BENCHES. With poppy-heads. – COM-
MUNION RAIL. C17. – PLATE. Chalice, Norwich, 1567;
Paten-Cover, London, 1788.

SLIPPER CHAPEL. The name has no antiquity. It implies that
from here the pilgrims to Little Walsingham walked barefoot.
The building had been in an unsatisfactory state when it was
bought by Miss Charlotte Boyd, who was later, in 1894,
converted to Catholicism. It was handed over to *Thomas
Garner*, himself a convert in 1896. He was commissioned to
restore the chapel, but it was only re-opened for worship in
1934. It is an oblong with much lavish decoration of the mid
C14 or just before. This decoration is essentially original, as
the elder Pugin's illustrations show. It is best preserved on the
W side. Doorway with niches l. and r. and niche above. Inside
two unexplained square holes l. and r. of the doorway, W window with tracery inside reticulation units. Also niches l. and r.
Gable with fleuron-band and three plinths, two of them square
and set diagonally. Along the long sides windows with the
motif of a four-petalled flower. Above frieze of two wavy lines
forming horizontal reticulation units. This frieze is largely
replaced, but correctly. The head of the N doorway is by
Garner. He also wholly re-did the E window and repeated the
gable from the W side. The roof timbers inside are partly Perp
and very impressive. Garner, during his restoration, found
traces of the original C14 roof which, he stated, must have had
the same double slope as the gable, i.e. in all probability a
clerestory in the timbers. Garner also found indications of a
Perp W gallery. The interior was restored again in 1934.* –
STAINED GLASS. E window by *Geoffrey Webb*, 1953 and
typical of his Comper-derived style.

MANOR FARMHOUSE, SW of the church. With shaped gable-
ends; probably early C18.

* I am greatly indebted to Mr H. Martin Gillett for most of the above
details.

HOVETON

ST JOHN. The W tower was built in 1765. It is of brick and has (rather surprising) four-centred arches over its bell-openings. The NE corner of the chancel is partly of carstone, i.e. Norman at the latest. Dec N doorway; Perp windows. – FONT. Octagonal, with panelled stem and bowl with shields on cusped fields. – SCREEN. Small, with two-light divisions and ogee arches. – BENCHES. Three original ones, with poppy-heads. – STAINED GLASS. In the chancel S window Netherlandish ovals. – PLATE. Gilt Chalice of the rare date 1562, made in London, and given to the church in 1824; Paten, 1797, by *J. B. C. Odiot* of Paris. – MONUMENTS. A number of Blofeld tablets.

ST PETER, 1 m. NNE. No more than a chapel. Of 1624, a time when not many churches were built. Three bays, brick with stepped gables and thatched. Porch with a stepped gable. The windows have Y- or intersected tracery, no doubt of the time of the restoration of 1884.* – PULPIT. A simple piece no doubt of *c.*1624. Plain panels, the top ones just with the typical Jacobean motif of a stylized palmette. – PLATE. Chalice with top, made in London, 1610; Paten, made in Norwich, *c.*1650–78. – (MONUMENT. Mrs Anfrere † 1750. Asymmetrical tablet. A putto holds drapery. NBR)

HOVETON HOUSE, ¾ m. SE. Built towards the end of the C17 and one of the most attractive, if not most perfect, houses of its time in Norfolk. It is a naive, but a most lovable design. Eleven bays and two storeys, red brick, with a steep three-bay pediment. In the pediment two long garlands squeezed under the sloping sides and a (later) oval window. The three bays with the pediment project a little and have attenuated unfluted giant Corinthian pilasters, as have the angles of the house. All windows have keystones, and all have aprons. The middle projection in addition has a doorway with fluted Corinthian pilasters and a fancy pediment with a lot of not very disciplined vegetable carving. The window above has pilasters with garlands. Hipped roof with dormers with alternating triangular and segmental pediments. At the back two projections with Dutch gables, i.e. shaped gables ending in a proper pediment. They can be only a little earlier than the grander façade. Inside fine fireplaces of *c.*1740, also a doorcase and a staircase with two twisted balusters to the tread. The gardens were laid out early in the C19 by *Repton*.

HOVETON HALL, ¼ m. N of St Peter. Early C19,* of grey brick, nine bays, of which three are part of a central bow window, two storeys. The three bays l. and r. on the ground floor replaced by one tripartite window.

HOVETON OLD HALL, ½ m. NW of St Peter. A handsome composition of c.1700, with its barn. The house has a seven-bay front of two storeys with a three-bay projection and brick quoins, also to the projection. Doorway with Ionic brick pilasters in front of rustication, and a segmental brick pediment. The roof is altered. The BARN has seven bays with horizontally placed oval windows, and below them blank vertically placed ovals under hood-moulds.

NORTH FARM HOUSE, 1¼ m. ENE of St John. Oblong block with a stepped gable. Four-storeyed step-gabled porch. Dated 1587 on a stone formerly in the cellar but now in the Hall. The windows remodelled in the late C17. They have wooden crosses and still the original leading.

COTTAGE, SE of Hoveton House. A charming little thing, of the late C17. Three bays with shaped gables and brick quoins. Broad doorway with pilasters, a pulvinated frieze, and a segmental pediment. On the l. side a lower attachment faced with chequer brick and also with a shaped gable.

HUNWORTH

0030

ST LAWRENCE. Norman W tower, originally unbuttressed.‡ On the N side a doorway and a window of c.1300 (Y-tracery). Most windows Perp. Perp S chapel. E.E. chancel of 1850. – PLATE. Decorated London-made Chalice, 1567; Norwich-made Paten, 1567.

HALL FARMHOUSE. Five bays, two storeys, whitewashed. Shaped end-gables. The house, until recently, carried a date 1699. On a barn the date 1700.

INGHAM

1020

HOLY TRINITY. A parish church, but on the N side interlocked with the former Trinitarian priory, founded in 1360 by Sir Miles Stapleton. He obtained licence for the parish church to be rebuilt and to become partly the church of the priory. The nave remained parochial, the chancel became monastic. So the

* Mr Cozens-Hardy says after 1797 and before 1825.
‡ The Rev. H. Welch tells me that a Norman window was recently discovered and exposed. It is in the S wall of the church.

building represents in its style the third quarter of the C14. Tall w tower, the base with flushwork panelling. Flushwork-panelled buttresses too. Doorway with thin shafts. Shields in the traceried spandrels, frieze of shields above in cusped triangular fields. Four-light w window. Very prettily traceried sound-holes with shields. Double-stepped battlements with flushwork decoration and pinnacles. s aisle and clerestory by *J. P. Seddon* (PF) 1876. The s porch is higher than the aisle. It is in fact three storeys in height, a great rarity. Inside the ground floor tierceron-vaulting in two bays. The upper floors may have been the living quarters of the parish priest, who was at the same time the sacrist of the priory. He may however have lived to the N, where domestic accommodation evidently existed between the church and the priory.

Of the PRIORY we can say little. There are traces of the cloister arches to the N of the nave, and obscure traces of rooms in several storeys. There are even two small mullioned windows in the chancel wall high up below the roof. Doorway from the priory into the nave, further E than the normal N doorway. This is an arrangement usual in wholly monastic churches.

The monastic chancel is all Dec. It was in fact probably built in the 1340s (*see* below). Five-light E window with flowing tracery, of a specially good design. Sedilia and Piscina are mostly Victorian. The arcades inside are typically Early Perp. Five bays, tall piers of quatrefoil section with thin filleted diagonal shafts. Polygonal capitals and abaci, moulded arches.

FURNISHINGS. FONT. C13, octagonal, of Purbeck marble, with the familiar two shallow pointed arches on each side. – SCREEN. Remains of a stone screen, i.e. really the pulpitum between the lay and the monastic parts of the church. – STALLS. With poppy-heads. – BENCHES. Ends with poppy-heads, mostly in the N aisle. – LECTERN. Very ornate, Victorian Gothic, of wood, triangular and ending in an eagle. It is by *J. P. Seddon*, probably of 1876. – PLATE. Chalice, Norwich-made, 1567–8. – MONUMENTS. Sir Oliver de Ingham † 1344, chancel N wall, originally under a sumptuous arch with buttresses l. and r. Of this very little is preserved. But the tomb-chest and the effigy are; and they are very good and very interesting. Against the tomb-chest twelve mourners, small figures. On the top Sir Oliver lying on a bed of pebbles (cf. Reepham) in a strangely convulsed attitude, characteristic of the Dec style. The r. hand on the sword on the l., the l. hand

reaching out across to touch the pebbles. Two kneeling angels
by his head holding his helmet. Sir Oliver presumably had the
chancel built, and is buried in this particular place for that
reason. – Knight and Lady of the de Bois family, late C14.
Tomb-chest with shields on quatrefoils and between them
three small stone statuettes. Against the end of the chest
Christ seated between two angels. The effigies sadly defaced. –
There were also three outstandingly good BRASSES at Ingham,
but of them one (Sir Miles de Stapleton † 1364, and his wife,
holding hands) has disappeared entirely, and of the others
only the indents and some fragments of the architectural surrounds are left. They are a Knight of c.1410 under a triple
canopy and Sir Brian de Stapleton † 1438 and his wife, 4 ft
6 in. figures. There was also the brass to his dog with a special
label JOKKE. – In the middle of the chancel floor brass inscription to Lady Elizabeth Calthorpe who, the inscription
says, died on July 33, 1536.

INGHAM OLD HALL. Mostly of 1904, but, hidden inside, a two-
light squint and some minor arches.

THE GROVE, ½ m. NW. Georgian, five bays, two storeys. Doorway with broken pediment.

INGWORTH

ST LAURENCE. Stump of a round tower, of which the upper
parts fell in 1822. Norman unmoulded arch towards the nave
on the simplest imposts. The tower is now linked to the nave
by the most curious buttress arrangement. Norman also the
nave, in spite of Perp windows; see the carstone quoins on the
NW and NE. The S side was widened. E.E. chancel, see the
narrow lancets on the N side. Perp S porch of two storeys.
Charming upper window. The gable repaired in the C16 in
brick with crow-steps. – FONT. Plain, octagonal bowl, stem
with vertical bands of quatrefoils. – FONT COVER. 1935. –
SCREEN. Part of the dado Perp. The top is C17 with sparse
thin balusters. – COMMUNION RAIL. C18, of slender balusters.
– ROYAL ARMS. Of William III, excellently carved. – BOX
PEWS. – STAINED GLASS. E window with a Flemish C15 panel,
much restored. – PLATE. Chalice and Paten with Elizabethan
stem and bowl of c.1620–30, Norwich-made.

IRMINGLAND

(IRMINGLAND HALL. 1609. Only the E wing remains. The
windows were sashed in the C20. B. Cozens-Hardy)

IRSTEAD

3020

St MICHAEL. Small; mostly Dec. Unbuttressed w tower. The body of the church thatched. The s aisle Perp and very rough. The arcade of three bays is indeed a minimum. Small fragments of a Norman zigzag arch in the N and s doorways inside. – FONT. Octagonal. Against the stem eight statuettes, against the bowl the Head of Christ (twice), the Lamb, the Hand of God, and four leaf motifs. – PULPIT. With linenfold panelling. (Attached to it a C13 STALL arm with stiff-leaf foliage and a 33a young head. NBR) – SCREEN. Against the dado on each side a broad panel with three painted Saints against a light patterned background. – BENCHES. Ends with poppy-heads. Some animals on arms. One back with linenfold panelling. – SOUTH DOOR. With a cross of ironwork round the knocker, the little brother of the cross at Tunstead and perhaps by the same craftsman. – PAINTING. On the N wall a St Christopher and a figure on horseback (?). – STAINED GLASS. Fragments in the E and s windows of the chancel. – PLATE. Chalice, Norwich, 1567–8; Paten unmarked, perhaps re-made from an older one to match the chalice.

IRSTEAD OLD HALL, ¼ m. SW. Partly Elizabethan or Jacobean. Two-storeyed porch with a pedimented window. Chimneys octagonal with star tops.

ITTERINGHAM

1030

St MARY. Unbuttressed w tower. Nave and chancel, the N side indicating an early C14 date. – PANELLING. In the chancel, Jacobean or a little later. Big square balusters framing arches in perspective. – BOX PEWS. – PLATE. Chalice, supposed to be pre-Reformation; Paten, undated.

See p. 390

MANOR FARMHOUSE, to the SE. An unusually perfect example of the late C17 house. Red brick, seven bays and two storeys, or rather six bays and the big doorway with its segmental pediment. Garlands and coat of arms in the pediment. Original panelled door. Windows with wooden mullion-and-transom crosses. Still shaped end-gables.

HILL FARMHOUSE, to the s beyond the bridge. Originally of the same type, but the windows reduced from seven to three bays.

MILL. Six-bay house of two storeys, brick, with sash windows. The dormer windows are later.

KELLING

0040

ST MARY. At present under repair. To the S the ruins of a S transept or transeptal chapel. One lancet window in the chancel. Otherwise Perp. The w tower with battlements faced with flushwork diaper. In the chancel a small but sumptuous Easter Sepulchre. Niche with four-centred head under an ogee arch. Panelled base and spandrels. Crenellated cresting. Close to the Easter Sepulchre, in the NE corner, part of a shaft with polygonal projections, perhaps a pedestal for a statue. – FONT. Perp, octagonal. On the bowl the emblem of the Trinity and the Instruments of the Passion, coats of arms, crossed swords, and crossed keys. Also an inscription. – STAINED GLASS. In the chancel lancet three small original figures, re-set. – PLATE. Chalice and Paten-Cover, London, 1671–2.

BECKHOUSE FARMHOUSE. Of c.1700. Red brick with a pattern of vitrified dark bricks. Five bays, two storeys, the middle window very narrow.

(KELLING HALL. Rebuilt for Sir Henry Deterding, c.1905–10. B. Cozens-Hardy)

BARROWS. For barrows on the w boundary of the parish *see* Salthouse.

KETTLESTONE

9030

ALL SAINTS. Much restored. Octagonal w tower. Dec with bell-openings with Y-tracery and openings in the form of quatrefoiled circles above them. N doorway and N arcade (five bays, low, octagonal piers, double-hollow-chamfered arches) Dec or c.1300. Perp nave windows, N aisle windows, and clerestory windows. Chancel 1869.* – FONT. Octagonal, Perp. Against the bowl the symbol of the Trinity, a cross, the crossed swords, the crossed keys, the arms of Norwich (three mitres), and the arms of England quartering France. – BENCHES. Some with poppy-heads. – PLATE. Paten on foot, 1702; Chalice, 1811; secular Salver, 1817.

KNAPTON

3030

ST PETER AND ST PAUL. The roof of Knapton church is one of the finest in Norfolk, and the font and font cover are almost as striking. The rest palls. Unbuttressed w tower probably of the early C14.‡ S porch and chancel of the same date or one or two

---

* By *F. Preedy* (PF).

‡ The WEATHER-VANE is said to have been designed by *Cotman*, when he gave a drawing lesson at Knapton House.

decades later. The porch has a handsome tripartite niche above
the entrance. As for the chancel, its s wall has two Perp windows and a little Perp porch to protect the priest's doorway.
Perp also the nave windows. A tomb-recess in the nave s wall.
The nave is wide and covered by a double hammerbeam roof,
datable to the year 1504 by an inscription to the then rector
('qui hoc opus fabricari fecit') quoted by Blomefield. Displayed against its various members is a total of 138 angels, all
with spread-out wings and certainly not all genuine. Wall-
posts with angels and above them little statuettes of Saints.
Wall-plate with two tiers of angels. Longitudinal arched braces.
Battlemented collar-beams. Angels even against the kingposts,
facing W as well as E. – FONT. Raised (when?) on three tall
steps with simple flushwork decoration. The font itself is of
the usual Purbeck type of the C13, i.e. octagonal with two flat
arches against each of its sides. – FONT COVER of 1704, a gay
piece with thin balusters and an ogee top. The Greek inscription means; Wash my sins and not my face only. – PULPIT.
With fine foliage carving along the bottom of the body. The
pulpit looks c.1730, but is said to be Victorian. – BENCHES.
Some, with poppy-heads, near the W end. – READER'S DESK.
Consisting of two bench ends and some Jacobean woodwork. –
SCREEN. With some old parts. – PLATE. Norwich-made
Chalice, 1567; Flagon, 1700; Paten, 1702. – MONUMENTS.
A large number of early coffin lids, some with decoration.

OLD HALL, ½ m. SW. Old the N part with stepped gable. The
large S part added.

LAKENHAM see p. 290

LAMMAS

ST ANDREW. All over-restored. Slender W tower. The bell-
openings with cusped Y-tracery. Nave and N aisle windows
Perp. Chancel of 1888, oddly out of plumb with the nave. –
FONT. Octagonal, buttressed stem, bowl with demi-figures of
angels on the underside, four shields and four flowers on the
bowl. – PLATE. Norwich-made Chalice of 1567, with the
bowl remade in 1640; Paten, Norwich, 1567; Tankard, London, 1690; Almsdish, London, 1730.

LAMMAS OLD HALL, SE of the church. A fragment, and much
pulled about. There remains a dormer with finials similar to
e.g. Barningham Hall, i.e. c.1600. The brickwork has dark
brick diaper. (Crinkle-crankle wall. NBR)

LAMMAS HALL, E of the church. A puzzling building, probably
of c.1690 with additions soon after. The doorway e.g. with
rustication of alternating sizes looks c.1730, as does the staircase with one slim turned and one twisted baluster to each step.
Carved tread-ends. On the other hand the shaped end-gables
and the steep gables of the dormers look late c17. Nice symmetrical shaped garden-walls l. and r.

LANGHAM

0040

ST ANDREW AND ST MARY. All Perp, restored in 1868 and
consequently lacking interest outside. W tower with flushwork-
panelled base and sound-holes in the form of a square with
three arched lights. S arcade c14. Four bays, octagonal piers,
double-chamfered arches. Mysterious big, shapeless blank
arch inside, E of the N doorway. Was there a chapel here? –
FONT. c13, of Purbeck marble. Octagonal, with two shallow
blank pointed arches on each side. – STAINED GLASS. E window 1856 by *King* of Norwich. – One N window by *Morris &
Co.*, designed by *Burne-Jones*: Spes and Fides, the same design
as used at Sculthorpe. – W window by *Kempe*, 1911. – PLATE.
Chalice, Norwich, 1566–7.
(LANGHAM HALL. Of c.1820, designed by the owner, the Rev.
Stephen Frost Rippingall. B. Cozens-Hardy)
The parish church of LANGHAM PARVA has disappeared com-
pletely. It was already decayed by 1602.

LESSINGHAM

3020

ALL SAINTS. Unbuttressed W tower. Nave and chancel in one,
thatched. The nave rebuilt in 1893. Divers windows, including
some with Y-tracery. – FONT. Octagonal, c13, of Purbeck
marble, with two shallow pointed arches on each side. –
SCREEN. Dado with twelve painted Saints. They belong to two
different periods. The seated Saints are earlier, of before 1400,
the others are on parchment and were pasted over. – In addition three detached panels. – PULPIT. Back panel and tester.
c17. – PLATE. Paten of the later c15 or early c16. Sexfoiled
depression with the head of Christ. – Elizabethan Chalice.
LESSINGHAM PRIORY. There seems to be no masonry left and
no published evidence. The priory was probably no priory at
all but no more than a grange. It was established from Bec in
1090 and then went to Ogbourne.

LETHERINGSETT   0030

ST ANDREW. Round tower with C14 top. Nave and chancel under one tiled roof. s porch by *Butterfield*, *c.*1875. Inside C13 arcades with quatrefoil piers and double-hollow-chamfered arches. The w responds are a head corbel and a corbel with a grotesque caryatid figure. The s doorway also C13. Chancel Dec, most windows Perp. – FONT. C13, of Purbeck marble, octagonal, with the usual two shallow arches on each side. – REREDOS, 1899. Of alabaster. – BARREL ORGAN, early C19, Gothic, from Hindringham. – STAINED GLASS. A jumble of old fragments in a chancel s window. In the chancel sw window two re-set panels of C15 glass. – *Kempe* glass in the w window (*c.*1895) and in s and N aisle windows (all early C20). – PLATE. Chalice, Norwich, 1566; parcel-gilt Cup, no marks; two Patens, no marks.

LETHERINGSETT HALL. Extension of an older house in 1832. The portico on the s side however is supposed to belong to the older part of the house, which was built about 1770. The portico is something of a mystery. It has five giant Greek Doric columns. Five and not four or six is a blatant solecism. The bottom part of the columns is left unfluted. Mr B. Cozens-Hardy, on the strength of certain family documents, insists on a date of *c.*1770 for the portico. But the very first Greek Doric columns in the West were Athenian Stuart's at Hagley. They are of 1768. When Soane in 1778 began to use them, this was still a revolutionary move. Clients before the late 1790s cannot be believed to have accepted them unless they were of the type of, say, the members of the Society of Dilettanti. At Letheringsett a date of 1832 would be infinitely more probable.

BRIDGE, E of the Hall grounds. Of cast iron, with big balusters; 1818.

THE LODGE, w of the church. N front of flint and brick. Five bays, the middle being a canted bay window. Georgian, with an older core. A s wing of brick, probably shortly after 1759.

KING'S HEAD INN, s of the Hall. Early C19, yellow brick, three bays with recessed centre.

LIMPENHOE   3000

ST BOTOLPH. 1881–2 by *A. S. Hewitt*. Medieval the base of the tower, with flushwork panelling, and the s doorway, Norman, with one order of shafts, decorated capitals, zigzag arch, and a scalloped frieze to the hood-moulds. Some windows seem to be medieval too, e.g. the small one with Y-tracery on the s side. – FONT. Octagonal, C13, of Purbeck marble, with two shallow pointed arches on each side. – TAPESTRY. Sacrifice of Isaac; Flemish, from Southwood. – PLATE. Chalice and Paten of 1567, also from Southwood; Chalice, inscribed 1693.

LINGWOOD

3000

ST PETER. The church seems to belong to the C14, with the nave windows later, the chancel and the unbuttressed w tower earlier. The nave has a roof on arched braces. – BENCHES. Some ends with poppy-heads. Two figures on arms. – COMMUNION RAIL. C17: cf. Burlingham St Edmund. – PLATE. Norwich-made Chalice and Paten Cover, 1567–8; London-made Flagon, 1729.

HOMELEA, I m. s. The former Workhouse. 1837 by *John Brown*. Red brick, still essentially classical; though the replacement of pediments by pedimental gables is a sign of the approaching Early Victorian style.

LITTLE BARNINGHAM

1050

ST ANDREW. Small, on a small eminence. Perp. Flint, partly knapped. – BENCHES. Ends with poppy-heads. – PEW. A 'Jacobean' pew with a skeleton in a shroud at one corner, knobs on the others. It is dated 1640 and part of the inscription says: 'As you are now, even so was I, Remember death, for ye must dye.' – PLATE. Chalice and Paten Cover, Norwich, 1567–8.

LITTLE HAUTBOIS *see* HAUTBOIS

LITTLE ORMESBY *see* ORMESBY ST MICHAEL

LITTLE PLUMSTEAD

3010

ST PROTASE AND ST GERVASE, a dedication unique in England. Norman round tower. Norman also the inside arch of the N doorway and indeed the nave masonry. Above the s doorway a Norman hood-mould with billet decoration. – FONT. Coarse C18 baluster, now outside the porch. – PLATE. Chalice, made at Norwich, 1567; Paten Cover, unmarked. – MONUMENTS. Sir Edward Warner † 1565. Brass, 3 ft long. In armour. – Thomas Penrice and Mrs Penrice † 1829. By *W. Hardy*. Large standing monument of white and black marble. Big base with

acroteria. Above big tablet, the top with a sarcophagus and urn.
PLUMSTEAD HALL (now Hospital). Built in 1889. Two-
storeyed, of brick, Elizabethan in style, with an untold number
of chimneys.

LITTLE RYBURGH   9020

ALL SAINTS. In ruins. Part of the w wall and of the s wall remain, the latter with the s doorway.

LITTLE SNORING   9030

ST ANDREW. The unsolved problem is why a church was begun
here in Early Norman (or, some say, pre-Norman) days and
then left unfinished or half demolished so soon that the successor, immediately to the N, is also in its beginnings still Norman. Were they perhaps two parish churches as close to one
another as e.g. at Reepham? The old church has a round tower
connected with the nave by a Norman one-step arch. The new
church has a Norman s and a Norman N window and a Late
Norman s doorway. This doorway was remodelled oddly and
ruthlessly in the C13. The stones were re-assembled, including
the zigzag at r. angles to the wall and the decorated hood-
mould, and what had been a broad round arch became a
narrow, sharply pointed one. On the N side a simpler Late
Norman doorway. Other windows of the church include
lancets and a two-light Dec design (w). The chancel is puzzling
again. It appears E.E. with its three widely spaced stepped
lancets, shafted inside. The angle Piscina confirms the date.
But the treatment of the E windows is surprisingly rough and
the result shapeless. – FONT. Circular, Norman, with foliage
medallions. – PULPIT. Simple. C18. – PLATE. Chalice,
Elizabethan, Norwich, and Chalice, probably early C17.

LITTLE WALSINGHAM   9030

ST MARY.* Dec w tower with bell-openings which have cusped
Y-tracery or two-light reticulated tracery. Recessed lead spire.
The tower is preceded by an extremely pretty w porch. Cusped
and subcusped entrance arch, hood-mould on big busts with
fleurons in the arch, cornice with fleurons, cornerstones above
this which indicate the former existence of a gable. Doorway
inside the porch with fleurons in the arch and the hood-mould

* In the night of 14–15 July 1961 the church was gutted by fire. The
steeple and s porch remain and inside the Sidney tombs.

which also stands on big busts. Two-storeyed s porch higher
than the aisle, vaulted inside with a tierceron-vault without
bosses. Two pairs of tiercerons each way. Entrance with a
niche. s and n aisle windows and clerestory windows all Perp,
with a preference for straight triangles instead of arches. The
chancel e window is of five lights with an embattled transom.
Perp six-bay arcades, not high, with piers, quatrefoil of broad
flat members and fillets. The arches are different in the n from
the s arcade. Later Perp chancel chapels of two bays. The piers
here have four polygonal projections and the arches are four-
centred. In the n aisle a pretty Perp piscina. The aisle roofs are
original (arched braces with tracery in the spandrels). – FONT.
Almost the perfect Norfolk font. It would be, if it were better
preserved. Three steps, the top step like a Maltese cross. All
three steps decorated with tracery motifs. Stem with shallow
statuettes, eight in the main divisions, eight very small ones on
buttresses against the angles. Against the bowl the Seven
Sacraments and the Crucifixion. – A former FONT in the N
transept. Octagonal with four unusually big figures standing in
the angles. This is also Perp.* – FONT COVER. Early C17. With
eight columns carrying an ogee cap. A dove at the top. –
SCREEN. In the n transept. One-light divisions. – DOORS. The
w and s doors have a pretty framing of bands of quatrefoils.
The w door has some more tracery too. – SCULPTURE. In the
n transept the top of a churchyard cross. In the s aisle at the w
end good figure of a seated angel. – STAINED GLASS. Some
C15 glass in the chancel window above the Sedilia. Two C17
roundels in a n transept window. – PLATE. Chalice, Norwich,
1567; another Elizabethan Chalice; Patens, London, 1627 and
1788. – MONUMENTS. Brasses to Margaret Stoke, c.1460, bust
(s aisle w), to Geoffrey Porter † 1485 and wife, 18 in. figures (s
chapel s, partly under the organ), to Henry Clederow † 1509
and wife, 20 in. figures (nave NW), to William Westow, a
chalice brass, c.1520 (below altar space, n chapel), to a Civilian
and wife, c.1540, 20 in. figures (n aisle w). – Dr Mott † 1699.
Tomb-chest with decorated pilasters and panels with skulls (n
chapel). – Sir Henry Sidney † 1612 and wife. Standing monuments. Alabaster. Two recumbent effigies, he in front and
below her. Coffered arch behind, flanked by two columns.
Strapwork cartouche and strapwork at the top (n chapel). –
Small tablet, Jacobean, with a white curtain hanging down and
closing all the rest. You can just see two columns l. and r. On

* Or was it the base of a churchyard cross?

top it says; 'Dormitorium Edwardi de Fotherbye'. He died in
1632. – Henry Lee-Warner † 1804, tablet with a large mourning female, and Mrs Lee-Warner † 1819, with a kneeling
maiden reading a book and putti above. Both by *Sir Richard
Westmacott* (chancel).

PRIORY. The Priory of Our Lady of Walsingham developed into
one of the most famous pilgrimage places in England. It seems
to have originated in a chapel built by Richelde of Fervaques
about 1150, *ad instar* of the house in Nazareth where the Annunciation took place. Her son Geoffrey had visited the Holy
Land and added to the chapel a priory for Augustinian canons.
That was about 1153, and a little later the priory became a
centre for pilgrimages, thanks, it appears, to the interest taken
in it by Henry III and Edward I, who visited Walsingham often
and gave presents. In 1236 Walsingham gave £3. 6. 8 in
feudal aid, Broomholm £5; in 1291 Walsingham had grown
richer than Broomholm. In the C15 it had become the richest
priory in Norfolk, except for Norwich.

Of the remains by far the most impressive piece is the E wall
of the CHURCH, with a very large window and two turrets. The
buttresses are lavishly and handsomely decorated with flushwork and three niches, one on top of the other. Of the S and N
walls of the chancel enough is recognizable to see that there
was a wall passage below the windows. There is plenty of evidence to show a busy building activity between 1360 (when
Lady Clare left bequests 'à l'overaigne de l'église') and 1390.
Nothing is visible of the transepts, which, oddly enough, did
not at all project, the crossing and crossing tower, or the nave
and aisles. Half buried the bases and what little survives of the
piers of the mighty W tower. So the church (like Wymondham)
had two axial towers, one at the W end, the other above the
crossing. The remains of the piers point to the later C13, a date
confirmed by the REFECTORY, which is as interesting as the
surviving parts of the church. The S wall is almost complete, a
very fine piece of late C13 architecture. The windows have bar
tracery, the ones to the S with two lights and a big trefoil over,
the large one at the W end with four lights arranged in two plus
two Y-fashion and with pointed trefoils and a large encircled
round quatrefoil in the tracery. The staircase also remains
which led to the reading pulpit. Behind it a plainer window
with Y-tracery. To the l. of the entrance to the refectory, which
was from the SW corner of the cloister, is the lavatorium niche.
Of the W range nothing is clear, of the E range the early C14

Dormitory UNDERCROFT, three bays, two-naved, with semi-circular wall-shafts but octagonal piers. Single-chamfered ribs. To the N of this was a PASSAGE and then the CHAPTER HOUSE, of which no more is above ground than two S corner shafts. They read together with the two N corner shafts of the passage.

The SHRINE, i.e. the Chapel of Our Lady with the venerated image of the seated Virgin, stood – this is the most likely suggestion – to the N of the N aisle. The house built by Richelde was surrounded by the chapel proper. There were in addition healing wells to the E of the church and, also to the E, a detached Chapel of St Lawrence. In that part a Norman DOORWAY has been re-erected.* In connexion with the position of the Shrine and the Wells the N porch can perhaps be explained which opened from the N chancel aisle. It would have led into the parts of the precinct visited by pilgrims. Finally the GATEHOUSE from the town, in line with the church and only a small distance from it. This was built in the C15. The outer front has a wide four-centred arch, no special pedestrian entrance, an upper cross-slit window with a niche l. and r., and on the top a quatrefoil with a fine head. To the inside there is a window with a mullion and transom cross and fleurons in the lintel and also a niche l. and r. The door was set across the middle between the two archways. The whole of the passage was vaulted.

ABBEY HOUSE. The house is built into the E (dormitory) range of the priory. It has a good late C18 brick front of five bays and three storeys. There is a three-bay pediment and a Tuscan porch. The last windows l. and r. on ground floor and first floor are of the Venetian variety. The back of the house later, with Gothic windows.

FRIARY (GREYFRIARS). The ruins belong to a private house and lie by the Fakenham Road, about 200 yds W of the church. The friary was founded in 1347. The principal remains are the stately GUEST HOUSE, with a tall upper storey. Both gable-ends survive, and the cross gable of the staircase up to the upper floor. To the S of this the present house and then the walls of the KITCHEN. To the E of the kitchen the charming LITTLE CLOISTER, which had a closed cloister walk with three-light windows. The upper apartments had their windows flush with these. To the E of the guest house was the great cloister. Of this and of the church very little can be recognized.

* It is not known where this came from. In the house there is also a small waterleaf capital, not *in situ*. These are the only pre-C13 remains.

The church had nave and aisles separated from the chancel, as at King's Lynn, by a corridor-like space with solid W and E walls carrying a steeple.

SHRINE OF OUR LADY OF WALSINGHAM. The new Anglican shrine was built in 1931–7. Design by *Milner & Craze*. It is a disappointing building, of brick, partly whitewashed, and looking for all its ambitions like a minor suburban church. Italianate brick portico. Campanile by the (ritual) E end. There is not sufficient evidence to justify the claim that the new shrine stands where the Holy House had been (*see* above). – (REREDOS. By *Comper*, 1959.*) – PAINTING. Madonna by *Sodoma* from the Mond Collection.

PERAMBULATION. Connected with this part of the Shrine is the COLLEGE OF PRIESTS, with entrance in KNIGHT STREET, a picturesque group of flint and brick houses of the C16 and later. From the S end of Knight Street, past the new Shrine and, turning W, along a street with the precinct wall on the l., one reaches the COMMON PLACE. In the middle the CONDUIT, C16, octagonal, of brick with a truncated stone pyramid roof. Nice houses on all sides, especially on the S the flint-faced SHIRE HALL and a long front next to it with an oversailing timber-framed upper floor. On the N side four similar houses. From here to the S the HIGH STREET. Here again a number of simple houses with timber-framed upper storeys, and also a C17 house with a shaped gable (E side) and two good Georgian houses of five bays with three-bay pediments, the HARVEST HOUSE and BARCLAYS BANK (both W side). Against the S end, diagonally across, a C17 brick house with shaped gable-ends. Now to the E, to the church, where, opposite the W tower, yet another pretty Georgian five-bay house, or to the W with the METHODIST CHAPEL (of 1793–4) lying a little back (arched windows, pyramid roof) and with access to the MARKET PLACE. The best house in this small secluded irregular space is ST HUGH'S HOUSE, red brick, Georgian, of five bays and two and a half storeys.

LITTLE WITCHINGHAM

1020

ST FAITH. Disused and ruinous. Unbuttressed W tower apparently of *c.*1300. Nave, chancel, and S aisle probably of about the same date. The arcade has the usual octagonal piers and double-chamfered arches.

* I owe this information to John Betjeman.

3010
LUDHAM

St CATHERINE. A large church. Of the C14 the w tower and the
chancel. The tower (buttressed later) has a Dec window, a
niche below, and also an arch towards the nave which has Dec
responds. The chancel has a five-light E window with reticulated tracery and sumptuous Sedilia with ogee arches on head
corbels and lush crocketing. Handsome capitals of the chancel
arch, one with leaves, the other with little caryatid demi-
figures. Perp arcades of six bays with octagonal piers and
double-chamfered arches. Perp aisle windows – one in the S
aisle singled out from the others by greater age. Perp clerestory
windows. N porch with big flushwork panelling and a niche
over the entrance. S porch two-storeyed. Spandrels with
shields on tracery. Two niches above the entrance. Good nave
roof with hammerbeams alternating with simple horizontal
beams starting from the apex of the longitudinal arched braces
which connect the wall-posts for the hammerbeams. No collar-
beams. – FONT. Octagonal, with four lions and four wild men
against the stem, and against the bowl small figures peeping
out from the underside and panels with four lions and the signs
of the four Evangelists. – SCREEN. One-light divisions. Ogee
arches within pointed arches. Eleven painted Saints and a King
on the dado, of exceptionally good quality. Above them blank
panels with quatrefoils and plants. Detached buttresses between the panels. Inscription and date 1493. – STALLS. Few
remain, with poppy-heads. – BENCHES. Ends with poppy-
heads. Also one length of an original back with pierced tracery.
– POOR BOX. Very big, assigned to the C15. – SCULPTURE. A
mysterious stone hand reaches out from the S aisle S wall. Its
purpose may have been to hold a taper. – PAINTING. On the
tympanum inside the chancel arch C15 painting of the Crucifixion, unusually creditably preserved. It rests on the ROOD
BEAM. When the Reformation had established itself, it was
apparently turned round, and on its back, now facing the nave,
the ROYAL ARMS of Elizabeth I were painted. – PLATE.
Norwich-made Chalice, 1567–8; Paten, 1710. – MONUMENT.
In the graveyard, SW of the S porch, tombstone to Frank
Harding Chambers † 1912, by *Voysey*. It is a plain pillar of
smooth grey stone tapering into a pointed top. Golden cross
carved on this and inscription below.

LUDHAM HALL. The house itself has a plain Georgian front of
six bays and two storeys with a two-bay pediment. But the
gable-end shows that this is only a remodelling of a Jacobean

house and, moreover, there is, at r. angles to it, a CHAPEL, built of brick, with a slender W tower and large arched windows, clearly of the C17. All this belongs to a house of the bishops of Lincoln which was burnt in 1611 and then rebuilt and enlarged by Bishop Harsnett. He added the chapel. The bishops of Lincoln came to Ludham because at the Dissolution Henry VIII did not strictly dissolve St Benet's Abbey (*see* below), but made the last abbot Bishop of Lincoln. To this day the Bishop of Lincoln is Abbot of St Benet's.

Ludham is an attractive village with a number of nice houses. The only one to be singled out is at Hull Common. It must be of the ending C17. It is of chequered brick and has wooden cross-windows and shaped end-gables. Later doorway.

WINDMILLS. One below Ludham Bridge, another 1 m. NW of the church, derelict too, but with sails and the external gearing. Also, ¾ m. NE of the church, stump of a tower mill.

ST BENET'S ABBEY, 1¾ m. SSW. The abbey was founded before the Conquest, but none of the scanty fragments that remain are early. The best-preserved part is the GATEHOUSE, though even that is a curiosity more than a monument of architectural beauty, owing to the fact that an C18 brick WINDMILL set itself up inside its ruins. The gatehouse has a wide and high two-centred arch flanked by niches towards the river Bure. To the outside there remains one polygonal turret. The other has disappeared. The decoration with raised square frames filled with squared knapped flint is almost Renaissance in character. The interior is vaulted, and two foliage capitals survive. A good deal further E on a slight eminence above the river the fragments of the CHURCH, i.e. the N wall of its nave and parts of the S wall. There were no aisles. Also a lump of the W façade and the outline of the N transept with a (no doubt) later large chapel to its E. The wall a good deal S, with diagonal end-buttresses, marks the chapter house. To its S the dormitory would have extended, and the reredorter, i.e. the lavatories, would thus have been conveniently near the river.

MANNINGTON

CHURCH. In ruins. Nave and chancel only. Under trees and[1030] surrounded by a curious romantic and picturesque display of antiquarian fragments, arches, a seated statue, etc. These were assembled by the second Earl of Orford of Mannington Hall (*see* below). Inside the church is his MONUMENT, a long, bare sarcophagus. He died in 1898.

MANNINGTON HALL. Licence to crenellate was given in 1451, and a house was under construction in 1460. Internal details are mentioned in Margaret Paston's will in 1505. The house was much interfered with by the second Earl of Orford (*see* above) who came into the title in 1846.* The house is most impressive from the s, where it appears behind the moat – which incidentally surrounds it on all sides. There are here two polygonal angle towers, the smaller on the r. containing the staircase, the larger on the l. apparently of domestic use. It adjoined the parlour, which in the customary way adjoined the Hall. The main entrance to the house with a small Perp doorway is on the w side, and the Hall fireplace with its large beam is still there. The screens passage has gone. So has the E exit, although there is an inexplicable two-centred arch close to and at r. angles to where it must have been. This may well have been brought in from a church. Its date seems decidedly earlier than that of the house. To the N of the Hall were buttery and pantry. The kitchen may always have been in a wing projecting to the w, which still has its original brickwork on the w side. There is a fine stone fireplace in the parlour and another in a room above the buttery. The house is of brick with brick window details cemented over. These details are puzzling. Has the house e.g. always had its second floor? Also some windows near the N end of the W front have cusped lights, others near the s end and on the s side uncusped ones. The detail of the latter seems later than 1500, the detail of the earlier is not usual in, but could be of, *c.*1460. The second-floor windows would be conservative for a date after 1550. In all this there is the additional uncertainty of the Earl of Orford's work. What he added to the house, and especially the s front (on the r.) and the back, is patent enough. The mysogynic inscriptions in black-letter are also evidently his, but how far has he made Gothic detail more Gothic ?‡ Inside, the

* He made his alterations in 1864.

‡ The inscriptions run as follows: On one side of the door – 'Trust your bark to the winds, do not trust your heart to girls. For the wave is safer than a woman's faith. There is no good woman, and if one attains to any good I know not how an ill-made thing becomes good.' On the other side of the door: 'A tiger is something worse than a snake, a demon than a tiger, a woman than a demon, and nothing worse than a woman.' A little way from the door is a third and longer inscription, which runs thus: 'Quid est Mulier hominis confusio, insatiabilis bestia, solicitudo continua, indesinens pugna, quotidianum damnum, tempestas domus, solicitudinis impedimentum, viri incontinentis naufragium, adulterii vas, inconcisum proelium, animal proximum, pondus gravissimum, aspis insatiabilis, humanum mancipium.'

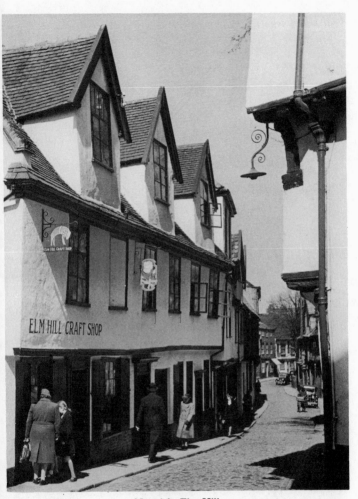

Norwich, Elm Hill

(a) *The Broads:* Horning

(b) Horstead, mill

(a) Cromer, from East Cliff

(b) *Coast Erosion:* Eccles, ruins of the church

3

(a) East Somerton, St Mary

(b) Mundesley, windmill

4

Norwich Cathedral

(a) Norwich Cathedral, north transept, before 1145

(b) Binham Priory, west front, before 1244

6

Great Yarmouth, St Nicholas, west front, thirteenth century

Norwich Cathedral, cloister, north-east doorway, *c.* 1310

Norwich, Carnary College, founded 1316, figure from hood-mould of west doorway

(b) Norwich Cathedral, cloister, 1297–c. 1430, east range

(a) Norwich, St Ethelbert's Gate, 1316

10

(a) Norwich Cathedral, cloister, south range

(b) Norwich Cathedral, cloister, north range

II

(a) *Church Exteriors, Decorated and Perpendicular:* Cley-next-the-Sea

(b) *Church Exteriors, Decorated and Perpendicular:* Worstead, mainly begun 1379, chancel earlier(?)

(a) *Church Exteriors, Perpendicular:* Norwich, Blackfriars, 1440–70

(b) *Church Exteriors, Perpendicular:* Brandiston

13

(b) Norwich, Erpingham Gate, 1420, detail

(a) Norwich, Erpingham Gate, 1420

14

Church Exteriors, Perpendicular: Norwich, St Peter Mancroft, begun 1430

15

(a) *Church Exteriors, Perpendicular: Norwich,
St Michael at Coslany*

(b) *Church Exteriors, Perpendicular: Cromer*

16

Church Exteriors, Eighteenth Century: Great Yarmouth, St George, by John Price, 1714–16

(a) *Church Exteriors, Eighteenth Century:* Gunton, by Robert Adam,
1769

(b) *Church Exteriors, Nineteenth Century:* Norwich, St John
Baptist, by G. G. Scott Jun. and J. Oldrid Scott, 1884–1910

(a) *Nonconformist Chapels, Exteriors:* Norwich, Old Meeting, 1693

(b) *Nonconformist Chapels, Exteriors:* Norwich, Octagon Chapel, by
Thomas Ivory, 1754–6

19

Church Interiors, Norman: Norwich Cathedral, chancel, before 1145; clerestory *c.* 1360–70, vault *c.* 1480–90

Church Interiors, Norman: Binham Priory

(a) *Church Interiors, Early English:* Burgh-next-Aylsham, *c.* 1220–30

(b) *Church Interiors, Early English:* Blakeney

(a) Bacton, Broomholm Priory, north transept, Early English

(b) Tunstead, sedilia, fourteenth century

23

Norwich Cathedral, cloister, after 1297, boss with St Luke

Norwich Cathedral, cloister, boss with the Sealing of the Tomb

(a) *Church Interiors, Perpendicular*: Norwich, St Giles

(b) *Church Interiors, Perpendicular*: Norwich, St Stephen

26

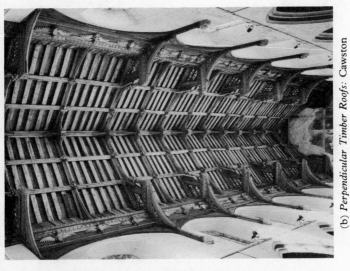

(a) *Perpendicular Timber Roofs: Salle*

(b) *Perpendicular Timber Roofs: Cawston*

27

(a) *Perpendicular Timber Roofs:* Norwich, St Mary at Coslany

(b) *Nonconformist Chapel Interior:* Norwich, Octagon Chapel,
by Thomas Ivory, 1754–6

Church Furnishings: Sloley, panel showing Confirmation from the Seven Sacraments font, Perpendicular

Church Furnishings: Trunch, font canopy, Perpendicular

(a) *Church Furnishings:* Taverham, communion rail, part of a
fourteenth-century screen

(b) *Church Furnishings:* Happisburgh, screen, Perpendicular

(a) *Church Furnishings*: Barton Turf, painted figure from the screen, mid fifteenth century

(b) *Church Furnishings*: Catton, pulpit, 1537

32

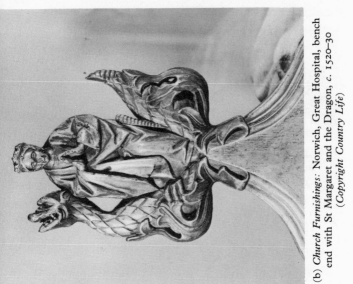

(b) *Church Furnishings*: Norwich, Great Hospital, bench end with St Margaret and the Dragon, *c.* 1520–30
(Copyright Country Life)

(a) *Church Furnishings*: Irstead, stall arm, thirteenth century

33

Church Furnishings: Norwich Cathedral, misericord, fifteenth century

Church Furnishings: Trowse Newton, pulpit with figures of King David and an angel, probably from an organ gallery

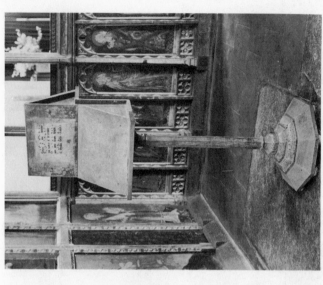

(a) *Church Furnishings*: Barton Turf, door into the tower. Perpendicular

(b) *Church Furnishings*: Ranworth, cantor's desk

36

(a) *Church Furnishings*: Norwich, St Gregory, door-knocker, fourteenth century

(b) *Church Furnishings*: Tunstead, south door, ironwork fourteenth century

37

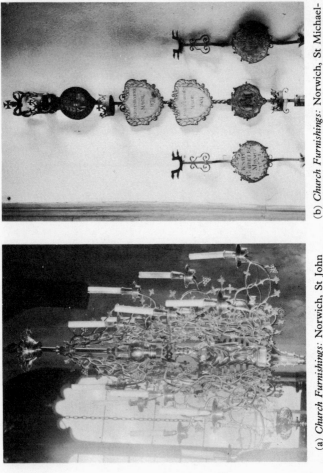

(a) *Church Furnishings:* Norwich, St John Baptist Timberhill, chandelier, probably

(b) *Church Furnishings:* Norwich, St Michael-at-Plea, sword and mace rests, eighteenth

38

(a) *Church Furnishings*: Felbrigg, Paten, with figure of St Margaret, c. 1500

(b) *Church Furnishings*: Burlingham St Andrew, chalice, 1567–8

(a) *Church Furnishings*: Potter Heigham, wall painting of one of the Works of Mercy, probably late fourteenth century

(b) *Church Monuments*: Norwich Cathedral, Herbert de Losinga(?) †1119

40

Church Monuments: Reepham, Sir Roger de Kerdiston †1337

41

Church Monuments: North Walsham, Sir William Paston, 1608 by John Key

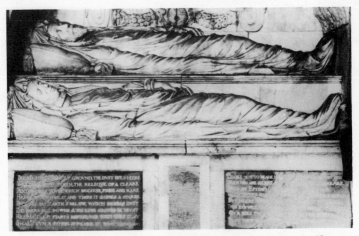

(a) *Church Monuments:* Spixworth, William Peck †1635 and wife
by Edward Marshall

(b) Blickling, mausoleum to the Earl and Countess of Buckinghamshire,
1793 by Joseph Bonomi

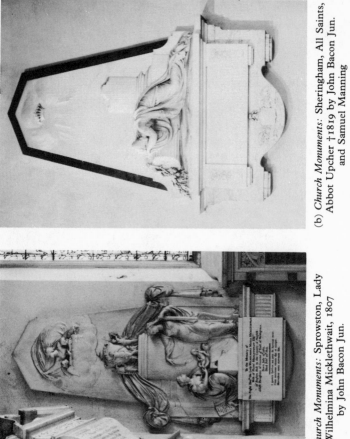

(a) *Church Monuments:* Sprowston, Lady Wilhelmina Micklethwait, 1807 by John Bacon Jun.

(b) *Church Monuments:* Sheringham, All Saints, Abbot Upcher †1819 by John Bacon Jun. and Samuel Manning

(a) *Norfolk Headstones:* Blakeney, †1772

(b) *Norfolk Headstones:* Cley-next-the-Sea, †1791

45

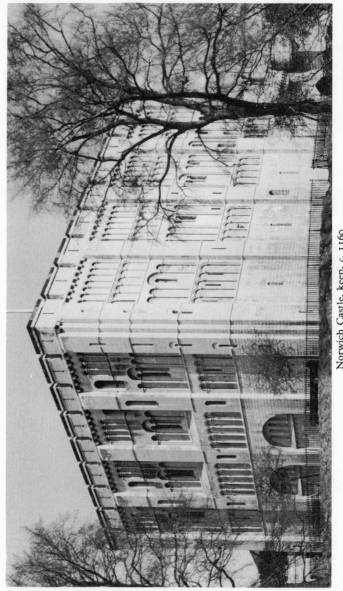

Norwich Castle, keep, c. 1160

(a) Norwich, Cow Tower, c. 1378

(b) Caister Castle, 1432-5

47

Norwich Guildhall, Council Chamber, completed 1535

(a) Carrow Abbey, Prioress's Lodging, early sixteenth century

(b) Blickling Hall, fireplace from Caister Castle, Early Tudor and eighteenth century

49

(a) East Barsham Manor House, *c.* 1520–3c

(b) Heydon Hall, 1581–4

(a) Barningham Hall, 1612

(b) Felbrigg Hall, *c.* 1620

Blickling Hall by Robert Lyminge, c. 1616–27

Blickling Hall, c. 1616–27, gallery

(a) Blickling Hall, detail of the ceiling of the gallery

(b) Blickling Hall, staircase, seventeenth century and 1767

54

Great Yarmouth, No. 4 South Quay, ceiling, c. 1600

(b) Felbrigg Hall, ceiling in the drawing room, 1687

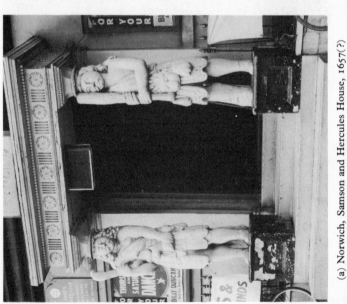

(a) Norwich, Samson and Hercules House, 1657(?)

56

Melton Constable, Melton Hall, c. 1664–c. 70

Norwich, Churchman's House, c. 1740–50, ceiling

Great Yarmouth, St Nicholas Hospital, by Edward Holl, 1809–11

Norwich, Messrs Jarrolds, by John Brown and Richard Parkinson, 1834

Holt, Home Place, by E. S. Prior, 1903–5

Norwich, Norwich Union, by G. J. Skipper, 1903–4

(a) Norwich, Royal Arcade, by G. J. Skipper, early twentieth century

(b) Norwich, Messrs Roberts, by A. F. Scott, 1903

63

Norwich City Hall, by C. H. James & S. R. Pierce, 1932–8

following further details are of interest: the overmantel in the Drawing Room which comes from Thwaite Hall, and the fireplace in the Morning Room, probably that originally in the Hall. The panelling in the Morning Room comes from Irmingland Hall, dated 1609.

MARSHAM
1080

ALL SAINTS. The S doorway is E.E., though somewhat altered. The chancel and the W tower seem early C14, but the chancel has a Perp E window. Aisle and clerestory also Perp, including the aisle arcades (five bays, octagonal piers, double-hollow-chamfered arches). The roof is delightful, especially if one tries to forget the later tie-beams. Without them it was an alternation of hammerbeams and simple horizontal beams, the latter placed on the apexes of the longitudinal arched braces. The transverse arched braces on the hammerbeams and the other horizontal beams rise to the ridge. Angel figures against both. – FONT. On two steps, the upper decorated with pointed quatrefoils. Octagonal with four seated figures and the signs of the four Evangelists against the stem, the Seven Sacraments and the Last Judgement (ingeniously condensed) against the bowl. – SCREEN. Tall, one-light divisions, the arches ogee, cusped. On the dado sixteen painted Saints. Below quatrefoils. Early C16. – BENCHES. Some, with poppy-heads. – SCULPTURE. Odd fragment in the N aisle perhaps from a churchyard cross. – STAINED GLASS. Chancel S by *Kempe*. – PLATE. Elizabethan Chalice and Paten.

(BOLWICK HALL. Two of the Nine Worthies in STAINED GLASS, Norwich School, late C15. Probably of the same origin as the roundels at Brandiston Hall. Woodforde) See p. 390

MARTHAM
4010

ST MARY. A substantial W tower with a lead-covered spike. Base with flushwork panelling. Transomed windows of Early Perp forms. Very tall tower arch with one moulding with suspended little shields. If the tower is Early Perp, so are the W responds of the arcade. They have the same familiar details as e.g. those of Great Walsingham. The arcades themselves, however, are fully C15 in their details. Piers roughly lozenge-shaped with thin shafts, only a minimum of capitals, and long shallow hollows in the diagonals. To this correspond the larger aisle windows with four-centred arches, identical on the N and s sides. They are set in giant arcading inside. The design of the windows is repeated in the three-light clerestory windows. The s aisle has a frieze of shields below the windows outside. s porch of two storeys with flushwork panelling l. and r. of the entrance, and above a three-light window flanked by niches. Tierceron-star-vault inside. But if one takes an impartial view, the *clou* of the church is the chancel, built in 1855–61 as a memorial to the Rev. Jonathan Dawson at the expense of Mrs Alice Langley. The architect was *Philip Boyce*, and neither money nor inventiveness were spared. The E window is a splash and the chancel arch even more so. The monument to Mr Dawson, in the form of the traditional Easter Sepulchre, the arcading of the E wall, the Sedilia, and the stone PULPIT are all in keeping. Nothing seems to be known about Boyce, except that an architect Boyce belonged to the Institute of Architects in 1848–52.* – FONT. Octagonal, with eight statuettes against the stem and the Seven Sacraments against the bowl. – ROOD SCREEN. Of wrought iron, part of the work of 1855–61. – BENCHES. Ends with poppy-heads. – SOUTH DOOR. Traceried and with a charming broad band of foliage trails. – STAINED GLASS. Many single C15 figures, re-set in the aisle E windows: also one Flemish panel (Mocking of Christ). – PLATE. Norwich-made Chalice and Cover, 1567–8. – (BRASS. Robert Alen † 1487; a heart with an inscription; 4½ in. long, chancel s.)

The village has a spacious Green and many attractive C18 houses.

MATLASK
1030

ST PETER. Round tower with Dec octagonal top. In the flint walling odd stretches of what look like Roman tiles. The chancel disappeared in 1726. The nave and s aisle Perp externally, but the arcade of three bays Dec. Octagonal piers, double-chamfered arches. Good, big stone corbel heads for the roof. – PLATE. Chalice, made in Norwich, 1567: Paten without marks.

MAUTBY
4010

ST PETER AND ST PAUL. Round tower with later octagonal top. Former s aisle of the C13. The arcade is preserved in the s wall and has octagonal piers, the bases with angle spurs, and double-

* Information kindly obtained for me by Mr Molesworth Roberts. Mr Peter Ferriday's Index (*see* Foreword) calls him of Cheltenham (*Builder* 1856, where it is said that he also rebuilt the arcades). The carving is by *M. Earp* (*Builder* 1861).

chamfered arches. It is a pity the aisle has not survived; for in
it was the monument commissioned by Margaret Paston,
daughter of John Mautby, widow of John Paston and writer of
so many of the Paston letters. The specification for the monument exists, but not alas the monument. Chancel of *c*.1300,
see the tracery of the windows and the mouldings of the
priest's doorway. Dec nave N windows, the middle one different in its tracery from the first and the third. Tall Perp tower
arch, remarkably tall for a round tower. – FONT. Simple,
octagonal, with four shields and four quatrefoils. – FONT
COVER. Partly medieval, with crocketed ribs. – SCREEN. Of
one-light divisions with ogee arches and panel tracery above
them. – STAINED GLASS. Good C14 canopies etc. (predominantly green and yellow) in the Dec nave windows. –
PLATE. Elizabethan Chalice and Paten. – MONUMENTS.
Knight, stone, with crossed legs, much defaced, in a low ogee-
arched tomb-recess. – Tablet to Richard Gay Lucas † 1771.
Pretty, and still more Early than Late Georgian in style.

MAYTON
1½ m. NW of Horstead
2020

BRIDGE. A C15 bridge of two pointed arches. At the NE and SE
ends of the parapet a little niche with a seat under a roof.

MELTON CONSTABLE
0030

ST PETER. The church lies in the grounds of the Hall. The
college which once extended to its S has gone. The church is
small but interesting, though not very precise in its message.
The Norman evidence is clear enough: a central tower, pre-
supposing a nave and a chancel. Norman windows in two tiers
appear outside. One Norman window also remains on the N
side.* Internally the W arch is intact, the E arch replaced. The
W arch is perfectly simple, unmoulded, and rests on the
simplest imposts. But above it, a first-rate surprise, is a double
opening with a Norman pier – not just a shaft – to separate the
two arched parts, a pier about 3 ft in diameter, as if we were in
a cathedral, not a small parish church. The later windows are
divers and not of special interest, except for the low-side
window in the chancel, to the W of which is a rough arched
niche with a seat, a very unusual arrangement. To the r. of the
arch, W of the central space, an ogee-headed crocketed recess
for the reredos of a former side altar. – FONT. An C18 baluster.

* The Norman doorway in the W wall is, needless to say, Victorian.

– PAINTING. Flemish triptych, attributed to *Rubens*. –
PLATE. Norwich-made Chalice and Paten on foot inscribed
1680; another Paten also *c*.1680. – HASTINGS PEW. This was
built in 1681. To the outside it appears odd, with its boulder-
like angle-stones not forming proper quoins. Inside raised by
some steps. – MONUMENTS. Many to members of the Astley
family. Not one of them either grand in scale or grandilo-
quent. All are tablets. The following may be singled out: Sir
Jacob † 1729, Dame Lucy † 1739, Sir Philip † 1739 (with two
portrait medallions, a sarcophagus below, and a pediment with
two reclining putti; by *Robert Page*), Lucy and Judith, 1742
(also by *Page*), Sir Jacob † 1760 (again by *Page*), Dame Anne
† 1768 (a l. half of a Rococo composition, as it were, i.e. completely asymmetrical – cf. W. Offley † 1767, St Giles, Norwich),
Sir Edward † 1803. All these are in the Hastings Pew. Also
Rhoda and Sylvia † 1808 and † 1807, by the younger *Bacon*
(with two draped sarcophagi and above a chariot rising into
the clouds), Lady Stanhope † 1812, of *Coade* stone, with a reclining female figure at the top, and Sir Jacob Henry Astley
† 1855 by *Manning*, with a big draped sarcophagus.

57 MELTON HALL. The essential part is the rectangular block of
brick with stone dressings which is said to have been built in
1664–*c*.70. All that is in fact known is that Sir Jacob Astley,
then still in his twenties, began to pull down the old house in
1664. Decoration was still applied in the eighties, as we shall
see. Sir Jacob's house is one of the most perfect examples of
the so-called Christopher Wren house, which has nothing to
do with him, but much with such older men as Pratt. The
model, later a doll's house, which is kept at the hall and which,
beyond differing in several minor details, has a cupola on the
hipped roof, makes this relation particularly clear. The house
is of nine bays by seven and consists of an ashlar-faced ground
floor treated as a basement and two upper floors. Nicely
framed windows. Three-bay projections in the centre of the
entrance and garden façades with pediments enclosing foliage
carving. The N (entrance) doorway may be altered, the S doorway, reached by an C18 staircase in two arms with wrought-
iron handrails, has fluted Corinthian columns. In the centre of
the W side, a terrace with four attenuated Tuscan columns was
added in 1757. On the E side a link of 1810, refaced on its S
side in 1887, connects the house with an Elizabethan service
range projecting far N. The Elizabethan evidence here and in
the stable yard behind was thoroughly disguised in 1810. To the

s of the stable yard and further s, as an extension of the garden side, additions of 1920–6. All this is of limited interest, whereas the c17 house is of far more than mere county importance.

Inside, only a few rooms have kept their c17 decoration. The Red Drawing Room, facing s, has a ceiling, dated 1687, which is a *nec plus ultra* in plasterer's artistry. The craftsman was probably the same who worked at Felbrigg in the same year and at Hintlesham in Suffolk *c.*1690. The ceiling at Melton contains game-birds and flowers and fruit in frames and panels, all most daringly modelled and undercut. The same brilliant craftsmanship on the ceiling of the NE corner room on the upper floor (now a bathroom) and on the staircase ceiling and the underside of the upper landing. The staircase itself has boldly twisted balusters, two to the tread, and carved tread-ends. The window placed high up gives on to the w side of the hipped roof. Several good later fireplaces, especially the one in the Saloon (formerly Chapel). This has putto caryatids and seems to be mid-c18.

In the grounds to the w the former MENAGERIE, castellated, with pointed windows, and probably late c18. Much further away, outside the grounds, beyond the Thursford Road, 1 m. N of the Hall, is what can only be described as a STANDING, i.e. an Elizabethan lookout tower. It is round and five-storeyed, has a pyramid roof, and must have had mullioned windows. Later the lower parts were encased into an octagonal shape, and this work carries the date 1721.

CULPIT'S FARM, ¾ m. SE of the church. With shaped c17 gables and a Georgian refacing of the front (three bays).

METTON

2030

ST ANDREW. Unbuttressed w tower of the early c14. Bell-openings with Y-tracery. An uncommon feature the N–S passage through the tower, made in all probability because the w boundary of the consecrated ground did not allow processions to pass further w. Chancel early c14 too. The tracery again Y, also intersected (E window). Piscina with ogee arch. Former Sedilia with shallow trefoiled ogee arches in the jambs. Of the original nave roof only the wall-plate is preserved. The roofs are now boarded, and the effect is intimate and not at all jarring. – ORGAN CASE. 1850, but still Grecian, i.e. pre-Victorian. – PLATE. Norwich-made Chalice of 1567 and Paten without date. – BRASS. Robert Doughty † 1493 and wife, 18 in. figures.

MANOR FARMHOUSE, NE of the church. Elizabethan or Jacobean. Flint and red-brick dressings. Small oblong without projections. One window mullioned and transomed. Several windows with pediments. Stepped gable.

0040   MORSTON

ALL SAINTS. The churchyard is large, without trees and with few graves. C13 W tower with original windows. The buttresses are a later addition. Late C13 chancel. Lancets and Late Geometrical and intersected tracery. Late C13 arcades of four bays. Circular piers with octagonal abaci and double-chamfered arches. The responds on head corbels. Clerestory with quatrefoils in squares. The aisle W windows and the S doorway also late C13 or c.1300. – FONT. Against the bowl the Signs of the four Evangelists and four seated Saints. – SCREEN. Eight Saints painted on the dado. Good carving in the spandrels, unusually many small figures. – PLATE. Chalice, Norwich, 1567–8; Cover, 1815–16, but foot is that of the old C16 Cover and is inscribed 1567. – MONUMENTS. Brass to Richard Makynges † 1596 (below the altar). – Susan Kinges † 1615. Alabaster tablet. The frame with strapwork, fruit, a skull, an hour-glass, the grave-digger's tools, a coffin, and a reversed torch. The inscription reads:

See
P.
390

> Though Gifts of Nature yet they Gifts of Grace
> The all-devouringe grave cannot Deface.
> Wittness they Godly life, they blessed End,
> Thy Conflicts and thy Conquest of ye feind
> When to thy Present Frindes Thy Dying Breath
> Did sounde they joyfull tryumph over death.
> Thy sacred ashes in the earth shall rest
> Till union make both soule and Body Blest.

3000   MOULTON ST MARY

ST MARY. Round tower with a conical roof. Nave and chancel seem to be of c.1300. Single-framed roof. The double Piscina in the chancel with a pointed sexfoil in the spandrel is the best feature. S porch of brick with brick entrance arch; C16. – FONT. C13, Purbeck marble, octagonal, with two shallow arches on each side. – PULPIT. Jacobean, with a pretty back panel and tester. It is undated, but the READER'S DESK obviously belongs to it, and this has the date 1619. – BENCHES. Ends with poor poppy-heads. – COMMUNION RAIL. C17. – PAINTINGS. On the N wall St Christopher, on the S wall the

Works of Mercy. Late C14 to *c*.1400. – PLATE. Chalice, Norwich, 1567; Paten, 1567; Dish, secular, London, 1662. – MONUMENTS. Brass to Thomasine Palmer † 1544, a small (7 in.) kneeling figure. – Edmund Anguishes, 1628. Alabaster tablet. Kneeling couple, and above, rather squeezed in below the arch, a third figure, a frontal bust, hands on a skull.

MUNDESLEY   3030

ALL SAINTS. Restored from a ruinous state in 1904 and 1914. At Ladbrooke's time one third of the w end was still roofed. The oldest original feature is a Norman (or Transitional) slit-window on the N side which has a pointed head. The fenestration Perp. – PULPIT. Jacobean, with tester. It was originally at Sprowston, Norwich. – PLATE. Paten, Norwich, 1567; Chalice, *c*.1680.

ROOKERY HOUSE. Queen Anne, but partly remodelled in the early C19. Five bays, two storeys, one-bay projection with doorway and pediment. The doorway has a scrolly open pediment. Is this part original?

Mundesley made an effort to develop into a second Cromer during the same 1890s when Cromer shot into prominence. Witness are the HOTEL CONTINENTAL of 1892 and the MANOR HOTEL of 1900 (by *Pearce*), both red brick and gabled. Close to the former, MEADOW CROFT, a pretty cottage with Tudor windows and wavy bargeboards. It looks *c*.1840, but is said to date from *c*.1760.

WINDMILL. A brick tower-mill, still complete with cap and 4b sails.

NEATISHEAD   3020

ST PETER, Three Hammer Common. Built in 1790, the windows altered in 1870. Above the w doorway fragment of the medieval church, perhaps from the porch. Frieze of shields and, in the middle, three figures in relief praying frontally. Medieval also the pretty Piscina in the chancel. – FONT. With panelled stem and bowl, two different patterns. – PULPIT. With linenfold panelling. – BENCHES. A few. – PLATE. Chalice and Paten Cover, Norwich, 1567.

BAPTIST CHURCH, ⅜ m. w. 1809. The façade of four bays with two entrances with broken pediments and two arched windows between.

WINDMILL, ⅜ m. sw. Stump of a brick tower-mill with conical roof.

NORTH BARNINGHAM

St Peter. A small church, damaged in the C18 and restored in 1893. The N aisle has evidence of *c.*1300 (Y-tracery). The chief contribution is Dec: the fine S window with intersected ogee tracery, the mullions having the characteristic moulding of the sunk quadrant, and the damaged Sedilia and Piscina which have buttresses and pinnacles inlaid in darker stone and even the cusps of the arch inlaid. Perp the W tower with a big, transomed window and the N arcade (four bays, low octagonal piers, double-chamfered arches). – TILING. In the nave floor the quite unusual device of a rose-window set out in tiles and stone. – PLATE. Chalice, engraved 1768. – MONUMENTS. To members of the Palgrave family of the Hall: Brass to Henry † 1516 and wife, he robust and swagger, she thin. 31 in. figures, with children at the base (N aisle, E end). – John † 1611, tomb-chest with shields, back wall alabaster with three small allegorical figures, inscription with strapwork decoration above. – Mrs Pope † 1621. Two angels in long garments hold up the curtains of the baldacchino under which she kneels. Big superstructure curving forward. – Sir Austin † 1639. Standing monument of grey, white, and pink. Two frontal busts of white marble in grey oval surrounds. Grey columns l. and r. carrying a big, almost semicircular pediment.

North Barningham Hall, ¼ m. E. Fragment of a large mansion, probably of the early C17 with some remodelling about 1700. From the position of the garden walls and the big chimneybreast one can assume that it was of H-shape and that the surviving wing was the kitchen wing. The Hall would have been at r. angles to it, and its entrance in axis with the gate-piers of the garden.

NORTH BURLINGHAM see BURLINGHAM ST ANDREW

NORTHREPPS

St Mary. The only Norman survival is some zigzag in stones at the E end, the only E.E. survival two lancet windows in the chancel, one of them oddly close to the E end. C14 the arcades of four bays with octagonal piers and double-chamfered arches and also the chancel arch. Otherwise the church is Perp. W tower with W doorway, a frieze over of crowned Ms for Mary and crowned IHSs for Christ. The same in the flushwork of the battlements. Sound-holes with simple tracery (four-petalled flower), three-light bell-openings. Nave roof with wall-posts, longitudinal arched braces, a quatrefoiled wall-plate, and transverse arched braces. Much of the roof is C19. – FONT. Panelled stem, quatrefoiled bowl. – SCREEN. Dado with double-cusped tracery and an inscription referring to John Playford and his wife. – (AUMBRY. Of terracotta.) – BENCHES. Ends with poppy-heads. – SOUTH DOOR. Big iron hinges. The cross in the middle is about 4 ft high. The work is probably C14. – PLATE. Plain Chalice of 1567, Norwich-made; Paten Cover, engraved 1567, but remade.

TEMPLEWOOD, 1 m. SE. Built by *Seely & Paget* for Lord Templewood (Sir Samuel Hoare) in 1938. The house was built as a shooting-box. It is small, single-storeyed, and very pretty. It incorporates C18 fragments from the Nuthall Temple near Nottingham (1754) and from Soane's Bank of England, and blends them by being itself in the Georgian style of Palladian villas. The garden carries on the theme by straight vistas. The whole looks in an engaging way like a stage-set for an Italian C18 opera, performed in England in the C20. The material is brick, painted a subdued yellow. The entrance is from the w. Attached portico of four columns with big pediment. The columns came from the Bank of England. Two sphinxes flank the terrace in front of the portico. They came from the Nuthall Temple. Behind and above the portico appears the raised centre of the house, containing the Saloon. To the s this centre has circular windows and below it is a recessed veranda with columns. The columns again from the Bank of England, the fine wrought-iron balcony railing above the veranda from the Nuthall Temple. From the latter place also the semicircular E terrace and the hanging garlands round one circular S and the circular E window.

THE COTTAGE, ¾ m. NW. *W. Wilkins Sen.* had made designs in 1792 for a house for Bartlett Gurney. They came to nothing and all that was built was The Cottage, a modest house, of flint and yellow brick with a Gothic doorway and Gothic glazing-bars.

NORTH WALSHAM

2030

ST NICHOLAS. A big town church, about 160 ft long. The w tower partly collapsed in 1724. It has never been rebuilt, and looks decorative enough as a crag dominating the town. It was a tower with a quatrefoil frieze at the base, but otherwise remarkably bare. Its original size was 147 ft, i.e. it was one of the tallest in Norfolk. The tower arch is very tall, and right up there the springers of a vault are preserved. To the N of the tower part of a former tower. What is its date? The body of the church is much restored. It is partly Dec and partly Perp. The tall arcades of seven bays came first. They have quatrefoil piers with fillets, thin filleted shafts in the diagonals, and still round, not polygonal, capitals and abaci. In the w wall of the N aisle is a small lancet window. The other aisle windows have mostly intersected tracery and thus correspond to the arcade. The s doorway also is evidently Dec. The chancel is Dec too, but the E window tracery dates from 1874. The s porch is a showpiece of the late C14. The heraldry confirms the date (Cautley : Edward III and John of Gaunt). Flushwork panelling on base and parapet. Flushwork shields on the battlements. Tall entrance. Shields in the spandrels in cusped fields. Niches l. and r. Above a niche and much flushwork panelling. It extends also into the gable, which is oddly like a pediment. Stone pinnacles l. and r. Inside an arch-braced roof. – FONT COVER. Tall Perp canopy, ending in a pelican. Much restored. Suspended from a cambered beam. – COMMUNION TABLE, s chapel. The inscription along the front is taken from the first Prayer Book of Edward VI and dates the table as between 1549 and 1552. – SCREENS. The rood screen has only its dado preserved. It showed twenty painted Saints. One has perished, two are now hidden. – From a second screen the broad panels in the s and N aisles with green and red grounds and an inscription. Complicated tracery. The little figures in the spandrels are excellently carved and obviously C14. – PLATE. Chalice, London, 1646; Chalice, c.1650; Paten, c.1670; Paten without marks; Paten and Flagon, 1723. – MONUMENTS. Brasses to Robert Wythe c.1500 (s chapel) and to Edmund Ward † 1519 (N aisle), both with chalices. – Sir William Paston, 1608 by *John Key*. Excellent standing alabaster monument. He lies comfortably, propped up on his elbow. Coffered arch behind with the inscription surrounded by graceful ribbonwork. Coupled mauve-coloured columns l. and r. Superstructure with three obelisks, two columns flanking the coat-of-arms and supporters l. and r. of the top obelisk. The price of the monument was £200. – Several tablets with urns and obelisks. Dates of death 1785, 1803, 1815.

FRIENDS' MEETING HOUSE. *See* Swafield, p. 326.

THE TOWN. There is little to see at North Walsham, and it can

best be seen by starting from the church. This lies nicely behind the Market Place with gardens or backs of houses facing
it. Only on the E a street runs along the churchyard, CHURCH
STREET, where one corner house has shaped gables. A little
further N, at the beginning of BACTON ROAD a five-bay house
with giant angle pilasters. Nothing of note in the MARKET
PLACE except the MARKET CROSS, an octagonal timber
structure rebuilt after a great fire in 1602. Rough posts, twice
truncated dome with double lantern lighting. The Market
Place has, however, the visual attraction of being funnel-
shaped and of then contracting to the W with a narrow passage
and a wider space, again funnel-shaped. From the narrow
passage a back entrance leads to the PASTON SCHOOL, i.e. the
Boys' Grammar School, whose original building dates from
1765. It is a plain red-brick range of seven bays and two and a
half storeys with a hipped roof. Nelson went to school here
from 1768 to 1771. Several later additions. To the W from the
Market Place in MARKET STREET on the l., recessed from the
street, a good three-bay house of grey brick with a Greek Doric
porch *in antis*, now part of the Girls' High School. The house
lies close to the corner of AYLSHAM ROAD, and here, on the W
side, first the ANGEL INN, three bays, two and a half storeys,
grey brick, with a one-bay pediment, and then, a little way on,
a handsome Georgian brick house of five bays and two storeys
with giant angle pilasters and a doorway with broken pediment
on attached, unfluted Ionic columns.

In VICARAGE STREET, the street running parallel with Market
Street to its N, close to the corner of Mundesley Road the
CHURCH ROOMS, built in 1828 as Fisher's Theatre.

INTRODUCTION

Norwich has everything – a cathedral, a major castle on a mound right in the middle, walls and towers, an undisturbed medieval centre with winding streets and alleys, thirty-two medieval parish churches, and a river – or really two rivers – with steamships (even if only small ones), and with motor-yachts and sailing-boats. It even has hills, though people tend to forget that, and they are steep towards the S and SE. It also has an almost complete ring-road, yet the traffic in the centre is as terrible as ever, and to enjoy the buildings of Norwich one has to go out on a Sunday morning early.

The city had about 120,000 inhabitants at the census of 1961, that is it is Britain's thirty-third city. But in the Middle Ages it was the second or third city of England, and only Bristol and perhaps York could compete with it. Already at the time of the

Conquest it was second in size (apart of course from London) to York only. Over 1,300 burghers are recorded. It is estimated that its population in the later C14 was about 5,000, at the time of Elizabeth I about 15,000, in 1700 just under 30,000. A hundred years later it had risen to about 40,000, in 1840 to over 60,000. Norwich received its first charter in 1158, and was granted a mayor in 1404. Trade was greatly helped by two streams of immigrants from the Netherlands, first c.1336, and again (promoted by the Duke of Norfolk) in 1565. The commercial prosperity of Norwich in the C14 to C16 is confirmed by the large number of essentially Perp parish churches (*see* Introduction to Churches, p. 234) and in addition by the houses of friars established in Norwich. The other orders had left Norwich aside – except of course for the Cathedral Priory. Carrow, the house of Benedictine Nuns, was outside the walls. The Franciscans arrived at Norwich in 1226, the Dominicans in the same year, the Pied Friars in 1253, the Carmelites in 1256, the Friars of the Sack c.1258, the Austin Friars c.1272. The prosperity of the city outlasted the late Middle Ages by several centuries. Celia Fiennes just before 1700 testifies to it (although she says that brick building is rare and only represented by some merchants' houses N of the river Wensum), and Defoe in 1723 testifies to it even more eloquently. On week-days, he says, the town seems deserted, because everybody is busy at the loom. So Norwich was still essentially a cloth, not a 'general-purpose' town. This changed only in the C19, as also the pattern of the town changed only then. The map of 1789 still shows hardly anything going on outside the medieval walls.

Today Norwich is distinguished by a prouder sense of civic responsibility than any other town of about the same size in Britain. It built a really monumental and for its date boldly modern City Hall between the two wars: it has its Assembly Room, and the Maddermarket Theatre, and it has four municipal museums. It has a good City Architect too, which is beginning to make itself felt, and some private architects whose work is of national interest.

The arrangement of Norwich in the following pages is that familiar from the treatment of other cities in *The Buildings of England*. Inner Norwich will be described first, Outer Norwich after. The boundary is to be roughly that of the walls, i.e. from the railway station S: Riverside, Carrow Hill, Queen's Road, Chapelfield Road (which remains outside), Grapes Hill, Barn Road, Station Road, Oak Street, Baker Road, Magpie Road.

Bull Close Road, Barrack Street (which remains outside), and back by Riverside Road.

As for Inner Norwich, the arrangement by Cathedral, Precinct, other churches, public buildings, perambulations is by now familiar to users of *The Buildings of England*. But the perambulations in this case need a word to themselves. Only the City of London and York can compare with Norwich in density of interesting buildings and intricacy of street pattern. Inner Norwich is about $1\frac{1}{2}$ m. from N to S and 1 m. from E to W, that is over a square mile, like London. This being so, it could do no good to enforce fixed walks. The arrangement had to be, as in the City of London, alphabetical by streets. The advantages of this are patent, but there is a disadvantage too. Some of the addicts of *The Buildings of England* like their conducted tours. For them three suggested itineraries follow here. They make mention of all the forty-nine streets listed under the Perambulations on pp. 266–80.

c. The Centre from the Market Place to the Cathedral.
Market Place and Hay Hill – Orford Hill – back by Davey Place – Exchange Street to the N – detour London Street to the E – St John Maddermarket and St Andrew's Hill – Princes Street and Elm Hill – Tombland and a detour into Queen Street, and then perhaps the Close.

N. To the North from the Cathedral to the Cathedral.
Palace Street – Palace Plain – Bishopgate (detour to Cow Tower) – back to Palace Plain – Cowgate – Fishergate – Fye Bridge Street – Magdalen Street (and the N parts of the Walls) – (St Augustine Street) – Gildencroft – Botolph Street – Colegate – Calvert Street to the N – St George Street to the S – the rest of Colegate – Pitt Street – Sussex Street (more of the Walls) – Oak Street – St Mary Plain – Coslany Street – Westwick Street – (Charing Cross) and back.

s,w. To the South and West from the Station to the Station.
Prince of Wales Road – Upper King Street – King Street – (S parts of the Walls) – Finklegate – Ber Street – All Saints Green – Surrey Street – Brigg Street etc. – Theatre Street – Chapel Field – St Giles Street to the E with Willow Lane to the N and Bethel Street to the SE – Pottergate to the W with Cow Hill (and the W parts of the Walls) – St Andrew's Hall Plain – St Benedict Street to the E – St Andrew Street – St Andrew's Hall Plain – Bank Plain and back.

Not everybody may have the stamina to perform these walks.

Some may wish to break up the three into five itineraries. To do it will prove easy and needs no guidance.

INNER NORWICH

THE CATHEDRAL

INTRODUCTION

Norwich Cathedral lies low, and if it were not for the spire which 5 rises above its crossing, it would not be more prominent in the picture of the city than is Winchester Cathedral. The spire makes the cathedral, as one approaches Norwich. When one is nearer and happens to have found a good vantage point, the other distinguishing features enter the picture: the exceedingly long nave and the strange geometrical richness of the decoration of the crossing tower. The interior is at its most powerful when one first sits down in the nave. The E part, as so often, cannot address us clearly, owing to the many ritually necessary interruptions of the visual impression. The styles contributing are the Norman and the Perpendicular, but both speak the same language. The palisade of closely crowding masts in the Norman walls, in spite of the arches between them, is as relentless as the bundles of closely crowding staffs that make the ribs, and the three parallel lines of bosses along the ridge shoot into the distance with the same straightness and the same never-halting tempo as the arcades. Rarely does the unity of English architecture from the C11 to the C16 carry so much conviction.

The cathedral in its original parts is built of Barnack and Caen stone. It is 407 ft long. The spire is 315 ft high.

Of the masons who designed and built it we know the following.* Members of the important *de Ramsey* family in the first half of the C14, that is on the cloister S and perhaps E walks, and also the Campanile (*see* below). Then *Simon Lilye* on the W walk of the cloisters in the 1340s, *Robert Wadham* on the cloister in the 1380s (W bays N walk?), *James Woderofe* and his brother *John Woderofe* in the first half of the C15 on the rest of the cloister and the Erpingham Gate, and *Robert Everard* on the spire and probably the nave vaults. The names do not help us much, because they do not cover with certainty any of the creatively important jobs, that is e.g. the E walk of the cloister or the presbytery vaults.

* The list and comments are based on Mr Harvey's *English Mediaeval Architects.*

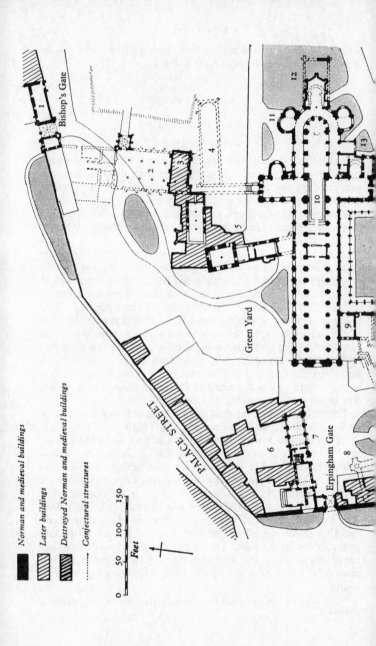

Norman and medieval buildings

Later buildings

Destroyed Norman and medieval buildings

Conjectural structures

Feet
0   50   100   150

Bishop's Gate

PALACE STREET

Green Yard

Erpingham Gate

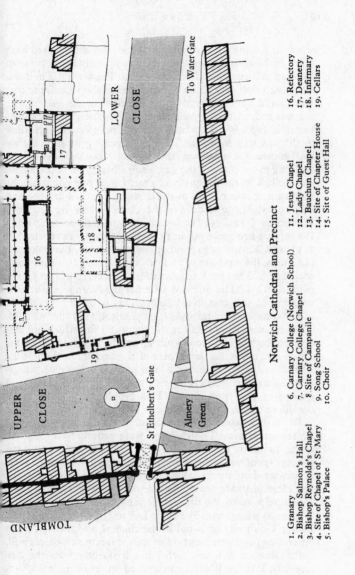

Norwich Cathedral and Precinct

1. Granary
2. Bishop Salmon's Hall
3. Bishop Reynolds's Chapel
4. Site of Chapel of St Mary
5. Bishop's Palace

6. Carnary College (Norwich School)
7. Carnary College Chapel
8. Site of Campanile
9. Song School
10. Choir

11. Jesus Chapel
12. Lady Chapel
13. Bauchun Chapel
14. Site of Chapter House
15. Site of Guest Hall

16. Refectory
17. Deanery
18. Infirmary
19. Cellars

HISTORY

Herbert de Losinga, a Lorrainer, but one who had reached high
office in Normandy, was raised in 1091 from being prior of
Fécamp to being bishop of East Anglia. The see was Thetford,
but in accordance with an order of Archbishop Lanfranc that
sees should be transferred to the big cities in the diocese, the
see was moved to Norwich in 1094. The new building was
begun in 1096. We know little of how it progressed. According
to the late C13 *Registrum Primum*, repeating what its author
had known 'ex relatione antiquorum', Losinga began the
building in the place of the C13 Lady Chapel, i.e. at the E end,
and built it to the Holy Cross altar, i.e. to one bay W of the
pulpitum or four bays W of the crossing. He died in 1119 and
was buried in the middle of the chancel, and his successor
Eborardus (1121–45) 'ecclesiam integraliter consummavit'.
However, a fire broke out in 1171, the damage was repaired in
1173, and, according to another late C13 source, Bartholomew
of Cotton, Bishop John of Oxford (1175–1200), 'consummavit
ecclesiam'. The final consecration, however, did not take
place till 1278. The question whether the Norman church, as
we know it, was completed before 1145 or after 1175, allows
of only one answer. Its style is emphatically not that of 1180.
The only confusing detail is the signs of a fire which are evident on the first and second piers from the E of the nave on the
S side and about the same part of the arcade on the N side,
where the stone is coloured a faint pink. It is these very parts
where also – in connexion with the fire or by accident – a
change of plan took place. This problem will have to be
considered later.

See
P.
390

Of further dates and approximate dates the following must
be recorded now. The cloisters were rebuilt from 1297 to
about 1430. In 1362 the spire fell, and for 1364 and 1369
moneys spent on the presbytery are recorded. This must refer
to damage done by the falling spire and to the building of the
new clerestory. Money was left for the new W window in 1449,
which helps to fix the date of the remodelling of the W front.
The vaults were put up by Bishop Lyhart (1446–72) in the nave,
Bishop Goldwell (1472–99) in the chancel, and Bishop Nykke
(after 1509) in the transepts. The spire was rebuilt by Goldwell.

Restorations followed each other frequently from the C18
onwards. *William Wilkins* e.g. worked on restoring in 1806–7.
Later the W front and the S transept were completely remodelled – and it is doubtful how accurately – by *Salvin* in the

1830s, and the crossing tower was restored by *John Brown* at about the same time.

See p. 391

EXTERIOR

As Bishop Losinga began at the E end, we are deprived of his earliest work. The Lady Chapel we see now was designed by *Sir Charles Nicholson* and built in 1930–2. It replaced a rebuilding of the C13 of which the straight E end E of the present chapel is exposed on the lawn. The shape of Losinga's E chapel is known from excavations.* It was the E chapel of a church planned on the principle of an ambulatory round the apse with radiating chapels and additional chapels E of the transepts, a principle established for cathedrals and abbey churches in France from the early C11 onwards or even earlier. Rouen Cathedral as begun in 1030 is an early example in Normandy. With the exception of the E chapel, the arrangement survives uncommonly completely at Norwich, and this is one of the church's architectural distinctions. Moreover, there seems no change of plan for quite a distance, and one is thus entitled to regard the whole E part and probably more as representing the plan laid down by Losinga's unknown master mason. It is a straightforward plan and elevation, a standard plan and elevation, one would be tempted to say, if it were not for the extremely curious shape of the SE and NE chapels. They consist of two parts each, both parts curved, the apse facing almost due E and an antechapel, as it were, facing almost due N and S. The E part is semicircular, the W part of a horseshoe shape. The parts are moreover connected with one another and with the walls of the chancel aisles to their W and of the E bays of the ambulatory to their N (the S chapel) and S (the N chapel) so that a composition of five curved surfaces results, undulating and somewhat ill-defined. The French did not do that sort of thing. They did not mind their SE and NE chapels facing SE and NE. The English were bothered by this ritual impurity and devised at Norwich and also at Canterbury, at Leominster, at Lincoln (St Hugh's Choir), and at Muchelney architectural impurities to overcome it.

Now for the system of the external elevation. What distinguishes it from most other Norman and, indeed, Europeanly

* During these excavations a smaller apse was found preceding Losinga's. Yet Losinga is supposed to have built on a virgin site. However, the late Dean Cranage has drawn attention to the fact that, according to Domesday, Losinga's predecessor Aerfast, a chaplain of King William, had already received property at Norwich 'ad principalem sedem episcopatus'.

speaking, Romanesque churches is that it has a gallery not only over the nave and chancel aisles but also covering the E chapels of the transepts, the NE and SE radiating chapels, and no doubt also Losinga's E chapel. Regarding elevational details as they can be gathered partly from the S, partly from the N side, they are as follows. Large shafted ambulatory windows, chapel windows and chancel aisle windows, all with billet mouldings. Big frieze of blank arcading on a nutmeg course. Small shafted single gallery windows. All the shafts have simple scallop or simple volute capitals. On these details the interior and especially the gallery will be more helpful. Above them, to improve lighting, straight-headed, apparently later C14, four-light windows of alternating designs (one has a row of reticulation units). For the Norman clerestory we must go further W. The whole part of the cathedral E of the crossing was given a new, much taller clerestory in the 1360s. This has tall four-light windows of typical Early Perp character; two-centred arches, and in the head still a motif reminiscent of the four-petalled flower. Steep, vigorous flying buttresses. Panelled battlements.*

6a
However, the TRANSEPTS help to finish visually the picture of the Norman E parts. The N transept is more helpful than the S transept: for the S front of the latter, which of course originally abutted on the E range of the cloister of the cathedral-monastery, was heavily restored and in its lower parts re-done by *Salvin* in the 1830s. Also to the E of the S transept there is a group of later structures; namely the Bauchun Chapel of c.1330, but with a Victorian four-light window, running S off the chancel aisle, and the former Chapel of St Catharine (now Dean's Vestry) of c.1250–75 running E off the transept and having small lancets to the S on two storeys and Victorian windows to the E. The original arrangement was, as has been said, an apse off the E side of the transept. On the N side this survives, although only in its lower storey. On both sides traces of the upper can still be seen. The lower arch on the S side is best examined from the staircase of the present E attachment.

The elevational system of the N wall of the N transept is this. On the ground floor a small doorway to the Bishop's Palace. Two orders of shafts. One single-scallop, one volute capital.
40b
Above a very interesting piece of SCULPTURE, a Bishop with crozier, tightly between two spiral-fluted columns and under

* On the N side traces can be seen of the roof of the former Relic Chamber and to its W the arch of a chapel. They will be referred to on p. 216.

an arch. The sides taper slightly towards the foot, and this has suggested to Clapham the attractive idea that we may have here the lid of the MONUMENT to Losinga, erected in the middle of the chancel after his death. If this is so, then we would have the most ancient of English funeral monuments. It is however improbable that the panel is entirely in its original state. Gabling has been cut away from the head and a dragon from the foot (A. B. Whittingham). To the l. and r. of the image are shafted windows. Above them tall shafted windows. Then a new motif which we shall not meet again for some time. Instead of the normal blank arcading of the chancel and the s transept there are here big intersected archheads. Then again tall shafted windows, and two more tiers in the gable. Square angle turrets. All the buttresses are flat and shafted too.

The w sides of the transepts show another sign of progress, and it comes only at clerestory level, i.e. at the end of operations. The clerestory is tripartite throughout with the big central window part raised – the usual English arrangement. Traces indicate that this was the way with the former clerestory of the E end too. But in the w walls of the transepts the minor arches have zigzag, the first in the cathedral, and the main arch has billet in the s, but a kind of barrel or bobbin motif in the N transept. In the s transept w wall these minor arches have the whole of the field below diapered – but it is not certain how far the motif was accurately renewed. Anyway, it must be remembered that at this stage a desire for ornamental enrichment made itself felt.

The CROSSING TOWER is more boldly decorated than that. In fact it is the only boldly decorated work of the Norman period at Norwich and, even so, not with any of the luxuriance which one is accustomed to in the Late Norman style. There is no abundance of motifs. The motifs employed are unusual and, if anything, austere: blank arcading, now also with intersected arches, and in addition between the bell-openings vertical strings of alternating lozenges and circles, and above the windows, very big and provocative, two tiers of again vertically connected circles or port-holes, as the upper ones served as bell-openings. The angle buttresses are square and over-closely shafted, almost reeded, but have on top polygonal turrets, also Norman. Only their crocketed spirelets belong to the C15 work, when the fine needle-spire was put on, with crockets up the edges and lucarnes in three tiers in alternating

directions. The spire is recessed behind battlements decorated
with shields.

In the Norman NAVE there are no external changes of any
significance against the system of the E parts. The gallery
windows are now part of a blank arcading of three even arches.
The N aisle windows are of the early C14 (cusped intersected
tracery). The larger upper windows introducing more light
into the nave are Perp.* The clerestory is tripartite as it was,
and the decorative enrichments of the transepts are not continued. The only change to be noted in the nave is that the
three w bays on the s side in the blind arcading below the
gallery windows again use intersected arches.

See
p.
391

The WEST FRONT, it must be admitted, is a disappointment.
Is this because a w transept was intended to be added as they
existed at Ely and Bury St Edmunds, and as Clapham, on
scanty evidence, regards as possible? Or is it because the
English were rarely at their best in Norman and E.E. façades?
As it is, the effect is lowered yet more by the admixture of C15
work, in itself of a high standard. The Norman façade had
three portals, the remaining aisle portals being lower than the
central one. Above them is again blank arcading (intersected
on the s side, which is not borne out by the illustrations of
1816) and a window over, flanked by blank arches. There are
square angle buttresses now crowned by turrets non-existent
before *Salvin*. As for the nave front, this has its ambitious
Perp portal with diagonally set niches and a shallow vault,
pairs of outer niches with small seated and kneeling figures
above, and then the nine-light w window. The tall Norman
shafts which now cluster round that window were not there in
1816, but remains were found when the porch was made
narrower. Clapham (*see* above) suggested that a w transept
was planned.

INTERIOR

20 We must again start at the EAST END, but we can now take it for
granted that the system was never changed to the very w front.
This system is one almost uniformly adopted in England (other
than the West), namely a nave (or chancel) with groin-vaulted
aisles, a gallery, a clerestory, a flat timber ceiling. The latter
we can only presume from the shafts which ran right up to it
to support the main beams. The clerestory has the arrangement with a stepped tripartite wall passage in front of the
window, as it was introduced at Winchester and taken over at

* Not Elizabethan, as the *Gent. Mag.* said in 1861.

Ely and everywhere in England. The gallery has unsubdivided openings, as it had been done at St Étienne in Caen
designed c.1065 and then in England, e.g. at Old St Paul's in
London. It is an impressive system, more uncompromising
somehow than the twin openings under one arch at Winchester, Ely, and Durham.

The details, once this has been established, are as follows.
At the E end of the ambulatory the tall twin arch with dog-
tooth decoration which now leads into the Lady Chapel of
1930 may well belong to its predecessor, the Lady Chapel
built by Bishop Walter de Suffield (1245–57), although the
dividing clustered shaft and the responds can be no earlier
than the later C14. The Norman ambulatory has broad unmoulded transverse arches on strong coupled shafts between
its groin-vaults. Wall arcading, that motif the English never
tired of, runs along the outer walls. The windows, where they
survive, are shafted. Capitals are of one or two scallops or have
primitive volutes.* Facing the entry to the Lady Chapel is
what seems a screen wall but is the retaining wall for the
Bishop's Throne (see p. 224). It has a deep niche with shafts
carrying capitals later than the surrounding ones. The adjoining bays continue this retaining wall, and they have intersected arches. So the Throne was not installed at once, but
only at the time when intersected arches became the fashion
at Norwich – say about 1120.‡

The SE and NE chapels look as weird from inside as they do
from outside. The relation between their groined vaults and
their plans ought to be observed particularly. The blank
arcading runs round the chapels as it does round the ambulatory. In the NE (Jesus) Chapel are five brackets for images,
one of them bigger than the others. They are probably Perp.
There is no change when it comes to the chancel aisles. Off the
S aisle the Bauchun Chapel runs S. The arch with semicircular
responds and semicircular capitals is typically Dec. An
identical arch opened into a corresponding chapel on the N
side. But the arch is blocked and the chapel has disappeared.
The Bauchun Chapel extended further E, as a blocked arch,
not visible from outside, proves. The Perp S window and the
vault prove also that the whole chapel was remodelled in the
C15 or early C16. The vault has exactly the same pattern as the
chancel vault (see below) and the same abundance of bosses.

---

* For more on this see under Gallery on p. 221.
‡ The first enthronement in the cathedral took place in 1121.

They deal with the legend of an Empress wrongly accused. In the E wall is an uncommonly big niche with a tall pedestal for an image, in the S wall a low tomb recess. To the E of the former N chapel a platform was erected which connected with the former Relic Chamber (see Exterior, p. 212, footnote). A spiral stair led down from it to the aisle and other steps to the chancel, but it served no doubt also as a watching point. The underside of the platform has heavy, single-chamfered ribs, rising on responds characteristic of the early C14.

The CHANCEL strikes one at once, as one enters, by its height. This is of course due to the altered clerestory, but the Norman wall treatment with its many sturdy shafts contributes much. The actual height is 83 ft. The apse piers have three shafts in steps to the chancel, but the sides to the aisle openings are treated as if they were part of a circular pier hidden by the shafts and steps. The design is the same at Ely.* The arches have two roll mouldings and a billet moulding. The gallery is large and undivided, with stilted arches. The clerestory is that of the C14. The system must have continued into the straight part of the chancel. The gallery is intact but the arcade level was completely recast in the Perp style, probably by Bishop Goldwell. The only indication of the Norman arcade still existing is the E respond of the NE bay of the chancel aisle and part of the base of the W respond. The arches were made four-centred by Goldwell, and the thickness of the wall which they pierce made the occasion for a display of tracery inside. Tracery in the spandrels too. Tall blank ogee arches between them with crockets. The new design just laps over into the gallery by means of a parapet of cusped lozenges, a pretty motif. On the gallery level traces remain between the arches which, in conjunction with what the nave will show, can be defined as the remains of shafts up to the roof. The traces make it certain that there was an alternation of twin shafts and single shafts. The Gothic clerestory keeps the stepped rhythm of the Norman tradition but simplifies it into low-high-low-high-low etc. The lower unit has an ogee head, and from this the lush palm fronds of Bishop Goldwell's vault spread. The harmony between the clerestory of *c*.1360–70 and the vault

* Whether Ely or Norwich is earlier, one cannot say. The motif survives at Ely only in the nave, which was begun shortly before or shortly after the consecration of 1106, but there is reason to assume that it existed also in the NE crossing pier in its original Norman form, and this must be of quite some time before 1106. Moreover the chancel may well have had it too. Ely was begun in 1083.

of *c.*1480–90 is perfect, so much so that one wonders how a timber roof can ever have looked satisfactory. Yet it was there, above the vault, till 1955. The vault, if one analyses it, is a rib-vault with diagonal and ridge ribs and three pairs of tiercerons in the N and S, one pair in the E and W walls. That far it is the system invented for Exeter two hundred years before. But the Norwich vault has a pattern formed by lierne ribs along the middle as well. The forms are a lozenge, an irregular, elongated eight-pointed star, a lozenge, etc. This in itself also was not a new idea. The Ethelbert Gate (*see* p. 232), and a few years after it the Ely Lady Chapel and Ely choir, had done very much the same well over a hundred years before, and it remains noteworthy that the Perp style could so successfully take over a Dec motif. The lierne part is studded with bosses. A few of them have figural subjects (Assumption, Trinity). In quite a number appears Bishop Goldwell's rebus. The line of the Norman roof can be guessed by the windows of the crossing tower visible inside.

The TRANSEPTS can be treated as one. They do not differ in essentials. The E walls are of necessity more varied than the others. Arcade and gallery (i.e. the arches from the chancel aisle) are as before. The clerestory now appears for the first time of a type no doubt also retained. It is the familiar stepped tripartite arcading in front of a wall passage. Some of the shafts of the N transept are decorated, the only ones in the cathedral if one excepts those of Losinga's effigy (*see* p. 212). The bay following that of the chancel aisle is virtually blank, as the staircases to the crossing tower go up behind it. On the N side the small doorway has a tympanum with a diaper pattern. Above the ground stage is tall blank arcading with billet and then a tall area of blank wall. On the S side this area is covered with more, very tall blank arcading, and that arcading is intersected. The fact may not be without significance. The level is almost the same as that of the intersected arch-heads noted (on p. 213) outside the N transept. So – to say it once more – perhaps, when that level was reached, there was a tendency to decorate a little more freely. The clerestory here has a single and a twin opening to the transept. Above this and above the lower arches of the stepped tripartite arrangement ran yet another band (an interrupted band) of blank arcading, a unique motif, almost resulting in the impression of a four-tier elevation. The last bay to the N is unpardonably irregular with only two parts of the tripartite

arrangement fitted in. In the s transept this is corrected by
Salvin, who inserted the s door, renewed the wall arcading,
and altogether treated the s transept ruthlessly. The end walls
of the transepts have large windows in two tiers. On the
ground floor of the N wall an anomaly occurs – corresponding
to the effigy outside. There are two lengths of billet moulding
arranged like twin Saxon triangle-headed arches, and a carved
head is placed between them, again with a little billet triangle
over. The feature looks very odd. For the w walls the s
transept is more helpful. The lower windows are flanked by
arched niches on the l. and r. The clerestory level is in the w
wall normal in the N transept as well as the s. The squeeze of
the E wall does not recur. The transept vaults were only put
up after 1509. Yet they continue the chancel (and indeed the
earlier nave) vaults without change. The bosses here represent the early life of Christ, and there are about 150 of them.
Off the s transept is the former Chapel of St Catharine, now
Dean's Vestry. This has E.E. rib-vaulting in three bays, the
ribs with one hollow chamfer. One boss has a beautiful
bishop's head in a wreath of stiff-leaf foliage.

The CROSSING TOWER could of course be built only when
the transepts and indeed the first bay or bays of the nave had
reached full height. Its upper parts are thus appreciably later
in style than the rest. This has already been emphasized when
the exterior was described. The crossing piers have three shafts
side by side in the E and W, two in the N and s arches. Scallop
and volute capitals still go on. The lantern is open. The first
tier is an arched wall passage, the second blank arcading in
pairs with near the angles a circle instead – the motif famous
from the outside. On the stage above the designer of this outside motif has done something equally surprising. The windows, which externally form minor incidents in a band of
arcading, are internally given the tripartite treatment, but with
absurdly narrow side-parts. The window itself is flanked by
fat shafts on which stand finer shafts, a motif which the clerestory of the transepts had already established.

The NAVE continues the same system entirely, except for
one attempt at a break. The system is no doubt still that of the
chancel, and it can now at last be fully summed up. In the
aisles there is no change at all. The arcade has piers with the
slightest alternation of supports. Curves towards the arch
openings as of a circular core alternate with triple shafts. The
former are continued in single shafts ending in capitals at the

springing of the gallery arches. The latter are continued in twin shafts right up to where the Norman ceiling beams ran across. Large, unsubdivided gallery, clerestory with wall passage and tripartite arcading. The gallery alone shows a change in decoration. Up to now no decorative friezes other than of billets and nutmeg have been found. Now zigzag occurs, a motif favoured in England from about 1115 or 1120 onwards. We have seen it arrive at Norwich very unobtrusively outside the clerestory of the transept on the w side. That stage in building may well have been reached at the same time as the first gallery arches of the nave.

The introduction of such a motif can hardly be called a break. But there is a real break, and this occurred a little further w and then at ground level, in a place which may well have been begun when the gallery arches and the transept clerestories were built. Its aim was again, but much more emphatically, to introduce decorative enrichment. The break occurs, or so it seems at first, at the fifth pier from the E. Here, instead of the pier with the curved surface towards the arch opening, is a very strong circular pier, vigorously spiral-grooved. It is short, and its circumference is about 7 ft 6 in. The motif is familiar and magnificent wherever it occurs. It was created at Durham in the plan of 1093 and taken over at Lindisfarne, Dunfermline, York (crypt), and also Waltham Abbey. It must have impressed someone at Norwich considerably to make him insist on a change of system. Who was it, mason or client? And when was it? The mason is unknown entirely, but if he was also responsible for the various zigzags, he was perhaps a new man starting about 1115. The other two questions introduce us to the principal historical puzzle of Norwich.

First of all, the change occurred before the fifth piers. In the third pier of the N side just such a round spiral-grooved pier has been partly exposed, encased in the present shape, which is the standard one. Those discovering this in 1898 pointed out rightly that the round pier showed unmistakable signs of a fire. Other signs of fire have already been referred to. The fire in question is, according to Mr Whittingham, that which occurred in 1463. But quite apart from the fire, the interesting fact is the change of system in this place, i.e. the place just w from where the future crossing tower had to be buttressed by arcade and gallery bays to be safe. It is a common experience that chancel, transepts, and first two bays of the nave form one

build and that the nave W of that point can follow later, as
being less important from the point of view of the clergy.
Losinga, we are told, built as far as the Altar of the Holy Cross.
That altar customarily stood W of the pulpitum which ran
across between piers there. In that place in fact excavations
have shown a rubble foundation wall running right across the
church. This must have marked the end of Losinga's work, i.e.
the year 1119. How high above the wall he reached is another
question. It has been noticed that the abaci change very
slightly between piers and shafts two and piers and shafts
three. To the E there is a slight convex member between the
vertical and the sloping part. To the W it is notched instead
and then chamfered. So everything points to a break at pier
three, and – we may add – at bay one in the gallery and at the
W clerestory in the transepts. The only snag is that the rubble
wall rises W of that line. It can, however, perhaps be suggested
that in spite of Losinga having marked the W termination of his
project the changes in the abaci and piers mark the start of a
new build. This could then be dated fairly securely to 1120.
There is no evidence to explain why and when the Durham
system was discarded and a return made to the former Norwich
system. The only minor change is that the capitals of the wall
arcading on the N side, after pier five, are much busier and
livelier. The same is not true of the S aisle, but the wall of this
may well have been built first, since it was needed for building
the cloister. In spite of these more varied capitals, the style
remains essentially as it had been before, and a post-fire date
is out of the question. Right up to the W front nothing can be
later than the deposition of Eborard in 1145. So one must reluctantly accept the curious accident that the temporary break
in the Norwich system and the effects of fire are visible in the
same part of the building. But do not such accidents happen?

The W wall of the nave shows the outline of the Norman
central portal, flanked by pairs of blank arches.

Of later contributions to nave and aisles the most important
is the vault. This was built by Bishop Lyhart, i.e. in the third
quarter of the C15, and is the pattern followed in the chancel
and transept vaults and the vault of the Bauchun Chapel. The
number of bosses is again prodigious (over 270), and they represent scenes from the Old and New Testaments, from the
Creation to the Last Judgement. Altogether well over 800
bosses have been counted in Norwich Cathedral (including the
cloister). Otherwise there is a very fine portal into the cloister

in the E bay. This dates from c.1310 and has shafts carrying a depressed two-centred arch.* There are also wall seats in two bays of the S aisle with cusped lozenges along the fronts. One of the S windows has pretty fleurons in jambs and arch. See p. 391

As a final confirmation of the findings so far expounded, a visit to the GALLERY is to be recommended. This is what it will show. The gallery was not vaulted. The only transverse arches were at the E end of the chancel aisles, i.e. the start of the ambulatory. The lean-to roof, still marked in the transept walls, made it necessary to run the twin shafts to much less in height against the walls than against the gallery piers. The whole of the E parts of the gallery, starting from the ambulatory, has far more volute capitals, also of quite playful shapes, than were used further W. The Norman gallery windows were shafted and set in a severe blank arcading of arches on broad pilasters, not colonnettes. This is specially impressive in the NE and SE chapels. The signs of fire are evident on piers one and two from the E in the S aisle gallery. From here, looking at the N wall of the arcade opposite, the discolouring of the stone is equally evident. See p. 391

FURNISHINGS

A topographical arrangement has been adopted, from E to W.

LADY CHAPEL. Several PAINTINGS of the Norwich School, of the highest value. They should be seen together with the Retable in St Luke's Chapel (see below, p. 223), as comparisons will prove illuminating. They are the following. In the chapel Retable of five parts given by, or at the time of, Bishop Despenser, i.e. c.1380–90, and the finest piece of East Anglian painting of its time. In the Lady Chapel a similar-looking Retable of five parts, but later and not originally a retable. It comes from St Michael-at-Plea and consists of the Resurrection which formed part of a retable and must be of c.1430–40, the Annunciation and the Crucifixion from the chancel screen, and two saints from a parclose screen. These four panels are about ten or twenty years earlier than the Resurrection. In addition there are in the Lady Chapel one more saint from the chancel screen of St Michael-at-Plea and two very good fragmentary scenes from the retable of St Michael-at-Plea; Betrayal and Crucifixion. These belong in date to the Despenser Retable, and the other panels from St Michael-at-Plea.

---

* For the other side of this portal see Cloister, p. 227.

The differences between the earlier and later pieces are evident. In the 1380s the colours are softer and subtler, the draperies have a gradual shading inspired by Italian Trecento painting, and the facial types are close to those of the same years in North Germany, especially the work of Master Bertram in Hamburg. Also, in the 1380s a patterned gilded background is all that sets the figures off. The Christ of the Resurrection is strictly frontal and his gesture conventional and hieratic, the sarcophagus appears as a diagonal on the picture plane rather than in depth. Fifty years later the scene of the Resurrection has become a scene indeed, placed in space and in landscape, with the sarcophagus unmistakably leading into depth, and Christ standing on it in a gently demonstrating pose. Yet conventions are certainly not yet discarded as they were to be in all painting influenced by the Flemish discoveries of the 1420s and 1430s, i.e. by the van Eycks, Robert Campin, and Roger van der Weyden. Thus e.g. the little structure in which the Annunciation takes place is just as fantastical as that of the Scourging of Christ of the earlier retable. Yet here again the figures certainly have more weight and substance, and also more charm. These child-like heads with large round foreheads and small features were an international fashion of the ending C14 and early C15. The bonier and perhaps uglier heads of 1380 allow for a more convincing presentation of tragedy and suffering.

AMBULATORY, from the E to the NW, including the NE (Jesus) Chapel. Of WALL PAINTING (of the C13 – probably largely after a fire in 1272) many traces survive here and especially in the chapel, where they are no doubt renewed. They appear, however, with their dark green columns and the red, light blue, and yellow of the capitals etc., quite convincing and in accordance with illuminated manuscripts. Even more important are the twelve Saints arranged around Christ in the vault of the bay converted into the balcony in front of the Relic Chapel. The conversion belongs to c.1275 (after the fire), but most of the figures, which must once have been very good indeed, are of the early C14.* – STAINED GLASS. In the E window of the Jesus Chapel, designed by *Sir T. G. Jackson* and made by *Powell's*. – MONUMENTS. Between chancel and E bay of the chancel aisle base of the monument to an un-

---

* But the accusing angel on the transverse arch must be of c.1275, and the same is true of the bishop's head on a capital below and some neighbouring ornamentation.

known person, C15, with ogee-headed panels. – In the same bay against the wall Elizabeth Calthorpp † 1582. Tomb-chest with tapering pilasters. No effigy. Semicircular top with shell fluting. – SCULPTURE. In a show-case fragments of exceedingly fine Norman capitals etc. of a style quite different from anything else in the cathedral. With nimble figures in various actions and entwined in foliage trails. They must be of c.1140 and probably belonged to the Norman cloisters. – In the arch towards the chancel of the next bay MONUMENT of Thomas Moore † 1779. Signed by *Thomas Ivory* and *J. de Carle*. Weeping putto under a medallion with palm fronds. – Under the same arch but on the E respond WALL PAINTING with many figures and many scrolls and, according to Mr Whittingham, the Virgin and St John to the l. and r. of a cross, and, above, the Fathers of the Church, the Evangelists, and God the Father surrounded by angels.

Now from the E to the SW, including the SE (St Luke's) Chapel. In the ambulatory STAINED GLASS window of St Brice, a large figure of the C16, probably French (from Langley Hall). – In the chapel E window medallions 1868 by *Hardman*, W window medallions 1881 by *Clayton & Bell* – a typical change of style. – In the chapel the painted RETABLE, which has already been discussed above, on p. 221. – Also in the chapel floor Victorian TILES by *Minton's*. – In the ambulatory W of the chapel FONT, a sumptuous piece of the East Anglian type, with eight seated figurines on the foot, eight standing figurines against the stem, and the Seven Sacraments separated by eight angels against the bowl. – MONUMENT. Richard Brome c.1500. Wall panel with ogee arch and panelling over. – Prior Bozoun. Low chantry chapel with a four-centred canopy, tracery-panelled inside. To the W of the chapel, long tomb-chest to Bishop Wakering † 1425, with small standing figures and shields in cusped circles. – In the Bauchun Chapel PAINTING. Adoration of the Magi, French, C17, good. – THRONE A former Bishop's Throne is kept in captivity here. It was erected by Dean Lloyd late in the C18 and is a piece of Gothic Revival, similar to the pew in the Great Hospital, even in the surprisingly Victorian character of the canopy. Pretty vault inside it. It might well be by *William Ivory*. – MONUMENT in the chapel to William Rolfe † 1754, by *Rawlins*. Varied marbles. With putto and skull before an obelisk. Very pretty. – Then between ambulatory and chancel large MONUMENT to Bishop Goldwell † 1499. It is really accessible from the chancel

and there forms a chantry chapel. Its composition is part of
Goldwell's remodelling of the chancel arcading. From the
(lower) ambulatory the tomb-chest seems excessively tall. On
it alabaster effigy. Big canopy, and its underside a traceried
shallow tunnel-vault.

CHANCEL. In the apse stands the BISHOP'S THRONE, restored in 1959. It faces W and is thus in the traditional Early
Christian position, familiar from Parenzo (C 6) but also to be
found north of the Alps (e.g. at Vaison). The details of the
arrangement are of 1959. The throne is a stone chair with
arms and low back. Against the arms, almost obliterated, coils
and beasts or dragons and perhaps birds. According to Mr
Ralegh Radford's recent research the two arms do not belong
together. Their sizes and their ornament differ. Both however
appear to be of the C8. The larger belonged in all probability
to the bishop's throne of that date, the smaller was the end of
a stone bench which ran around the apse and in the middle of
which the throne was placed. This is exactly as it is at Parenzo
etc. If date and function are assumed correctly, then the two
arms must have come from North Elmham, the see before
Thetford. – DEAN'S CHAIR, presented in 1922. In the middle
of the back painted relief medallion of the Emperor Maximilian, dated 1512. The rest C17 engraved ivory panels,
perhaps also German. – Goldwell Monument, see above. – In
the E clerestory windows STAINED GLASS, many small
figures, by *Warrington*, 1847.

STALLS. The sixty-two Norwich stalls have changed their
places more than once. They are now divided between the
chancel, the crossing, and the choir, and are therefore discussed together. Traceried fronts, canopied backs, straight
top-cresting, MISERICORDS and arms with human figures,
human heads, animals, and monsters. The stalls are of the C15,
but not of one date. The division between those of *c.*1420 and
those of *c.*1480 is too complicated to be summarized here.*
The difference between the canopies W (1420) and E (1480) of
Nos 16 S and N is easily seen. For the style of the misericords
one ought to contrast any of the first eight on the S or N sides
with most of those further E. The later ones are decidedly
busier. There is a difference in the front edge of the misericords too.

CROSSING. The wooden PULPIT here was designed by

---

* Users must be referred to the booklet by A. B. Whittingham and E. C.
Le Grice.

Seddon in 1889 and made by *Hems* of Exeter. – BISHOP'S
THRONE, designed by *Pearson* and unveiled in 1895. –
LECTERN. Of brass, Flemish, late C15. The three statuettes
between the thin buttresses and flying buttresses were called
new in 1841. Pelican (not eagle) at the top. – SWORD AND
MACE RESTS. Wrought iron, C18, not more sumptuous than
those in the parish churches.

SOUTH TRANSEPT. SCREEN with doorway to the chancel
aisle. Of stone, filling the Norman arch. Perp, with plenty of
close panel tracery. In the jambs and arch of the doorway
pedestals for statuettes. – CHEST. Of sandalwood. North
Italian, late C16. In the lid Crucifixion, Scourging, and Resurrection, drawn in pokerwork. – CLOCK JACKS. Small,
probably C17.

NORTH TRANSEPT. SCREEN, a Victorian paraphrase of the
S transept screen. – SCREEN to the E chapel, neo-Jacobean;
1920. – STAINED GLASS. W window, designed by *Burne-Jones*
and made by *Morris & Co.*, *c.*1901–2. – MONUMENTS. Bishop
Bathurst, by *Chantrey*, 1841. White marble. Seated peacefully
with folded hands. – Bishop Pelham, by *James Forsyth*, 1896.
White recumbent effigy on an alabaster tomb-chest. – Violet
Morgan, by *Derwent Wood*, 1921. White kneeling maiden.

NAVE AND AISLES. PULPITUM. Rebuilt by Bishop Lyhart
after the fire of 1463, but completely remodelled by *Salvin* in
1833. On it ORGAN, the case by *S. E. Dykes Bower*, designed
in 1939. – Against the N side of the pulpitum are parts of
the Perp stone SCREEN formerly between ambulatory and
Jesus Chapel. – Against the S pier by the pulpitum MONU-
MENT to William Inglott, organist, † 1621. Painted. Inscription with strapwork surround. – In the S aisle at that point
MONUMENT to Thomas Gooding; Elizabethan. Painted skeleton with inscription including the familiar 'As you are now
Even so was I'. – Then CEILING PAINTING in the vault,
good but very faded work of *c.*1175. Professor Tristram refers
to an Adoration of the Magi with shepherds in the W compartment and three medallions with stories of Bishop Losinga in
the W arch. – Then in the N aisle MONUMENT to Sir John
Hobart † 1507. Tomb-chest with the brasses missing. – In the
next bay STAINED GLASS window († 1849) by *Warrington*. –
Back into the S aisle for the MONUMENT to Dean Gardiner
† 1589. Illegible inscription. Tomb-chest with two shields;
pediment on pilasters; no effigy. – MONUMENT to Bishop
Parkhurst † 1575. Plain, with black lid. The brass is missing.

Back panel to the E with curly top-gable. – In the nave stone
PULPIT of 1889, designed by *Carpenter & Ingelow*. – Then
the MONUMENT and its surround which Bishop Nykke
erected for himself. He died in 1536. It consists of two bays,
though the tomb-chest in the W bay of the two is not his but
that of Chancellor Spencer. The whole of the two vaults in
the aisle was faced with shallow rising tunnel-vaults decorated with panel tracery. In the E bay a low base with panel
tracery and shields, and against the E pier three niches with
pedestals for images. Chancellor Spencer's tomb-chest is low.
– STAINED GLASS. Five-light window signed by *O'Connor*,
1864. – Three-light window by *Wailes*, 1859. – MONUMENT.
Dean Fairfax † 1702, by *William Stanton*. Inscription with
flanking columns and outside them piles of books with oil-
lamps burning on them. Good quality all round. – Again into
the N aisle. Blocked DOORWAY with a four-centred arch,
and in the spandrels centaurs and leaf; very pretty. – Then
MONUMENT to Sir Thomas Wyndham † 1521. This is between N aisle and nave. Tomb-chest of Purbeck marble. Three
shields in quatrefoils. Three brasses missing. – Finally in the
W window an enormous expanse of STAINED GLASS. Six large
scenes still treated completely pictorially. It is signed by
Hedgeland and dates from 1854, a date surprisingly late for
this interpretation of the art of the glass-painter.

GALLERY. MONUMENT. Thomas Ivory, the sculptor-archi-
tect, † 1779, by *J. Ivory*. Simple tablet with urn at the top.

PLATE. All made in London and not locally: Chalice, 1614–
15 ; Paten, 1660–1 ; Almsdish (gilt) and Candlesticks, 1665–6 ;
two Cups and Covers and two Flagons, 1707–8 ; large gilt Cup,
1743–4 ; Spoon, 1744–5.

CLOISTER AND SURROUNDINGS

Nothing can actually be seen of the Norman cloister, although its
existence is clear from the one small window above the later
entrance from the E bay of the S aisle and also from the position
of the refectory and its windows. The pretty mid-C12 capitals
now in the ambulatory come probably from the cloister. It was
rebuilt from 1297 onwards. Progress was slow and completion
achieved only about 1430. Yet the system never changed,
though the tracery of the openings and the style of the sculptured bosses did. The system is a two-storeyed elevation, a
most unusual thing,* the lower part vaulted on wall-shafts of

See p. 391

* On the N side the upper storey is a dummy.

three detached shafts clustering round a stronger one. Round
capitals and tierceron-vaults with delicately moulded ribs and
an unparalleled wealth of bosses. There are nearly 400 of them. 24
In the s and w ranges they illustrate scenes from the Apoca- & 25
lypse, in the N and part of the E ranges from the Life of Christ.
But there is also a bay of the N walk with the Life of the Virgin
and another with the story of St Thomas Becket. The tracery
of the openings in the E range is of trefoiled arches with a tiny 10b
ogee flip at the top and in the head spherical triangles and trefoils upside down. In the s range there are three cusped ogee 11a
arches and in the heads an alternation of two motifs of the
four-petalled flower with two cinquecusped quatrefoils. The
outer arch mouldings are different too. The w range is similar,
though the motifs in the heads are different. The N range 11b
clearly came last. It starts from the w with flowing tracery and
continues with Perp motifs. The last bay before the NE corner
is the junction of 1300 and 1430. The tracery is of the type of
the early E walk, though not quite the same, but the outer arch
moulding is as in the rest of the N and in the w and s walks,
and the bosses belong to the late not the early style of sculpture.

To this we must now turn: for in the corner bay is one of
the most beautiful portals of the budding Dec style, erected 8
probably about the year 1310. Four detached shafts, and in
the arch figures under crocketed ogee gables arranged radially:
Christ seated in the middle, between angels, and then four
more figures. Against the E wall three deep niches with
crocketed ogee gables on head corbels. In the vault Christ in
Limbo, a praying bishop and a praying monk, and foliage still
naturalistic. There are also very fine bosses immediately
against the wall, notably the four Evangelists. They are, like
the ones just mentioned, perfect examples on a small scale of
the style of sculpture in the early c14. In the E wall further on
the blocked doorway to the slype, again with a crocketed
ogee gable. The arch here is both cusped and subcusped.
After that comes the chapter house entrance, tripartite as
usual, with two wide twin windows and a twin entrance (i.e.
with *trumeau*). The room itself has unfortunately disappeared,
as has indeed the whole E range. It is now simply a lane leading to the s transept and will as such be described later. But
the chapter house entrance can best be seen from that side.
All arches are ogee-headed and the motifs in the spandrels
between them have ogee tops too. From the same vantage
point one can also observe what remains of the w wall of the

dormitory, which was on the upper floor of this range. From the SE corner to the S another doorway with an ogee gable, cusped and subcusped. It leads into the DARK ENTRY. This is Norman and tunnel-vaulted and has in its E wall a doorway with a finely moulded early C14 arch. In the W range of the cloister, close to the former refectory entrance two bays converted into a lavabo with the fronts decorated with a delightful trail pattern. Arches with quatrefoils behind and three canopied niches per bay for sculpture. In the NW corner the other usual entrance into the aisle. Niches with nodding ogee canopies up one moulding of jambs and arch, six niches in all.

In the middle of the cloister garden the TOMBS of Deans Willink and Cranage, completely plain.

The S and W ranges round the cloister must also be studied principally from outside, i.e. the close. The S range contained, as was customary, the REFECTORY. Of this the N wall stands to full height, with twenty-three shafted windows, closely set, then to the E one on its own, and then, marking the wall between the Refectory and the Dark Entry, a broad, flat buttress and after that the doorway to the Dark Entry. Above this is another Norman window. S of the refectory some remains of the INFIRMARY, enough to confirm the late C12 date of which the *Registrum Primum* tells us. John of Oxford, according to the *Registrum*, built it, and he ruled from 1175 to 1200. The piers which stand belonged to the S arcade of the infirmary hall. The piers alternate between compound and circular. The compound piers consist of four lobes set diagonally and a thin roll between two spurs in the cardinal directions. The capitals, which must once have been good, are decorated with upright leaves. To the W followed another room connected with the infirmary. Part of the S wall also survives, with a blocked round and a blocked pointed doorway. In the adjoining house (No. 64 The Close) are walls of other later additions to the infirmary, partly hidden, partly exposed.

The W range is now less articulate. Only the N chamber, adjoining the W front of the cathedral, exists in full. It was the OUTER PARLOUR and is now the SONG SCHOOL. Norman, with three sweeping round arches on short wall-piers. The E wall was remodelled in the later C13 with a lancet and an inelegant plate tracery window and a doorway. They are connected inside by handsome shafting and moulded wall arches. To the S followed the GUEST HALL. Nothing remains except the E wall and the W doorway inside a porch added in the C13. This is shafted and has a finely moulded arch. There is also the r. jamb of a large contemporary window to its l.

One postscript to the W range: In what was the E wall, close to the C13 stair-turret of the song school, is a small circular window, of the type always considered Saxon in Norfolk churches. When this evidence was published in 1879 traces were also mentioned of five more windows of the same type. *See* The wall is 180 ft long and has on its E side, superimposed, the $^{P.}_{391}$ interlaced Norman arches characteristic of the parts of the cathedral close to its W end. What the wall can have belonged to, no one has yet ventured to suggest. There is a hint in Domesday Book of a Saxon establishment at Norwich prior to the transfer of the cathedral-priory from Thetford. Circular windows not in towers occur also at St Julian Norwich and at Coltishall and Witton-next-the-Sea.

Independent of the W range, further S and further W and not in axis with it, were the CELLARS, a long range, featureless except for a Perp doorway close to its N end and on the W side, and a rounded staircase tower on the E side.

For the PRIOR'S LODGING *see* below, under Deanery.

BISHOP'S PALACE

The Bishop's Palace is a distressing building of flint and red brick dating from 1858–9 and perpetrated by *Ewan Christian*. It is not easy to pick up what is left of ancient evidence. In the E wall of the N–S range, visible from inside, is a Norman window. Other medieval windows appear, or have left traces, outside. One of them is Norman too. In the same range is the vaulted kitchen of four bays with octagonal piers and hollow-chamfered arches. This is C13 work. S of it is a tunnel-vaulted room. The range at r. angles to this, i.e. running W–E, has externally a blocked Late Norman doorway to the S. This led to an undercroft which still exists and serves as a chapel now. It is of twice three bays with single-chamfered ribs dying into short piers. On the first floor of the palace a panelled room. The panelling, it is said, came from St Benet's Abbey when the last abbot, William Rugg, became bishop in 1536, and it is most interesting. It contains the medallions with fancy profiles which were so fashionable, but gives them such outrageous names as Julius Caesar, Ulysses and Penelope, Solomon and Sheba, Aurora and Cephalus, and also Pyramus. *See*
To the NE of the palace Bishop Salmon built a new HALL. $^{P.}_{391}$

He obtained licence to buy the land in 1318. Of this hall, a match for Bishop Burnell's slightly earlier hall at Wells, nothing stands except the glorious E PORCH. Against its W wall traces of the giant blank arcading of the hall itself. The porch is two-storeyed, of two open bays with very steep arches and tierceron-vaults on bundles of shafts, and big foliage capitals just turning bossy. To the l. and r. of the W doorway an ogee-headed niche. Hood-mould of the E doorway on head corbels. The E face is very corroded. There were niches l. and r., and there remain shapeless figures. Stair-turret in the NW corner. The hall extended to the S, and its S wall is marked by the S wall of Bishop Reynolds's CHAPEL built in 1661–76. The windows are undoubtedly Dec. They cannot be a case of Gothic revival of the Reynolds time. The E window with shafts in front of the mullions and naturalistic foliage is more elegant, the side windows are somewhat blunt. The flowing tracery is decidedly later than Salmon's in his porch or the Carnary College. The explanation is that the windows come from the former chapel which lay to the S of Bishop Salmon's Hall and therefore are not tied to the date of the hall. To the N of the hall incidentally there were buttery and pantry and a passage to the kitchen between. Inside the chapel MONUMENT to Bishop Reynolds † 1676. Black and white marble. Bust in an oval recess. Columns l. and r. Segmental pediments.* To the NE of Salmon's porch a new BISHOP'S HOUSE was completed in 1959. It is by *J. Fletcher Watson*, in his agreeable Neo-Georgian, of pale-purple brick, but to the S brick and cobbles (cf. his church at Bawdeswell).

Close by the BISHOP'S GATE, built probably a little before 1436 and decidedly simpler than the other precinct gates. To the inside it has two polygonal turrets and a wide archway with a two-centred head. Traceried spandrels. Attached to it on the W the porter's apartments. The archway has a tierceron-star-vault with one figured boss. Towards Palace Plain there are two entries, one for carriages, the other for pedestrians. Both have two-centred arches, but only the larger one has traceried spandrels. On the upper storey, just as in church porches, a niche between two windows. Battlements with tracery and shields. – Both outer DOORS appear to be original.

To the E of the Bishop's Gate the former GRANARY, C15 on C13 arches.

* PLATE. Norwich-made Set of the 1660s and Mace of about the same time.

DEANERY

The Deanery (or former Deanery, as the Dean no longer lives in it) was before the Reformation the PRIOR'S LODGING. It lies E of the E range of the cloister, or now E of the lane replacing the E range. The E wall of the cloister has a blocked doorway with a four-centred head and the W wall of the Deanery two blocked doorways, but neither is quite in line with the former. Altogether the evidence of the Deanery is not easily pieced together. The most valuable feature is the two windows of the hall, obviously late C13, of two lights with a trefoil upside down in a circle and shafted inside. Remains of more tall windows in the same wall. From the hall a doorway to the W led to the offices. More doorways and arches. In the present entrance hall a good fireplace with a four-centred head, probably reset.*

CARNARY COLLEGE now NORWICH SCHOOL

The premises lie within the precinct, just W of the cathedral and N and NE of the Erpingham Gate (see below, p. 232). The College was founded by Bishop Salmon in 1316. The chapel is an extremely fine piece of that date, oblong and with polygonal angle-turrets at the SW and SE angles. It is distinguished by its spacious undercroft, with large, circular, beautifully cusped windows. The undercroft itself is of twice four bays with heavy piers of shallow chamfered projections and thick single-chamfered ribs dying into them. The upper chapel is lofty and has Perp N and S windows (and a shapeless E window) but the fine shafting and fine small leaf capitals of the founder's time (cf. E window of Bishop Reynolds's Chapel). There are also hood-moulds on head stops. Piscina with buttresses and a crocketed gable, again with leaf capitals. Doorway from the W, also with leaf capitals. Hood-mould with extremely delicate seated figures. Stoup with crocketed gable to its r. The staircase up to this doorway, which is the most distinctive feature of the group of buildings, was altered by Bishop Lyhart to connect the college with the chapel. The college is now SCHOOL HOUSE. Its façade dates from c.1830–5, but hides C14 and C15 details, introduced by the very good doorway with hood-mould on head-stops. To it corresponds inside a larger doorway from the N. This must have been the outer entrance, and one would assume that the two doorways were

* Professor Tristram reports richly painted ceiling beams below the ceiling over the Prior's Hall, a rare example of C13 domestic decoration.

connected by the screens passage. However, it was the Parlour that lay to the E. At its NE end, behind Lyhart's stair, remains of a newel stair and odd doorways. Bishop Lyhart's staircase, turning through 90 degrees at an intermediate landing, has an irregular rib-vault, but at its upper end, to allow for the early C14 doorway into the hall, the rib-vault suddenly turns up vertical and continues in relief as a wall facing the doorway. The DOOR is original early C14 work, including its beautiful iron hinges and decoration. The Hall of the college projected to the N, i.e. NW of the screens passage. Buttery and pantry entrances in part survive, and on the upper floor remains of a tall hall window now visible from a passage.

A specially attractive addition to the chapel, and indeed to the W front of the cathedral, is a homely timber-framed cottage with a stepped gable to the S, nestling right under the E window of the chapel. The additions made to the N by the school cannot be called attractive. They spoil the NW part of the precinct beyond hope of redemption.

THE CLOSE

The Close is approached from the town by two great gates. One of them is in fact known as *the* Great Gate. It is also called St Ethelbert's Gate.

10a ST ETHELBERT'S GATE. This dates from 1316 and was in its top parts much restored by *Wilkins*. From the outside it has a large archway with a two-centred arch. One outer moulding with large square fleurons. Wide niches l. and r. Above it a flourish of niches and steep gables. No ogees are used. Wilkins's top proudly displays three large rose windows in flushwork. They are the result of heavy restoration, but the same pattern was there before Wilkins (*see* Britton, 1815). Old WALL to the l. and r. This is in fact Early Norman walling. Inside, the archway is vaulted in two bays. The vault has lierne ribs, an enterprising thing still at the time. To be more precise, there is a tierceron star and round its centre an octagon of lierne ribs. The pattern, once introduced, was to be of great importance for the cathedral. The vault rests on tripartite shafts. The inner façade is much simpler, but has much major flushwork, especially two blank windows l. and r. of the upper window. All three display reticulated tracery.

14a
& b ERPINGHAM GATE. Built in 1420. It is one of the proudest of cathedral gateways, with its very tall arch towards Tombland. The arch is flanked by polygonal buttresses, and but-

tresses and arch are covered with sculpture and heraldry, fortunately preserved in their entirety. On the buttresses panelling, the lowest tier with trees carrying shields, the next with a chain keeping shields together, the third and fourth with standing figures under leaf canopies. This same motif is used all up two mouldings of jamb and arch, which makes a total of fourteen plus twelve figures, plus the four of the buttresses. Their style has often been compared with that of the Morley monument at Hingham, but without justification. The arch spandrels have much big tracery. The gable is faced with knapped flint and has a niche. The archway inside is completely plain and plastered, and towards the cathedral the façade is also simple. Two big diagonal buttresses with flushwork panelling. Arch with fine mouldings.

BISHOP'S GATE and WATER GATE, *see* pp. 230, 234.

Now the Close itself. As one enters through the Great Gate there are mostly Georgian houses to one's l. and r. To the l., that is along the w wall of the Close, the backs of houses in Tombland, namely one with a pretty door-lintel with pelicans, and then a stately one of grey brick with a broad canted bay window and a Georgian doorway. After that a successful recent house by *Feilden & Mawson*, 1955. After this follows a gabled C16 or C17 house, but with no original details. It was here that in the C13 a big broad CAMPANILE was built, not at all in line with cathedral and cloister. Such detached 'clochers' were less exceptional than they seem to us today. Westminster had one, Salisbury had one, and Chichester still has one. The houses here face on to an oblong open space* and beyond it the monastic cellars (*see* above).

To the s of the Great Gate first a big house of 1702 with seven bays and two and a half storeys above a basement. It has a parapet and a doorway with Tuscan columns set against rustication and crowned by a segmental pediment (a rarity at Norwich). Nos 3 and 4 are brick-faced but older, with windows with the typical wooden crosses of the later C17. The houses are dated 1701. They have three storeys and gables. No. 5 is similar, with three plastered gables. No. 6 has two provocative shaped gables side by side towards the cathedral and two more further back at r. angles facing E. There is a very pretty door-case with Early Renaissance decoration. Altogether the houses in this corner of the Close stand all at ease, not in line and not

* With the STATUES of Nelson by *Thomas Milnes*, 1847, and Wellington by *G. G. Adams*, 1851.

even in one direction. Then Georgian discipline imposes itself.
No. 7 starts it, five bays and two and a half storeys, and after
that Nos 8–12 are one terrace and face a tidy oblong square
whose opposite side is also, after the irregular Deanery (*see*
p. 231), an even terrace (Nos 51–56), though, as the flintwork
shows, composed of pre-Reformation houses. Nos 9–12 are in
fact one nine-bay composition. Nos 13–15 are an interjection
of about 1883, three villas in the style of George & Peto, all
different and yet all the same. The E side of the square is filled
by Nos 32–33, originally the priory brewhouse, a fine eight-
bay house with a big hipped roof and the date 1682. In spite of
this the house has also its medieval past, see a buttress at the
NW corner of No. 34. From this house the Close ceases to be a
close and becomes two parallel streets or lanes running E. The
southern of the two shall be explored first. Nos 32–29 all have
flint parts showing their medieval pasts. After that some nice
minor doorways, Nos 29, 27, 26. So on to the WATER GATE,
which was built in the C15. It makes an eminently picturesque
group with the C16 FERRY HOUSE of Pull's Ferry. This was
the approach by water to the precinct, a mode of transporta-
tion more natural to the Middle Ages than to us. The Water
Gate consists of one very wide segmental archway and a
pedestrian archway by its side. The outer moulding of the arch
is of two chamfers and a roll. Round tower to the N outside,
polygonal turret inside.

The lane to the E from the N end of No. 33 is no more than a
lane in any small town. Yet there is one special house here,
No. 50 with three gables and a three-storeyed porch, the
ground floor of which is now open and has four Tuscan
columns. The house has a staircase with arabesques on the
newel-posts and flat balusters, Jacobean probably. From the E
end of the lane one can turn to Bishopgate.

There is now no more to be added to the Close than the
faux-pas of No. 57, built in 1862, very Gothic and completely
insensitive to the demands of the E view of the cathedral. In
the gatepiers SHIELDS said to come from the tomb-chest provided for Bishop Losinga's remains in the C15 right in the
centre of the chancel. To the N of No. 57 more modest houses,
again with medieval walling.

CHURCHES

As has already been said, Inner Norwich still possesses thirty-
two parish churches of the Church of England, including six not

in use at the time of writing.* To these must be added four
ruined ones‡ and the twenty which Blomefield quotes as no
longer in evidence at his time. There is no Georgian church in
Inner Norwich: they are all medieval. Walk along the 500 yds of
St Benedict Street, and you will pass St Gregory, St Laurence,
St Swithin, St Margaret, and the round tower of St Benedict.
You can repeat the experiment in other directions. If the population of Norwich was about 10,000 in 1500, and if there were about
fifty parish churches then – there were more – one must assume
that two hundred was enough to form the congregation of a
church. The parish churches of Norwich are predominantly
Perp and in every respect a Norfolk Perp. They have however
also certain details which, while not absent in Norfolk otherwise,
are more typical of Norwich than of the county. Such are: flushwork patterns of shields and lozenges in the tower parapets,
porches continuing the aisles instead of in front of the aisles,
porches two-storeyed, porches vaulted, and porch entrances with
figures in relief in the spandrels.

ALL SAINTS, All Saints Green. Unbuttressed early W tower with
    Perp (Victorian?) top. Dec chancel, Perp nave and N aisle.
    Windows with four-centred heads. Arcade of four bays with
    octagonal piers and four-centred arches. – FONT. Especially
    good. Octagonal. Against the stem eight standing figurines,
    against the bowl sixteen (cf. St James), including St Michael
    and St George. – STAINED GLASS. Canopies etc. in N windows.
    – PLATE. Chalice of Elizabethan type, given in 1669; London-
    made Paten, 1701–2, and Flagon, 1753–4.
ST ANDREW, Broad Street. Placed a little above the street. Perp
    throughout. The W tower, which has no proper parapet nor
    battlements, was built in 1478, the rest – see the inscription of
    1547 inside, on the W wall of the S aisle – in 1506. Only the
    frieze of shields above the E window is older and re-set. The
    heraldry connects it with Appleyard, the first Mayor of
    Norwich, who lived in what is now the Bridewell Museum just
    opposite to the S and died in 1419. That the W tower is earlier
    than the present church is evident from the way the porches

* St Edmund, St Mary the Less, and St Swithin are used for storing, St
Peter Hungate is a museum, Blackfriars a civic hall, St Simon and St Jude a
Boy Scout Hall.
‡ St Peter Southgate was mostly demolished in 1887, St Benedict and St
Paul lost all but their towers (and the tower of St Paul's has since been pulled
down); St Julian was in almost the same position, but has since been rebuilt;
of St Michael at Thorn there is virtually nothing left. The last four of these
five are victims of the Second World War.

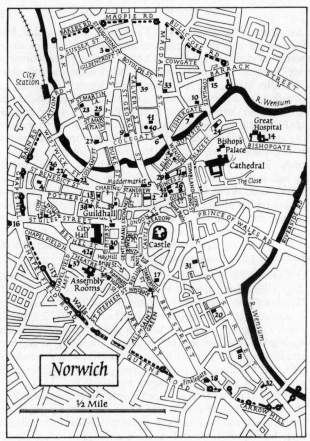

Norwich: plan of the centre of the city

Key to Churches

1. All Saints; 2. St Andrew; 3. St Augustine; 4. St Benedict; 5. Black-friars; 6. St Clement; 7. St Edmund; 8. St Etheldreda; 9. St George; 10. St George (R.C.); 11. St George Tombland; 12. St Giles; 13. St Gregory; 14. St Helen; 15. St James; 16. St John Baptist (R.C.); 17. St John Baptist Timberhill; 18. St John de Sepulchre; 19. St John Maddermarket; 20. St Julian; 21. St Laurence; 22. St Margaret; 23. St Martin-at-Oak; 24. St Martin-at-Palace; 25. St Mary at Coslany; 26. St Mary the Less; 27. St Michael (St Miles) at Coslany; 28. St Michael-at-Plea; 29. St Peter Hungate; 30. St Peter Mancroft; 31. St Peter Permountergate; 32. St Peter Southgate; 33. St Saviour; 34. St Simon and St Jude; 35. St Stephen; 36. St Swithin; 37. Congregational Church; 38. Friends' Meeting House; 39. Methodist Church; 40. Octagon Chapel; 41. Old Meeting; 42. St Peter's Methodist Chapel; 43. Princes Street Congregational Church.

from the s and N lead against walls of the tower meant to be
visible – see the base frieze. The aisles continue the porches to
the E, i.e. the doorways from the porches into the church lead
E. The tower has panelled buttresses. Some flushwork decoration on the N side. A frieze of shields above the w doorway.
The aisles, clerestory, and chancel are ashlar-faced, the
porches have exposed flint. The porch entrances have traceried
spandrels. In the N porch also a tall niche above it. Frieze of
shields at the base of the chancel. Specially pretty tracery in
the chancel N and S windows. Large four-light aisle windows.
Clerestory with eleven closely set windows. Tall five-bay
arcades, the piers with four shafts and in the diagonals four
long shallow hollows. Four-centred arches. Blank panelling
above them. Very tall tower arch dying into the imposts. The
aisle windows are set in wall-arches. – Much of the FURNISH-
INGS is High Victorian, especially the FONT, the stone
PULPIT and low stone SCREEN of 1870, the REREDOS etc. of
1856, and the ORGAN CASE of 1908. – The FONT COVER is
dated 1637. Four columns, openwork obelisk in the middle,
octagonal canopy with a ball at the top. – PLATE. Elizabethan
Chalice (Norwich); Paten Cover inscribed 1568 (Norwich);
very ornate Chalice and Cover (London) 1617–18; Paten
(London) 1670–1; Almsdish and two Flagons (London)
1704–5. – MONUMENTS. Unusually many. In the chancel
Brass of a Civilian, early C16, the figure 3 ft long. – In
the N chapel: Robert Suckling † 1589, with the usual
kneelers facing one another; Francis Rugge † 1607, in flat
relief without effigies; Robert Garsett, 1613, frontal bust
under arch with two small kneeling figures l. and r.; also Sir
John Suckling (to his wife who died in 1613). This is a standing monument of alabaster with her recumbent and him reclining on his elbow. Stiff figures. They lie on a black slab
which is not the lid of the tomb-chest but carried by four
skulls on the tomb-chest. Columns l. and r. carrying a super-
structure. Children kneel by their heads and feet, others
against the tomb-chest. Many inscriptions, large and small;
for instance SPARISCO with a flame rising out of an urn, and
SCIOLTA with a dove released from a cage. Also, where the son
kneels; 'Frater mater nostra non morta est sed dormit'. – In
the S aisle Dr Thomas Crowe † 1751 by *Robert Page*, with arms
in front of an obelisk, and John Custance † 1752 by *Rawlins*,
also in a very nice Rococo. – In the N aisle Hambleton
Custance † 1757, also by *Rawlins*. This has a weeping putto in

front of an obelisk. – On the w wall Richard Dennison † 1768.
Turning neo-classical. – (Also canopy of the lost brass of John
Gilbert † 1467, children from brass of John Holly † 1527.)

ST AUGUSTINE, St Augustine Street. A large church, at the N
end of the old town. Stately w tower of brick with clasping
buttresses. This was built in 1726, but the traceried sound-
holes must come from the predecessor. The aisle windows are
Dec and simple. The rest is later Perp, including the arcades
of aisles (three bays) and chapels (two bays). Octagonal piers,
four-centred arches. Four-light clerestory windows. Wall-
posts and longitudinal arched braces frame them and support
the arched braces for the cambered tie-beams of the roof. –
SCREEN. Only one painted panel remains (N aisle w). – WEST
GALLERY. High up, with dumb-bell balusters. – PLATE.
Chalice (Norwich) 1565–6; Paten (Norwich) given in 1697;
Flagon (London) 1705–6; Spoon, 1820–1. – MONUMENTS.
Several minor tablets; of architectural interest the plain inscription plate to Matthew Brettingham, the builder of Holk-
ham, who was buried here in 1769.

ST BENEDICT, St Benedict Street. Only the round tower remains, polygonal on the bell-stage.

BLACKFRIARS, see St Andrew's Hall (Public Buildings), p. 260.

ST CLEMENT, Colegate. Slender Perp w tower. Against the
parapet, in flushwork, shields in lozenges. Nave and chancel
Perp, except for the Dec E window. Aisleless interior. Wall-
arches in the chancel. The chancel roof has arched braces and
longitudinal arched braces on angel-busts. – FONT. Octagonal.
Panels with fleurons on the stem, flowers and leaves on the
bowl. – PLATE. Norwich-made Chalice and Paten, 1566–7;
London-made Paten, 1712–13; two Flagons, 1739–40; Almsbowl, 1744–5: Spoon, 1815–16. – MONUMENTS. Brass to
Margaret Pettwode † 1514, 39½ in. long (nave floor). – A
number of good, largish tablets.

ST EDMUND, Fishergate. Disused and now a factory store. All
Perp. w tower with traceried w sound-hole. s aisle, and s
chapel. Arcades with four-centred arches. Curious rhythm:
two bays, then a small window-like opening in the wall, then a
third bay (with foliated little capitals), then another such
opening, then the two-bay chapel.

ST ETHELDREDA, King Street. Round tower with an octagonal
top with brick trim. Aisleless nave. s doorway Norman, but
very much renewed. One capital which is in a good state of
preservation is reminiscent of those on show in the ambulatory

of the cathedral. On the s and N walls lengths of a Norman zigzag course. – FONT. With shields on the bowl and small heads against the underside. – PLATE (partly from St Peter Southgate). Chalice and Paten (London) 1612–13; Chalice (Lynn); Paten (Norwich) 1627–8; two Almsdishes (London) 1753–4; two Spoons (London) 1755–6. – MONUMENTS (from St Peter Southgate). William Johnson † 1611. With groups of kneeling figures in relief facing each other. Framed by shaped tapering pilasters. Obelisks on top. – John Paul † 1726. Tablet with books in the 'predella'.*

ST GEORGE, Colegate. Several dates are recorded: nave and tower of c.1459, chancel c.1498, aisles and chapels 1505 (N) and 1513 (S). Tall w tower, the doorway decayed. Remains of flushwork panelling to its l. and r. and of a row of shields above. Tall three-light bell-openings. Battlements with flushwork decoration: shields in lozenges. Late Perp aisle windows, clerestory ashlar-faced. Two-storeyed s porch attached to the w end of the s aisle. Entrance with St George and angels on the l., the Annunciation on the r. A niche between the upper windows. Three-bay arcades with piers of the four-shafts-four-hollows section; four-centred arches. In the s aisle wall-arches. In the clerestory six closely set windows. Between them the wall-posts for the roof. They rest on angels. Longitudinal arched braces above the windows. Cambered tie-beams on arched braces. In the s aisle arched braces too. s chapel of one bay, separate, i.e. with an arch from the aisle, but of the same style. – FONT. Octagonal, C13, of the Purbeck type with two shallow arches to each side, but not of Purbeck marble. – REREDOS. Of dark wood with columns and pilasters, i.e. of a late C17 type, but in fact late C18. – WEST GALLERY. On Tuscan columns. Earlier, it seems, than the reredos. – ORGAN CASE. 1802. Oddly enough, the Apollo Belvedere, gilt, on top. A Fame now in the s lobby, half-naked, may have been on the organ-case originally. – PULPIT. An important C18 piece, with back-panel and tester. Only one panel of the pulpit is decorated – with handsome flower and leaf carving and with tarsia. – Three sets of SWORD AND MACE RESTS. – STAINED GLASS. In the E window copy of Reynolds's New College allegories but in strident early C19 colours. Probably by *Willement* (cf. Welney, vol. 2). – PLATE. Paten of c.1720; Cup, Paten, Almsdish, and two Flagons (London) 1738–9. – MONUMENTS. Unusually many. Brass to William Norwiche † 1468 and wife;

* (Also a brass to a priest, c.1485.)

34 in. figures (N chapel). – Excellent Early Renaissance tomb-chest of terracotta to Robert Jannys, erected in 1533 or 1534. Evidently by the same craftsman who worked at Oxburgh and Wymondham. Tall tomb-chest with baluster pilasters and prettily decorated panels. – Thomas Hall † 1715 by *Thomas Green* of Camberwell. Nothing special. Two small putti l. and r. of the pilasters flanking the inscription. Open, broken segmental pediment. – Thomas Pindar Sen. † 1722. By *Robert Singleton*. Standing monument with semi-reclining figure – not the deceased, however, but a cherub. – John Calvert † 1744. With portrait medallion in front of an obelisk. – Timothy Balderston † 1764. By *Thomas Rawlins*. A putto standing on a curvaceous sarcophagus, holding a parchment with the inscription. – John Herring † 1810. By *John Bacon Jun*. With mourning woman leaning over a sarcophagus which is placed at an angle. Obelisk behind. – Many more worthwhile tablets.

ST GEORGE (R.C.), Fishergate, *see* Perambulation, p. 271.

ST GEORGE TOMBLAND. Several legacies for the building of the tower in 1445. Repair of the tower 1645. It has a niche below the W window, and traceried sound-holes. The flush-work decoration of the battlements with big lozenges and shields might well be C17. Two-storeyed S porch. Parapet with flushwork quatrefoils. Tierceron-star-vault inside with a boss of St George in the centre. Two-storeyed N porch with the N aisle attached to its E. Plainer vault, without tiercerons, though with ridge ribs. In the N one window with Dec motifs, framed by two Perp ones. Yet they belong to the same build. Coarse arcades with octagonal piers and triple-chamfered arches. The one-bay N chapel has a four-centred arch. – FONT. Octagonal, C13, of Purbeck marble, with two shallow arches to each side. – FONT COVER. Jacobean or later. Eight columns and an openwork obelisk in the middle. – REREDOS and chancel PANELLING. Good early C18, with an open segmental pediment on Corinthian columns. – PULPIT. C18 with panels of lively shape and a big tester. – COMMUNION RAIL. With slender twisted balusters. – SWORD AND MACE RESTS. Wrought iron; C18. – SCULPTURE. Relief of St George, German (?), *c.*1530. – Statuette of St George on horseback, on the font cover; Baroque. – PLATE. Large set, made in London, 1750–1. – Also, from St Simon and St Jude, Chalice 1632–3 and Paten 1634–5, both made in Norwich. – MONUMENTS. Alderman Anguish, by *Nicholas Stone*, 1617, but not of special interest. The usual composition with kneeling

figures facing one another. – Mary Gardiner † 1748. A cherub
stands and lifts a cloth off a portrait medallion. Obelisk background. The corbels are placed diagonally. – Thomas Maltby
† 1760. Cherub in front of an obelisk. – Many more tablets.
ST GILES, St Giles Street. The tallest tower of any Norwich
parish church, 120 ft high, and building up beautifully when
seen from the E above the chancel and nave gables. On the top
is a pretty little cupola, effective from afar. This dates from
1737. The church was built in the late C14, but if the chancel
built by *Phipson* in 1866–7 represents anything of the original
state, it must have been Dec. Perp aisle and clerestory windows, Perp W doorway with niches, Perp W window of five
lights, Perp four-light bell-openings with transom. The S
porch is ashlar-faced; it has a top frieze with shields in running tendrils, a pretty cresting, and a fan-vault inside. So this
must be a hundred years later than the rest. Arcades of five 26a
bays. The piers have an odd design. Four shafts and many
thin mouldings in between, but more towards the nave than
towards the aisles. The chancel arch corresponds to the arcade
arches. Three tiers of niches l. and r. of it. Beautiful hammerbeam roof with the bosses supporting the hammerbeam and
the braces rising on it constructed in one unbroken curve from
the wall-posts to the top. No collar-beams. The angels against
the hammerbeams cut across the braces and finish at the wall-
posts. This is an early stage of the hammerbeam roof, as
Cautley and Crossley explain. – FONT. Faces on the underside; flowers and little shields against the bowl. – SWORD
RESTS. Five sets of them. – PLATE. A large London-made set
of 1738–9. – MONUMENTS. Brasses to Richard Purdaunce
† 1436 and wife, 45 in. figures, and to Robert Baxter † 1432
and wife, 39 in. figures, both uncommonly good (nave). –
(Chalice Brass to John Smyth † 1499.) – Thomas Churchman
† 1742 by *Sir Henry Cheere*, tablet with a very civilized frame
and three cherubs' heads below. – William Offley † 1767. By
no means Rococo in spiritedness, but violently Rococo in
composition, i.e. demonstratively asymmetrical. The 'predella', oval inscription plate, and ledge for the top urn create
a most unexpected zigzag movement upward. The monument
is nearly identical with the Dame Anne Astley at Melton
Constable † 1768 (*see* p. 196). – Sir Samuel Churchman † 1781.
By *Rawlins*. Good and neo-classical. On the sarcophagus a
relief. Against the obelisk above, a portrait in an oval medallion.
– Several other tablets are enjoyable.

ST GREGORY, Pottergate. W tower tall, with flushwork-panelled
battlements. The spire was demolished in 1840. W doorway
inside a shallow little porch with a quadripartite vault. The
doorway has panelling up one moulding of jambs and arch.
All windows in the body of the church Perp with two-centred
arches. The arcade piers (four-bay arcades) indicate a date
between Dec and Perp: four strong shafts and eight very thin
ones in the diagonals. Castellated polygonal capitals. Two-
centred arches. The clerestory, with eight closely set windows,
concurs. The window tracery is still Dec. Two two-storeyed
porches, attached to the W walls of the S and N aisles. The S
porch has two bays of quadripartite vaulting with ridge-ribs
and bosses. Niche above the entrance. The N porch is simpler.
The chancel projects one bay beyond the aisles. Very tall
windows. The chancel was rebuilt in 1394 at the expense of the
Cathedral Priory. A passage runs from N to S under the chancel
(cf. St Peter Mancroft). The most enjoyable feature of the
interior is the inside of the tower. There is a vault high up and
a stone gallery looks down whose underside is also vaulted.
Both vaults are tierceron-stars, with two pairs of tiercerons
and a big bell-hole, but the upper one has strictly speaking no
diagonal ribs. Instead three ribs rise from the corners; they
are then cut off by a diagonal, and the rest of the vault is continued from there. Traceried STOUP under the tower. – FONT.
At the foot four rather alarming, grotesque busts and four
lions' heads. Against the bowl shields in cusped fields. – FONT
COVER. Jacobean. Low with volutes. – SCREEN. Only two and
a half panels of the dado remain; with painted figures. –
STALLS. Four in the chancel. The MISERICORDS have a lion,
two angels, and a bearded man. – Eagle LECTERN of brass,
East Anglian, dated 1496. It belongs to the same type as the
lecterns of Oxborough, Lowestoft, Oundle, and also Holy
Trinity Coventry, St Michael Southampton, Southwell and
Newcastle Cathedrals, and Urbino Cathedral. – DOOR-
KNOCKER. Now in the S chapel. An outstandingly good piece
of the C14 with a lion's head devouring a man. – WALL
PAINTING. Large, N aisle W. It represents St George, dates
from the mid C15, and is in an unusually good state. –
STAINED GLASS. A few bits in a N aisle window. – TEXTILES.
C16 pall with the repeating motifs of an angel holding a soul
in a napkin and a dolphin. – Also an earlier piece of a cope. –
PLATE. Chalice and Paten (London) 1609–10; Flagon (Nor-
wich) 1627–8. – MONUMENTS. Francis Bacon, 1659. Big

37a

tomb-chest (s chapel). – Sir Joseph Payne † 1668. Tablet with a broad frame illustrating military equipment. Compact garland below the open segmental top (chancel N). – Sir Peter Seaman † 1715. By *Thomas Green* of Camberwell. Demifigure in a niche pointing forward with a baton. Putti l. and r. (N chapel). – Joseph Chamberlin † 1762 by *Thomas Ivory*. In an elegant architectural frame (nave W). – Several more good Georgian tablets.

ST HELEN, *see* Great Hospital (Public Buildings), p. 264.

ST JAMES, Cowgate. Not big; all Perp. A curious feature is the W bay, tripartite inside, with the middle part carrying the short tower on an E, a S, and a N arch. The tower has a brick top, showing all headers. S porch attached to the S aisle. Little seated figures as pinnacles. Arcade of three plus two bays. Octagonal piers, four-centred arches. – FONT. Octagonal. With eight little standing figures against the stem and sixteen in shallow relief against the bowl (cf. All Saints). Against the underside of the bowl pretty tree-branches with leaves. – SCREEN. The dado alone is preserved, with ten painted figures, quite good. The screen was formerly dated 1505. – STAINED GLASS. A number of Flemish C16 panels and two C15 Norwich heads. – PLATE. Chalice and Paten (Norwich) 1566–7, the latter re-made in the early C18; Paten (London) 1701–2. – (COPE. Late C15.)

ST JOHN BAPTIST (R.C.), St Giles' Gate. An amazing church,₁₈ₓ proof of Victorian generosity and optimism – optimism in this case concerning the future of Catholicism in Norwich. The church was built by the Duke of Norfolk, begun in 1884, completed in 1910. It was designed originally by *George Gilbert Scott Jun.* and continued after his early death in 1897 by his brother *John Oldrid Scott*. The nave is by the elder brother, the chancel was designed by both. The church is of cathedral size, all ashlar-faced, 275 ft long and over 80 ft high inside the chancel. The nave is of nine bays, the chancel of four, the transepts of three with an E aisle, and there are a polygonal chapel attached to the E side of the N transept, and a tall crossing tower. The style is E.E., with all windows lancets and fine if conventional combinations of them, with flying buttresses for the clerestory, with a triforium inside, and with stone vaulting throughout, quadripartite in the nave (which was built first and finished in 1894), with ridge-ribs and tiercerons in the chancel. Sumptuous portals with black marble shafting, the same in the wall arcading and more in the E parts, and stiff-leaf capitals everywhere. The church is of course an end, not a beginning. It belongs to Pearson (not to Sir G. G. Scott Sen. incidentally), that is to self-effacing historicism. It has nothing of the new freedom and licences of Sedding or Caröe, i.e. the Arts and Crafts. – The thing which gives the interior its peculiar holiness is the STAINED GLASS, by *John Powell* of Hardman & Powell, and, for the E parts, his son *Dunstan Powell*. Its colours are dark and glowing, its composition designed on the principle of C13 cathedral windows – historicism here too and not Arts and Crafts, but supremely well done.

ST JOHN BAPTIST TIMBERHILL, Ber Street. The tower collapsed in 1784. Perp throughout, except for the E window. All windows renewed. S porch two-storeyed, vaulted inside. Arcades of three bays. Quatrefoil piers with octagonal capitals and triple-chamfered arches. One-bay N and S chapels with four-centred arches, the N responds semicircular, the S responds polygonal. – CHANDELIER, S chapel. Of *c.*1500 and probably German. A small figure of the Virgin in the centre. The arms bristle with branches, leaves, and grapes. – SWORD REST. Of wrought iron; C18. – PLATE. Norwich-made Chalice of 1565–6 and Paten of 1566–7; Paten (London) 1697–8. – MONUMENT. Robert Page † 1778 by *Robert Page*. With a weeping putto in front of an obelisk.

38a

ST JOHN DE SEPULCHRE, Ber Street. W tower, aisleless nave with transeptal chapels, chancel. All Perp. Tall tower arch. Wall arches along the nave walls. Two-storeyed N porch. Tall niche between the upper windows. A frieze of shields and one of flushwork separates the storeys. Elementary tierceron-star-vault. – FONT. Against the stem four lions, against the bowl four lions and four demi-figures of angels. – NORTH DOOR. Traceried. – PLATE. London-made Chalice of 1776–7 and Paten of 1795–6. – BRASSES. Civilian and wife of *c.*1530, the man palimpsest of a monk under a canopy behind a grille.

ST JOHN MADDERMARKET, St John Maddermarket. W tower, nave and aisles. The chancel seems to have been demolished already in the C16. Its E window must have been set back to become the E window of the church. It is a sumptuous Dec piece of forms more fantastical than customary in Norfolk. The N aisle E window has cusped intersected tracery, but may not be original. All the rest is Perp. The W tower is squeezed in between houses and has a passage through from N to S. Traceried sound-holes, little figures on the pinnacles. Two-storeyed porches, that on the S with a damaged vault inside, that on the N (now a chapel) with the usual tierceron-star but in addition a circular rib to connect the bosses. The entrance to the N has two sets of suspended shields up one moulding of jambs and arch. The interior is of three bays with slim Perp piers with thin shafts and long wave mouldings diagonally between them. The clerestory has eight windows closely set and is faced extensively with ashlar. Roof with ribbed coving, the rest ceiled. This dates probably from c.1864 (after an explosion). In the N aisle wall-arches. – REREDOS. A sumptuous early C18 piece with detached columns carrying a tester or canopy. It is said to come from Corton in Suffolk but supposed to have been in St Michael at Coslany originally. – STAINED GLASS. Old fragments in two N windows. – PLATE. Chalice (Norwich) 1566–7; Paten, inscribed 1568; Paten, 1705–6; two Flagons, 1715–16; Spoon, 1738–9, all London-made. – MONUMENTS. Brasses (under the gallery at the W end) to Walter Moneslee † 1412 and wife (18 in. figures), John Toddenham c.1450 (16 in. figure), Ralph Segrym † 1472 and wife (3 ft figures), William Pepyr † 1476 and wife (28 in. figures), Johanna Caux † 1506 (28 in. figure), John Terry † 1524, wife and children, on brackets (25 in. figures), John Marsham † 1525 and wife (30 in.), Robert Rugge † 1558 and wife (3 ft; palimpsest of an early C14 abbot), Nicholas Sottherton † 1540 (inscription only; palimpsest of a nun of c.1440). – Christopher Sayer † 1600, Thomas Sotherton † 1608, both tablets with kneeling figures facing one another across a prayer-desk. In the frame of the former to the l. and r. figures of Pax, Vanitas, Gloria, and Labor (a workman). – Tablet to Walter Nugent Monck † 1958, founder of the Norwich Players and the Maddermarket Theatre.

ST JULIAN, St Julian's Alley, off King Street.* Mostly destroyed in the Second World War and rebuilt by *A. J. Chaplin*. Of the round tower a stump has been left standing. The N wall however was sufficiently intact to preserve three windows revealed during repairs. They are Anglo-Saxon: two circular and one oblong and arched but perhaps originally also circular. In the tower traces of circular bell-openings could be seen too. The Norman doorway, now inside, comes from St Michael-at-Thorn. One order of shafts, single-scallop capitals, zigzag in the arch. – FONT. Octagonal, with demi-figures of angels. – PLATE. Chalice and Paten Cover, inscribed 1669; Almsdish (London) 1765–6.

* Julian of Norwich was an anchoress here.

ST LAURENCE, St Benedict Street. Perp. w tower 112 ft high
with flushwork-panelled two-step battlements and higher stair-
turret ending in a spirelet. w doorway with spandrels with
reliefs of St Laurence grilled and St Edmund shot at. Simple
two-storeyed N and S porches. The N porch has a lierne-vault.
Aisles with four-light windows. Clerestory of eleven closely
set windows. Buttresses to E and W with canopies. The E
window is Victorian. Interior without a chancel arch. Arcades
of three plus two bays. The chancel aisles have piers with a
normal Perp section. Four shafts, but only those towards the
arch openings with capitals. Chamfer and long shallow hollow
in the diagonals between. The aisle piers are very odd and
probably altered. They are octagonal but all angles are
rounded (cf. St Margaret) and the capitals are undulating.
The aisle and chapel windows are set in wall arches. – FONT.
Stem panelled and with fleurons. Bowl with demi-figures of
angels in square, framed and cusped fields, but placed so that
their heads reach above the top frame, an unusual and very
successful motif. – DOOR. The entrance door to the S porch is
traceried. – STAINED GLASS. Mosaic of old bits in the N aisle
E window. – PLATE. Chalice and Paten Cover (Norwich)
1565–6. – BRASSES. John Asger Sen. † 1436 (35 in. figure),
John Asger Jun. † 1436 (17 in.), and John Stylle † 1483 (20½
in.); in the nave floor. – Geoffrey Langeley † 1437, Prior of
Horsham St Faith. The figure is 31 in. long and stands on a
bracket. Of the canopy little is preserved (N aisle). – Thomas
Childes † 1452, a skeleton (22 in.) – (John Wellys † 1495.)

ST MARGARET, St Benedict Street. Of moderate size. Dec w
tower with flowing tracery in the bell-openings, plain battlements and traceried sound-holes. Late Perp aisle windows of four
lights with four-centred arches. Two-storeyed S porch attached
to the W end of the S aisle. In the spandrels of the entrance St
Margaret and a monk (?) amid branches. Simple tierceron-
star-vault. S aisle and S chapel of two plus two bays. Octagonal
piers with concave sides and rounded angles (cf. St Laurence).
Four-centred arches. – FONT. On a high traceried step. Bowl
with shields in quatrefoils. – REREDOS. The former reredos
with painted Moses, Aaron, and Ten Commandments, C18,
now above the S door. – CHEST. C15. With blank windows in
two tiers and bands of four-petalled flowers as a frame. – WEST
GALLERY and TOWER SCREEN. Parts of the former communion rail. With dumb-bell balusters. Dated 1707. –
PLATE. Chalice and Paten Cover (Norwich) 1566–7; Alms-

plate (London) 1763–4. – MONUMENT. Low tomb-chest with brass to Anne Rede † 1577. The brass is a palimpsest of three different brasses, English c.1370, English c.1470, and Flemish c.1560 (S chapel).

ST MARTIN-AT-OAK, Oak Street. Built before 1491, the date of death of Thomas Wilkyns who, according to an inscription reported by Blomefield, 'istam E^{lam} sumptibus suis de novo in omnibus fieri fabricavit'. Much damaged in the Second World War. Stump of the unbuttressed W tower. Nave, S aisle, and chancel. Four-bay arcades, the piers of a typical Late Perp section: four shafts separated in the diagonals by a wave and a long shallow hollow. Arch-braced roof. – PLATE. Chalice and Paten (Norwich) 1566–7; Paten and Flagon (London) 1723–4. – MONUMENTS. Jeremiah Revans † 1724. No longer complete. It had two largish kneeling figures, not in relief.

ST MARTIN-AT-PALACE, Palace Plain. Unbuttressed W tower, much restored in 1874. During a previous restoration in 1851 damage was done to the chancel, and that explains the Victorian look of the chancel chapels. They have two bays and piers and arches of the mid C14. The nave and aisles are Perp, but the windows again look entirely Victorian, except for the W window (with stepped embattled transoms). The N arcade is convincingly Dec too (three bays), the S arcade is shapeless. Two-storeyed S porch with the rebus of Bishop Lyhart, i.e. third quarter of the C15. – FONT. Octagonal, C14. The stem with shafts and blank little two-light windows between. Quatrefoils on the bowl. – CHANDELIER. Of brass, a fine piece, inscribed 1726. – PLATE. Chalice with Paten Cover (Norwich) 1567–8, specially beautiful pieces; Paten and Flagon (London) 1730–1. – MONUMENTS. Lady Elizabeth Calthorpe † 1578. Tomb-chest with shields in strapwork fields separated by pilasters. Four-centred back-arch between pilasters. In the spandrels medallions and leaf. Top with shields under triangular and semicircular heads.

ST MARY AT COSLANY, St Mary Plain, off Oak Street. Anglo-Saxon round tower. The triangular heads of the twin bell-openings and the far receding shafts are unmistakable. In the chancel one Dec N window and traces of a Dec E window superseded by the present Perp one. The rest Perp (of 1477, says Cox), the windows with two-centred arches. The transept windows are specially tall. There are no aisles. Two-storeyed S porch. Niche between the upper windows. Simple tierceron-star-vault inside. Chancel with wall-arches. Arch-braced roofs

28a in nave and chancel resulting in the crossing in an arrangement as of diagonal ribs (cf. St Peter Hungate and Stody, also Honiton, Ilsington, and Luppitt in Devon). In the centre boss with the Virgin surrounded by rays. Angels against the intersections around. Chancel roof also arch-braced but panelled, each panel with a richly cusped quatrefoil. The E bay with gilding as a ceilure above the altar. – FONT. Octagonal, panelled stem, bowl with shields in cusped fields. – FONT COVER. Later C17. Tall, with four columns and tall bold volutes above. – STALLS. Six with simple MISERICORDS. – COMMUNION RAIL. Later C17. With fully-fashioned dumbbell balusters. – HOUR-GLASS STAND of iron, attached to the pulpit. – SWORD AND MACE RESTS. – PLATE. Norwich-made Chalice and Paten Cover, 1567–8; London-made Flagon, 1728–9; Almsdish, 1736–7; Almsdish, 1745–6. – MONUMENTS. Martin van Kurnbeck † 1579 and wife (chancel N). Flat four-centred arch. Spandrels with branches and medallions. The figures incised in the back-wall. Pediment at the top. – Clement Hyrne. Tablet with kneeling figures as usual. – Thomas Hurnard † 1753. By J. Ivory.

ST MARY THE LESS, Queen Street. Disused and a furniture showroom at the time of writing. W tower, aisleless nave and chancel. In the nave late C13 windows, in the chancel C14 windows, E purely Perp, S at the transition between Dec and Perp. Arch-braced chancel roof. Angle piscina.

ST MICHAEL (ST MILES) AT COSLANY, Coslany Street. All
16a of c.1500 and the most enthusiastic display of flushwork. In the tall W tower admittedly it is not used (parapet with shields in lozenges), but the S aisle (or what remains of it) is covered by it and so is the chancel (refaced in 1883*). The N side is left plain but faced with ashlar. The motifs include whole blank windows. Four- and five-light windows under four-centred arches. Also stepped-up-and-down, embattled transoms. Four-bay arcades (on the S side the first two missing). The piers have a characteristic Later Perp section: four shafts and in the diagonals a wave and a long shallow hollow. Four-centred arches. – FONT. Octagonal, simple, with quatrefoils. – DOORS. The W door is elaborately traceried and was illustrated by Cotman. – Traceried also the door to the sacristy. – SWORD AND MACE RESTS (vestry). – SCULPTURE. The four supporter figures over the W door are probably Jacobean and come from

* When the S and E walls received their flushwork to harmonize with the original N side.

the chapel of Oxnead, the Paston mansion. – STAINED GLASS.
E window by *Heaton, Butler & Bayne*, 1884. – Fragments of
original glass in the N aisle E window. – PLATE. Chalice and
Paten, Norwich-made, 1566–7; Flagon, 1731–2, two Almsdishes, 1734–5, and Almsbowl, 1761–2, all London-made. –
MONUMENT. Brasses to Henry Scottowe † 1515 and wife; in
shrouds, 26½ in. figures (N chapel). – Henry Fawcett † 1619.
Four-centred arch; the monument is incomplete. – Between
chancel and N chapel defaced tomb-chest, probably of William
Ramsey † 1502, who founded the N chapel. – Edmund Hooke
† 1784. Large and good, with a bust and books l. and r., in
front of an obelisk. Putto-heads at the foot. – More enjoyable
Georgian tablets.

ST MICHAEL-AT-PLEA, Queen Street. All Perp. W tower
lowered (no bell-openings) but with thick crocketed pinnacles.
N and S transepts, S chancel chapel, two-storeyed S porch with
niches l. and r. of the entrance, St Michael and the Dragon in
its spandrels and a niche between the upper windows. Base
frieze of shields in N aisle and N transept. Nave roof arch-
braced with embattled wall-plate, longitudinal arched braces,
and angels along the ridge. – FONT. Octagonal, simple, with
demi-figures of angels against the underside. – FONT COVER.
C17. With eight columns, an openwork obelisk in the middle,
and a tall top with an obelisk and a dove. – COMMUNION
RAIL. Jacobean or a little later. With vertically symmetrical
balusters. More of them are re-used in the WEST GALLERY. –
SOUTH DOOR. Excellently traceried. – SWORD AND MACE 38b
RESTS. Wrought iron; C18. – PLATE. Chalice given in 1691;
two Flagons (Norwich) 1667–8: Almsbasin, inscribed 1694;
Paten (London) 1708–9. – MONUMENTS. Jacques de Hem
† 1603. Inscription in black-letter and, to its r., panel of the
same size with kneeling figures incised, a pediment over the
whole with shovel, pick, skull, cross-bones. The odd thing is
that the monument is folded round an obtuse angle at the W wall.

ST MICHAEL-AT-THORN, Ber Street. Only remains of walls,
after a bomb fell on the church in the Second World War.

ST PETER HUNGATE (now a Museum), *see* Public Buildings,
p. 262.

ST PETER MANCROFT, Market Place. Begun in 1430. A large 15
donation towards the building of the chancel in 1441. The
church was consecrated in 1455. St Peter Mancroft is the
market church, as they say in Germany, of Norwich and the
Norfolk parish church *par excellence*. It lies in a splendid

position, a little above the market place and facing it broad-wise. It has a mighty W tower and is 180 ft long and ashlar-faced, all symptoms of prosperity and ambition. The tower, however, it must be reluctantly admitted, is more rich than aesthetically successful. Every motif has been lavished on it, and in the end this very prodigality has defeated its object. Yet the details must be enumerated. First the tower gains by the processional way through it, i.e. the N and S arches in addition to the W entrance and W doorway inside. The space between these four arches has a tierceron-star-vault with a big circle in the middle. The buttresses are mighty but ill-defined, polygonal below but with spurs as if of set-back buttresses. There is a base frieze of flushwork and a frieze of shields above that. The arches have shields in cusped fields up a moulding of jambs and arch. The W window is of five lights with a frieze of niches below. There are niches and shields also higher up by the window. The buttresses have niches in three tiers with big pedestals. The lower stage of the wall is flushwork-panelled, the upper stages have three tiers of stone panelling with bases for many statues. Bell-openings of three lights, niches to the l. and r., more panelling over. Short polygonal turrets and a small lead-covered spire or spike with dainty flying buttresses, too playful to make a stand on this tower. It was added in 1895 by *A. E. Street*. It raises the total height of the steeple to 146 ft.

The aisles and transepts have four-light windows with two-centred arches. Base friezes of flushwork panelling and of shields, buttresses with niches. N porch of two storeys. Stoups and shields l. and r. of the entrance. Niche above. Lierne-vault inside and finely shafted doorway. The S porch is a little simpler. It has the usual tierceron-vault inside, but with two plus two pairs of tiercerons. Doorway with two mouldings studded with fleurons. In the transept end walls simply rusti-cated doorways with four-centred heads, probably of *c*.1650 (*see* below). Chancel aisles of two bays, chancel projecting by one bay with a passage from N to S under it. The E wall was damaged in 1648 and repaired by *Martin Morley*. The present E window is of seven lights and flanked by polygonal turrets. To the E of the chancel and accessible from it by two small E doorways a three-storeyed vestry and treasury. But the finest motif of the church, as seen from the market place, is the clerestory with its seventeen windows.

The interior is dominated by the tall arches of the eight-bay

arcade, the immensely tall tower arch, and the tall transept
arches. There is no chancel arch. The arcade piers are quatrefoil with small hollows in the diagonals, and the arch mouldings
have sunk waves, C14 rather than C15 motifs. The W bay is
squeezed in by the tower buttresses, another proof that the
tower invaded the nave. Beautiful hammerbeam roof. The
hammerbeams rest on long wall-posts between the clerestory
windows, and these in their turn rest on busts. Flat niches in
the stonework beneath. The hammerbeams are not visible.
They are concealed by a ribbed coving like that of a rood
screen (cf. Ringland and also Framlingham, Suffolk). Many
bosses. Aisle roofs arch-braced with tracery. The tall square
transepts, or rather transeptal chapels, have lierne-vaults of
wood.

FURNISHINGS. FONT. Shafted stem, the reliefs of the bowl
hacked off. – FONT CANOPY. A canopy, not a cover, cf.
Trunch and also Durham Cathedral. Four square supports,
and on them an octagonal canopy so that the diagonals come
forward to a point, stressed by a pendant. Big octagonal super-
structure with crocketed cap. A pelican on top. – REREDOS.
1885 by *Seddon*, but remodelled and enlarged by *Comper* in
1930; neo-Gothic and neutral. – A few STALLS with simple
MISERICORDS. – LENTEN VEIL, that is the curtain to cover
the rood during Lent. The pulley wheels and boss are
still in position. – ORGAN GALLERY AND LOBBY. Of c.1707.
Fine woodwork, as in a City church in London. With
fluted columns and pediment. – BENCH. One plain one (S
chapel). – WEST DOOR. Traceried. – Three sets of SWORD
AND MACE RESTS. – SCULPTURE. One small C15 alabaster
panel with female saints (chancel). – PAINTINGS. Liberation
of St Peter by *Charles Catton*, 1768 (N aisle). – Barnabas by the
Cross and Moses on Pisgah, by *William Blake Richmond*. –
STAINED GLASS. The E window a bible of East Anglian C15
glass, though not made for this window. Forty-two panels
with stories of Christ, the Virgin, St Peter, St John Evangelist,
St Francis, etc. – In the S chapel E window good glass of 1921,
in the style of Eric Gill. By *H. Hendrie*. – TAPESTRY (S aisle
W). Resurrection, Flemish, dated 1573. – PLATE. A veritable
treasure. Very fine, London-made Chalice and Cover of 1543–4
with a classical figure at the top; Sir Peter Gleane's Cup and its
Cover (London) 1565, very sumptuous; Cup and Paten
(Norwich) 1566–7; two Flagons (London) 1612–13; Almsbasin inscribed 1635; Paten-Dish (Norwich) given in 1657;

Flagon (London) partly 1683, partly 1741–2; Paten (London) 1689–90; Spoon (London) 1711–12; Chalice (London) 1738–9; Almsbasin (London) 1753–4; Paten (London) 1779–80; Knife (London), Late Georgian.

MONUMENTS. Brass to Sir Peter Rede † 1568, but in armour of the late C15. Palimpsest of a better late C15 Flemish brass. The figure is 33 in. long. The inscription records that Peter Rede served the Emperor Charles V at the conquest of Barbaria and the siege of Tunis (chancel floor).* – Francis Windham † 1592. Big tomb-chest with Tuscan columns and shields in strapwork surrounds. On it the demi-figure of the deceased, frontal, and over it canopy and curvy top. An uncommon composition. – Augustine Curtis and Augustine Curtis Jun., † 1731 and 1732, carvers. By *James Barrett* (N aisle W). A column in front of an obelisk. Cherubs' heads to the l. and r. half concealed by drapery. – Many more good tablets.

St Peter Permountergate, King Street. A number of benefactions (no doubt in connexion with the rebuilding) in 1486. W tower with a doorway with two seated figures in the spandrels. A row of shields above it. Traceried sound-holes. Aisleless nave with four-light windows. The chancel windows also of four lights. An E vestry of two storeys attached to the chancel (cf. St Peter Mancroft). Two-storeyed S porch. – FONT. Octagonal, with four lions against the stem and four lions and four demi-figures of angels against the bowl. – SCREEN. The N half of the dado is original. In the spandrels nicely carved leaf, animals and figures (including St Michael and the Dragon). – SWORD AND MACE REST. – PAINTING, now above the S door. St Peter and the Cock. By *Joseph Brown*, 1740. – STAINED GLASS. E window. Probably mid-C19. Sharp colours; not bad. – PLATE. Chalice (Norwich) 1565–6; Spoon inscribed 1613, a very early date; Paten or Dish (Norwich) inscribed 1679; Flagon and Paten (London) 1765–6. – MONUMENT. Richard Berney, 1623. Four-poster against the wall. Recumbent effigies. Big top-structure with angels on the corners.

St Peter Southgate, King Street. The church was demolished in 1887, and only a shapeless part of the tower remains, up some steps to the S of a play-yard.

St Saviour, Magdalen Street. Of modest size, with a short W tower. Aisleless Perp nave. Dec chancel with reticulated

* (Also groups of children of the brass to Richard Aylmer †1512.)

tracery. – FONT. Beasts' heads, rather frighteningly, at the foot. Stem with nodding ogee arches coming forward round the shafts supporting the bowl. Against the bowl quatrefoils. – Two SWORD RESTS. – PLATE. Chalice and Paten (Norwich) 1564–5; Flagon (London) 1735–6; Almsdish (London) 1736–7. – MONUMENTS. Many minor ones, starting with one † 1610.

ST SIMON AND ST JUDE, Wensum Street. Disused, and now a Boy Scout Hall. Unbuttressed W tower, half-collapsed. Wide aisleless Perp nave. Chancel, early C14, with three-light windows with cusped intersected tracery. Encased in the chancel arch earlier tripartite responds. No furnishings.

ST STEPHEN, Rampant Horse Street. N tower with porch, the ground floor (see the entrance) C14 – as is also the S doorway. The ground floor is vaulted in two bays with a big circle in the middle and two figured bosses of which one represents the Stoning of St Stephen. Above this ground floor the tower is the result of a remodelling dated in large figures 1601.* Knapped flint friezes. Two-light bell-openings flanked by large blank two-light flushwork windows. Above on each side a circle, a lozenge, and another circle. In spite of this the tower appears still essentially Perp, and this is also true of the rest of the church, of which the chancel was indeed built in 1501–22, but the rest after the Reformation. Above the W doorway runs a frieze of small lozenges with, in the middle, the date 1550. Yet the W window of six lights under a four-centred arch is as convincingly Perp as the E window of five lights under its two-centred arch. The clerestory, with its splendid sixteen windows on each side, is internally as convincing, though externally the little buttresses between the windows have a post-Reformation touch. W and E walls are ashlar-faced.

The interior of the church is impressive. There is no chancel 26b arch, so that the arcades run without any break for eight bays. The piers are octagonal, and their details are clearly no longer Perp. They have sunk concave panels in each side. Many-moulded four-centred arches. Panelling above the arches in the East Anglian way. Hammerbeam roof with tracery in the spandrels and no motif betraying the real date of the work. – STALLS. Just four are left, one with a minor MISERICORD. – STAINED GLASS. In the E window a jumble of old glass culminating in five large figures and groups of 1511 from the monastery of Mariawald near Heimbach in the Ruhr valley. Also English C15 fragments and others. – In the head of the w

* The figures were unfortunately removed in 1960.

window many small figures in clear colours, according to the *Ecclesiologist* 1865 by *Heaton, Butler & Bayne*. – In a s aisle window glass by *Kempe*, 1905. – PLATE. Chalice and Paten (Norwich) 1567–8; two Flagons (London) 1626–7; Chalice and Cover (London) 1631–2; Almsbasin (Norwich) given in 1694; Paten or Dish (London) 1718–19; Spoon dated 1753. – MONUMENTS. Brass to a Lady, early C15. – Brass to Thomas Bokenham † 1460. – Brass to Thomas Cappe † 1545 (2 ft figure). – Brasses to Richard Brasyer and his son, who was Mayor in 1510. Also to Robert Brasyer and wife (28 in. figures) made *c.*1510–15 (all chancel). – John Mingay, 1617, tablet with kneeling figures facing each other across a prayer-desk. – Charles and Mary Mackerell. By *John Ivory*. She died in 1747. A very fine architectural tablet. – Elizabeth Coppin † 1812. Of Coade stone, signed *Coade & Sealy*. Gothic below, but with a normal Georgian chubby putto by an urn above.

ST SWITHIN, St Benedict Street. Disused and at the time of writing a furniture store. The tower was pulled down in 1881. The little Victorian stone bell-turret which replaces it is very pretty. Nave and chancel in one. No structural division. Four bays of piers made cruciform and classical. At the same time the arches were made round. The aisle windows are Dec, simple, of two lights, the E window also has the Dec reticulation motif, but a four-centred arch. – FONT. Octagonal. Against the stem four lions, against the bowl four lions and four demi-figures of angels. – STALLS. A few, with MISERICORDS. – PLATE. Chalice (Norwich) 1565–6; Paten, Paten-Cover, Almsdish, Flagon (London) 1721–2.

CONGREGATIONAL CHURCH, Chapel Field. 1858 by *Joseph James* of London. Grey brick. Deplorably Norman, and with two thin towers set back behind the centre of the front.

FRIENDS' MEETING HOUSE, Gildencroft. Built in 1699, destroyed by fire in 1942, and rebuilt on the old lines in 1958. It was one of the largest and stateliest of the early Quaker Meeting Houses and clearly followed the pattern of the Old Meeting (*see* below). Brick, eight bays and two storeys. Big hipped roof, windows with wooden crosses and a curious punctuation by giant Doric pilasters set between windows two and three and three and four and then five and six and six and seven. Galleries inside.

FRIENDS' MEETING HOUSE, Upper Goat Lane, off Pottergate. 1826 by *J. T. Patience*. Quite a composition on a restricted site. Grey brick. The centre with a one-storeyed portico of two pairs of short, sturdy, unfluted Doric columns. Arched windows and pilasters above. Two projecting wings with broad pilasters. The back is of ten bays with a centre with – a somewhat painful arrangement – five giant pilasters.

METHODIST CHURCH, Calvert Street. 1810. A pleasant façade. Five bays with arched windows on two floors and a hipped roof of low pitch. Doorway with Tuscan columns *in antis* and a segmental fanlight.

OCTAGON CHAPEL, Colegate. 1754–6 by *Thomas Ivory*. Built 19b for Presbyterians; after 1820 it became Unitarian. Of brick, with a one-storeyed pedimented portico of four unfluted Ionic columns. Three arched windows over, two in each of the other sides. Octagonal pyramid roof and in it little dormers, or 28b bull's-eyes with curly surrounds, which are the only light relief of an otherwise, not stern, but reticent building. Interior with eight giant Corinthian columns and wooden galleries between them. Perfect FITTINGS altogether, especially good the surround of the entrance. The pulpit and organ wall was re-done in 1889. – SWORD AND MACE RESTS. – PLATE. Six Patens dated 1713. – Several agreeable MONUMENTS. – Outside to the E the former MARTINEAU MEMORIAL HALL, 1907 by *H. Chatfield Clarke*. Red brick, still in the Norman Shaw style.

OLD MEETING, Colegate. 1693. Congregational. A beautiful 19a façade of red brick, lying far back from the street. Five wide bays and two storeys with hipped roof. The centre with four monumental Corinthian brick pilasters with stone capitals. Doorways in the outer bays with straight hoods on carved brackets. Windows in raised frames. They were, Mr Briggs reports, the earliest sash windows at Norwich. Interior with galleries on three sides. Tuscan and upper Ionic columns. Flat ceiling. The original ritual and seating arrangements are all preserved. – PLATE. Bequeathed in 1737.

PRINCES STREET CONGREGATIONAL CHURCH. 1869 by *Boardman*. Big and still classical. Grey brick, three bays. With giant pilasters carrying a pediment. Arched windows. An office building on the r. is part of the same composition.

ST MARY'S BAPTIST CHURCH, Duke Street. 1951–2 by *Stanley J. Wearing*.

PUBLIC BUILDINGS

CASTLE. The castle was made shortly after the Norman Conquest by heightening an existing hill and digging a ditch. But nothing is known of a stone keep at that time. The ditch is 100

ft wide, the mound 33 ft high. The KEEP was built about 1160.
It is *c*.95 by 90 ft and *c*.70 ft high, nearly as large as the White
Tower, and unique in its consistent external decoration. The
only comparable keep in this respect is also in Norfolk, Castle
Rising, no doubt built in imitation of Norwich and by no
means as thorough in the application of blank arcading, the
one decorative motif on which they both relied and on which
Norman masons were so often satisfied to rely exclusively.
The Norwich keep as we see it today was re-faced completely
in 1833–9 (by *Salvin*). It was done in Bath stone as against the
original Caen stone and carstone, and that alone makes it look
rather like a model. But the motifs were all there and can be
trusted, and the most remarkable thing in any case is the fact
that a military, that is entirely utilitarian, building was decorated externally at all. France e.g. has nothing to compare with
Norwich. To go more into detail, there is an unbroken ground
stage, and above this follow three, and on other sides four,
tiers of blank arcading with the windows set in irregularly
where they come. The tiers are not regular in themselves
either. They differ in height, and the arches in width. The
whole system is of course articulated by the broad, flat Norman
buttresses. The base courses of the various levels are carried
round them. The only decorative motifs, apart from the
columns with their plain scallop capitals, are occasional
pilasters instead and billet friezes with big oblong billets
rounded on the face, and some diapering inside the top
arcading on the w side. There is only one exception to this re-
ticence: the main portal at the N end of the E wall, and this was
protected by a fore-building, just as at Castle Rising. The fore-
building, as it is now, is entirely renewed, but it still stood,
even if badly treated, at the time of the restoration. The portal
is not in a perfect state, but shows enough to place it fairly at
the date given here to the whole keep, and to recognize it as the
most ornate piece of Norman decoration at Norwich. There
were three orders of shafts. One of them carries the beakhead
motif which is also continued into the arch. The capitals, as
far as they survive, had lively decoration with little people and
beasts, apparently in fighting scenes. In the best preserved one
a man with a sword and a dog are attacking an animal. On another a boar can be recognized. The abaci were decorated too,
and the arch had, apart from rolls, panels with foliage, interlace, again little animals, etc. in no order. Finally the whole
portal was surrounded by a much wider arch with panels with

four-petalled flowers. This no doubt marked the line of the vault of the vestibule. As it is so much wider than the portal, one blank arch was fitted in to the r. of the portal.

The keep was entered at the level of the main hall. The situation is confusing now, because the keep was open to the sky for a long time and when adapted for the use of a museum was horizontally and vertically subdivided differently from what it had been originally. The present main level is half-way up the basement and the floor level of the main halls is that of the present gallery. What used to be the hall galleries, i.e. wall passages, is now not accessible. Also, today's division by columns must be in one's mind replaced by a solid wall such as survives in the White Tower in London. This adjustment having been made, one can try to visualize the interior of the keep as it was. The main floor contained two halls and certain interesting subsidiary chambers. The halls are known as the Soldiers' and the Knights' Hall (for no special reason). The former had the N, the latter the S half. The portal led into the Soldiers' Hall. In the W wall each hall had four garderobe (or lavatory) shoots whose openings to the exterior were one feature of that side. There was one spiral stair in the NE corner, a second in the NW corner, and a third in the SW corner, so that both halls were served. The kitchen fireplace can be seen across the NW corner. In the SE corner was the chapel. The irregular groined vault of its apse and its NE and SE windows are preserved. In the SW corner are a strong respond and the springing of a vault. It has been suggested that this was part of the governor's private room.

No medieval buildings other than the keep exist now in the inner bailey, nor any in the roughly semicircular outer bailey, which extended where the old Cattle Market is. The former was 3¼ acres in size, the latter 4½. The buildings which are there now are connected with the use of the castle as a gaol in the late C18 and early C19 and with its present use as a museum. The gaol was made in 1789–93 by *Sir John Soane*. The one-storeyed LODGES date from 1811 and are by *Francis Stone*.* The BRIDGE is of c.1825 but replaces a stone bridge of the C12. The granite walls, much more theatrically medieval than the keep, and the Great Gatehouse attached to the keep on its E side are of c.1825 (by *Wilkins*). At the foot of the gatehouse one can see the base of the C13 gatehouse with its mighty round

---

* Information received from Mr Nairn. The iron RAILINGS, so Mr Paget Baggs tells me, are also by *Stone*.

towers. Then, from *c*.1889, conversion into a museum began (under *E. Boardman*) and new low buildings of red brick were gradually provided (partly on the foundation of the gaol), the most recent one in 1951.

WALLS. The length of the walls of medieval Norwich is about 2¼ m., no less than that of the walls of London. They were probably first built in the C12, but rebuilt systematically between 1294 and 1320 – so Blomefield says. They surround the town, except where it is protected by the Wensum, i.e. from Carrow at the SE end to the Cow Tower NE of Bishopgate at the NE end. They were about 20 ft high and had arched recesses at the foot in some parts, but not in others. The towers were circular or semicircular, and occasionally semipolygonal. Remarkably much is preserved, even if no longer in as good a state as e.g. at York or Chester or Newcastle. The best stretch is at the S end, starting with the BOOM TOWERS flanking the river near CARROW BRIDGE. On the Thorpe side a round tower, on the Carrow side an open semicircular one and a stretch of wall with indications of the wall-walk. The wall goes on behind the Jolly Maltsters and rises steep up CARROW HILL. One tower stands half-way up, another, called BLACK TOWER, on the top.* The wall can then be followed along Carrow Hill and BRACONDALE. Behind No. 1 Bracondale remains of the battlements at the top of the wall survive. At the S end of BER STREET there is a sudden turn. This marks the corner of the former Ber Street Gate. The wall then follows the line of QUEENS ROAD and CHAPELFIELD ROAD, shows its arched recesses well from BULL LANE, and is specially fully exposed along CHAPELFIELD GARDENS and from COBURG STREET reveals recesses, a semicircular tower, and a tower semicircular at the back, but polygonal in front. When the DRILL HALL was built at the corner of Chapelfield Road and Chapelfield North a wall-tower was incorporated in the composition, just l. of the gateway. Much can also be seen again further N in WELLINGTON LANE, just E of Grapes Hill. At the S end of BARN ROAD the wall ceases and only appears again along its N stretch, that is S of BAKER ROAD and MAGPIE ROAD. W of the corner of OAK STREET and Baker Road is a tower. Recesses are W and E of ST AUGUSTINE STREET, i.e. N of St Martin at Oak Lane and Catherine Wheel Opening. At the E end of this, i.e. at the corner of MAGDALEN STREET and WALL LANE, there is again a better preserved

* The inscription records the making of the street Carrow Hill in 1817.

piece ending inside a public lavatory. After that a polygonal
tower in WALL LANE just N of BARRACK STREET and S of
the corner of BULL CLOSE ROAD and Silver Road. Finally, at
the NE corner, again by the river, there is the last and most
spectacular tower, COW TOWER, 50 ft high and 36 ft thick, 47a
with a strong batter and remains of battlements. This is an
early example of the use of brick in Norwich. Bills exist of
1378 for the purchase of the brick and the making of the stone
arrow-slits. The bricks are 9 by 9¼ by 2 in. in size.

SHIRE HALL, Castle Meadow. 1822–3 by *William Wilkins*, refaced in 1913. Neo-Tudor, red brick, two-storeyed, low and
symmetrical. Polygonal angle-turrets to centre and sub-centres.

GUILDHALL, Market Place. The Guildhall was built in 1407–
13, perhaps by *John Marwe*, and a new Council Chamber was 48
provided at the E end after the old one had collapsed in 1511.
It was completed in 1535 and is the one spectacular feature of
the building. Of knapped flint below, of the gayest, almost
carnavalesque diaper flushwork above, and crowned by a
pretty turret of 1850. Below the window a panel and two coats
of arms, separated by balusters, or rather semi-Gothic, semi-
Renaissance finials.* The older part has less of original work.
The pretty SW doorway came from a house in London Street.
It has niches in the jambs and spandrels with sumptuous
foliage. Between the two parts, the porch projects. The whole
of this S front is the design of *T. D. Barry* and dates from 1861.
On the W and N side also all windows are C19. On the W side
there were in the Middle Ages two towers, but they collapsed
in 1508. Inside there is one C15 doorway on the first floor. The
Council Room has a low-pitched roof with beams with pendants and in the E windows a fine display of much (brought-in)
STAINED GLASS of the C15, and in addition very good original
PANELLING, partly linenfold, partly with Early Renaissance
arabesques, and SEATING with beasties and grotesques
(especially for the Lord Mayor's Seat). Otherwise the few
features of interest are mid-Georgian: a screen of Roman
Doric columns, the door surround of the Sword Room, and
the STATUE of Justice in the Sword Room.

CITY HALL, Market Place. 1932–8 by *C. H. James & S. R.* 64
Pierce. In spite of its frankly admitted dependence on Sweden,
the Norwich City Hall is likely to go down in history as the

---

* Below this C16 part is a C14 CRYPT with brick vaulting. This belonged
originally to the Tolhouse. Single-chamfered ribs dying into the walls. The
turret mentioned above is by *Robert Kerr* (Messrs Baggs and Young).

foremost English public building of between the wars. It lies
in an enviable position, raised above the spacious market
place, and it makes the best of that position. Its tower, 202 ft
high, is a beacon from everywhere, and it is successfully con-
trasted against the stretching front with its slender portico.
The building is of greyish-red brick and yellow Ketton stone.
The whole ground floor is stone-faced. The portico starts
above it, and, with its attenuated polygonal pillars, derives
clearly from Tengbom, as the asymmetrically placed tower and
even such motifs as the little copper canopies over the
principal windows near the ends of the façade derive from
Östberg and his Stockholm City Hall. The interior has no
climax to match the façade, neither a monumental staircase
nor a monumental hall. Flanking the outer staircase up to the
main entrance a pair of fine bronze lions by *A. Hardiman*.

13a ST ANDREW'S HALL, St Andrew's Hall Plain. This should
really be listed as a church; for it was the Dominican or Blackfriars' church of Norwich, and its survival is extremely valuable, as it is the only English friars' church which has come
down to our day so complete – in spite of what Norwich did to
it (and had to do) to use it as a public hall. The chancel has not
suffered from that treatment and is the most impressive part of
the building. The Dominicans arrived at Norwich in 1226 and
moved to the site of the present church in 1307. This present
church however is not that of 1307. It was begun in 1440 and
completed in 1470. It is 265 ft long and consists of a nave and
aisles, the usual cross-space with walls to W and S, and an aisleless chancel. Originally an octagonal tower rose above the
centre of the cross-space (cf. King's Lynn). The tower collapsed in 1712. The church was much restored by *T. D. Barry*,
the city surveyor, in 1863. Due to him is the W wall and W
doorway (which had not existed), the S porch, and the arch at
the E end of the nave. The church is Perp throughout, except
for the S aisle windows and the chancel E window, which is a
splendid seven-light piece. These windows must be of the Dec
building, and Mr Eliston Erwood is of the opinion that they
are *in situ*. The other chancel windows are tall and large too,
of five lights with embattled transoms stepped up and down.
The N aisle windows are of four lights and Perp. The clerestory
is East Anglian in that it has twice the number of windows as
compared with the bays inside, i.e. fourteen. It is ashlar-faced.
The arcades carrying this clerestory are tall and have piers
with four shafts and four long shallow concave curves in the

diagonals. Two-centred arches. – MONUMENT. John Elison
† 1639. Largish, simple architectural tablet.

From the N aisle one descends into the former CLOISTER.
This is assigned to the C14 by Mr Eliston Erwood. The walks
are buttressed and vaulted and have an upper storey. The
arches are of brick, quadruple-chamfered. One cusped single-
light upper window remains. The E wall of the E range is also
still in existence. It contained the chapter house, which was
three bays wide and two bays deep and projected to the E. It
had circular piers. The dormitory was as usual in this range
on the upper floor. One of its windows (to the W) and one tie-
beam of the roof remain. The N range has entirely disappeared,
but the W range is complete.

Between the E walk of the cloister and the chancel lies an
undercroft formerly known as BECKET'S CHAPEL. It has a
stone pier in the centre and brick vaulting.

ASSEMBLY ROOMS, Theatre Street. On the site of the Assembly
Rooms stood the College of St Mary-in-the-Fields. This had
been founded before 1250. Small fragments are in the W wing
of the present building. The College was dissolved in 1545.
The church was demolished, but the collegiate buildings
could be used as a mansion. The Assembly Rooms stand on
the site of the centre of the mansion. Norwich can be proud
of its Assembly Rooms. No other town of its size in England
has anything like them – except of course for a spa like Bath.
They were built in 1754 by *Thomas Ivory* as a speculation,
and he also built the theatre a little further W.* The building
is of five bays and two storeys with a one-bay pediment and
long projecting wings, not regular in their façades. These
wings are not in accordance with Ivory's design. They are
younger but incorporate older masonry, especially the W wing.
This was recently converted into a cinema by *Rowland Pierce*.
The Assembly Rooms proper consist of a middle room in line
with the entrance and ending in a polygonal bay and, to its r.
and l., the ballroom and banquet room with elegant plasterwork.
Both have a gallery above the entrance supported on columns.

AGRICULTURAL HALL (now Anglia Television), Prince of
Wales Road. 1882 by *J. B. Pearce*. Red brick. Remarkably
restrained for its original (and present) purpose.

* On a drawing in the Victoria and Albert Museum, however, *James
Burrough* of Cambridge is named as the designer. Also Mr Ketton-Cremer
tells me of a letter from a Cambridge don, dated 1755 and quoted in 1831,
which says that Burrough 'designed the apartments'.

POST OFFICE, Prince of Wales Road. 1866 by *P. C. Hardwick*.
Built as a bank. With a portico of coupled Ionic columns
carrying a terrace. A design one would date 1880 or later.

BRIDEWELL MUSEUM, Bridewell Alley, behind St Andrew's
Church. The house became the Bridewell only in 1583. It was
built about 1370 as a private house by the father of William
Appleyard, first Mayor of Norwich. He died in 1419. The
front to the street is of knapped flint with irregular and heavily
renewed fenestration on two floors. The house for its present
function has four ranges round a garden of which the street
front belongs to the N range. The hall was in the E range, but
nothing of the internal arrangements appears to survive except
for the two-centred archways from the former screens passage
to the offices, until one descends into the basement and here
sees the complete vaulted substructure of the hall and the
front ranges. What makes these vaults so memorable is the
fact that they are of brick with brick ribs, the earliest example
of the use of brick in Norwich, as they antedate that at the
Cow Tower, if the assumed date of Appleyard's house is
correct. The hall range has twice six bays with middle piers
and quadripartite vaults, the front range five bays without
middle piers and with vaults, sexpartite in the two E bays,
octopartite in the others. The ribs are double-chamfered. The
other features of the house, doorways and the like, come from
other buildings.

ST PETER HUNGATE MUSEUM, Elm Hill. Unbuttressed W
tower with low pyramid roof. Two-storeyed S porch. Nave
and transepts with tall four-light windows. In the nave they
are in wall-arcading. The date 1460 appears on a buttress of
the porch. The most interesting thing about the church is the
roof, with hammerbeams and arched braces. They are set
diagonally in the crossing so as to intersect. – FONT. Octagonal,
simple, with quatrefoils on the bowl. – STAINED GLASS.
Much in the E window, also whole figures of the late C15 and
early C16. A mosaic of bits in the chancel S windows, fragments in the chancel N. – PLATE. Chalice and Cover, Norwich-
made, richly embossed, *c.*1620; Paten (Norwich) inscribed
1675; two Flagons (London) 1680–1; Almsbasin (London)
1680(?); Cup and Cover (London) 1734–5; Paten (London)
1735–6.*

---

* The exhibits of ecclesiastical art from Norfolk churches are of course not
included in this list of furnishings.

STRANGERS' HALL MUSEUM, Charing Cross. The street front is of 1621 and very uneventful, but behind it, in the little courtyard, the varied and interesting story of the house is at once sensed. Its showpiece is the hall, raised above a basement and built in the mid C15 by a merchant, William Barley. The porch at the top of the stairs, however, with its tierceron-star-vault, the roof of the hall, and the high bay window to the s, i.e. the garden, are the result of a remodelling by Nicholas Sotherton, a grocer, c.1530. The bay window is canted and has tall traceried windows and a tierceron-star-vault. The roof has tie-beams on arched braces with tracery and kingposts. The two arches to the offices are probably of Barley's time, the wooden screen is Sotherton's but made of panelling from another place. Sotherton's arms appear also in the large fireplace of a room to the w of the courtyard, above the so-called kitchen. The original kitchen lay to the se of the hall. However, this C15 house was built in replacement of an older, a late C13 or early C14 hall, built by Ralph de Middleton, and of this the undercroft still exists, at r. angles to the hall and below the room called the Parlour which faces the courtyard near to the hall staircase. The undercroft is of three vaulted bays with hollow-chamfered ribs on semi-octagonal wall-piers. To its E remains of the C14 entrance at ground-floor level, the porter's lodge, and the squint from it to the doorway. The other rooms are less important. Mention may be made of those remodelled by Sir Joseph Paine, a hosier, and dated by him in fireplaces 1659, and also of the main staircase in the hall and the bay which became necessary when the staircase was built. The staircase has the date 1627. The balusters are massive.

SUCKLING HOUSE, St Andrew Street. The house is essentially an early C16 merchant's house, though the front does not tell us so. In the present entrance hall a pretty fireplace with nice surround. To the r. the hall. Tall arch to the former bay window in the s wall. Roof with tie-beam and kingpost. Plain doorways of entry and exit into the hall, i.e. the former screens passage and access from it to the w into the offices. One and a quarter of the arches are left. The rest is replaced by a big doorway of c.1700, connecting with the corner house in St Andrew's Hill. But a little later to the N the vaulted buttery is still there, with three bays and double-chamfered ribs. The corner house is of four bays out of a former five and has rusticated quoins and a parapet. The extensions of Suckling House to the E are recent.

CENTRAL LIBRARY, Bethel Street and forming a new square
with the City Hall and St Peter Mancroft. 1960–2 by *David
Percival*, the City Architect. The building consists of four
ranges round a pretty *patio* or inner courtyard. Three ranges
(News Room, Reference Library, Americana, and offices) are
one-storeyed, the fourth is high and contains the stacks above
the Lending Library. The basement is all archives. An excellent composition.

TECHNICAL INSTITUTE, St George Street. 1899 by *A. F.
Collins*. Tall, red, with a long frontage to the river and a domed
corner. Mixed stylistic components, including polygonal buttresses and round arches. Attached to it on the s is the former
Middle School, built in 1861, yellow and red brick, Gothic
and clumsily picturesque. By *J. S. Benest*.

GREAT HOSPITAL, Bishopgate. The Great Hospital was
founded in 1249 by Bishop Walter de Suffield. It was intended
as a house for decrepit chaplains and also to look after any
poor sick people. In spite of later additions and sweeping
alterations the original plan can still be made out, with a long
aisled infirmary hall followed by an aisleless chancel – the
usual arrangement of cathedral and monastic infirmaries as
well. It was a remarkably large building, over 200 ft long. It
adds to the usual certain unusual features, first the s tower
projecting to the w beyond the w wall (money was left for it
c.1375), second the s porch (Limbert's Porch), three vaulted
bays long, with plain, single-chamfered ribs and quite possibly
of the C13,* and third the vaulted s transept. The latter two
features are connected with the most extraordinary arrangement at the Great Hospital, namely the fact that the part
reached by the s porch and including the s transept constituted
and still constitutes a parish church, the church of St Helen.
This is also the only part which is now easily accessible. The
chancel, rebuilt by Bishop Despenser *c*.1380, has been horizontally divided to form the women's wards, the w parts of the
nave to form the men's wards. This dubious arrangement is
Elizabethan, but the windows must be Georgian. The ceiling
of the chancel, however, survives as the ceiling of what is now
Eagle Ward. It is a half-dodecagon in section and has panels
filled with 252 spread eagles and many bosses at the intersections. The church was rebuilt by Bishop Goldwell, i.e.

---

* The upper floor was repaired in 1754 and then received its window with
intersected tracery.

about 1480, and still has three bays with quatrefoil piers with thin polygonal shafts in the diagonals and polygonal capitals. The style looks later C14. The s transept chapel has a sumptuous lierne-vault, close in style to the vaults of the cathedral but different in pattern. Among the bosses are the Coronation of the Virgin, Nativity, Annunciation, Ascension, and Resurrection, and also Saints and Apostles. The original colour is preserved. In the w wall of the s aisle a tiny Perp three-light window, like a miniature model. This is original and appears to be *in situ*, in which case the E bay of that part of the s aisle which is now wards must in the C15 already have been walled off. Of the other parts of the church the 'nave' w window was very large. It is now blocked in brick and has four tiers of mullioned and transomed windows. The chancel E window is Early Perp, of seven lights, as corresponds to its date, and the N windows alternate between a purely Perp pattern and one still reminiscent of Dec (four-petalled flower). – BOX PEWS and raised PULPIT at the E end. The IVORY PEW in the s transept, dated 1780, and inscribed with the names of *William Ivory* and his wife, is also a box pew, but it is Gothic, not of the dainty Strawberry Hill kind, but oddly heavy, as if it were Victorian. The details, even the lettering, have the same flavour. – BENCH ENDS. Quite a number, with poppy-heads, and one with St Margaret on the Dragon and 'hec' beneath for Hecker, who was Master of the Hospital in 1519–32. – SWORD AND MACE RESTS. C18. Of wrought iron. – BANNER STAFF LOCKER. W of the entrance from the cloister. – PLATE. Chalice (Norwich) 1566–7; Chalice and Paten (London) 1758–9. 33b

To the N of the Infirmary Hall lies the CLOISTER. This was built about 1450. It has straight-headed three-light openings. Two doorways in the E wall, one smaller one in the N wall. The w range is the most interesting. This was the MASTER'S LODGING, and his hall with the three doorways from the former screens passage to the kitchen and offices survives. The hall has tie-beams with tracery with dragons and foliage and kingposts. To the NE of this, as part of the original offices, a rib-vaulted room of two bays. The ribs are single-chamfered.

To the w of this a flint range was added in the C15. But this is now entirely changed. At r. angles to it stands a nine-bay red-brick building of two storeys, with a three-bay pediment. This is by *Thomas Ivory* and dates from 1752–3. – In the present Chaplain's House on the N side are two DOORS of c.1530 no doubt belonging to the Hospital. They have Early

Renaissance decoration, three inscriptions, of which two are
IHS and MARIA, and linenfold panels.

To the E of the old buildings additional ranges, single-
storeyed, of grey brick, and of the accepted almshouse type.
They date from the 1820s and later.

BRIDGES. The only medieval bridge is BISHOP BRIDGE at the
E end of Bishopgate. It is assigned to c.1340 and has three
arches. Next in date is *Soane*'s BLACKFRIARS BRIDGE, in St
George Street. This was built in 1783. Stone arch and a simple,
but effective cast-iron railing, no doubt later. It must be of the
same date as that of the neighbouring DUKE'S PALACE
BRIDGE in Duke Street, and this, which is entirely of iron, is
of 1822. Between Wensum Street and Fye Bridge Street is
FYE BRIDGE, again similar. This is of 1829 and by *Francis
Stone*. But the earliest iron bridge in Norwich is COSLANY
BRIDGE by *James Frost*, 1804, a stone rather than an iron
design. The bridge in front of Thorpe Station, FOUNDRY
BRIDGE, is of 1844. Its iron railing has little quatrefoils in
circles. The bridge was built in the eighties.

PERAMBULATIONS*

ALL SAINTS GREEN (S,W). The N end forms part of the dull
new Norwich just emerging (cf. Brigg Street). But by Surrey
Street there remain some Georgian properties, notably ST
CATHERINE'S CLOSE of shortly after 1778 with a very pretty
curved Adamish porch and the ground-floor windows with
blank tympana. Canted bay windows to the S. On the other
side of the street an earlier Georgian house of five bays and
three storeys with a parapet. Doorway with rusticated pilasters
and a semicircular top. The ground-floor windows have, in
harmony with this, blank tympana. (This house is by *Thomas
Ivory*. A. Paget Baggs)

BANK PLAIN (S,W). BARCLAYS BANK is surprisingly monumental, considering the size of Norwich. It was designed by
E. Boardman & Son and *Brierley & Rutherford* of York and
built in 1929–31. Its façade is the length of a whole block, it is
entirely symmetrical, and it is not an office building but quite
clearly the envelope of a large banking house. The style is a kind
of Renaissance as handled perhaps by McKim, Mead & White

* The letters N, S and W, and C (for Centre) stand for the locations of the
streets and correspond to the three perambulations proposed on p. 206.

in America. The hall is apsed at both ends and has giant pilasters and a tunnel-vault with penetrations from the windows.

BEEHIVE YARD, see Palace Plain, p. 274.

BER STREET (S,W). A strikingly wide street on a ridge falling to the E. It led to the Ber Street Gate. There is little to watch for, except at the S end: some minor Georgian (Nos 101–129) and, opposite, the grim neo-Norman façade of 1868 of the former Wesleyan Chapel (by *Boardman*). Then, facing the E end of St John de Sepulchre, a better group: No. 156, BLACKS HALL, half-timber with moulded bressumer, No. 158, BER HOUSE, a Georgian double house of seven bays and two and a half storeys with the doorways in the first and last bays, and No. 160, again with a moulded bressumer.

BETHEL STREET (S,W). A few commendable Georgian houses. No. 33 with a doorway with Roman Doric columns and decorated metopes. – Nos 38–40, of much higher pretensions: five bays, two and a half storeys, brick quoins of intermittent rustication, doorway with carved frame, two unfluted Ionic columns, a pulvinated frieze, and a pediment. Staircase with two twisted balusters to the step. In a ground-floor room overmantel of c.1740. – No. 61. Probably C17. Windows with hood-moulds. Georgian doorway with Ionic columns and rusticated lintel.   *See p. 391*

BISHOPGATE (N). The W end has turned slummy, with factories. But soon one is out of them. At the junction the ADAM AND EVE with a shaped gable, then ST HELEN'S HOUSE, a good early C19 villa of grey brick with a nice doorway with columns placed in the bow window in the middle. Charming rounded anteroom with grisaille painting. (Staircase with glazed oval dome. NBR) Then, opposite, Nos 43–44, insignificant from the street, but with three shaped gables to the S. After that the GREAT HOSPITAL, see p. 264, the access to the COW TOWER, see p. 259, and the WATER GATE of the cathedral precinct, see p. 234.

BOTOLPH STREET (N). Here lies the most interesting factory 63b building in Norwich, a discovery of Mr Nairn. It is now Messrs ROBERTS, Printers, but was a clothing factory. It is dated 1903, and there was little in England and indeed in Europe quite so functional and unfussy then. Yet it is by no means purely utilitarian. The façade consists of three wide bays separated by broad brick pillars with rounded angles. The bays are lit by unmoulded mullioned and transomed windows, eight lights each, and ground floor and first floor with three transoms, top floor with one. Did the architect, *A. F. Scott*, know Mackintosh's Glasgow School of Art?

BRIGG STREET (S,W). Around this area of the Market Place and to Westlegate and the top of Ber Street, All Saints Green, St Stephen's Street, and Rampant Horse Street a new Norwich is being built, looking much like any new shopping district in any unenterprising town of the size of Norwich. It is a pity.

CALVERT STREET (N). Connecting Colegate with Botolph Street. The neighbourhood has come down in the world, but No. 1 of six bays with rusticated quoins must have been quite stately when it was built about 1700. (Inside staircase with three turned balusters and carved tread-ends. Also a nice mid-C18 overmantel. NBR)

See p. 391 (CASTLE HILL. The showrooms of Messrs PANK, built *c.*1868, have a remarkable cast-iron and glass front. A. Paget Baggs)

CASTLE STREET, *see* Market Place, p. 274.

CHAPEL FIELD (S,W). A large triangular green space. On the E side No. 15, late C18, has a broad doorway with Tuscan columns against a rusticated background and a broken pediment. S of this the factory of John Mackintosh & Sons. Behind its older buildings a recent one by *A. J. Mathewson*, 1955–6. On the N side No. 4 of three bays and three storeys, plastered white, with a gratifying first-floor veranda of cast iron and Doric columns *in antis* flanking the doorway. Until 1947 there stood in Chapel Field one of the most gorgeous Victorian cast-iron monstrosities of England, the PAGODA, designed by *Jekyll* for the Philadelphia Exhibition of 1876, and not looking in the least like a pagoda, nor indeed like anything else.

COLEGATE (N). Colegate runs from E to W, parallel with, and N of, the Wensum, connecting Coslany with Magdalen Street. No. 3, opposite St Clement, is Georgian, of five wide bays and one and a half storeys with plastered quoins. Doorway with a carved frame and a pediment on carved brackets. Then, opposite, what little remains of ALDRICH'S HOUSE, now Employment Exchange, that is the flint ground floor of a C16 house built round a courtyard. After that two of the best early C18 houses in Norwich, the first of seven bays and two storeys with a central dormer, plastered quoins, nicely carved eaves, and a doorway with a carved frame, fluted Ionic columns, a pediment, a keystone head, and vermiculated spandrels. Next to it, L-shaped and forming an irregular courtyard with it, a house with monumental giant Ionic pilasters

and a parapet.* The former house has a staircase with two
slender twisted balusters to each step, the latter a Jacobean
ground-floor ceiling with ornamental ribbing and a mid-c18
fireplace with two cherubs on the pediment. A doorcase goes
with this, and these features are said to come from the Duke of
Norfolk's palace by Duke Street (cf. St Andrew Street, p.
276). Nos 27–29 is timber-framed and plastered with a number
of the usual dormer gables. BACON'S HOUSE has in its W gable
(towards St George) two small medieval two-light windows
with hood-moulds. The four-light windows are renewed or
new. To Colegate the upper floor shows its timber-posts. Doorway with decorated spandrels and wicket-door with its own
little decorated spandrels. The decoration here is Early Renaissance. S of St George the Norvic factory, W of the church
(St George's Plain) two more Georgian houses, Nos 47 and 51,
the former with Tuscan pilasters to l. and r. of an arched
rusticated doorway, the latter with an Adamish door surround
with decorated frieze. Opposite, No. 52 has a nice doorway
too. No. 57 is humble but may be mentioned because one of
the pediments of its two shallow oriels is dated 1660.

COSLANY STREET (N). At the S end a typical industrial scene.
First BULLARD'S BREWERY, chiefly of the 1860s, then the
bridge across the river, with industrial views l. and r., then
Barnard, Bishop and Barnard's NORFOLK IRON WORKS,
probably of 1855, and adjoining them in a semi-ruinous condition a C17 house with overhangs and five gables and a fine
early C18 house with giant brick pilasters and brick-rusticated
pilasters l. and r. of the doorway.

COWGATE (N). At the SE end, i.e. immediately by the river
Wensum, Messrs JARROLD'S works. They include two un- 60
expected and very different things, one small, one large. The
large one is their splendid wedge-shaped, five-storeyed old
building, of red brick with a dome at the W corner. This was
built for a yarn mill in 1834 etc. The architect was *John* *See p. 391*
Brown, County Surveyor. Mr Nairn called it 'the noblest of
all English Industrial Revolution mills', and Messrs Richards
and de Maré have put it on the dust-jacket of their book on
the vernacular of industrial architecture. Yet the dome is not
really vernacular in the way in which the parapet rises towards it, nor is the stress on the third floor by way of blank

---

* Mr Paget Baggs informs me that the former house has arms referring to
c.1730, the latter a date 1743 on a rainwater head. Both houses are thus very
conservative.

tympana over the windows, a motif familar from Norwich
Georgian houses (cf. e.g. All Saints Green and Surrey Street)
and e.g. from Soane's work at Ryston. Nestling below the
works is the one remaining fragment of the Norwich WHITE-
FRIARS, founded in 1256, a two-centred arch with mouldings
suggesting a later C14 date.

COW HILL (S, W). Between Pottergate and St Giles Street. Near
the N end Nos 15–17, HOLKHAM HOUSE, by *Matthew* or
Robert Brettingham, a surprising little composition which the
architect built for his brother. Grey brick like Brettingham's
Holkham. Recessed centre, the wings with broken pediments, the
centre with a straight top but Palladian half-pediments l. and r.

DAVEY PLACE (C). A remarkably successful pedestrian shopping
street running from the Market Place to Castle Meadow, down
and up again and in a line connecting visually the portico of
the City Hall with the keep of the Castle.

ELM HILL (C). This is the most picturesque street in Norwich.
It winds from Princes Street and St Peter Hungate to Wensum
Street. At the start No. 4 with its plaster rustication and gables.
No. 9 at the NW corner of the churchyard is distinguished by
its position. It has a medieval doorway with a two-centred
head towards the churchyard, but is otherwise timber-framed.
Behind on the W rises the chancel of the Blackfriars, and on
the NE is a pretty triangle with an elm tree. No. 12 opposite
is timber-framed too. Then a fine sequence of houses with
overhangs along the N side, especially the STRANGERS'
CLUB, early C16 and C17, with a dainty Perp frieze in the
wooden lintel of the carriageway on the l. and large mullioned
and transomed windows further r., one of six, one of two lights.
Brick-nogging on the upper floor. At the back in a wing
extending at r. angles a brick doorway with two-centred head.
On the first floor moulded beams and a fireplace obtained from
a house nearby. Opposite, No. 41, PETTUS HOUSE, also
timber-framed. On the upper floor prettily traceried Perp
windows. Again opposite, No. 36 (FLINT HOUSE) with a
flint ground floor with one small C17 wooden window and an
overhanging upper floor. Adamish door surround with
curious, somewhat rustic capitals (cf. Barracks). There is not a
single house in Elm Hill which could be disturbing.

EXCHANGE STREET (C). Only two buildings to be noted. The
former CORN EXCHANGE, 1863 by *T. D. Barry*, not detached,
tall and like a prosperous Nonconformist chapel. The composition like Italian churches with nave and aisles expressed;

but astylar. Bands of grey and red brick. Gaudy Baroque detail. Further N NORFOLK HOUSE, set back and detached, quite a good modern design. Red brick, by *Alec Wright*, 1950.

FINKLEGATE (S,W). On its S side and around the S side of St John de Sepulchre good and pretty council housing by the City Architect *David Percival*, 1959–60.

FISHERGATE (N). The R.C. church of St George uses the former BOYS' HOSPITAL SCHOOL, founded in 1620. That explains the steep shaped gable of the porch. (The school is by *Benest*, 1864. A. P. Baggs and D. M. Young)

FYE BRIDGE STREET (N). The S continuation of Magdalen Street. At the corner of Fishergate, i.e. the river, a newly done-up shop, but above nice early C19 work, with wide windows and coupled giant pilasters. Opposite in No. 8 (WINE VAULTS) a small fireplace dated 1599.

GENTLEMAN'S WALK, *see* Market Place *and* Hay Hill.

GILDENCROFT (N). S of St Augustine's church. An impressively long, even row of two-storeyed timber-framed cottages with overhangs; C16 or C17.

GUILDHALL HILL, *see* St Giles Street, p. 277.

HAY HILL (C). Really the imperceptible continuation of the Market Place, if one considers St Peter Mancroft as an island building in an open space. MONUMENT to Sir Thomas Browne, 1905 by *Henry Pegram*. On the W side Messrs LAMBERT'S, an unashamed Georgian warehouse, four storeys, eleven bays long, and completely plain. Opposite, really that is in Gentleman's Walk, CURAT'S HOUSE, the front five-bay Georgian with a neo-Gothic shop front, but at the back medieval, with a doorway with two-centred head and an oriel window. Inside rooms with moulded beams, fireplaces with surrounds, and overmantels not *in situ* and including some typical panels of *c*.1535–50 with profile heads in roundels (cf. Bishop's Palace, p. 229).

KING STREET (S,W). King Street is very mixed now, with some important old domestic buildings and quite a number of less important recent industrial ones. The following may be listed. Nos 56–60, brick, three-storeyed, with shaped gables. – No. 79, five bays, with a Venetian window above the Tuscan doorway. – Nos 86–88 half-timbered with overhang. – HOWARD HOUSE, now part of Morgan's Brewery. This has a fine if small staircase through two storeys, with openwork panels instead of balusters. They have strap and leaf motifs. The date probably *c*.1630–40. The S façade of *c*.1690, four bays with hipped roof. Built into the walls of FLEUR DE LYS HOUSE a little further S is an early C14 stone arch, belonging probably to the AUSTIN FRIARS. – No. 115 etc. and the old BARGE INN belong together. The latter has to the S a C14 stone doorway in a C15 surround and several more stone doorways inside. No. 115 itself has under the steep roof two trusses of a grand tie-beam roof with kingposts and four-way struts spanning about 30 ft. No. 167 is the MUSIC HOUSE. The façade divided into a stone-faced, featureless l. part and a r. part with mullioned and transomed windows with pediments, dating probably from the early C17. Behind the stone part lies what remains of a private house of the C12. The entrance porch was to the S, and was obliterated by the later building. What survives, however, is the lower part of the N respond, now in the vaulted undercroft of the C17 house. The mouldings are unmistakably of the later C12. The undercroft of the C12 house is in good order. Oblong rib-vaults with broad transverse arches between. Originally these rooms were on ground-level, not below ground. The hall, i.e. the principal room, was on the upper floor. Opposite, No. 170 etc. is the PRINCE'S INN, with a carved beam containing the name and Early Renaissance decoration. – Much further S a range belonging to READ'S FLOUR MILL but built as the ALBION MILLS for spinning yarn. The date of the building is 1836–7, and it has the same dignity as Jarrold's of the same date in Cowgate, though it is smaller. It is four storeys, eight by three bays, and the first floor has the characteristic blank tympana above the windows.

LONDON STREET (C). For Jarrold's and Burton's shops *see* Market Place, p. 274. Further E is the NATIONAL PROVINCIAL BANK, 1924 by *F. C. R. Palmer* and *W. F. C. Holden*, a building that will be noticed on account of the portico and the somewhat Wrenian turret and cupola at the sharp corner of London Street and Bedford Street. One would assign a much earlier date to it.

MAGDALEN STREET (N). Magdalen Street, the main street N out of Norwich and the shopping centre for the old town the other side of the river, has recently – in 1958–9 – received a much publicized face-lift. Colours, lettering, street-signs, street lighting, etc., have been brought up to date, on the suggestion of the Civic Trust – its first public venture in doing, not pleading – and with the help of designs by *Misha Black* and *Kenneth Bayes*. While all is still fresh it is a great, if deliberately modest, success, that is, it does not look as if imposed

by anyone. The impression is that many shopkeepers have
suddenly seen the light and that everyone then has chosen his
own colour and lettering; that is, variety has been preserved,
which is what a shopping street needs. Of old buildings the
following deserve a glance or more. For the s end *see* Fye
Bridge Street, p. 271. Then No. 24 of two and a half storeys,
plain but with a nice doorway, No. 29 with a doorway dated
1612 in one of the spandrels of its four-centred head, and so to
No. 31, GURNEY COURT, where Elizabeth Fry and Harriet
Martineau were born, the perfect example of a Norwich back
court. Several pedimented doorways, all windows sashed. The
climax is No. 44, one of the most ornate Georgian houses in
Norwich. It is structurally one with 46 and 48. Giant pilasters
and a third storey above the cornice. Doorway with Tuscan
columns, a decorated metope frieze, a keystone head, and
lively foliage in the spandrels. A Venetian window over. The
most likely date is *c*.1740–50.

MARKET PLACE (C). Few cities in England can boast a market
place like Norwich. It is exactly as a child pictures it, large,
full of booths, and with the proud parish church on one side,
the old-fashioned Guildhall on another, and the proud modern
city hall on a third. Moreover the city hall as well as St Peter
Mancroft lie elevated above it, and nothing could be prouder
than the two towers of both and the row of upper windows of
the church. Finally Davey Place has been cut through so un-
erringly that it connects in a straight line the market place of
the city with the keep of the kings. In the Middle Ages,
though, this spacious market place did not exist. There was of
course no city hall, and between St Peter and the s side of the
Guildhall there were houses and lanes. This was still so into
the C20. On the sides of the Market Place there are no buildings for worship and administration and there is little to make
a show of, nor indeed is anything needed visually. The following may be listed. The most rewarding is the funny SE corner
with two high-looking houses on an island site in front of the
chancel of St Peter Mancroft, one with an overhang but a
Greek Doric shopfront, the other with a bow window to the N
and one to the E. On the N side a nine-bay range, not entirely
regular, with quoins and a hipped roof. The centre window
has a pediment. Is it all of *c*.1700? On the E side (strictly
speaking called GENTLEMAN'S WALK*) in the corner of

---

* Gentleman's Walk has recently had a face-lift of the same kind as
Magdalen Street: *see* p. 272.

Exchange Street and London Street JARROLD'S Baroque
shop by *Skipper*, 1903–5 (but the corner and the façade
to Exchange Street are later, and the building in London
Street, which was Skipper's own office, dates from 1896
and was only purchased recently), then BURTON'S Gothic
premises, then HOPE'S, according to Mr Nairn formerly
Barnard's and with minor ironwork designed for them by
Thomas Jekyll, DOLCIS of 1959 by *E. E. Somake*, and then
the ROYAL ARCADE by *Skipper*, perfectly innocent in the
front* but very naughty once its back is turned. The front is
a debased-classical house perhaps of *c.*1850, and only the
ground floor suggests the real interest of the arcade. The
interior is harmless too, but the back in CASTLE STREET,
63a   with the attached pub on the l., is a spectacular display of
English Arts and Crafts, when, in spirit though not in form, it
came nearest to Continental Art Nouveau: coloured tiles with
flower and tree motifs, tracery of a fat, curly Gothicky kind,
lettering that could not be made more telling. Finally, to return
to the Market Place, Nos 27–29, nine bays and three storeys
with a fourth and a gable in the middle and raised oblong
plaster panels between the windows. This again may be of
*c.*1700. If one continues s there follows Hay Hill immediately.

OAK STREET (N). The interest is Nos 98–112, N of Station Road,
a group of timber-framed plastered houses with overhang, and
No. 121 opposite, with entrance from FLOWER POT YARD,
badly war-damaged. This was a hall-house of the early C15,
remodelled in the early C16. Doorway with four-centred head.
Gable to Oak Street. It is remarkable how far N the medieval
Norwich went. It evidently filled in the space within the walls
pretty completely.

ORFORD HILL (C). Opposite the Bell Hotel a three-bay Early
Victorian house with a big stag on the top against the sky. It
was put up by a gun-maker about 1890.

PALACE PLAIN (N). The E continuation of Palace Street, by St
Martin-at-Palace. No. 7 is Cotman's house, five bays, two and
a half storeys, simple doorway. No. 10 at the corner of Cowgate is half-timbered, of three storeys, irregular. In BEEHIVE
YARD‡ on the l. ERPINGHAM HOUSE with a five-light
window of *c.*1409. The house is derelict at the time of writing.

PALACE STREET (N). The street faces the NW part of the cathedral precinct. Nos 1–5 timber-framed with overhang, No. 15

---

* By *Joseph Stannard*, of the 1840s (A. Paget Baggs).
‡ The entrance to the Yard faces the gates of the Gas Works.

is of brick, five bays and *aufgestockt*. Brick quoins, door surround with Doric pilasters, metope frieze and pediment. Arched middle window with rusticated surround.

PITT STREET (N). Running N from Duke Street to St Augustine Street. The fact that the best houses are close to the N end shows once more that Norwich in the C17 and C18 filled out its ample walled space. No. 65, opposite No. 68, is of the early C18, with five bays and three storeys, the third above the cornice. There are giant pilasters flanking bays one and five. Short pilasters in the top storey as well. All windows have segmental heads. Aprons below the first-floor windows. The doorway is altered, but the window above it emphasized by an arched head and pilasters. Two later C18 doorways inside the wide entrance.

POPES BUILDINGS (C) has its main front to the N like that of a large garden-house. Windows in blank arches, those on the l. and r. wide and segmental. To the street a doorway with Gibbs surround. Opposite also one or two nice doorways.

POTTERGATE (S,W). Parallel to St Giles Street s and St Benedict Street N of it. The three are, however, on different levels descending N towards the river, which is effective for the churches. No. 7, at the corner of St John Maddermarket, has a pre-Reformation brick doorway with two-centred head, No. 8 a sudden Venetian window. No. 17 is probably early C18. Seven bays and two storeys, with brick quoins also to the three-bay centre. Castellated parapet, no doubt castellated later. Doorway with heavy Tuscan columns and a pediment. Then the BLUEBELL at the corner of Lower Goat Lane, with overhang and gable. Nos 61–63 is of six bays and three storeys with a central double doorway with rusticated pilasters. No. 65 of the early C18 is recessed from the street. It had seven bays (but only six are left) and three storeys. Rusticated quoins flanking bay one and the missing bay seven. Doorway with rusticated pilasters and a rusticated lintel. Opposite, No. 64, Early Georgian, of five bays with a doorway whose pediment is carried on two brackets and a female head.

PRINCE OF WALES ROAD (S,W). The wide street winds and rises from Thorpe Station towards Castle Meadow. Two curious features: one row of trees along the middle of the upper part of the street, and the terrace of houses Nos 30–52, of grey brick and each with a gable of low pitch, like an unimaginative seaside terrace. These houses were put up about 1865. At the top the ROYAL HOTEL, tall, red, and turreted, by *E. Boardman & Sons*, 1896–7, but looking like Waterhouse.

PRINCES STREET (C). Connects Tombland with St Andrew's Street and Blackfriars. The N side is one of the best street sequences in Norwich. The best houses are Nos 24 and 14, half-timbered with brick-nogging and overhang, No. 24 with a big mullioned window, No. 14 with two provincially heavy Ionic doorcases. No. 16 has a pedimented Gibbs door-surround, No. 6, at the corner of Elm Hill and St Peter Hungate, built *c.*1619, is gabled and has rusticated blocks imitated in plaster. The corner house to Redwell Street, opposite, has a rounded corner, two and a half storeys high with a doorway with Tuscan columns *in antis* and a segmental fanlight. Finally GARSETT HOUSE, No. 1, facing down St Andrew's Plain. This is timber-framed and dates from 1589. It has two overhangs, both with carved angle brackets. There are also remains of mullioned windows, and there is a shaped gable to the S and a nicely *ingénu* Greek Doric porch to the W. The house is now the seat of the Norfolk and Norwich Archaeological Society.

QUEEN STREET (C). Off its N side BANK OF ENGLAND COURT, with a seven-bay house of two and a half storeys at r. angles to the street. Three-bay pediment. Doorway with pediment on Corinthian columns. The rest of the court less regular, but with two more Georgian doorways.

REDWELL STREET (S, W). For Garsett House, *see* Princes Street, above. A little higher up, opposite St Michael-at-Plea, the new building of the EASTERN DAILY PRESS, 1958 by *Yates, Cook & Darbyshire* of London.

ROYAL ARCADE, *see* Market Place, p. 274.

ST ANDREW'S HILL PLAIN. For Garsett House *see* Princes Street, above, for Suckling House *see* Public Buildings, p. 263.

ST ANDREW'S HILL (C). For Suckling House, i.e. the NE corner, *see* Public Buildings, p. 263. A little further S, on the other side, a Perp doorway with carved spandrels. Above it, not *in situ*, a traceried fanlight, i.e. a length of tracery.

ST ANDREW STREET (S, W). Nos 6–12 are a long half-timbered house with eight gables, artless and not attractive. Opposite in an alley-way a BILLIARD CLUB which meets in what was the DUKE OF NORFOLK'S CHAPEL. Five arched windows W, five E, ceiling with minor stucco decoration. Just W of the new Telephone Exchange, lying back, the fragment of a half-timbered pre-Reformation house. Upper floor with brick-nogging. Archway with arched braces and a moulded lintel.

ST CATHERINE'S CLOSE, *see* All Saints Green, p. 266.

ST GEORGE STREET (N). For Nos 35–39 *see* Bacon House, Colegate. Up to about Nos 70–80 there were evidently well-to-do houses in the C18. Where No. 89 now is, John Crome had his house.

ST GILES STREET (S, W). A fine, straight Georgian street leading from the Market Place to the impressive E view of St Giles church. But the start is far from straight, at least aesthetically. At the corner of Lower Goat Lane, strictly speaking in GUILDHALL HILL, a timber-framed house with an overhang but a long shopfront with Roman Doric columns and a metope frieze. *See* p. 392 Then at the corner of Upper Goat Lane an office building, typical of about 1900, with artificial stone, white and brown, a typical turret with a typical spike, a corner dome, short bulgy columns, etc. Then the Georgian sequence starts. It starts very well with No. 28, though the real façade of the house turns away from the street to the S. There it has a tripartite doorway, a Venetian window with pilasters, and a tripartite lunette window. Staircase with turned balusters and carved tread-ends. No. 36 has a doorway with a nicely carved frame and Tuscan columns carrying the usual pediment. Nos 29–39 are a minor terrace, but Nos 31–33 have a double entry with three recessed Tuscan columns, and No. 35 has a nice staircase, with three twisted balusters to each step and carved tread-ends. It also has a good overmantel and two good doorcases on the first floor (of *c.*1740) and stands on a vaulted undercroft. Sexpartite vaults, chamfered brick ribs. No. 43, TELEPHONE HOUSE, is by *Skipper*, the Norwich Union *en miniature*, i.e. not detached, yet with projecting first and last bays and a projecting centre, and very Baroque indeed. It is dated 1906. No. 45 is of five bays and two and a half storeys, with Tuscan columns and a broken pediment around the doorway. No. 49 must be by *Skipper* again. The doorway and ground-floor windows with alternately blocked surrounds, the upper floor with attached columns. No. 48 is the Y.M.C.A. Seven bays, two and a half storeys, three-bay pediment. Four of the ground-floor windows with blank tympana. Doorway with Roman Doric columns and decorated metopes. Dated 1792. No. 49 is much altered but has another doorway with Roman Doric columns and decorated metopes. Nos 50–52 are of eight bays and two and a half storeys. Plastered, with quoins and moulded window frames. The date on the rainwater head is 1727. Then the church is reached, and the street bends round it. Here at once No. 68, CHURCHMAN'S HOUSE, one of the finest in Norwich. It dates from *c.*1740–50.* Seven bays, two storeys, three-bay projection with quoins and a pediment with a tripartite lunette. Doorway with Tuscan columns, decorated metopes, and a pediment. The window over it is segment-headed and has curves rising up to it. Inside is a room with amazingly luxurious decoration, both of the walls and the ceiling. On the walls paintings in elaborate Rococo framings (which remain, however, symmetrical). Two of the paintings may be called school of *Bellucci*. On the ceiling stucco with an oval landscape centre, very gay and pretty. The fireplace with excellent small-scale sculpture. Then No. 74, timber-framed with three dormers, but with a doorway with Tuscan columns in front of rustication. The columns carry a pediment. Finally No. 94, of five bays and two and a half storeys. Good doorway with Ionic columns set in front of pilasters and a pediment.

58

ST JOHN MADDERMARKET (C). N of the church No. 20, and next to it No. 7 ST JOHN'S ALLEY, both timber-framed and quite picturesque.

ST MARY PLAIN, off Oak Street (N). One building alone calls for a visit, PYKERELL'S HOUSE, SW of the church. This is Early Tudor in date. The thatched hall-wing lies behind the front, accessible by an archway. The doorway remains, and the outlines of large hall bay windows to the S and N. The parlour is to the W, the kitchen etc. to the E of the hall, i.e. facing the street with its back wall.

ST PETER STREET, *see* Market Place, p. 273.

SURREY STREET (S,W). A Georgian street of distinction, though one may for a moment forget about it, knocked down by the smashing NORWICH UNION building which, without any doubt, is one of the country's most convinced Edwardian office buildings. It is by *G. J. Skipper*, a local architect but every bit as competent and inventive as any in London. The date of the building is 1903–4. It is stone-faced, buff to yellow, and only five bays wide, but much happens around the five bays, for instance one-storeyed wings coming forward and ending in heavily rusticated niches with canopies and the statues of Bishop Talbot of Oxford – a surprise that – and Sir Samuel Bignold. There are also deep recesses between bays one and five and the centre, which has columns above the ground floor and a pediment. Rustication is heavy everywhere

b2

* Lease date, according to Mr A. Paget Baggs, 1751.

in surrounds and at quoins. Inside, in the fanlight of the doorway some STAINED GLASS including two oval panels signed by *Henry Gyles* of York and dated 1697. Coat of arms and inscription about Vigani, 'Veronensis Chymicorum princeps'. He became professor of chemistry at Cambridge in 1703. The main hall of the building is low and has a large skylight. Various marble facings. Behind, a new eight-storeyed building is being got ready for the Norwich Union. This is by *T. P. Bennett & Sons* and lacks the punch of its predecessor. It is restless but undramatic, and the idiom of today is used without the conviction Skipper wielded in his day. Opposite, also part of the Norwich Union, one of the largest Georgian houses in Norwich, yet completely plain. It is by *Robert Mylne*, 1764, and consists of five bays and two and a half storeys with quadrant wings. Good sturdy cast-iron railings and gates, of heavily Grecian forms.* Further on, No. 11, also detached, also five bays and two and a half storeys, but with two one-storeyed wings in line with the façade. Door surround with bulgy Tuscan columns. This is by *Matthew Brettingham*. It has cast-iron rails too. Nos 25–35 by *Thomas Ivory* are a very urban terrace, three and a half storeys high. They date from 1761–71. The deep porches must be later. Then building becomes definitely looser and more suburban, cf. All Saints Green. The end is the Georgian house with a pretty Adamish porch and a two-bay pediment which forms part of NOTRE DAME CONVENT.‡ Opposite, as proof of how loose building was, terrace of 1881.

SUSSEX STREET (N). Built up about 1830. Near the E end there is a terrace of two-and-a-half-storeyed houses with modestly decorated doorways. The nicest is No. 21 with Greek Doric columns *in antis*. No. 17 has a richly carved surround clearly not *in situ*. Name-plate at the NE corner. On the S side two-storeyed cottages.

THEATRE STREET (S,W). The *clou* of course is the Assembly Rooms, *see* p. 261. To their E, in THE CHANTRY, a doorway with curious C17 carved brackets, probably from the oversailing upper floor of a timber-framed house. To the E of this CHANTRY COURT, a typical Norwich court, with a late C18 iron gate with honeysuckle motifs and two pedimented

---

* These are of 1883; so Mr Paget Baggs tells me. He also gave me Mylne's name for this house.

‡ The date 1820 on a pump.

doorways inside. Minor Georgian further E. The term Chantry refers to the College of St Mary-in-the-Fields which adjoined to the W (*see* Assembly Rooms).

TOMBLAND, W of the Precinct (C). The name has nothing to do with tombs. On the S side an even row of Georgian houses of two and a half storeys (Nos 26–29). Two of them have brick quoins. The W side is more varied. No. 3 has a Greek Doric porch, No. 4 is Early Georgian, with segment-headed windows, vertically 'laced'. No. 5 is of seven bays with a deep Adamish porch and a nice staircase (twisted balusters). The E side is of course dominated by the precinct gates. Between them only one remarkable house, ST ETHELBERT'S (Purdy's Restaurant), 1888, by *E. P. Willins* (according to Mr Nairn), rather wildly Norman Shavian, but symmetrical. To the N the space narrows, and now on the W side No. 14, built by Augustine Steward, Mayor of Norwich, *c.*1530. The house is half-timbered, with overhang and an underpassage to the churchyard of St George. Then the four-gabled SAMSON AND
56a HERCULES HOUSE, so called after its porch with the two most debonair and sleepy of English strong men. The house is said to have been built in 1657. Underneath it some arches of medieval rooms. The N end of the space is the MAID'S HEAD HOTEL, with a Georgian brick front on the r., a wholly redone half-timbered part on the l.

UPPER KING STREET (S,W). No. 17 lies back from the street. Georgian, five bays, two and a half storeys. Door surround with Tuscan columns and pediment.

WESTLEGATE. *See* p. 392.

WESTWICK STREET (S,W), just off and below St Benedict Street. Incorporated in Messrs Bullard's brewery is GIBSON'S FOUNTAIN, dated 1578, a graceful recess with a four-centred head, a semicircular top, and decoration still in the Early Renaissance style.

WILLOW LANE (S,W). Off St Giles Street to the N of St Giles church. First the R.C. SCHOOL, formerly a Catholic chapel, 1827 by *J. T. Patience*. Grey brick with pediment and a porch of two pairs of Ionic columns. Then No. 16, a simple double cottage of brick from the street but most surprisingly adorned at the back – i.e. towards the churchyard – with a Late Gothic oriel window whose provenance is unrecorded.* Its neighbour No. 18 has a stepped gable also towards the churchyard.

---

* It is said that it comes from a hermit's cell in the SW corner of St Giles's churchyard. Mr Whittingham, however, considers the window C19.

OUTER NORWICH

CHURCHES

St ALBAN, Grove Walk. 1932–8 by *Cecil Upcher*. In the Maufe succession. – FONT. From Knettishall in Suffolk. Octagonal, with tracery patterns on the bowl, much damaged. – ALTAR PAINTING. By *Jeffery Camp*, 1955.

St BARTHOLOMEW, Heigham, Waterworks Road. The church was destroyed in the Second World War and only the tower stands: unbuttressed with flushwork-panelled battlements.

St CATHERINE, Mile Cross, Aylsham Road. 1935 by *A. D. R. Caröe & A. P. Robinson*. Pale purple and brown brick with a big w arch and an e tower with saddleback roof. Sheltered under the w arch the shallow, low projection of the baptistery. Round concrete arches inside and side chapels with transverse arches. The chapels are connected by passages.

CHRIST CHURCH, Church Avenue. 1873 by *J. H. Brown & Pearce* (GR). With an apse and an asymmetrically placed e bell-turret. The w porch an obvious addition. It dates from 1913. The s aisle with its Perp windows is of the same date. Interior with an assertive N arcade of short round piers with heavy square capitals and a lot of nailhead decoration in the arches. In the windows mostly plate tracery. – STAINED GLASS. Some C15 fragments in the porch window.

CHRIST CHURCH, New Catton, at the N end of Magdalen Road. 1841–2 by *John Brown*. Grey brick. In the lancet style, with a heavy bellcote and heavy pinnacles. Nave, transept, and tripartite chancel. A poor timber roof. – To the s the funny Gothic church SCHOOL, also of grey brick. This is of 1850 (by *J. S. Benest* and *A. Newson*) but was enlarged in 1882 (bellcote).

HOLY TRINITY, Essex Street. 1860–1 by *W. Smith*. The church builds up well from the street, with a tall e tower rising above the apse and ending in an octagonal top and spire. Plate and bar tracery in the windows. – PLATE. Paten (London) 1764.

St MARK, Hall Road. 1844 by *John Brown*. The apse and vestry by *J. H. Brown*, 1864. Flint and yellow brick, w tower with polygonal buttresses and turrets. Wide barn-like nave with three galleries on iron shafts. – PLATE. Set of 1843, made by *Barnard* of London.

St MATTHEW, Rosary Road, Thorpe. 1851 by *John Brown*. Neo-Norman, of ragstone. – PLATE. Two Chalices of 1829, made in London.

ST PHILIP, Heigham, Heigham Road. 1871 by *Edward Power* of London. With plate tracery windows and a NW tower. – PLATE. London-made set of 1836.

ST THOMAS, Earlham Road. 1886 by *Ewan Christian*. Red brick, with lancet windows and without a tower. Definitely Late and no longer High Victorian, i.e. restrained, not showy. Low and wide inside. The nice ceiling was put in after war damage in 1954.

PRESBYTERIAN CHURCH, Unthank Road. 1954–6 by *B. M. Feilden*. In the new mid-century Expressionism with a steep gable and sharp angles otherwise also, where possible, including the paving pattern of the forecourt. Only the tower does not participate. The church itself is on the upper floor with staircase and subsidiary rooms below. The timber ceiling of the church again broken into angles.

CEMETERIES. *See* p. 392.

PUBLIC BUILDINGS

POST OFFICE SORTING OFFICE, Thorpe Road. 1955–6 by *T. F. Winterburn* (Senior Architect, Ministry of Works). A good example of current architecture, nicely grouped and with much curtain-walling. It deserves mention in a town so far poor in worthwhile contemporary buildings.

SWIMMING BATHS, Aylsham Road. 1959–61 by *David Percival*, the City Architect. Good, with a series of tall segment-headed windows above and behind a low windowless range.

LAZAR HOUSE (Branch Library), 219 Sprowston Road. The Lazar Hospital was founded by Herbert de Losinga. A Norman range is preserved with two doorways, one to the W with one order of shafts, the other to the S, much damaged and apparently originally with two orders. In the W gable, right at the top, two tiny round windows with carstone surrounds.

CITY COLLEGE, Ipswich Road. 1949 by the then City Architect, *L. G. Hannaford*. Three-storeyed, thirty-one bays long, of pale brick and entirely neutral.

HEWETT (SECONDARY TECHNICAL) SCHOOL, Hall Road. 1956–8 by *David Percival*, the City Architect, an impressive, loose group, stretching out one-storeyed along the road, but with a two-storeyed pavilion at the l. end and a four-storeyed slab of classrooms receding at r. angles.

HEARTEASE SCHOOLS, Heartsease Lane. Junior and Infant Schools, completed in 1956 and 1960. Similar in character to the above and equally attractive. Also by *David Percival*.

EARLHAM SCHOOLS, *see* p. 289.

ST ANDREW'S HOSPITAL, Thorpe, 1¼ m. E of Thorpe village church. The oldest part is by *Francis Stone*, 1811–14, grey brick with a three-storeyed seven-bay centre, a three-bay pediment, a one-storeyed porch of two pairs of heavy Tuscan columns, and long lower wings l. and r. in the same direction and with arched windows. The hospital is supposed to be the oldest public mental hospital in England.

NORFOLK AND NORWICH HOSPITAL, St Stephen's Road. 1770–5 by *William Ivory*. A new wing was added in 1802 to complete the original design. The design was H-shaped with a centre facing S, nine bays long and two storeys high with a projecting, pedimented centre. It was quite a monumental composition. The most substantial addition was made in 1879. It is by *E. Boardman*, consultant *T. H. Wyatt*, and consists of a centre like a town hall with a turret over the middle and wings with sturdy polygonal turrets at the corners towards the street. More additions since.

BRITANNIA BARRACKS, Britannia Road. 1885–7. In the Norman Shaw style, which is a surprising thing for barracks.

NELSON BARRACKS, Barrack Street. Built in 1791 as the Cavalry Barracks. Red brick. Symmetrical composition. The centre is a nine-bay house of two and a half storeys. Doorway with rather rustic Adamish capitals. To the l. and r., in the same direction, extend long, lower staff ranges.

DRILL HALL, Chapelfield Road. 1866 by *J. S. Benest*. Flint and red brick, castellated and with a menacing 'gateway'. To its l. a tower which incorporates one of the towers of the town wall (*see* p. 258).

SPORTS CENTRE, South Park Avenue, Eaton Park. Circular, with colonnades and a domed pavilion in the centre. A formal lake in front. Designed by *A. Sandys-Winsch* and built after 1924.

CATTLE MARKET, Hall Road. By the City Engineer, *H. C. Rowley* and the City Architect, *D. Percival*, 1958–60. A thirty-two-acre job, well-planned. The livestock buildings and pens are on the N side, shops, offices, and a restaurant in the SW corner arranged to form a kind of market square in the middle of which is a water tower. In the middle of the site three cattle sale rings with shallow tunnel-vaulted roofs.

THORPE STATION. 1886 by *John Wilson*. Red brick and yellow stone. Classical and symmetrical but with a French pavilion roof

PERAMBULATIONS

A coherent perambulation can only be done to the SE, S, and SW in the sector between Bracondale and the Newmarket Road. For the rest no more is needed than a mention of a few places.

To the E Thorpe within Norwich and Thorpe without merge imperceptibly, or just perceptibly. Along THORPE ROAD one notices the detached Norwich villas of c.1830 or so, such as THE LAWNS (with a Tuscan porch), and also houses immediately on the street still with nice doorways, e.g. No. 73. THORPE LODGE, at the corner of Harvey Lane, has a crinkle-crankle or undulating forcing wall. Then rather bigger Victorian villas culminating in PINE BANKS of the 1880s, with a tall picturesque folly tower which looks earlier (c.1850?) and, opposite the entrance, another folly-bit with a Gothic two-light window. Here the expansion of Norwich meets the expansion of Thorpe village with Thorpe Hall and the Town House Hotel, see pp. 291–2.

In ROSARY ROAD, N of the Norwich end of Thorpe Road, similar Latest-Georgian developments, e.g. THE MOUNT (No. 91), of yellow brick with a Greek Doric porch. Also a group of pleasant new flats and houses by *David Percival*, the City Architect, 1958–9.

Further N, i.e. now NE of the centre, in BARRACK STREET Messrs Steward and Patteson's BREWERY. The former brewer's house is of the early C19; the principal brewing buildings were erected in 1891 and 1906. Due N, i.e. in SPROWSTON ROAD, N of Gertrude Road, the LAZAR HOUSE, see Public Buildings, p. 282.

Then NW, again a feeler, in HEIGHAM STREET the so-called Bishop's Palace, later DOLPHIN INN, badly damaged in the Second World War and recently rebuilt. It had in one gable a date 1595. L-shaped. The recessed part symmetrical with two canted bay windows. It carries the date 1615. The windows transomed but still with arched lights. Small doorway with four-centred head.

Now, turning to the more fruitful direction, the position is this. Bracondale was the Georgian West End, but after 1800 well-to-do houses also went up along Ipswich Road, Newmarket Road, and Unthank Road. Moreover, at the same time terraces of cottages and houses were built closer to the centre. Examples are in and around CHAPELFIELD ROAD, especially THE CRESCENT, which dates from c.1820 and is not crescent-

shaped. Immediately behind here, incidentally, that is around
VAUXHALL STREET, new developments have started in 1959,
well-designed blocks of flats by *D. Percival*, the City Architect.
Also BISHOP HERBERT HOUSE, for young, disabled people,
one-storeyed, round an inner court.

Then, to dispose of these further three feelers quickly and be
able to concentrate on Bracondale: in UNTHANK ROAD Nos
41–47 are a grey-brick terrace of about 1830–40, and similar
terraces are in side streets too. Building at that time went as
far as Gloucester Street. Further E, off Unthank Road and off
Upton Road, is UPTON CLOSE, a good recent house by *John
Winter*. Yet further E, EATON HALL, to the N of Unthank
Road. This must now be reached from Pettus Road, off
SOUTH PARK AVENUE. It is a grey-brick house, not regular,
apparently Late Georgian. Doorway with recessed fluted
columns, ground-floor windows set in blank arches.

Next the Ipswich and Newmarket Roads. Here again early C19
houses in gardens as well as terraces. At the junction FOUN-
TAIN with the figure of a young woman with a child. By *J. E.
Boehm*, 1874. A few examples: in IPSWICH ROAD No. 10 of
three bays with a one-bay pediment. Then TOWN CLOSE
HOUSE. The rusticated quoins in three places look as if this
had been an early C18 house, altered in Late Georgian days.
Door with Greek Doric porch. More in the NEWMARKET
ROAD, e.g. Nos 12–18, two pairs of semi-detached four-bay
houses with two-bay pediments. Then No. 45a, SUNRAYS,
grey brick, with giant pilasters and wreaths in the frieze. After
that No. 65 etc. and 77–81, the former a unified composition
with a pediment in the centre, the latter with Greek Doric
porches.

So that leaves BRACONDALE. There was some *ante-muros*
building here even in the C16 and C17; for there are Tower
House and the Manor House. TOWER HOUSE (No. 58) has
behind an C18 front an Elizabethan tower or indeed tower
house with a flat SW front of one large and one small window
on one floor, all pedimented. Behind the small window is the
staircase. As the terrain rises much, there are two more storeys
of basement below, the lower one of them tunnel-vaulted.
Nothing is known about the house. The MANOR HOUSE (No.
54) is dated 1578, with a middle projection, shaped gables,
and pedimented windows. Then the Georgian activity, starting from the town end. Here there are the same types of houses
and terraces with pedimented doorways or porches as we have

found in the s and sw, e.g. Nos 51–57 where the porches have
Greek Doric columns. No. 58, Tower House, must here be
mentioned again. Its front part is a big, three-bay Late
Georgian house. THE GROVE (Nos 59–61) is grey brick and
Early Victorian, but Nos 62–64 have a nucleus which must be
Early Georgian. They are a pair with heavy doorways and still
have shaped end-gables. No. 66 is again prosperous Georgian.
It has canted bay windows. After that one enters the Colman
domain. Messrs Colman's CARROW WORKS are at the
bottom end of KING STREET. The chief constituents now
which are of interest here are the satisfactory new office block,
done in 1959 by the firm's architectural department, and the
Early Victorian villa of grey brick which adjoins it and still has
its large conservatory. This must have been built before 1856.
The next gate after that to the villa, and now back in Bracondale,
leads to CARROW ABBEY, or to be more correct, Carrow
Priory. As one approaches the house, it seems another Colman
house, this one Late Victorian. In fact what one sees is the
PRIORESS'S LODGING, enlarged and somewhat prettified by
a Colman son-in-law in 1899–1909 (after having been
Martineau property). The Priory was founded for Benedictine
nuns in 1146, and something of the Norman buildings survives, as we shall see. But the last Prioress, Isabel Wygun, had
built herself a house to the w of the cloister which, in its
sumptuousness and worldliness, almost seems to justify the
Dissolution. Her house, which is of flint with brick dressings,
remains *in toto*, and can easily be appreciated if one takes away
in one's mind the r. (s) half of the present house and starts only
a little to the r. of the porch. This was the main entrance even
in the early C16. The large doorway has in the spandrels of its
wooden frame the rebus of the prioress, a Y and a gun. It
repeats in other places. The doorway led into the hall, which
has a five-light window and a seven-light bay window, both
with wooden frames and a transom. To its l. (N) follows the
parlour, and at the far end of the parlour, projecting towards
the cloister, the spiral staircase up to the bedroom (which has
an oriel window). Moulded beams and doors remain inside,
and the huge fireplace of the parlour.

Provided with the knowledge that the prioress's house ran
along w of, and parallel with, the w range of the cloister, one
will easily find one's way among the fragments of the nunnery.
Of the church the straight E wall can be detected by the bases
of its shafted Norman buttresses. The chancel had aisles and a

later N chapel. The SE crossing pier is easily recognized. So is the S transept W wall with its wall shafts. The S wall of the S aisle stands up, i.e. the wall between church and cloister. Of the ranges surrounding the cloister the best-preserved piece is the E wall, i.e. the former dormitory wall. The doorway is complete which led to the day-stair from the cloister just S of where the chapter house was. More complete excavation and public access would be very desirable.

Opposite the gates to Carrow Abbey are the gates to BRACON-DALE LODGE, another Martineau, later Colman, house, and this is best visible from MARTINEAU LANE. It is a Late Georgian villa of only three bays, but as the middle one is an ample bow and ends in a dome of ever so slightly Oriental-Brighton-Pavilionish outline, the sight is very pretty.

Martineau Lane forms part of the Norwich ring-road, which visitors will find useful to approach the various outer items without the ordeal of driving in the centre.

NORWICH VILLAGES

Of the villages described in following pages, Earlham, Eaton, and Lakenham are inside, and Catton, Hellesdon, Sprowston, Thorpe, and Trowse Newton are outside the City boundaries.

CATTON 2010

ST MARGARET. Round tower. Octagonal top, with yellow brick trim and traceried Perp bell-openings. Aisles and N transept of 1850–2. Chancel Perp, with a pretty little niche N of the E window. A larger niche inside, S of the chancel arch. – FONT. Octagonal, with four cusped fields in each panel. – PULPIT. A very interesting piece, dated 1537. Linenfold panels, separated by balusters, and above the linenfold small panels with Early Renaissance arabesques. – PLATE. Elizabethan Chalice (Norwich); Paten, by *Peter Peterson*, 1567; Ladle (London) 1818. – MONUMENTS. Green family *c.*1745. Standing monument with sarcophagus in front of an obelisk. Two sad putti. By *Robert Page*. – Jeremiah Ives † 1820. By *Sir Richard West-macott*. He signs with his London address (South Audley Street) – a sign of how with the C19 the monumental sculptor becomes a firm. Seated mourning woman with her hair down, by a sarcophagus carrying the inscription. – Lady Bignold † 1860. By *Stanley Stevens*, with a faith-inspired woman. – Many more tablets.

CATTON HALL. A dull Late Georgian house, plastered, with two bow windows symmetrically arranged. Large grounds. *Repton* laid them out and calls them his earliest job.

THE FIRS, 71 St Clement's Hill. A beautiful five-bay house of two and a half storeys. Lower two-bay extensions with arched windows. Doorway with pediment on unfluted Ionic columns. Staircase with two twisted balusters for each step and carved tread-ends. Exuberant plasterwork on the ceiling. The date must be *c.*1750.

One or two other houses with good doorways in ST CLEMENT'S HILL. Also, a good deal further N, in LODGE LANE, No. 2, of six bays and two storeys, and the OLD HALL, late C17 with mullioned windows in two floors arranged symmetrically and with a central doorway. The brickwork is Flemish bond.

2000

EARLHAM

ST MARY. A small church. W tower of knapped flint and red brick. Yet there may be a very old core, if the S window in its internal Norman form can be trusted. The W wall of the nave in any case shows blocks of carstone which look Norman. Nave and chancel; S porch with stepped gable. – FONT. Octagonal, with quatrefoils. – SCREEN. With broad, ogee-headed one-light divisions, cusped and subcusped, and with short four-light miniature windows over; quite good. – LECTERN. A coarsely carved angel, probably from the hammerbeam of a roof. – SCULPTURE. Circular wooden relief of the Annunciation; Baroque and Continental. – PLATE. Chalice (London) 1674; Chalice, Paten, and Almsdish from Bowthorpe (Norwich), given in 1680; undated Paten Cover (Norwich). – MONUMENT. Bacon children; the latest death recorded is 1678. Tablet with two putti and with carved garlands. From St Giles-in-the-Fields, London.

Just N of the church CHURCH FARMHOUSE, facing the churchyard. Early C17. Timber-framed, with polygonal chimneys.

EARLHAM HALL, S of the church in generous grounds. An odd house with many accretions. Flint and red brick. It looks a different date from every side. The W is dated 1642 and has two straight gables. The S, i.e. the principal, front with its three shaped gables is probably of the late C17, but the one-storeyed pavilion may be Georgian. The entrance, i.e. N, front is Georgian, but has two projecting wings with canted bay windows which seems to indicate that here a C17 house under-

lies too. Star-shaped chimneytops also survive. A DOVECOTE
nearer the church.

EARLHAM SCHOOLS. A group of three schools for over 1400
children. Two of them are linked up. They were completed in
1954 (Bluebell), 1957 (Earlham), and 1959 (Blackdale). By the
City Architect's department (City Architect now *D. Percival*).

UNIVERSITY. Earlham is the suggested site for the university
to be established at Norwich. A pity the site by Ber Street
was not preferred. It would have been a good thing to have
one of the new universities in the centre of a town and not in
splendid isolation.

Along Earlham Road the former village merges into the town. It
is doubtful whether CURFEW LODGE, No. 129, C 19-Tudor
and pretty, ought to be listed with the former or the latter.

EATON   *2000*

ST ANDREW, Church Lane. This is the biggest of the Norwich
village churches, and it still lies in the open country. Perp W
tower with flushwork panelling against the battlements. Nave
and chancel in one, thatched. The windows are all small
lancets, and the body of the church must indeed be of the C 13.
E window of three lights with intersected tracery. Restoration
by *Thomas Jekyll*, 1860–1. The single-framed roof is certainly
not original, but may represent the original. – Bowl of the
PILLAR PISCINA with big nobbly leaves. – PLATE. Chalice
and Paten (Norwich) inscribed 1684.

To the E of the church OLD HOUSE, of five bays and two and a
half storeys, with a rusticated, pedimented doorway and
stuccoed lintel stones above the windows. The present appearance is Late Georgian and would go with the date 1822 on a
gatepier. However, the house is called 'de novo aedificata' in
1689. It would deserve some study. Opposite another Georgian
house, three bays, plastered, with a doorway with fluted Ionic
columns.

From the W end of Church Lane slightly to the W the RED
LION, a good inn of the late C 17. Brick, two storeys, with
shaped end-gables, very widely spaced pilasters between the
(altered) windows on the upper floor, and raised window
frames. Opposite yet another three-bay Georgian house,
plastered, with pedimented doorway and above it an arched
window with alternatingly rusticated surround.

BARROWS. On the golf course E of Eaton are two bowl barrows,
survivors of a group of four.

1010
HELLESDON

ST MARY. Small, with a lead-covered bell-turret crowned by a
spire, and with a prominent two-storeyed s porch. Inside the
porch, vault with diagonal and ridge-ribs and bosses. The N
aisle windows are Dec but not old, the chancel windows Perp.
Two-bay arcades with a pier of four shafts and four hollows
between. – FONT. Octagonal, with quatrefoils. – PLATE.
Chalice (Norwich) 1567; Paten unmarked; Almsdish (London)
1738. – MONUMENTS. Brasses to Richard de Heylesdone and
wife, later C14, demi-figures 14 in. long; Richard de Tasburgh,
1389, a figure 29½ in. long (N wall).

2000

LAKENHAM

ST JOHN AND ALL SAINTS. On a steep hill above the old
village nucleus, which is by the Yare bridge. Unbuttressed w
tower. Nave and chancel in one and very low. The chancel E
window has cusped intersected tracery.* The s aisle is of brick
and has wooden arcade piers. This dates from 1825. – FONT.
Octagonal, panelled stem with fleurons, bowl with two angels,
the signs of the Evangelists and the Instruments of the
Passion. – PLATE. Chalice (Norwich) 1567–8; Elizabethan
Paten Cover; Oval Dish (London) 1792. – MONUMENT.
Tablet to William Crowe † 1779. Signed by *M. Crowe.*
Below by the bridge the POST OFFICE, a cottage with some pedimented windows, Jacobean or later. Several other minor old
houses nearby.

2010

SPROWSTON

ST MARY AND ST MARGARET. C18 brick tower. The clerestory
of the nave was clearly also remodelled at that time and later
re-gothicized again. The chancel has a clerestory too. C14
arcades of four bays. Octagonal piers, double-chamfered
arches. The s arcade earlier than the N arcade, it seems. –
STAINED GLASS. E window 1865, and quite good. Probably by
Hardman. – PLATE. Chalice and Paten, Norwich-made, 1568.
– MONUMENTS. An unusual number. First the Corbets in the
N chapel. John † 1559. Tomb-chest with three shields in
cusped lozenges. Back wall with kneeling brass figures. – Miles
† 1607. Tablet with kneeling figures facing one another across
a prayer-desk. – Thomas † 1617. Recumbent effigies on a
tomb-chest with pilasters decorated by strapwork. – The
monument in the N aisle with a recess, many small kneeling

---

* The chancel was rebuilt by *J. Brown* (*Builder* 1864; PF).

figures, and no inscription is to Christopher Knolles † 1610. –
In the chancel Sir Thomas Adams † 1667 and wife. Large
standing monument with both effigies semi-reclining, he
below and in front of her, lying rather stiffly, she in a precious
pose. Tomb-chest with lush acanthus and a good cartouche.
Reredos background with columns. Weeping putti l. and r. –
Sir Paul Paynter † 1686. Black and white marble tablet.
Drapery lifted for the inscription and looped round the
columns. – Nathaniel Micklethwait † 1757. By *Robert Page*.
Good; with a bust between the arms of an open scrolly pediment and in front of a pink-marble obelisk. Against the
obelisk a putto with a wreath. – Lady Wilhelmina Mickle-44a
thwait, 1807 by *Bacon Jun*. White marble. A group of two
women and a baby below an urn with the three Graces very
small. Above in clouds woman with two babies.

THORPE 2000

ST ANDREW. Of the old church the s porch tower remains, and
parts of the s and w walls. One goes through the porch to reach
the new church, which was designed by *Thomas Jekyll* in 1866
(GR). Knapped flint, red brick, and stone. In the plate-tracery
style. Nave and s aisle, apse and tower with a pyramid roof.
The aisle arcade is monstrous, short round piers on high bases
with square capitals and abaci, i.e. Transitional, but with
colossal capitals, with some semi-Norman motifs but also a
pelican and busts of angels. – PLATE. Chalice and two Salvers *See*
(London) 1754. – MONUMENT. Elizabeth Meadows MartineauP.
† 1810. By *Coade & Sealy*. Tablet with a reclining woman. 392
THORPE HALL, Thorpe Road. An early C17 house, said to incorporate the remains of a quadrangular late C14 house. What
there is now is one range with mullioned and transomed
windows and a lower range at r. angles to it. At the time when
this was built or rebuilt the house belonged to Sir Edward
Paston, who died in 1630. The ground-floor windows have
pediments. Star-topped chimneys. One room inside is well
preserved, the room N of what must have been the hall. It has
a fireplace and a fine surround still in the Early Renaissance
taste and an overmantel with fluted pilasters. The walls are
panelled, also with fluted pilasters. In the garden wall towards
the street a small doorway and a small bit of C15 or C16
tracery, re-set. The house indeed still had until quite recently
parts of the late C14, including a chapel. It belonged to the
bishops of Norwich.

Several old houses worth noting near the church in Thorpe Road. Between it and Thorpe Hall the TOWN HOUSE HOTEL, with a remarkable circular domed conservatory, probably of *c.*1820–30. Closer to the church a five-bay house with a pedimented Gibbs door-surround and shaped end-gables (derelict at the time of writing). E of the church GARDEN HOUSE, much renewed, but basically Tudor: timber-framed with brick-nogging. Two-storeyed porch. Original chimneystack. Then No. 103 and No. 105, Georgian.

PINE BANKS, *see* Outer Norwich, p. 284.

2000   TROWSE NEWTON

ST ANDREW. The great architectural interest of the church is its E window. This, though renewed, represents the state recorded by Ladbrooke about 1825 and is datable by an inscription in the E wall which reads 'WILELMUS DE KIRKEBEI PRIOR NORWIC ME POSUIT', etc. He was prior of Norwich Cathedral from 1272 to 1288, and so the tracery of the window represents a stage reached before 1288. The window is of three lights with trefoil- and cinquefoil-cusped lights, and above two unenriched quatrefoils slightly tipped inwards and a large diagonally placed quatrefoil, also unenriched, above that. The E window of Lincoln Cathedral must date from *c.*1275 and is still entirely pure. Here certain impurities begin to appear in Geometrical tracery which were in the end to lead to its disintegration in the Dec style. The chancel Piscina is original and less restored. The church is otherwise not specially attractive. Unbuttressed W tower, two-storeyed S porch with a rib-vault of diagonal and ridge-ribs inside. N aisle and N arcade of 1901. – FONT. Octagonal. Four lions against the stem; four lions and four demi-figures of angels holding shields (emblem of the Trinity and Instruments of the Passion, three crowns, three chalices) against the bowl. – SCULPTURE. Seated most inappropriately around the pulpit three Baroque life-size figures, David with his harp and two angels blowing trumpets. They come from an organ-case most probably. – PAINTINGS. Ascension of Christ, the altar-painting of St Michael at Coslany. Said to be by *C. Heins*. Is it *John T. Heins*, who died in 1771, or his father *D. Heins*? St Michael was refurnished in 1739, and the painting is mentioned by Blomefield, i.e. cannot be later than *c.*1740–5.* The painting is in its original frame.

* Information kindly volunteered by Mr P. Hepworth.

Also l. and r. of the altar and in Gothick frames around their original frames, four large single figures from the same reredos. – PLATE. Paten, pre-Reformation, the central aperture removed. – Norwich-made Chalice of 1567–8 and Paten inscribed 1681. – Flagon, London-made, 1769.

CROWN POINT HALL (Whitlingham Hospital). In the Elizabethan style by *H. E. Coe*, c.1865 (date on the lodge). Red brick, but the staff wing half-timbered. (Additions of 1902 by *Boardman*.)

WINDMILL, ¾ m. s of Crown Point Hall. A derelict tower-mill without sails.

In the street from the s entrance of the Crown Point estate to the bridge on the NE side TROWSE OLD HALL, in the Gothick taste, said to be of 1721 but, if so, clearly externally remodelled, say about 1775. Crenellation, pointed windows and one cinquefoil one, some rocky rustication round the windows, also very thin giant pilasters with thin bands of rustication. A little further NW GOTHIC COTTAGE, also Gothick. Then, at the widening into the large open GREEN along its s side, RUSSELL TERRACE, four identical terraces of eight houses each, red brick, very simple, but solid and not without dignity. They date from the 1880s but look a good deal earlier.

NEWTON HALL, ⅝ m. NNW of Crown Point Hall, at the N end of the four-line avenue of trees. Ruins of a pre-Reformation manor house which became a residence of the Deans of Norwich until long after the Dissolution. Demolished about 1860. What details survive point to a Perp date, e.g. the remains of cusped lights in a large window facing N and a Perp doorway facing s. The house has never been sufficiently published.

The BARROW 300 yds NE of the Arminghall henge (*see* Bixley, vol. 2) is a bowl barrow with twin concentric ditches now cut through by a road. Excavations showed the mound 80 ft in diameter to be a natural gravel knoll encircled by a penannular ditch. The outer ditch was incomplete. Of three central pits one contained a necked beaker and another earlier, secondary Neolithic sherds as found at Arminghall. A fourth pit lay somewhat off centre.

WHITLINGHAM

ST ANDREW. On a ridge above the river. The round tower, one window with cusped Y-tracery, and the E window remain.

ORMESBY ST MARGARET

St Margaret. Norman s doorway of heavy design with one order of shafts, the bases in the form of reversed capitals, arch with two zigzag and two billet friezes. Perp w tower with flushwork panelling on the base and triple-stepped battlements also with flushwork panelling. Figures on the pinnacles. Tall arch to the nave. Two-storeyed s porch. N aisle of 1867. The details of the church mostly of that time. Inside Sedilia and Piscina Dec; recut. Easter Sepulchre Dec and more ornate, with a cusped and subcusped arch and spandrels with close tracery; also re-cut. Recess in the E wall of the N aisle with traceried spandrels, not *in situ*. – PAINTING. Virgin; the Baroque frame is genuine. Is it Spanish? – PLATE. Elizabethan Chalice. – MONUMENTS. (Brass demi-effigy of a lady holding her heart; *c*.1440.) – Brass to Sir Robert Clere † 1529 and wife; 35½ in. figures. – Several tablets to Lacons of Ormesby Hall.

ORMESBY HALL (also called Ormesby Old Hall), E of the church. Fine Early Georgian front of brick headers only. Seven bays, two storeys, with a pedimented three-bay projection. Angle brick quoins. Partly parapet, partly balustrade. Doorway with Tuscan columns and a metope frieze.

ORMESBY HOUSE (also called Ormesby Hall), ¼ m. w of the church. A Georgian house with a bow to which in 1810 Gothic additions were made to the design of *Mark Graystone Thompson*. They included polygonal angle shafts with pinnacles and of course battlements. On the s side a Gothic conservatory. Vaulted entrance hall.

To the E of Ormesby Hall two cottages with shaped gables, one of one, the other of two storeys.

At East End THE GRANGE, with shaped end-gables but a Late Georgian front of three bays with a one-bay pediment and a Roman Doric porch. There is in fact an inscription with the date 1796.

At the N end of the village a nice Georgian five-bay house with a rusticated door surround of alternating sizes and a hipped roof.

About ¾ m. NW of the church the MANOR HOUSE, also Georgian, also of five bays. Two and a half storeys, the half-storey above the cornice. Rusticated angle pilasters of brick. Hipped roof. Low one-bay attachments.

ORMESBY ST MICHAEL

St Michael. Not large. Unbuttressed, much repaired w tower. Thatched nave. Nave and chancel windows late C13 in style, but all renewed or new. They include (chancel s) one with bar tracery, a quatrefoil in a circle. The nave has an arch-braced roof with a castellated wall-plate. – STAINED GLASS. Designed by *Henry Holiday* the s chancel window with Faith, 1898, the N chancel window 1911–13, and the E window 1919–20 – the continuation of a style still dependent on Burne-Jones. – PLATE. Elizabethan Chalice; Elizabethan Paten. – MONUMENTS. Tablets to Peter Upcher † 1796 (with a classical urn), to Elizabeth Upcher, 1806 (an excellent tablet by *Bacon Jun.* with one allegorical figure in a roundel at the foot), and to Hester Manning † 1805 (by *Gray & Jaynes* of London, with a coat of arms in front of an obelisk).

(ORMESBY MANOR. Built originally *c.*1800, the rear a little earlier than the front and tower. The tower had a glass dome.)

OULTON
1020

ST PETER AND ST PAUL. Perp w tower, not centrally placed. A nave w window with pretty tracery is placed to its N. Perp s windows. Former N and s chapels. The chancel has straight-headed transomed Perp N and s windows of two lights. Nicely cusped and subcusped priest's doorway with fleurons in the spandrels. – PAINTING. A fish remains of the scene of St Christopher carrying the child Christ (N wall). – PLATE. Paten, *c.*1520. In a sexfoil a decorated circle and in this the face of Christ with rays. – Chalice, Norwich, 1567–8. – MONUMENT. Coulson Bell † 1800. Tablet with urn in front of obelisk.

CONGREGATIONAL CHURCH, ½ m. NNE. Hidden by trees. Late C18. Four bays, two storeys, red brick. The doorways in bays one and four. Two main columns or posts inside.

OULTON HALL. Georgian, whitewashed, of seven bays and two storeys. Wide Roman-Doric porch with metope frieze. Stabling on the l. with cupola.

OVERSTRAND
2040

ST MARTIN. The church had become ruinous in the C18. It was partly restored, partly rebuilt in 1911–14. Perp w tower with small sound-holes and flushwork-panelled battlements. A small oven for baking wafers has a flue coming out near the top. The aisleless Perp nave with big windows was enlarged by a N aisle during rebuilding. The N doorway was kept in its original position, i.e. appears now inside the church – a nice, unexpected effect. The N porch was re-erected on the s side. –

PLATE. Norwich-made Chalice of 1567 and undated Paten. –
MONUMENTS. Tablet to Sir Thomas Fowell Buxton, the
philanthropist, † 1845, by *T. Marsh.* – Sir Edward North
Buxton † 1856, by the same and identical.

CHRIST CHURCH, the church built in 1867 to take the place of
the bigger, ruinous church, has been pulled down.

METHODIST CHURCH, at the E end of the village. 1898 by
Lutyens. A very curious design. Simply an oblong, but with a
clerestory, and, whereas the ground floor of two colours of red
brick is nothing startling, the clerestory is pebble-dashed and
consists of four lunette windows to the S, four to the N, and
one each to the W and E. This must be the only Nonconformist
chapel designed by Lutyens.

BELFRY SCHOOL, opposite the church. The old part, one-
storeyed, of pebble with a Greek Doric porch at the end, dates
from 1830.

OVERSTRAND HALL (Convalescent Home). Built by *Lutyens* in
1899 for Lord Hillingdon, a partner in Glyn Mills, the bankers.
Overstrand Hall is one of his most remarkable buildings, at the
time when he had reached maturity but still believed to the
full in his own inventiveness. The entrance side especially is a
masterpiece of free balance and unexpected juxtaposition of
solid and void. The contrast between the deliberately insignificant arched doorway, the long band of windows above,
and the bold, bald chimneybreast on the r. ought to be
savoured at leisure. The garden façade, with two half-
timbered gables, is more conventional. Inside a circular court
with curved steps and a curved fountain.

THE PLEASAUNCE (Christian Endeavour) is also by *Lutyens* and
dates from 1897–9. It was adapted from two existing houses
for Cyril Flower, first Lord Battersea, who had married a
daughter of Sir Anthony de Rothschild. It has more capricious
inventions than Overstrand Hall, notably the two curious
cloisters to the S and N of the hall. To the S it is not really a
cloister, only one detached covered walk with heavy buttresses
instead of pillars and a very big roof. To the N the cloister is
three sides of an oblong with low arches and in the centre of
the N side a pebbledashed clock tower. The inspiration from
Voysey which meant much to Lutyens in the late nineties
appears very clearly here. The house itself is red brick with
some tile-hanging. The lower N wing with six little oriel
windows and six little gables is especially successful.*

* The garden was laid out by *Gertrude Jekyll.*

SEA MARGE, at the E end of Overstrand, is in contrast the conventional large half-timbered house of the same period. It was
built in 1908–12, and the name of the architect could not be
traced.*

OXNEAD

2020

ST MICHAEL. Much added to in brick, namely the tower top
(C17?), the N porch (C17?), the S porch (C18), and the stepped
E gable. – PLATE. Two London-made Flagons, 1637; Chalice
and Paten, 1662; Almsdish, 1687. All the plate is silver gilt.
– MONUMENTS. Sir Clement Paston † 1597. Alabaster. Tomb-
chest with two shields and the kneeling figure of his wife.
Recumbent effigy on a half-rolled-up mat (a motif of Nether-
landish origin). – Lady Katherine Paston † 1636. By *Nicholas
Stone*. Grey and white marble. Base with paterae oddly broken
off at the corners. White, rather dull bust on a pedestal with
two volutes. On this the two putti may have reclined originally.
Arched white inscription plates l. and r. Segmental top pediment.

OXNEAD HALL. The principal house of the Pastons. When their
fortunes had declined under the first and second Earls of Yarmouth and the estate had been sold to Admiral Anson in 1731,
most of the house was demolished. The Hall was called 'in
utmost Ruins' in 1744. What remains is a service wing (cf.
Blickling) in good order, with symmetrically arranged doorways (blocked) and mullioned windows. To this a C19 wing
was added running parallel to the S and so that its W wall
touches the E wall of the service wing, an odd arrangement.
Both ranges have polygonal angle shafts and pinnacles. Of the
house itself cellars of the W wing exist and bumps in the grass
indicate where the centre was. Inside the stables HORSE-
BOXES with acanthus decoration of the late C17(?). Of the
statuary bought from *Nicholas Stone* nothing is left. It included a Hercules (now at Blickling, see p. 99), a Jupiter, a
Mercury, and a Venus. In the grounds below the house to the
S a fragment of a summer-house or gatehouse. Brick with three
arches, two of them belonging to niches.

PALLING *see* SEA PALLING

PANXWORTH

3010

CHURCH. Thin, unbuttressed W tower. Battlements with flushwork panelling. Nave and chancel designed by *James Watson*
(GR) and built in 1847.

* Information received: 'He came from London and was knighted; name
unknown.' *Sic transit.*

PASTON

ST MARGARET. A thatched church. Dec almost throughout.
Y-tracery cusped, three stepped lancet lights under an arch,
intersected tracery, also flowing tracery. Contemporary nave
roof: single-framed and scissor-braced. In the chancel pillar
piscina with credence shelf. – FONT. Octagonal. Panelled
stem, two ogee arches on each side of the bowl. – SCREEN.
Little of it is old. – READER'S DESK. Two bench ends with
poppy-heads. Traceried ends and front. – (BENCH ENDS,
some with poppy-heads, some with grotesques.) – COMMUN-
ION RAIL. The very ornate balusters of bulbous shape and
with small foliage nearly all-over come from a house in Norfolk, and presumably a staircase. – PAINTINGS. Large St
Christopher, late C14. Also, further E, remains of the Scourging of Christ (?) and the story of the Three Quick and the
Three Dead. – PLATE. Paten of c.1450–c.1540. Hand of God
issuing from clouds in a circular halo. – Chalice, Norwich,
1567. – Flagon, London, inscribed 1664. – MONUMENTS.
Three plain tomb-chests, no doubt of Pastons, the one at the E
end said to have been brought from Broomholm Priory.* All
these have shields in lozenge-shaped fields. – Brass to Erasmus
Paston † 1538 and wife, made c.1575; chancel (25 in. figures,
partly palimpsest, English as well as foreign). – The only two
major monuments are by *Nicholas Stone*. He made the first of
alabaster in 1629 and received £340 for it, the second of stone
and black marble in 1632. The first is in the Jacobean tradition, the second so faultlessly classical that one would like to
assume consultation with Inigo Jones. The first is for Dame
Katherine Paston. She is represented in a semi-reclining
position. Double arch on two pink columns behind. Pediment
with two reclining allegorical figures. Two more on black
columns outside and behind the pink ones. The second is for
Sir Edmund Paston, † 1632. Completely plain urn on a bare
base in an aedicule of black Tuscan columns carrying an open
segmental pediment. Coved and coffered ceiling of the recess
thus formed. Above the inscription small open segmental
pediment ending at the top in volutes. – Contemporary railing
for both monuments together.
Of the mansion of the Pastons only the BARN is preserved. It is

---

* This monument may well be what is left of John Paston's, who died in
1466. His funeral involved 13 barrels of beer, 27 of ale, 15 gallons of wine,
1300 eggs, 20 gallons of milk, 8 gallons of cream, 41 pigs, 49 calves, etc.

of flint and in length – 163 ft – superior to any other in the
county.

PENSTHORPE

1¾ m. ESE of Fakenham

CHURCH. A cowhouse of the farm to the S of Pensthorpe Hall is
built into part of the walls of the former church.

PLUMSTEAD

ST MICHAEL. Chancel of c.1300 (the windows with the Geometrical tracery are Victorian). Late Dec W tower. Flushwork
panelling at the base and on the battlements. Perp S arcade,
blocked to the outside. Three bays, low octagonal piers, arches
with one chamfer and two hollow chamfers. Blocked also the
clerestory. Fragment of a small vaulted Easter Sepulchre. –
STAINED GLASS. Some C15 figures etc. in the E window, some
C16–17 glass in the S windows, including a big C16 angel. All
this glass came from Catton Hall, Norwich, in 1952. – PLATE.
Chalice inscribed 1567, but perhaps c.1680: Paten, unmarked.

POSTWICK

ALL SAINTS. Chancel of the late C13. The exterior over-
restored, but inside good Piscina with twin arch and stiff-leaf
capitals. Dec and Perp windows in the nave. The W tower Dec
with flushwork at the base of the buttresses and on the battlements. – FONT. Octagonal. Panelled stem, heads against the
underside, cusped panels against the bowl.

POTTER HEIGHAM

ST NICHOLAS. Round tower with an octagonal C14 top. Nave
and chancel thatched. The chancel is mostly Perp and distinguished by exceptionally tall three-light clerestory windows.
The aisle windows have the motif of an embattled horizontal
running above the three lights and separating them from the
panel tracery. On the S porch above the entrance in a niche a
rustic demi-figure. The chancel masonry is clearly earlier than
that of the nave, and there are indeed indications inside of the
existence of a Norman window with a deep splay, and a jamb
of a C13 window is exposed. Perp arcades of four bays with
octagonal piers and double-chamfered arches. Good nave roof
with wall-posts on stone brackets with demi-figures of angels.
Longitudinal arched braces. Hammerbeams with tracery.
No collar-beams. The ROOD BEAM is preserved. – FONT.

Octagonal, of brick – no wonder at Potter Heigham – and apparently with some panelling or tracery of moulded bricks. – PULLEY for the font cover. – SCREEN. One-light divisions. Arches originally with tracery in two tiers in depth, much damaged. Against the dado eight painted Saints. – BENCHES. A few ends with poppy-heads. – COMMUNION RAIL. C17. – 40a PAINTINGS. In the aisles; defaced. The Works of Mercy in the S aisle can at least partly be read. They seem to be late C14. – PLATE. Silver-gilt Chalice, Norwich, 1567–8; also from Norwich the Paten of 1638.

BRIDGE. A medieval bridge with an unmoulded (later) round arch flanked by two shorter triangular ones with chamfered ribs.

WINDMILL, 1 m. SW. Stump of a tower-mill.

2010   RACKHEATH

ALL SAINTS. All early C14. Unbuttressed W tower. Much Y-tracery, S clerestory with quatrefoil windows. Flushwork panelling along the clerestory is preserved only (or was commenced only) at the W and E ends. Arcade of three bays with octagonal piers and double-hollow-chamfered arches. The chancel arch and the capitals of the responds are of the same style. A tomb-recess in the chancel N wall also of c.1300. – FONT. Octagonal. Heavily profiled, with angel-heads and a coat of arms. – BANNER STAFF LOCKER. – PLATE. London-made Almsdish, 1621; Flagon, 1743; Cup, 1755. – MONU-MENTS. Tablets of the Pettus family, 1698, 1723, 1746 (the latter by *J. Chapling*).

RACKHEATH HALL, 1½ m. S. Large square mansion of 1850, yet not fully Victorian in character. Nine-bay front with one-bay projection. The ground floor with rather wild rustication – a post-Georgian sign. At the angles of the projection giant pilasters. Top balustrade. Porch and, round the corner, porte-cochère, both with Tuscan columns. Swell cast-iron GATES on the Wroxham Road. Made by *Barnard's* and shown at the 1851 exhibition.

3010   RANWORTH

ST HELEN. Tall W tower. Base frieze of chequer flushwork. Traceried sound-holes. Battlements with flushwork panelling. Very tall arch towards the nave. Embattled nave. Tall Perp windows. Shields on some buttresses. Two-storeyed N porch, one-storeyed S porch with a niche above the entrance. In the chancel the E window and the N windows are Dec, so are the S porch windows. The chancel S windows are Perp. But are they reliably renewed? Tall chancel arch. Chancel roof with arched braces. – PULPIT. With linenfold panels perhaps not *in situ*. The tester is C18. – SCREEN. The finest screen arrangement surviving in Norfolk. One-light divisions. Pretty cusping in two layers in depth. Ribbed and painted coving. Rood-loft preserved, though without its parapet. Against the dado twelve painted Saints. To the l. and r. side altars separated from the rood screen by partition walls again with painted panels. Detached from these to the W posts with holders for tapers. They are very prettily linked to the partition walls by flying buttresses. The reredoses of the two side altars again have painted figures. All this work is supposed to be connected with a will of 1419 leaving money for 'cancelli'. – CANTOR'S DESK. An improbable survival. Simple lectern used presumably on the rood loft. But painted on its back an eagle with the first words of the Gospel of St John, and on its front a versicle in plainsong. – STALLS. The return stalls have poppy-heads and simple MISERICORDS. Also CANDLE-HOLDERS on the stalls. – COMMUNION RAIL. C17. – DOORS to N and S traceried.* – PLATE. Chalice, Norwich, 1567; Paten, without marks. – MONUMENT. Thomas Holdiche † 1579. Small (nave, S wall). With fluted columns and a four-centred arch. By the same hand, it seems, as the Wodehouse Monument at Waxham.

OLD HALL. Two fragments of a C16 brick house perhaps of E shape. The porch now stands detached. Its upper window is still entirely Gothic and can hardly be later than *c*.1530. The round-headed doorway, however, with its pediment, looks Elizabethan, and the l. wing, with large mullioned and transomed windows and a stepped gable, could even be Jacobean. Not much is known of the house and its history.

REEDHAM

ST JOHN BAPTIST. Big Perp W tower. The lower parts of a rough, effective flint and stone chequer. Flushwork panelling at the base. Doorway with traceried spandrels, big W window, traceried sound-holes, three-light bell-openings. The rest of the church mostly of *c*.1300, see the windows, especially the E window with intersected tracery, and also the vestry E window.

---

* The church also possesses an ANTIPHONER bequeathed in 1478 and re-bought in 1912.

The vestry doorway has an ogee arch on head-stops, and this ought to be a little later; cf. the priest's doorway with its hood-mould on a head and a dragon, which takes us back again to c.1300, the most probable date also for the arcade between chancel and s chapel (two bays, octagonal pier, double-chamfered arches). There must have been a s aisle as well, but this was removed to widen the nave so that now chancel arch and chapel arch both open into the nave. Arch-braced roof in the chapel. The chapel received a third taller and narrower arch towards the nave (castellated abacus), probably at the time when the first of the MONUMENTS was installed. This is a tomb-chest with three shields in cusped lozenge fields. Recess with four-centred arch and decorated cresting. The date probably c.1500. – The neighbouring monument is to Henry Berney † 1584. This is a tomb-chest with Tuscan colonnettes. There is still a four-centred arch to the recess above, even if it is flanked by fluted Ionic columns. Under the arch in relief the kneeling family. The top is a coat of arms under an entirely Gothic ogee arch with a pointed quatrefoil in the spandrel. Is that survival or tentative revival? – Brass to Elizabeth Berney, late c15, the figure 2 ft 10 in. long (floor). – Against the e wall of the chapel a brass inscription to Alyce Yelverton † 1502, palimpsest of a brass inscription referring to Nicholas Lathe, a 'parchmyner', without a date of death. Lathe is called Senior, and this is the reason why the brass was rejected. Another was made and installed at St Simon and St Jude Norwich. The date of death is only two months earlier than that of Alyce Yelverton. So quick were the craftsmen in making use of waste material. – STAINED GLASS. In the s chapel e window large pieces, probably from the Netherlands, c16. – PLATE. Chalice, London, 1568–9, an exceptionally fine piece.

(REEDHAM HALL. Built c.1775–80. Dates on outbuildings 1779 and 1781. B. Cozens-Hardy)

WINDMILLS. There is a gay stump e of the Ferry, another stump 1¼ m. sw of the village, and a more complete tower-mill 1½ m. w of the village. Three more mills c.1¼ m. ne. But the best, one of the best in the county, is the BERNEY ARMS MILL, 3 m. ne of the church. This is in perfect order. It is over 70 ft high, i.e. the highest marsh mill in Norfolk or Suffolk. It was built in 1870.★

★ For further details see the Ministry of Works leaflet by Rex Wailes.

REEPHAM

In the churchyard of Reepham stood three churches touching each other, or almost touching each other, and two still stand. Of the third, HACKFORD CHURCH, ruined since 1543, there is only one wall left. This stands s of St Michael.

ST MICHAEL. St Michael, facing the Market Place with its tall tower, is the parish church of Whitwell, not of Reepham, a curious anomaly. It has a tall Perp w tower with a transomed w window, to N and s small pointed-quatrefoiled openings, and panelled battlements. The rest of the exterior is depressingly over-restored. The chancel is connected with Reepham parish church by the vestry and a stone staircase. Interior with deep w gallery. No aisles, but blank arcading framing the windows. Good Jacobean chancel roof. – PULPIT. Jacobean, with tester. – PLATE. Chalice, Norwich-made and inscribed 1681; Paten, London, 1692.

ST MARY. The parish church of Reepham, hidden by St Michael. s tower with bell-openings with Y-tracery. The fenestration otherwise appears Dec but is all too much restored to be trusted. Four-bay arcades. Octagonal piers, double-chamfered arches. The s arcade C13, the N arcade C14, but the E and W responds on the s side going with the N arcade. – FONT. Square, Norman, of Purbeck marble. Each side with four of the usual shallow blank arches. – BENCHES. A few, with poppy-heads and small animals on the arms. – SOUTH DOOR. C15? With much scrolly ironwork. – SCULPTURE. Head of a churchyard cross with the Virgin and St John squeezed under the arms of the cross. – STAINED GLASS. E and SE by *O'Connor*, † 1867 and 1871. – PLATE. Chalice and Paten-Cover, Norwich, 1567. – MONUMENT. Sir Roger de Kerdiston 41 † 1337, an important and beautiful monument. Recumbent effigy. He lies on big pebbles (cf. Ingham). The meaning of this is not certain. It may be self-mortification or may be an allegory. His attitude is singularly tense. The r. hand grips the sword on the l., the l. crosses over and touches the pebbles. Against the tomb-chest eight small figures of mourners or weepers. They must once have been of a delicate, lyrical character. Tall canopy. Two arches with a pendant between. The arches are cusped and subcusped. Ogee gable, the top part with a band of panelling behind, a remarkably early case of the use of this Perp motif. – Brass to Sir William de Kerdiston † 1391 and his wife. Good figures, 5 ft 2 in. long, under two concave-sided canopies.

The MARKET PLACE is pleasant to look at, especially the row of red brick houses along the N side. This starts with an excellent house of *c*.1700, DIAL HOUSE (or Brewery House), and continues with minor Georgian houses. Dial House is of seven bays and two storeys and has a broad porch with fluted Corinthian columns, a carved frieze, and a segmental pediment also with carving. Staircase with slim twisted balusters. On the S side the KING'S ARMS, and in the narrow street behind it a house with exposed timber-framing and overhang. (C17 staircase inside. MHLG)

HACKFORD HALL, 1½ m. WSW. Handsome Late Georgian house of yellow brick; five bays, two storeys. The centre a one-storeyed porch of coupled columns and angle pillars, the first and last windows on both floors tripartite.

OLD MONASTERY, ½ m. NE. Modest house of *c*.1700. Five bays, two storeys. Door with straight hood on big carved brackets.

REPPS

₄₀₁₀

ST PETER. Round Norman tower with a bell-stage added in the later C13. Four twin bell-openings, divided by round shafts. The arches pointed-trefoiled, and in the spandrels a pointed quatrefoil, a stepped Greek cross, etc. The bell-openings are connected by two bays of blind arcading, the tympana again decorated with quatrefoils of different shapes and a St Andrew's cross. Later flint and brick battlements. Unmoulded tower arch and blocked doorway (or just a long opening?) over. S porch of brick, probably early C17. Chancel of brick; C18. The chancel windows are a Victorian alteration. – FONT. Perp, octagonal, with simple decoration. – SCREEN. Not much of it is old. – PLATE. Chalice, Norwich, 1567–8; Paten Cover, without marks.

RIDLINGTON

₃₀₃₀

ST PETER. W tower Early Perp with traceried sound-holes. Big, transomed W window. On top instead of pinnacles the signs of the four Evangelists. Nave and chancel, the window tracery mostly intersected, but that may be due to restoration. The E wall brick. – FONT. C13, octagonal, of Purbeck marble, with two shallow pointed arches on each side. – PLATE. The Chalice, made in London in 1769, is a secular cup.

ROLLESBY

ST GEORGE. Round tower; otherwise mostly early C14, i.e. two
tall top-stages of the tower (cusped Y-tracery; battlements
with flushwork chequer), windows with cusped Y-tracery in
the aisles, delightful cusped and subcusped arch of the S doorway, S side of the clerestory with quatrefoil windows. Later the
N side of the clerestory, the chancel with its fine E wall enriched by pinnacles on the angle buttresses, and the N porch
with a four-centred arch and a niche over. The interior is
interesting. The N and S arcades of four bays have a circular W
pier with details more C13 than early C14 and then two octagonal piers. The arches have two hollow chamfers. More interesting still the unexplained cubicle in the SE corner with an
entry (with four-centred head) from the altar as well as the W.
It is only 4 ft 6 in. by 3 ft 6 in. and 6 ft 8 in. high, i.e. very
small for a vestry and not well guarded for a treasure-chamber.
– PLATE. Chalice, Norwich, 1567–8; Flagon, London, 1728. –
MONUMENTS. Rose Claxton † 1601. Of the monument only
the tomb-chest and the effigy, on her side propped up by her
elbow, are preserved. – Leonard Mapes † 1619. Alabaster, and
well done. Kneeling figures, also children behind the parents
and in the 'predella'. – Amphillis Ensor † 1830. Nice tablet
with urn, oil-lamps, and shells. – Thomas Baker † 1841 and
Mrs Cook † 1840, identical, with an urn on a concave-sided
pedestal.
(ROLLESBY HALL. Jacobean Hall with hall, panelling, and
screen. In the Parlour a fireplace dated 1620. White brick
wing added in 1824. Recently demolished.)

ROUGHTON

ST MARY. Not big, but with tall two-light clerestory windows.
Anglo-Saxon round tower with two circular double-splayed
windows, one to the S, the other to the N. The carstone below,
it will be noticed, is laid herringbone-wise, a technique which
for some time now has been regarded as Early Norman rather
than Late Saxon. Tall twin bell-openings. Triangular heads
instead of arches. The dividing pier is built up roughly of
drums of carstone. The tower arch is altered. But the curious
feature of a doorway above it, often to be met in Saxon towers,
is preserved. Saxon also the SW quoin of the nave. Dec chancel
with an E window with reticulated tracery, Dec N porch and
Dec E window of the S aisle. In fact the aisle arcades (octagonal

pier, double-chamfered arches) may also be Dec, although they are more likely to be of the late C14. The clerestory was built at the same time, see the pretty shafting inside, with fillets. Perp aisle windows, s porch, and probably the former N chapel or N vestry. The wall arches which survive may indicate that it was vaulted. – FONT. Octagonal, C14. Plain stem with eight attached shafts, two ogee arches against each side. – PLATE. Chalice, Norwich-made, 1567; Paten, unmarked.

4010   RUNHAM

ST PETER AND ST PAUL. N tower with flushwork panelling on the base, sound-holes with tracery including a wheel of mouchettes, and double-stepped battlements with pinnacles. Money to the building of the tower was left in 1501. The nave has early C14 windows. As for the chancel, the notable features are the shields and quatrefoils on the buttresses and a low-side window made by extending downwards one of the lights of the sw window and dividing it vertically. N porch with niche above the entrance. – BENCHES. Very little old work. – PLATE. Elizabethan Chalice.

WINDMILLS. There are to the s and SE of Runham along the river Bure five drainage mills, all brick tower-mills, with and without sails. From certain points the view is much like in Dutch C17 landscape paintings.

1040   RUNTON

HOLY TRINITY, West Runton. E.E. w tower, with a vault or projected vault inside, lancet windows, and bell-openings with Y-tracery on a circular shaft. Only the w window is Dec. Dec also the chancel, in spite of the two surprisingly big Perp s windows. The N aisle with Y-tracery in all windows may be a little earlier, though here too the w window is Dec. Four-bay arcades with octagonal piers and double-chamfered arches. Ungraceful Sedilia and Piscina. – FONT. Octagonal, with many small ogee-headed panels, perhaps Dec. – STAINED GLASS. A few early bits in a chancel s window. – PLATE. Parcel-gilt Paten of the later C15 or early C16 with the IHS of Christ; Chalice, 1633, London-made; Flagon, 1712.

PAVILION. By *W. F. Tuthill*, 1938, plus additions. In the late C17 style.

WINDMILL, East Runton.

ST BENET'S ABBEY *see* LUDHAM

SALHOUSE

ALL SAINTS. The N aisle arcade is the interesting part of the church. Of five bays, with octagonal piers and double-chamfered arches, as usual, but the capitals with bands of large, bossy foliage and one with separate heads instead. The dating is not easy. Cox and Cautley both plead for a Dec date. The bosses on which the arch-braced roof of the aisle rests must belong to the same style. Later than the aisle arcade anyway the W tower, which was begun with the intention of making it part of a roomier church. The tower is placed in front of the former W wall, whose thickness can still be seen to the W of the N arcade. The nave S wall was set far enough S, but the N arcade was never demolished to make way for a corresponding N extension. Even the tower itself was not completed; it now ends above the traceried sound-holes and has no bell-openings. The church thus remained most oddly lopsided. The windows are all renewed, but it looks as if the chancel had been of *c.*1300. – FONT. From Woodbastwick church. Octagonal, with panelled stem. – PULPIT. With Perp and Early Renaissance panels. – BENCHES. Some with poppy-heads. Also one minor STALL. – HOURGLASS STAND.

METHODIST CHURCH. 1775. Façade with arched doorway, two arched windows, and a pediment.

SALHOUSE HALL. Probably mostly of *c.*1860–70. Symmetrical, heavily castellated brick mansion with polygonal angle-shafts carrying heavy battlements too.

SALLE

ST PETER AND ST PAUL. Salle is not only an exceptionally complete Perp church, it is also historically exceptionally important in that it can be dated with fair accuracy. By the W doorway of the tower occur the arms of Henry V, which gives a date *c.*1405–20. In a S window existed glass with an inscription referring to Thomas Boleyn, who died in 1411. According to a will, the S transept existed in 1444. The N transept was the chapel of Thomas Rose, who died in 1441. A window in this transept had the date 1440. The church deserves in every respect to be examined closely. It stands all alone and is dominated by its tall W tower (126 ft high). Richly decorated battlements. Large sound-holes with complicated tracery. Four-light transomed window to the W. Doorway with a quatrefoil band up jambs and arch. Two angels in the spandrels. A frieze of shields above it and three niches around it. Looking at the church from the W one sees with the tower the two identical porches, both two-storeyed and both with flushwork battlements and turrets rising above the roof. In the front a niche between two single-light windows on the S, a three-light window on the N. The front of the N porch has moreover quatrefoils running up jambs and arch of the entrance, a big ogee gable, panelling to its l. and r., and niches in two tiers l. and r. In the entrance halls of both porches tierceron-vaults with bosses. The N porch has in addition a lierne-vaulted upper room again with bosses. In the E wall a piscina with shelf. The N and S aisles have tall three-light windows and again flushwork battlements. S and N transepts, the latter projecting two bays. The S transept has a four-light S window, the N transept an E window with stepped transoms in the tracery above the heads of the three lights. The S side of the S transept on heraldic evidence re-done in the late C15. In the chancel angels as supporters. Seven-light E window. Pretty N doorway with shields and fleurons up the jambs. Pretty little niche in the N transept with an inlay of darker stone.

Interior with six-bay arcades. The piers with four shafts and four hollows. Moulded four-centred arches. Clerestory. Very tall tower arch. Roof with short arched braces. Angels against the crossings of principals and purlins. Aisle roofs with a little tracery by the arched braces. Beautifully panelled low-pitched transept roofs. Chancel roof boarded, with bosses, those along the ridge with scenes of Annunciation, Nativity, Circumcision, three Magi, Entry into Jerusalem, Last Supper, Crucifixion, Resurrection, and Ascension. Beautiful caryatid figures on the brackets for the rood high up l. and r. of the chancel arch.

27a

FURNISHINGS. FONT. On two steps. The inscription records the donor.* The figures on the base have been chopped off. Against the bowl the Seven Sacraments and the Crucifixion. – FONT COVER. A very tall Perp canopy. Not completely preserved, but very impressive with the remaining fin-like radially-set members. The PULLEY on its big arm also survives and is connected with the BALCONY in the tower. All Perp wood-carving. – PULPIT. Perp, but back-panel, tester, and the three-decker arrangement Jacobean. – SCREENS. Tall rood screen with tall dado. The figures faded. – Parts of other screens variously re-used. – STALLS. Excellent, with outstandingly good minor carving. Poppy-heads, faces and monsters on the arm-rests. On the MISERICORDS flowers and faces,

* Who died in 1489.

also good flowers in the supporting l. and r. pieces. – BENCHES.
With poppy-heads. – DOORS. Original traceried doors W,N,S,
and in both doorways to the porch staircases. The W door alone
has a framing band of quatrefoils as well. – COMMUNION
RAIL. C17. With vertically symmetrical balusters. – STAINED
GLASS. In the S transept S window heads six original figures. –
In the E window also several figures. – The N transept glass by
Bryans, c.1895, good, sensitive, period-conscious work. –
PLATE. Later C15 or early C16 Paten, badly preserved. Mono-
gram of Christ in a circular depression. – Norwich-made
Chalice, 1567. – MONUMENTS. Many brasses. Civilian, c.1420
(S aisle), upper part only. – Geoffrey Boleyn † 1440 and wife
(2 ft 4 in.; nave). – Thomas Roose † 1441 and wife, standing
on a big bracket. The sons form part of the plate cut for him,
the daughters part of hers (18 in. figures; N transept) – John
Funteyn † 1453 and three wives. Only two wives remain.
Scrolls emanate from the mouths (length of the figures 17 in.;
N transept). – John Brigge † 1454, skeleton in shroud (26 in.).
– Tablets with urns in front of an obelisk: Mrs Evans † 1798
(by *Ivory* of Norwich), Mrs Hase † 1801.

SALLE PARK. Built in 1761. Brick house of seven bays and two See p. 392
and a half storeys. Three-bay pediment. Simple doorways. On
the entrance side charming low attachments.

(MANOR FARMHOUSE. Brick. With a C17 staircase. MHLG)

MOOR HALL, ¾ m. SW. The front probably late C17. Knapped
flint and red brick. Windows with wooden mullion and transom crosses. Steeply gabled dormers. Stepped end-gables. A
brick pilaster indicates a former decoration of the two-storeyed
porch. (A medieval stone window re-set. MHLG)

SALTHOUSE
0040

ST NICHOLAS. On an eminence broadside to the sea. Somewhat gaunt in its loneliness. The church has a short W
tower with Dec bell-openings. The rest is of the late C15
and completed in 1503. Long nave with closely set clerestory
windows. Extremely large E window of five lights with transom.
Aisle windows of two lights only but unusually long. All
windows much renewed. S doorway with shields and tracery in
the spandrels. Bare, impressive, tiled interior. Five-bay
arcades. The piers have four shafts and four hollows in the
diagonals. Shields at the apexes of the arches. Roof with
arched braces to the ridge. Wall-posts with circular shafts and
connected by longitudinal arched braces. Wall-plate with

shields and quatrefoils. The curious thing about the arrangement of the interior is that the chancel projects only by one
short bay so that the ritual chancel takes in some of the nave.
On the piers by the rood screen diagonally-set brackets. Seats
in the recesses of the aisle windows. The vestry to the N of the
chancel was in ruins in the C18 but restored in 1929. – FONT.
Four lions against the stem, the signs of the four Evangelists
and the Instruments of the Passion against the bowl. –
SCREEN. The dado only remains. Painted on it sixteen Saints.
The date of the screen is 1513. – STALLS. Partly in order,
partly with bits of old woodwork. – ALTAR. N aisle. Also old
woodwork used. – PLATE. Parcel-gilt Chalice, Norwich, 1567;
Paten, Norwich, 1567. – BRASS. Chalice Brass to Robert
Fevyr † 1519, on the floor, E of the screen.

In the NW corner of the churchyard ruin of a CHAPEL. (It
had a Piscina and an altar.)

SALTHOUSE HALL, W of the church. Two storeys, red brick,
c.1700–10; see the rhythm of normal and very narrow
windows.

Salthouse was a port in the Middle Ages. The Salthouse Mayne
Channel was made useless by the C17 reclaiming of the
fens.

BARROWS. On the Heath in this parish and the parishes of
Kelling and Cley are at least ten barrows of various periods of
the Bronze Age, including a fine disc. A number of the smaller
mounds belong to the Late Bronze Age.

0030   SAXLINGHAM
                         Near Holt

ST MARGARET. Mostly Perp. Much restored in 1896. Plain W
tower. Nave and chancel under one lead roof. No aisles. –
CHANDELIER. Of brass, believed to be C18. – PLATE. Chalice
of 1567 made in Norwich, and Paten probably belonging to it.
– MONUMENT. Lady Heydon † 1593. No more is preserved
than the kneeling alabaster figure. In addition, perhaps belonging to it, an open book of alabaster with 'I am sure that my
redeemer liveth', etc. – i.e. the pre-Authorized text.

HEYDON HALL, E of the church. A total ruin. Recognizable still
the N front with one three-light straight-headed C15 window
and the adjoining porch with its entrance arch and the inner
doorway, also pre-Reformation. The house was quadrangular,
and fragments of walls survive plentifully.

SAXTHORPE

ST ANDREW. Unbuttressed W tower, Dec chancel windows. Perp the other windows, the S aisle W window particularly pretty. Perp also, it seems, the arcades of four bays with their tall octagonal piers and double-chamfered arches. – FONT. The stem panelled. – FONT COVER. Small, Jacobean, with some decoration, a charming if modest piece. – SCREEN. Not big. One-light divisions, panel tracery above. On the dado eight panels with painted brocade. – BENCHES. One with openwork tracery patterns in the back. One end with a recessed panel containing a lamb. A few others with other motifs or just with poppy-heads. – COMMUNION RAIL. Late C17 and very unusual. Balls like cannon-balls on the posts. The top rail curves down between the posts. Flat, cut-out balusters. – SOUTH DOOR. With an iron plate for the ring and on this a small and dainty band of trefoils. – STAINED GLASS. In a N aisle window some quite good, if naive glass of c.1888. – PLATE. London-made Chalice, 1812.

SCO RUSTON

ST MICHAEL. What remains of the W tower is a cliff. Nave and chancel in one, with bellcote probably of 1860. – BENCHES. Two complete benches with robustly traceried backs and poppy-heads. Also ends re-used for the reader's desk. – SOUTH DOOR. With the very unusual motif of an inscription carved in to commemorate the donor and his wife. – PLATE. Paten, 1710; Chalice, London, 1803.

SCOTTOW

ALL SAINTS. Slender W tower, base frieze of flushwork panelling. Perp W window. Perp S porch, two-storeyed. The ground floor vaulted with simple diagonal and ridge-ribs. Green man boss. Flushwork parapet. Aisles Perp, chancel Dec with flowing tracery. Five-light E window. Even the Piscina has mildly flowing tracery (mouchettes). Of the arcades the N side is Dec, the S side Perp. The latter is one bay shorter, because the S porch takes the place of the first bay. Six bays on the N, quatrefoil piers with fillets and deep hollows in the diagonals. Moulded arches. S arcade, octagonal piers with castellated abaci and double-hollow-chamfered arches. Arch-braced roof, high collar-beams. A similar roof in the N aisle. Across the nave still the ROOD BEAM, a rare survival. It is on arched

braces and marks the ritual division of chancel from nave. –
FONT. Of the octagonal Purbeck type of the C13, but probably
a copy. – FONT COVER. C18. A baluster and four dolphins, a
curious conceit. – ORGAN CASE. Covered with any number of
C16 and C17 pieces of ornamental woodwork, English and
foreign. – LECTERN. Probably also made up. C17 parts; not
English. – BOX PEWS. – PAINTING. St Christopher, nave N
wall, the upper half lost. – PLATE. Chalice and Paten, Norwich,
1567. – MONUMENTS. (Chalice Brass to Nicholas Wethyrley,
c.1520.) – Davy Durrant † 1757, by *George Storey*. Big, rather
clumsy standing monument. Base with extremely bulging
balusters. Big obelisk with three cherubs' heads and arms.
Back wall with wide open scrolly pediment.

SCOTTOW HALL. Irregular, long front, the l. part gothicized.
Stables with wooden lantern. In the garden a big piece of ornamental stone carving probably from a pediment of the late C17
(cf. Hoveton House).

4020

SEA PALLING

ST MARGARET. Not large. Unbuttressed w tower, nave and
chancel. The nave windows are Perp, but not original. But the
wide present nave is no doubt Perp indeed; for it is the
successor of a Dec nave-and-aisles arrangement of the same
total width of which evidence is the two w windows and the
two doorways. The chancel Piscina proves a Dec chancel too. –
FONT. Octagonal, C14, with flatly modelled tracery patterns.
Those on the bowl are like a pattern-book, including pure Dec
(reticulation) as well as pure Perp. – SCREEN. The dado partly
original. – BENCHES. Ends with poppy-heads. – SOUTH DOOR.
With tracery. – BANNER STAFF LOCKER, NW, a feature more
customary in Suffolk than in Norfolk. – PLATE. Chalice and
Paten, Norwich, 1567–8.

WINDMILLS. One derelict tower-mill, tall, 1 m. w, another,
only a stump, with a conical roof, yet a little further w.

0030

SHARRINGTON

ALL SAINTS. Former aisles of three bays, now blocked up, with
circular capitals and abaci. Double-chamfered arches. All this
indicates a C13 date. About 1300 the chancel, see the windows,
including the E window of four lights with its intersecting
tracery and the pretty section of the mullions. See also the
angle Piscina and the priest's doorway. Dec w tower. Low
triple-chamfered arch. Perp N and S nave windows. –

BENCHES. Some ends with poppy-heads. – PLATE. Chalice, Norwich, 1567; Paten, Norwich, c.1695. – BRASSES (chancel, s wall) to a Knight probably of the Daubeny family, c.1440, a 3 ft figure; to John Botolff † 1486, priest, an 11½ in. figure; to a Lady of c.1520 (12 in.); and to Christopher Daubeny † 1587 (12 in.).

SHARRINGTON HALL. Flint and red-brick dressings. Elizabethan or Jacobean. Gabled porch with four-centred doorhead. Gabled l. wing with blocked mullioned and transomed windows. Polygonal staircase projection to the r. (Panelled rooms inside. MHLG)

CROSS. SE of the church. Base and part of the shaft.

SHERINGHAM

Sheringham consists of Upper Sheringham, the village on the hill, and Lower Sheringham, the seaside resort.[1040]

UPPER SHERINGHAM

ALL SAINTS, Upper Sheringham. W tower of c.1300, see the arch towards the nave (double-chamfers dying into the imposts), the cusped lancet windows, and the cusped Y-tracery of the bell-openings. Flushwork panelling on the buttresses. Early C14 arcades. Octagonal piers, double-chamfered arches. Chancel arch of the same kind. Contemporary probably also the fine clerestory, a minor relative of Cley. Alternating circular quatrefoiled windows and normal two-light windows. The clerestory has an E window above the low chancel. Aisle windows Perp. The S porch with its façade of regularly knapped square flints and the pedimental gable looks c.1800. – Upcher Mausoleum, N of the chancel, early C19. – FONT. Octagonal, Dec. Bowl with divers tracery patterns. – The support for the former font cover is a BEAM on arched braces across the nave. Traceried spandrels. – SCREEN. Of two-light divisions with ogee arches and panel tracery. A separate beam on arched braces (with dragons in the spandrels) carries the rood-loft, whose traceried parapet is preserved. – BENCHES. With poppy-heads and some animals (e.g. a cat) on the arms, also a baby in swaddling clothes. – COMMUNION RAIL. C18. – PLATE. Chalice and Paten-Cover, Norwich-made, 1567. – MONUMENTS. Brass to John Hook † 1513 and wife (19½ in. figures; s aisle). – Abbot Upcher † 1819. By *Bacon Jun.* and *Samuel Manning.* Hanging monument of considerable size. White marble. A disconsolate woman lies over a broken column and a dead branch. Behind and above obelisk with a coronet.

In front of the church RESERVOIR, given by Abbot Upcher 'anno pacis', i.e. in 1814. Walled-in basin with access under a broken pediment. Pebble and yellow brick. To the W the former WORKHOUSE, built in 1805.

SHERINGHAM HALL. Built in 1812–17 to the design of *Humphry Repton* and his son *John Adey Repton*. The uncommonly well preserved grounds are the father's, the architecture of the house probably more the son's. Repton's 'Red Book', specifying the alterations and buildings he proposed, is kept at the house. He later called Sheringham his favourite work. It was built for Abbot Upcher and has remained in the Upcher family. The house is quite simple and not large. It has two storeys and a roof of low pitch. Undecorated windows. Porch with two pairs of Tuscan columns to the W, veranda of four pairs of the same columns to the S. Inside, three rooms to the S front, with a large library on the r. taking up the whole E front of the house, the smaller breakfast room, the entrance hall, and the study or Justice Room behind it on the l., and a corridor and the staircase behind the music room in the centre. The staircase projects to the N, and has an apsed N end with niches for statuary in the corners. The corridor is tripartite and repeats on the upper floor, where it has two circular skylights. Most of the furnishing was done in the Early Victorian years, after the house had stood empty for over twenty years. The bookcases in the library are specially characteristic of the rather heavy Latest Classical of *c.*1840. Much of Regency and Early Victorian furnishing has been added recently and with great discrimination. Beautiful grounds with splendid rhododendrons and judicious screening against the N winds from the sea.

LOWER SHERINGHAM

The place was chiefly developed in the 1890s and the early C20, i.e. it looks very much more cheerful and civilized than, say, Hunstanton, which was built in the 60s and 70s.

ST PETER. 1895–7 by *St Aubyn & Wadling*. Flint and red brick, with shingled bell-turret. E.E. in style. Octagonal brick piers, also brick arches. Open timber roof.

ST JOSEPH (R.C.), Cromer Road. 1910–36 by *Sir Giles Gilbert Scott*, an early and a very remarkable work of his. Tall red-brick building with low aisles and without a tower. The windows high up and with fancy flowing tracery. The (ritual) E window, a rose, yet higher up, faces the street. Only the (ritual) w window is normal. Inside very tall, narrow proportions and an odd rhythm of the arcades. Low, oblong, rounded piers. After two bays a much smaller and lower arch, then three more of the former bays. – STAINED GLASS. w window by *Hardman*, after 1936 (designed by *Dunstan Powell*).

Of buildings connected with the Sheringham holiday season only a few need be mentioned: the GRAND HOTEL (Grand Court), 1898 by *H. J. Green*, with two domes at the corners, the Sheringham Hotel (now SHERINGHAM COURT) of 1890–1 (by *Skipper?*), and a streamlined terrace in white and green on top of the cliff (1936 by *R. L. Martindale*).

SIDESTRAND

ST MICHAEL. Moved inland from its site in 1880. The old site would by now have been ruined by the advancing sea. Round tower of 1881, the upper part octagonal as it had been before it collapsed in 1840. The E window of 1881. The other windows partly Dec, partly Perp. – PULPIT and SCREEN. With the use of Jacobean panels. – SANCTUARY PANELLING. Jacobean, but bought in. – ORGAN CASE. The part facing w is a charming piece of mixed Georgian and Gothic of *c.*1800. – STAINED GLASS. E window designed by *Holiday* and made by *Powell's*. – SCULPTURE. The statuette of a Saint with a chalice, now above the s doorway, comes from the gable of the E wall. – CROSS. A strange cross in the nave E wall, its stepped ends looking oddly Anglo-Saxon, in spite of an inscription referring to a man of the C15. It is not known what the meaning of the cross was. – PLATE. Chalice, Norwich, 1567*; Wafer Box, undated, Dutch. – WAR MEMORIAL. By *Seely & Paget*; with the use of a niche which was bought in an antique shop.

SKEYTON

ALL SAINTS. A C13 church. Unbuttressed w tower with much carstone in the walling. Nave fenestration Perp, but N doorway of *c.*1300. In the s wall a blocked lancet. The church probably had a N aisle, for which the C13 N wall was demolished. Hence the asymmetrical position of the tower. – SOUTH DOOR. With a good iron knocker. – PLATE. Norwich-made Chalice of 1567 and Paten of 1638.

THE LODGE. Shaped gables, but an early C19 façade of three wide bays with a broad porch on Tuscan columns.

* Inscribed 1593.

SLOLEY

ST BARTHOLOMEW. Exterior over-restored. NW tower with
Dec window and Perp bell-openings. The chancel is of *c.*1300,
see one N window and the Piscina. Perp arcades of four (N) and
three (S) bays. Octagonal piers, double-hollow-chamfered,
four-centred arches. The N arcade could contain re-used C14
material. Arch-braced roof. – FONT. Four small lions on the
corners of the foot. Four statuettes against the stem. Well-
29   preserved representation of the Seven Sacraments and the
Baptism of Christ against the bowl. – PLATE. Chalice of 1567,
made in Norwich. – MONUMENTS. Gothic tablets by *Burgess*
of Yarmouth (1826) and *J. Stanley* of Norwich (1845, 1852).
(SLOLEY HALL. White brick; *c.*1810. B. Cozens-Hardy)

SMALLBURGH

ST PETER. The tower fell in 1677. The chancel has now only a
bellcote put up on a broad buttress in 1902. The nave is of the
most usual Perp Norfolk type. The chancel is Perp too, the
Dec E window being Victorian. Prettily traceried Piscina inside. – SCREEN. Eight painted Saints against the dado of the
former rood screen. Also three detached panels of diminishing
size. – SOUTH DOOR. With remains of tracery. – PLATE.
Norwich-made Chalice of 1567 and Paten of *c.*1590.
HOLLY HOUSE, opposite the church. Fine grey-brick house of
the early C19. Three bays, the ground-floor windows set in
blank arches. Greek Doric porch.

SOUTH BURLINGHAM *see* BURLINGHAM
ST EDMUND

SOUTHREPPS

ST JAMES. A big church, originally with N as well as S aisle, and
with a W tower 114 ft high. The tower is lavishly decorated.
Flushwork base frieze, flushwork panelling of the buttresses.
Above the base frieze another of carved shields alternating
with the shells of St James. Big W doorway. Traceried spandrels with shields. Niches l. and r. A frieze also below the six-
light W window. Sound-holes with a grid of panel-units.
Three-light bell-openings. Dec chancel, and Dec the aisles
(pulled down in 1791), as the arcades show inside (octagonal
piers, arches with one chamfer and one hollow chamfer). The
chancel has large windows with intersected tracery, shafted
inside and with hood-moulds on head-stops. Sedilia with ogee

arches. Charming figures l. and r. of the inner hood-mould of
the priest's doorway and equally charming figures in the place
where the sill frieze of the chancel climbs up to avoid the
priest's doorway. – FONT. Simple, Perp, with quatrefoils. –
SCREEN. Ornamental painting on the dado. – STAINED GLASS.
One original fragment in the chancel, s side. Chancel N by
Mayer & Co., c.1900. – PLATE. Parcel-gilt Chalice and Paten
Cover, Norwich, 1567.

s of the church BUCKLANDS FARM of 1744. Five bays and two
storeys with brick quoins and brick rustication round the
upper middle window. Later doorway. (Original staircase.)

The same motifs are employed on the larger SOUTHREPPS
HALL, 1 m. WNW. This is of seven bays and has a contemporary doorway with rusticated pilasters and a pediment.

SOUTHTOWN *see* GORLESTON

SOUTH WALSHAM   3010

Two churches lie in adjoining churchyards, St Lawrence partly
in ruins, St Mary as the present parish church.

ST MARY. A good deal of the church is Dec, the w tower (with
traceried sound-holes and flushwork-panelled battlements),
both arcades (five bays, octagonal piers, double-chamfered
arches), the w and E windows of the s aisle, and the chancel
arch and chancel s windows. Perp N aisle windows, and Perp
s porch. Two storeys, flushwork panelling. Entrance with the
Annunciation in the spandrels. Niche above, between the
windows. In the niche group of the Coronation of the Virgin.
The niche is vaulted and much crocketed. – FONT. Bowl with
tracery and a top band of quatrefoils. – SCREEN. Of two-light
divisions. Ogee arches and above them panel tracery. Dado
with ornamental painting and an inscription commemorating
the donor, John Galt, who had been a serf and was set free in
1437. – BENCHES. Many ends with poppy-heads. – BANNER
STAFF LOCKER. Chancel N wall. – STAINED GLASS. One
window in the s aisle represents Astronomy. It is by *R. O.
Pearson*, of 1907, a talented piece of work. The lettering may
incorporate old pieces. – PLATE. Elizabethan Chalice and
Cover. – MONUMENTS. Incised slab to Richard de South
Walsham † 1439, Abbot of St Benet's Abbey. The upper half
lost. The slab went to be a doorstep in the Duke of Norfolk's
house in St Andrew Street at Norwich. When this was
demolished, it found its way into a sham ruin in Bracondale

Wood and was obtained for South Walsham church in the
1940s (s of the altar). – William Jary † 1810. By *J. Watson* of
Norwich. Black and white tablet with an inscription scroll
hanging down.

St Lawrence. Burnt out in 1827. The chancel re-opened in
1832. The large Perp windows must be either original and renewed or Victorian. The w half of the tower stands up to the
very battlements with their flushwork panelling. – PLATE.
Chalice and Cover, Norwich-made, 1567; Almsdish, London-
made, and surgeon's Cupping Dish, both 1679.

3000
SOUTHWOOD

St Edmund. In ruins. Unbuttressed w tower repaired in brick.
Nave quite overgrown, chancel mostly collapsed.

Southwood Hall. On the wall a very attractive SUMMER
HOUSE, late C17, square, with pyramid roof, red brick with
rusticated brick quoins. The windows have wooden crosses.

0010
SPARHAM

St Mary. Much of the church is early C14. The chancel side
windows and the priest's doorway demonstrate that date, even
if the e window (with stepped embattled transoms above the
lights in the tracery) is Perp. The arcades inside also seem to
be early C14. They are of four bays with octagonal piers and
double-chamfered arches. The widths of the arches vary
curiously, and as one of the piers on either side is a considerably
elongated octagon, the fact is probably that building started
from the e, that the elongation indicates the w wall of a preceding church, that calculations as to the spacing of the arches
went wrong, and that finally the present w bay was an extension
beyond the previous building. The early C14 building also had
a clerestory. This was of quatrefoils in circles, as can still be
seen from the aisles. It was well below the present Perp
clerestory with its quick rhythms of windows. There is an e
window as well. The n doorway and n aisle w window are also
early C14. Perp notably the w tower. This has below the w
window a pretty niche with a little vault, and against the top
battlements flushwork panelling. Perp aisle windows.* Perp s
porch. Good Perp roof with arched braces up to a high collar.
Angels against the collars. – PULPIT. Perp; much restored. –

* The s aisle was given by Joanna Butte in 1481.

SCREEN. On the dado, apart from the Saints, scenes from the Dance of Death, rare and interesting. One panel contains two skeletons in fashionable costume, a man and a woman. One scroll reads 'Sic Transit gloria mundi', the other has a passage from Job. On the panel a skeleton clothed in a shroud and standing in a church with a font on the l. Above the font on a scroll: 'De utere'. On the other scrolls again passages from Job. – BENCHES. Many ends with poppy-heads; also two traceried fronts. – Two lengths of dainty carving, quatrefoils etc., in the N aisle E window. They may come from the benches and the wall-plate of the roof. – ORGAN CASE. Gothick, probably of c.1800. – PLATE. Chalice, Norwich, 1567. – BRASS to William Mustarder, rector, c.1490.

SPIXWORTH 2010

ST PETER. A very odd sight. Nave and chancel of a piece, Dec, with reticulated, flowing, and other tracery and, incidentally, depressed window heads. But the nave front is only the l. half of a composition continued by the S aisle front with only a very small, not centrally placed, doorway and then a spindly unbuttressed W tower. It looks as if this might be the remaining part of a smaller, older church. Its upper part is later (brick). The S arcade is Perp (three bays, thin octagonal piers, double-hollow-chamfered arches). – FONT. Norman, of cauldron-shape, on five supports. – PLATE. London-made Chalice of 1567, Paten inscribed 1721, and Flagon of 1730. – MONUMENT. William Peck † 1635 and wife. By *Edward*[43a] *Marshall*. Large alabaster monument. The effigies recumbent, in their shrouds, and represented naturalistically as dead. He lies behind and a little above her. Two black columns, a coffered arch with an inscription plate against the back wall. This has garlands, as has the top of the monument, a wide open curly pediment and a shield between. On the pediment reclining putti.

SPROWSTON *see* p. 290

STAININGHALL 2010
½ m. SE of Frettenham

CHURCH. In ruins already in 1600. Only the W wall of the tower and part of the S and N walls.

STAININGHALL FARM. The farm has an astonishingly monumental C18 BARN, with blank arcading and the entrance flanked by giant pilasters.

STALHAM

ST MARY. Very big, but squat, unfinished w tower. Dec nave,
i.e. its arcades with octagonal piers and double-chamfered
arches, and its clerestory with quatrefoil openings alternating
with two-light blind flushwork windows. Dec also the s aisle
E window and the chancel (reticulated tracery; rebuilt 1886).
The N aisle windows (if old) are entirely Dec. Perp s porch
with flushwork panelling on the front. – FONT. An excellent
piece. On three steps, two of them finely traceried. On one a
repeating motif of catherine wheels. Foliage trail on the foot.
Statuettes on the stem. Ribbing on the underside of the bowl.
On the bowl itself Trinity, Baptism of Christ, and six pairs of
Apostles. – SCREEN. (Five original panels, under repair at
the time of writing.) – PLATE. Paten, 1716; Chalice and Paten,
1718. – MONUMENTS. (Brass to a Civilian and wife, c.1460.)
– Tomb-chest with black lid. Against the front bulgy balusters
and two panels with cherubs. Probably of c.1700.
The church faces with its s side the main street of the little town,
a street with a number of nice, modest Georgian brick houses.
STALHAM HALL, at the E end of the street. A remarkable house
of c.1670, not yet affected by the classical style of Wren and
his contemporaries. Five wide bays, two storeys. Ends still
with stepped gables. Central porch with steep gable. The
façade is entirely divided by two orders of paired brick
pilasters, the upper standing on flat bulgy bases, reminiscent
of Dietterlin rather than 1670. But decidedly of c.1670 are the
casements of the windows, of the so-called Ipswich type
(named after Sparrow's House at Ipswich), tripartite with the
centre arched, the sides transomed. Staircase through to the
attic, with dumb-bell balusters.
WINDMILL. No more than a stump. $\frac{3}{8}$ m. s.

STIBBARD

ALL SAINTS. Short w tower. Chancel of c.1300. The E window
is interesting. It is of five lights with intersected tracery; but
this regular pattern is interrupted to insert a quatrefoiled
circle. Windows otherwise also of c.1300, of c.1350, and Perp.
Arcade of four bays with octagonal piers and double-chamfered
arches. The clerestory windows now give on to the N aisle roof.
– SCREEN. The dado remains, and some fragments used in the
pulpit. – BENCHES. With poppy-heads, a few also with animals

on the arms and one with a little figure. Two backs with pierced tracery. – STAINED GLASS. Many original fragments in the chancel N window. – PLATE. Paten, 1824.

STIFFKEY

9040

ST JOHN BAPTIST. W tower, nave and chancel. Perp, except for the chancel windows, which seem of the late C13 and early C14; but the chancel was drastically restored in 1848. Tall nave windows. Parapet with chequer flushwork panelling, two shields in octofoils, and brick and flint chequerwork in the gable. Rood turret with spire on the S side at the E end of the nave. – STALLS. Simple, only three, with two simple MISERICORDS. – STAINED GLASS. Mixed original bits in a S window. – PLATE. Chalice of 1567; Paten given in 1762; Flagon made in London in 1772. – MONUMENT. Nathaniel Bacon. A black marble cloth hangs over the sarcophagus. Simple back-wall decoration with a single needle obelisk. No effigy. The monument was placed before Nathaniel died in 1615. It could well be by *Maximilian Colt*.

STIFFKEY HALL. Built by Nathaniel Bacon, son of Sir Nicholas, Keeper of the Great Seal and husband of a natural daughter of Sir Thomas Gresham.* The estate had been bought by Sir Nicholas in 1571, and in 1578 Nathaniel was busy building. The house was originally U-shaped with long projecting wings, four circular corner towers, and in addition two circular towers in the re-entrant angles. That is a type rather of *c.*1550 than of *c.*1575, the type of Long Melford, Kentwell, and Rushbrooke, all in Suffolk. The four angle towers, though square and not oblong, had however also been part of the pattern of Gresham's Osterley Park, a house he had bought in 1562. Of the building of Stiffkey Hall only the W range and half the N or hall range are intact. The other half, containing the hall, is gutted, and of the E range only traces survive. There is in addition to the S, i.e. the river, an oblong gatehouse, dated 1604. The gardens, with a walled terrace and again circular towers at the E corners, lay to the E of the house.

Stiffkey Hall is of flint with brick dressings. The original windows have mullions and transoms. The lights are no longer arched. The entrance and exit doorways of the hall are small, with four-centred heads and without porches. There is a newel staircase in the remaining inner tower and in addition a longer square staircase projecting on the W side close to the SW

* His mother moreover was a sister-in-law of Gresham.

tower. The two-light windows in both towers are set so as to express the rise of the stairs.

The gatehouse is flat, with a narrow pedimented doorway from the s. The polygonal buttresses to its l. and r. look a little suspicious. To the N the side bays have entrances too.

WARBOROUGH HILL is an Iron Age barrow, now much destroyed, with early primary cremation and later pottery.

0030

STODY

St MARY. Round tower with Dec bell-openings and flushwork panels in the battlements. Nave and chancel long and low, under one lead roof. Dec chancel, see the windows, that on the E of four lights with intersected tracery, those on N and s still with Late Geometrical tracery but ogee arches. Perp nave and transept windows. Only the doorways are – as so often – earlier. Fine arch-braced roofs in nave, chancel, and transepts. The meeting of the four results in a timber rib-vault with diagonal and ridge-ribs. – FONT. C13, octagonal, of Purbeck marble, with the usual two shallow arches on each side. – BENCH ENDS. With poppy-heads, not well preserved. – STAINED GLASS. In the nave N windows and the s transept E window small figures in the tracery heads. – PLATE. Parcel-gilt Chalice, Norwich, 1567; Paten, Norwich, 1567.

VALE HOUSE, midway between Stody and Hunworth churches. Flint and red brick. Asymmetrically placed gabled porch. Brick doorway with low segmental arch.

CASTLE. On Hunworth Castle Hill. Remains of a medieval earthwork.

4010

STOKESBY

St ANDREW. Unbuttressed W tower. Bell-openings with Y-tracery. Triple-stepped brick battlements of the C16. The nave windows are all Dec, except for one large Perp window inserted no doubt to provide better light for the pulpit. Brick s porch, probably C18. The nave roof probably of the same date as the nave windows. Single-framed, with scissor-braces. – BENCHES. Backs with openwork tracery. Ends with poppy-heads, and on the arm-rests animals; also a kneeling woman. – SOUTH DOOR. With a cross-shaped surround for the knocker; C14. – PLATE. Chalice, made at Norwich, inscribed 1678; Paten, 1689, originally probably Elizabethan. – BRASSES (all chancel floor). Edmund Clere † 1488 and wife, 25½ in. figures. – (Thomas Gerard † 1506.) – Anne Clere † 1570 with an

inscription in Latin distichs (e.g. 'Inter Parrhasidas lustrent
sua nomina luces/Dum trahit elapsum coerula biga diem.')
24½ in. figure. On the back a Flemish inscription. – Fragment
of brass to a Lady in Elizabethan dress, also palimpsest, also
with a Flemish inscription.

Opposite the church to the s GLEBE FARMHOUSE, with a
medieval stone doorway with a four-centred head.

WINDMILLS. In the village itself one without caps and sail.
Several drainage mills near by, one with sails 1 m. SE, another
without 1 m. W, a third 1½ m. NW.

STRATTON STRAWLESS

2020

ST MARGARET. Very broad w tower with mighty diagonal
buttresses, obviously intended to be higher. Money was left to
the building of the tower in 1422. Figures instead of pinnacles.
s aisle brick, rebuilt in the C17 for the Marsham monument.
Is the arcade of three bays also of that date? (octagonal
piers, double-chamfered arches). The E window is of 1883. –
FONT. Octagonal, with quatrefoils. – STAINED GLASS.
Figures and canopies in two N windows. Bits in a s window. –
PLATE. Chalice, probably Norwich, inscribed 1619; Paten,
probably belonging to the Chalice. – MONUMENTS. Effigy of
a Lady, wearing a wimple, c.1300. – Thomas Marsham † 1638.
Standing monument. Effigy comfortably semi-reclining,
though in his shroud – an early case of this attitude in England.
At the foot a glimpse through a grate into the charnel-house;
l. and r. the grave-digger's tools. Black columns l. and r. above
and two reclining figures at the top. – Henry Marsham † 1692
with wife and son († 1678). All three kneel frontally, with not
enough space to kneel in. A standing-up babe on the r.
Columns l. and r. and an open scrolly pediment. Plaques with
rhymed inscription below.

STRATTON STRAWLESS HALL. Built c.1800. Very plain six-
bay front with two-bay pediment. The façade was lowered
recently. The most remarkable feature is an arched three-bay
loggia, i.e. recessed entrance with Tuscan columns, a French
rather than an English motif. Inside two rooms, apsed at both
ends, one of them being the staircase.

STRUMPSHAW

3000

ST PETER. Long thin w tower and long low nave and chancel
under one roof, a curiously rigid appearance, made more so
by the arrangement of the churchyard. Chancel of c.1300.

Windows cusped lancets or with Y-tracery. Also a good
double Piscina. This has stiff-leaf stops, one with a tiny dragon.
N doorway also of c.1300, but the nave windows Perp. Plain
tomb-recess in the nave wall. – FONT. Octagonal. Four lions
against the stem, four flowers and four shields against the
bowl. – SCREEN. With one-light divisions. Concave-sided
crocketed gables. Panel tracery above. Dado with ornamental
patterns. Much of the colour is preserved. Cautley has pointed
out indications that originally side altars were placed against
the screen, as at Ranworth, and that detached buttress posts or
partition walls stood between them and the entrance, also as at
Ranworth. – BANNER STAFF LOCKER. E of the N doorway. At
its foot a re-used piece of a C13 FONT of Purbeck marble. –
PLATE. Elizabethan Chalice; London-made Paten, 1733.

2030   SUFFIELD

ST MARGARET. Late C13 chancel with a handsome double
Piscina (trefoil in the spandrel) and a low-side lancet. Dec the
E bay of the N aisle (N window segment-headed, E window with
reticulated tracery). Perp first of all the tall W tower, lacking a
parapet. Flushwork chequer pattern on the base. Traceried
sound-holes. Tower arch tall and with a rere-arch (strengthening arch?) set oddly far back. Perp N aisle with arcade (octagonal piers, double-chamfered arches) and N windows. The
S aisle arcade and windows look what the antiquaries used to
call 'debased', i.e. as if they might be late C16 or C17 work.
Aisle roofs with arched braces. – FONT. Octagonal. Demi-
figures of angels against the underside holding shields with the
Instruments of the Passion. – SCREEN. Eight panels painted
with Saints are preserved. Nice carving of figures and foliage
in the spandrels. – STALLS. Some with poppy-heads. – SOUTH
DOOR. Traceried arch with a band of cusped circles. –
STAINED GLASS. Bits in a N window. – PLATE. Paten of
c.1480 with a sexfoiled depression holding the face of Christ
in a circle. – Chalice, inscribed 1567. – MONUMENT. John
Symonds † 1584. Tomb-chest with fluted columns (mostly destroyed). Some modest strapwork in the frieze. No effigies.

1030   SUSTEAD

ST PETER AND ST PAUL. Slim round tower with brick battlements. SW quoin of the nave of big carstone blocks, Norman
or pre-Norman. Dec S aisle, see the one window, nicely shafted

inside. Dec s porch with a curious flourish at the top, consisting of two blown-up mouchettes. Windows with Y-tracery.
Dec also the chancel. The s windows here are quite exceptionally pretty, with shafts and tiny foliage capitals. Tiny foliage
also outside. Double Piscina with much shafting and ogee
arches. The chancel roof with pleasant recent painted decoration on the rafters. Dec N transept, demolished. The arch
however remains, with typically Dec responds. Dec s and N
doorways, the latter with an ogee gable with finial inside.
Later only some windows and the brick rood-stair turret
(with a flint diaper). – FONT. Octagonal. The stem with simple
panelling, against the bowl exactly carved coats of arms. –
Stem of a second FONT (?) with statuettes, defaced. – PULPIT.
A rustic C17 piece with angel faces in the spandrels at the corners above the usual blank arches. – SCREEN. With narrow
one-light divisions. Only partly old. – STAINED GLASS. Original bits in the heads of the s windows. – Chancel s two windows in the Arts and Crafts style, c.1897 and c.1899. –
PLATE. Norwich-made Chalice, 1567; Paten without marks.
W of the church a house with a shaped gable towards the street.
SUSTEAD HALL. The façade towards the road rebuilt after col-
lapse in 1888. To the back a pair of C17 brick windows with
mullion and transom crosses under one hood-mould. The
front may have had regular fenestration throughout. The date
of the house is 1663. (Good staircase and panelling.)
HALL FARMHOUSE, ½ m. E. With stepped gable and remains of
mullioned brick windows.

SUTTON

ST MICHAEL. Not large. Unbuttressed W tower. This is probably early C14, as seem to be the s arcade (four bays, octagonal
piers, double-chamfered arches) and the s and N doorways and
the s aisle windows (Y-tracery, cusped intersected tracery).
Late Perp N windows. Late Perp s porch, formerly two-
storeyed, with a brick entrance arch. – FONT. Octagonal.
Eight attached shafts and simple panel units against the stem,
ogee arches, two to each side, against the bowl. – PULPIT.
Jacobean; humble. – PLATE. Chalice, Norwich, 1567–8;
Paten probably the same; Flagon, London, 1728. – MONU-
MENT. Mary Bygrove † 1822. Big sarcophagus; in the church-
yard.
WINDMILL, ½ m. E. Tower-mill, derelict, with damaged sails.

SWAFIELD

St Nicholas. w tower of the early c14, formerly probably unbuttressed. Tower arch triple-chamfered, dying into the imposts. The rest all Perp, with identical three-light windows. The roof-line of the former church visible against the tower E wall inside the church. Nave roof with arched braces. Bosses against the ridge. – screen. Eight painted Saints against the dado. – south door. Knocker and plate probably early c14. – plate. Chalice, Norwich-made, and Paten, both undated. – monument. Isaac Horsley † 1803. Tablet with an urn in front of an obelisk.

Swafield Hall. Early brickwork and stepped gables, but thin giant angle pilasters. The s front sashed.

Mill House, s of the river, w of the B-road. Three bays, two and a half storeys, red brick. Giant angle pilasters.

Friends' Meeting House. Three bays, two storeys, pyramid roof. Interior with a gallery on Tuscan columns.

SWANNINGTON

St Margaret. Broad w tower, embraced by the aisles, its detail not corresponding to that in Ladbrooke's drawing. The details in the body of the church also over-restored, but some, it seems, correctly. The pair of transomed Dec chancel windows e.g. is an accurate reproduction. Internally the arcades are of three bays with quatrefoil piers and double-chamfered arches. The details differ, but N as well as s aisle must be of dates about 1300. The tower was built into an existing nave. Its arches towards nave and aisles are Perp, and it is a nice feature to see them doubled in depth. The s porch is Perp too. It has flushwork decoration of crowned letters along the base of the front, and above the entrance of letters which read IHS NAZARENES. In the spandrels of the entrance a dragon l. and several figures r. The N aisle roof has arched braces with tracery, the chancel roof cambered tie-beams on arched braces with tracery above the tie-beams. In the chancel on the s side sumptuous Dec Sedilia with ogee arches and large leaves in the spandrels. The Piscina is of pillar type, using a Norman capital with St George and the Dragon. The w part of the N wall of the chancel has blank arcading. – font. Octagonal, of Purbeck marble, c13, with shallow blank arches on each side. – benches. Many old poppy-heads, including a number in the vestry. – communion rail. Specially nice, probably about 1660, with the posts supported on six balusters set in three pairs in depth. – PAINTING. St Christopher, s aisle, N wall. – PLATE. Chalice, Norwich, 1639; Paten, London, 1763.

SWANNINGTON MANOR. Of *c.*1700, brick, with brick quoins and windows with wooden crosses. Shaped end-gables. Inside quite a collection of STAINED GLASS and woodwork, not originally belonging to the house. The glass includes some C15 pieces, said to come from Heydon church, and much minor foreign glass. Among the WOODWORK the most interesting is a spectacular STALL END with a large bird and three panels of Early Renaissance mythological scenes with the initials of William Rogers, M.P. in 1541, mayor of Norwich in 1542 and 1548. There are also many C16 to C18 panels.

COTTAGE, w of the church. Timber-framed.

BARROW. The barrow on Alderford Common (now cut into by a chalk and gravel pit) is of Middle Bronze Age date, to judge from the lugged food-vessel which has been found in it.

SWANTON ABBOT

2020

ST MICHAEL. Dec w tower, Perp s porch with a niche above the entrance, Perp nave windows, three on either side, the middle ones more cusped than the others, Perp chancel. Arch-braced nave roof. – FONT. Octagonal, with panelled stem and a bowl with quatrefoils and with faces on the underside. SCREEN. One-light divisions, tall, painted Saints on the dado panels, now at the back. Of the carving not much is old. – PEWS. At the back rising as in a lecture-theatre. – SOUTH DOOR. Iron plate with knocker, perhaps C13. – PLATE. Chalice and Paten, London, 1786. – BRASS to Stephen Multon, a priest, † 1477. The figure is 18 in. long (chancel).

SWANTON NOVERS

0030

ST EDMUND. Unbuttressed w tower, rebuilt in 1960–1, evidently with old materials. w window with Y-tracery and a niche below. In the nave traces of a former s doorway with round head. Can it have been Norman? The masonry looks it. One window with Y-tracery. Chancel and N aisle apparently Victorian. Nice ogee-headed Piscina in the chancel. In the spandrel two Ws surrounded by rings with fleurons. The same Ws but surrounded by crowns of thorn recur in the FONT.

Octagonal. Also with the four symbols of the Evangelists. –
PLATE. Paten by *Nathaniel Lock*, 1712; Chalice, London,
1728; Paten on foot by *John King*, 1787.

1010

TAVERHAM

ST EDMUND. Round tower with octagonal top and flushwork-
panelled battlements. Nave and chancel thatched. The nave
has a plain Norman N doorway and also carstone quoins which
confirm the date. Dec chancel. The E window has the motif
of the four-petalled flower. A blocked N doorway in the chancel formerly went to a vestry. Also a fragment of the Sedilia,
which were of the dropped-sill type. What remains is two little
arches in the window jambs. The S aisle and S arcade are of
1863. The nave has a single-framed roof. – FONT. Octagonal,
with eight statuettes against the stem, the signs of the Evangelists against the underside of the bowl, and plain shields
against the bowl. – SCREEN. With one-light divisions and ogee
arches. – STALLS. With poppy-heads, traceried fronts, and
two animals on arms. – BENCHES. Two with poppy-heads in
31a   the porch. – COMMUNION RAIL. With much Flamboyant
tracery of great delicacy, obviously coming from a church
SCREEN. The most likely date is the C14, as other Norfolk
screens of the C14 have the traceried roundels which appear
here and also the reticulation unit with much internal
tracery. – STAINED GLASS. In a N window Crucifixion,
Norwich *c*.1450. – In the E window by *O'Connor*, 1873. –
PLATE. Chalice, Norwich, probably late C17; Paten, Exeter,
1730. – BRASS. Small chalice brass to John Thorp, rector,
† 1515 (chancel floor).

TAVERHAM HALL. 1858–9, by *David Brandon*. Red brick, neo-
Tudor, with a tall, symmetrical S front and an asymmetrical E
(entrance) side with a turret.

TEMPLEWOOD *see* NORTHREPPS

0020

THEMELTHORPE

ST ANDREW. Unbuttressed W tower, probably built in the C13.
Nave and chancel in one; no chancel arch. The windows
again point to the C13. At the E end three single stepped lancets; otherwise e.g. Y-tracery. – BENCHES. Several ends with
poppy-heads. – PLATE. Norwich-made Chalice, 1567. –
(BRASS to William Pescod † 1505.)

THORNAGE

ALL SAINTS. Drastically renewed in 1898 and 1904. The masonry at the NW corner looks like an indication of Saxon long-and-short work. Three Norman windows (one blocked) in nave and chancel. Unbuttressed W tower. Early C14 the chancel, see the E window (three stepped lancet lights under one arch), the priest's doorway, and the angle Piscina. The S aisle blocked up. The arcade had two bays. Octagonal pier, arches with two sunk quadrant mouldings. – BENCHES. Some ends have Perp poppy-heads. – PLATE. Chalice, Norwich, with inscription referring to 'ye gifte of John Butes and Margret hys wyfe 1456 whych died in 1477'; Paten, inscribed 1563. – MONUMENTS. Sir William Butt † 1583. Tomb-chest with fluted pilasters and shields in the panels. Plain recess with pilasters and depressed arch. – Lady Anne Heigham † 1590. Nice incised slab with kneeling effigy.

THORNAGE HALL. A former grange of the bishops of Norwich, and a very curious fragmentary survival. One oblong range with buttresses. Two doorways in the same front, one more elaborate than the other. Two original windows with panel tracery, both large for their date, but the last one to the r. excessively large. Lower part divided by a transom from the upper, which represents the whole size of the other windows. There is no explanation for so large a window in such a place, and it may well be a C19 enlargement. However, it is in a drawing of 1851. The l. hand large transomed window dates from after 1851. Above windows the emblems of the see of Norwich and of Bishop Goldwell who ruled from 1472 to 1499 (a scallop and well). Similar windows at the back and traces of a blocked bay window. Big square DOVECOTE of brick. To increase the number of nesting places there are four internal buttresses or fins reaching forwards towards the centre.

THORPE see p. 291

THORPE MARKET

ST MARGARET. Built (by one *Wood*) in 1796, a rare date for Norfolk. The little church is a plain oblong with four short turrets carrying spirelets. The windows have Y-tracery with original glazing-bars. Modest porches in front of the first and last bays to the S. The interior is given its character by the coved, thinly ribbed ceiling and the SCREEN, which all one's sympathy cannot prevent one from calling gimcrack. Very

thin woodwork, the diapering of iron, the panes of glass painted with the figures of Moses and Aaron. – FONT. Perp, octagonal. Originally on eight attached shafts. Against the bowl two ogee arches on each side (cf. Felbrigg). – PLATE. Chalice, Norwich, 1567; Paten, 1726; Flagon, 1825; Alms-dish, 1828. – MONUMENTS. Three tablets of very similar composition, commemorating deaths in 1671, 1711, and 1749, are entertaining to compare. – Two brothers Marden, 1796 by *Regnart*. With a putto standing by, and pointing to, an urn.
GREEN FARMHOUSE, ½ m. NW, on the Green. Elizabethan. Front with two stepped gables and a lower stepped-gabled porch between. The windows had pediments, and some of these are preserved. Groups of four big polygonal chimneys.

9030

THORPLAND
2 m. NE of Fakenham

ST THOMAS. In ruins, just SE of Thorpland Hall. No more than one corner stands up, apparently the SW corner.
THORPLAND HALL. One of the finest pieces of C16 brick architecture in Norfolk. What survives is a complete range, with polygonal angle buttresses and a porch projecting in the middle. The porch has polygonal angle buttresses too. But the unforgettable spectacle is the chimneyshafts, round, decorated in various ways, and crowned by the most daring star tops. Only the stepping of the gable and the panelling and quatre-foiling of the top of the porch – apart of course from the de-tails of fenestration and of the top cornice – are C19 embellish-ments.

4010

THRIGBY

ST MARY. W tower Dec, see e.g. the details of the tower arch. Good Dec S doorway. One order of shafts with foliage capi-tals; finely moulded arch; hood-mould with fleurons on head-stops. The S windows and the E window apparently of *c*.1800, pointed.* At the time of writing creeper covers them com-pletely and spreads a very attractive green light through the church. – FONT. Octagonal, plain, with two patterns of quatre-foils. – PLATE. Elizabethan Chalice.

1030

THURGARTON

ALL SAINTS. Thatched and now towerless. Remains of the tower are still visible, and l. and r. of them two small lancet

* But the *Building News* 1896 reports restorations including Dec window tracery and the chancel arch (PF).

windows belonging to the nave. The s windows and the N window of the nave are Dec, with reticulated tracery. Dec also the chancel (E window altered), with an odd passage through the SE buttress. Plain two-storeyed s porch. – FONT COVER. Modest, Jacobean. – BENCHES. With poppy-heads and a few figures, also twice a tun and once an elephant and castle. The blocks of benches taper away to the W to give more space round the font. – SCULPTURE. Fragment of an alabaster panel of the C15. – PLATE. Paten of the late C15 or early C16, with a rather crude head of Christ in a sexfoiled depression; Chalice, Norwich, 1567.

THURGARTON HALL, W of the church. Five bays, two and a half storeys; plain. Dated 1733 by Kelly.

THURGARTON OLD HALL, ¾ m. NW. Shaped gable-end of red brick on the W side, with a date 1733, but front of yellow brick. Six bays, two and a half storeys, and a Greek Doric porch, i.e. early C19. A date 1828 is in fact at the back of the house. Moreover a bigger mid-C19 addition of four bays on the E side.

THURNE

4010

ST EDMUND. Unbuttressed W tower, the doorway to the nave indicating an early C14 date. Later top of brick and flint chequer with pretty triple-stepped battlements. Nave and chancel. The N doorway seems early C14 too. The rest is mostly Perp or Victorian. N porch with a niche above the entrance. Arch-braced nave roof with crenellated wall-plate. – The ROOD BEAM is preserved. – COMMUNION RAIL. Late C17, the balusters of dumb-bell shape. – PLATE. Norwich-made Chalice of 1567–8; Paten Cover, Elizabethan and altered.

WINDMILLS. Two drainage-mills of the brick-tower type with caps and sails. Both immediately W of Thurne, and very picturesque by the river Thurne.

ASHBY HALL. *See p. 75.*

THURNING

0020

ST ANDREW. Unbuttressed W tower with a W lancet and bell-openings with cusped Y-tracery. The chancel has disappeared, except for the ruins of its N wall. The priest's doorway and the E window were re-set in the nave E wall. They are clearly late C13. Nave s windows Dec (reticulation). The N aisle humble Perp, the arcade, much restored, with octagonal piers and double-chamfered arches. – Three-decker PULPIT, BOX

PEWS, sanctuary PANELLING, and three-sided COMMUNION RAIL all of 1742 and some or all from the chapel of Corpus College, Cambridge. The furnishings were designed by *James Burrough* and given by Sir Jacob Astley (*see* Melton Constable). The chapel was pulled down in 1823. – MONUMENTS. Elizabeth Wake † 1759 by *W. Tyler*, Caleb Elwin † 1776 by *E. Holl*, both tablets, and the latter specially handsome with an obelisk at the head and two cherub heads at the foot.

THURNING HALL. Georgian, five bays and two and a half storeys, with a parapet.

ROOKERY FARMHOUSE, ¾ m. N. With a pair of shaped gables.

9030
THURSFORD

ST ANDREW. Simple N doorway of *c.*1200. W tower early C14. The same date applies to the N aisle E bay. The S transept and the ambitious chancel are of 1862.* The chancel is really the most interesting part of the church, with its High Victorian stepped tripartite arcade of columns two-deep with shaft-rings and stylized bracken capitals. The N aisle pier is a Victorian disgrace, the S arcade is strange and hard to date. Octagonal piers with square bases and capitals. Can this also be Victorian, or can it be Perp? – STAINED GLASS. The glass in the E window, designed by the *Rev. Arthur Moore* in 1862, is one of the most beautiful of its time in England, or indeed Europe, as good as the early Morris glass, which is saying much. It is more reminiscent of progressive work of the 1920s than of anything in the C19. – Chancel N and S 1873 by *Powell*, designed by *Wooldridge*, also good, relatively speaking. – PLATE. Norwich-made Chalice and Cover of 1567–8; London-made Chalice and Paten of 1798 and Paten of 1817. – MONUMENT. Black and white marble sarcophagus to Sir Thomas Gaybon † 1666. Signed by *William Stanton*.

THURSFORD HALL. Of an Elizabethan building one can see nothing. Of the big Victorian building facing S there is also nothing left, except for a minor wing with the date 1857. To the E of the buildings circular DOVECOTE. To the SW STABLES with stepped gables.

1030
THWAITE

ALL SAINTS. Norman round tower with C14 bell-openings (Y-tracery). Norman W quoins to the nave (carstone). On the

* By *W. Lightly* (PF).

N side of the nave one Dec window. The s aisle has mixed Dec windows and bits of decoration on the buttresses. However, the arcade (three bays, octagonal piers, double-chamfered arches) seems Perp. Chancel and N chapel apparently Victorian. – PULPIT. Dated 1624. Plain, with back panel and tester. – SCREEN. Only the dado exists now. – BENCHES. Very primitive flat poppy-heads; C17? – PLATE. Norwich-made Chalice and Paten, 1567–8. – MONUMENT. Brass to John Puttok † 1442 and wife † 1469, 25 in. figures (s aisle E). He is said to have rebuilt the s aisle.

TRIMINGHAM   2030

ST JOHN BAPTIST. Short w tower without parapet. Its E buttresses stand beside the nave. The chancel windows are 'debased' Perp. – FONT. Octagonal. Stem with eight attached shafts. Bowl with two ogee arches on each side. – SCREEN. One-light divisions. Delicately cusped tracery in two layers in depth. Paintings of eight Saints, c.1500. – PLATE. Norwich-made Chalice, 1567.

TROWSE NEWTON see p. 292

TROWSE NEWTON see p. 292

TRUNCH   2030

ST BOTOLPH. Trunch will always remain in one's mind as the church with the font canopy. There is however much else to be enjoyed. It is a Perp church throughout, and probably Early Perp. Tall w tower. The aisle windows have purely Perp windows flanking a middle window still with reminiscences of the Dec. Arcades of four bays with octagonal piers and double-chamfered arches. Fine tall s porch entrance. Chancel with the curious feature of the middle s buttress standing on a porch built in front of the priest's doorway. Warham St Mary and Beccles in Suffolk are the only other examples of this arrangement. The nave has a good hammerbeam roof on wall-posts and longitudinal arched braces. Horizontal angels against, and tracery above, the hammerbeams. No collar-beams. – So to the FONT. It has a flushwork-panelled stem and a bowl with tracery patterns. This modest font is guarded by the glorious FONT CANOPY. There are only four font canopies 30 in England. The other three are at St Peter Mancroft Norwich, at Luton, and, of the C17, at Durham Cathedral. The canopy at Trunch is in two stages. It is encrusted with vegetable decoration. The lower stage has eight posts decorated with foliage trails of divers patterns. Vine, lily, and thistle are recognizable. There are also twisted branches. This stage ends in a fan-like vault with a pendant and very much cusped fields. The upper stage has eight big, somewhat heavy, tripartite, hanging vaulted canopies. They are too broad to have contained only one figure each. They seem originally to have been connected with the posts below by flying buttresses. Crocketed ogee top. – SCREEN. Two-light divisions with cusped ogee arches. Nice delicate cusping. Carved cresting. Much remains of the original colouring. Against the dado twelve figures of Saints. Decorated top rail of the dado, with a painted inscription scroll dating the screen 1502. – STALLS. With poppy-heads and some tracery. Also six MISERICORDS, with three demi-figures of angels and three heads. – PLATE. Norwich-made Chalice of 1566 and Paten Cover of 1567; London-made Paten of 1748. – (BRASS. Heart and scroll, c.1530.)

MANOR HOUSE, ⅛ m. E. Elizabethan or Jacobean. Thatched, with two stacks of three octagonal chimneyshafts with startops. Porch, and to its l. an original wooden mullioned and transomed window.

IVY HOUSE, to the NW of the former. Late Georgian. Five bays, two storeys, with two Tuscan porches and windows with Gothic glazing-bars.

TUNSTALL
4000

ST PETER AND ST PAUL. Largely in ruins. The chancel alone is still in use. The chancel arch was blocked by a brick wall as early as 1705. The W tower is overgrown, and no details are recognizable. The nave has had Dec windows, but the tracery is broken out. The chancel had a S chapel, but no details of it survive. The chancel roof is single-framed with upper scissorbracing. – FONT. Octagonal, with simple tracery patterns, including a wheel of three mouchettes. – PLATE. Chalice, Norwich, 1631.

TUNSTEAD
3020

ST MARY. A big church, 140 ft long. The distinguishing feature is the flushwork arcading along the windowless clerestory. Early Perp W tower. Wavy base frieze. Doorway with a trail in the hood-mould. Three-light window. Two-light bell-openings. In the tracery still traces of the Dec style. The aisle windows still Dec, but the aisle arcades definitely Early Perp.

The piers are quatrefoil with fillets and fine double-waves in
the diagonals. Niches for images in the spandrels. One must
assume that the windows and the arcades belong together, i.e.
that a symbiosis of Dec and Perp took place in the second half
of the C14. Stone benches along the aisle walls. Perp chancel
with arch-braced roof. Sedilia and Piscina with ogee arches 23b
and little variety. The most surprising thing in the chancel,
and one that is probably unique in England, is the raised
PLATFORM along the E wall. It is only just over 3 ft wide.
Below it a low, windowless, tunnel-vaulted chamber or passage accessible from the sanctuary by a simple doorway which
corresponds in position to the steps up to the platform. The
only light which reaches the chamber is by a grating in the
platform floor. The platform may have been used for the exhibition of relics, the vaulted chamber as a strong-room.
Against the wall of the platform two fragmentary niches, remains of the stone REREDOS of the former altar. Some of the
original colour is preserved. – SCREENS. Rood screen with
one-light divisions. Ogee arches set in round arches. Two-
layer cusping. Sixteen painted Saints. Remains of the floor of
the rood-loft. – Tower screen with some old woodwork. – The
ROOD BEAM survives, nicely painted. – STALLS. One end of
the return stalls is preserved. – DOORS. The door into the
chamber below the platform is original. – The S door to the 37b
church has a cross of iron, about 4 ft in size, fabulously enriched by trails with trefoil leaves boldly detached from the
ground. It is certainly C14 work. – PLATE. Paten, Norwich,
1568; Cup, Norwich, c.1675; Chalice, London, 1734.

TUTTINGTON   2020

ST PETER AND ST PAUL. Small, with a round tower. The rest
built in 1450 (Kelly). Solid two-storeyed S porch. Nave with
three tall windows each side. The middle ones are Perp with
decided Dec reminiscences, the others are purely Perp (cf.
Brandiston). The chancel seems to be Dec. – FONT. Octagonal, Perp, with shields in cusped quatrefoils. – FONT COVER.
Simple, Jacobean in style; dated 1638. – PULPIT. Plain,
panelled, with attached iron HOURGLASS STAND. – BENCHES.
With poppy-heads and figures, in many cases l. as well as r. of
the poppy-heads. Among the unusual representations are St
George and the Dragon, the elephant and castle, a musician
with a drum, a musician with a lute, a woman making butter,
a woman with a basket and a pig, a dragon devouring a man. –

PLATE. Later C15 or early C16 Paten, parcel-gilt. In a lobed depression the monogram of Christ in a circle. – Chalice of 1567, Norwich-made.

TWYFORD

0020

ST NICHOLAS. Norman – see the window in the W gable. Late C13 chancel, with lancets and at the E end three stepped lancet lights under one arch. Humble but quaint brick S porch tower, dated 1757. It has a wooden cupola. – PLATE. Chalice, a secular cup, made in London, 1738.

UPTON

3010

ST MARGARET. All Perp, quite large, and much restored, though the details of the windows seem accurate. Those in the nave have the characteristic motif of a horizontal between the three lights and the panel tracery. Arcades of four bays. The piers have a section of four shafts and four hollows. The same in the chancel arch. The W tower had long been ruined and was rebuilt in 1928–9. In the stoup a re-used Norman capital. Nave roof with tie-beams on arched braces; much restored. – FONT. On three steps, the topmost decorated by a quatrefoil frieze and little lions at the corners. Stem with eight statuettes. Bowl with the signs of the four Evangelists, two broad, seated young angels with shields and two with musical instruments. – PULPIT. Perp. (Unused; in the N aisle.) – SCREEN. With eight painted figures on the dado and part of a former inscription. – BENCHES. A few ends with poppy-heads. Also one front (or back) with pierced tracery. – PLATE. Norwich-made Chalice, 1567; Paten, unmarked.

WINDMILL, 1 m. NE.

WALCOTT

3030

ALL SAINTS. All Late Dec to Early Perp and probably one of the cases of the overlap by which decidedly Dec and decidedly Perp forms appear side by side as part of the same building campaign. Big W tower. Base and double-stepped battlements with flushwork panelling. Doorway with traceried spandrels with shields. Shields on the W buttresses too. The buttresses have flushwork panelling in addition. Four-light Perp W window. Traceried sound-holes. Bell-openings with Dec tracery. Three large windows in the nave to the S, three to the N. S porch entrance Early Perp-looking. Chancel windows Dec (the E window is Victorian).* Yet the mouldings and the but-

---

* Restoration by *Phipson* 1854 to 1877 (PF).

tresses the same in nave and chancel. Sedilia and Piscina partly
without, partly with ogee arches. – FONT. Octagonal, C13, of
Purbeck marble, with the usual two shallow blank arches on
each side. – SCREENS. The rood screen with one-light divisions. Ogee arches and very elongated tracery above, all
nicely restrained. – Tower screen with Jacobean balusters. –
PLATE. Chalice, Norwich, 1567; Paten, 1567, perhaps made
out of an older Paten.

WALSINGHAM see GREAT WALSINGHAM and LITTLE WALSINGHAM

WARHAM ALL SAINTS   9040

ALL SAINTS. The W tower has disappeared. It had a low arch to
the nave. The aisles have also disappeared, except that their
last bays were allowed to stand as transepts. The arcades had
octagonal piers and double-hollow-chamfered arches. The
curious base of a shaft to the N of the NE respond may have
been for a Pillar Piscina. The chancel is early C14, see the
(renewed) E window and the angle Piscina. Arch-braced nave
roof with high collar-beams. – FONTS. There are three, a
Norman square one with angle colonnettes and on the other
sides flat blank arches and one knot, another Norman square
one, cut to an octagonal shape and originally displaying the
Labours of the Months and the Tree of Life (cf. Burnham
Deepdale), and an C18 baluster font. – MONUMENTS. Defaced effigy of a Civilian, of c.1300, carrying a horn or a roll. –
Brass to William Rokewod † 1474. An 18 in. figure (near
SW door).

WARHAM ST MARY   9040

ST MARY. Norman N doorway, blocked, with one order of
columns carrying one-scallop capitals. Roll-moulded arch.
Odd small nave W window just S of the tower. How does it
connect with the other evidence? The tower is Dec, but the
battlements with a chequer trellis of flint and stone may be
later. In the chancel a priest's doorway placed in an attractive,
unusual, though not unique way inside a little gabled porch on
which rises the chancel S buttress. On the N side of the chancel
the utilitarian Turner Mausoleum of brick. It dates perhaps
from the time when the nave was ceiled and the BOX PEWS and
the very complete three-decker PULPIT were installed. – The
FONT is a baluster and could also be of the same time. – COM-
MUNION RAIL. C18. – The church contains much foreign

STAINED GLASS, mixed up with local fragments. The foreign glass, German or Flemish, is mostly of the Early Renaissance. – MONUMENT. One († 1836) with a putto on the base of an urn is by *Gaffin*.

GROVE FARM. The unusually attractive appearance is largely due to the recent addition of two pyramid-roofed single-bay pavilions to a simple Georgian three-bay house.

WARHAM CAMP. An Iron Age FORT, nearly circular, of 3½ acres, lies by the river. Originally double-banked and ditched with an inner rampart and timber palisade, the defences are now single towards the river. Excavations in 1959 showed the occupation to start in the period *c.*50 B.C.–A.D. 50, with a certain amount of later CI A.D. rubbish from Romanized peasants. The W side has been destroyed by C18 landscaping.

WARHAM BURROWS. NE of Warham Camp is a rectangular enclosure, visible only from the air, 275 ft long with an E causeway. This is an unfinished Iron Age fort with a 10-ft-wide marking-out ditch.

WAXHAM

4020

ST JOHN. The chancel is in ruins, and the W tower in a precarious state, with most of its details obliterated. Flushwork panelling on the top parapet. The nave is at least partly Norman, see one blocked S window. In the N wall a small lancet window. In addition on the S side three later C13 windows with Y-tracery. Two-storeyed S porch. Entrance with traceried spandrels with shields. Lozenge frieze above, also with shields. Is the late C13 W window of the porch re-set? – FONT. Plain, Perp, with quatrefoils. – BANNER STAFF LOCKER, N wall. – PLATE. Norwich-made Chalice, 1567–8; Paten, Elizabethan, no marks. – MONUMENT. Thomas Wodehouse † 1571, a good typical Early Elizabethan monument, i.e. without an effigy and with comparatively restrained classical detail. Four-centred arch flanked by Corinthian columns. Tomb-chest with shields.

WAXHAM HALL. Long enclosing wall with polygonal angle buttress shafts crowned by finials. In the middle of the NE front a C15 gatehouse. Four-centred archways with tracery in the spandrels. Again polygonal buttress shafts and finials l. and r. From here by a 90-degree turn to the NW a second gateway is reached, and this is Elizabethan. It has a subsidiary pedestrian entrance. The main entrance is flanked by columns. Near by one of the largest BARNS in Norfolk.

WINDMILL. A drainage mill. Fragmentary tower-mill 1 m. SW.

WELLS-NEXT-THE-SEA

St NICHOLAS. A large, townish Perp church, damaged in its appearance by the fact that it is nearly all a rebuilding after a fire of 1879.* Tall, broad w tower, E window in the chancel of six lights, rood turret at the E end of the N aisle, s porch and w tower with panelled battlements. Arcade of five bays with quatrefoil piers with fine hollows in the diagonals and moulded arches. One-bay chancel chapels. – DOOR. Chancel, N, with tracery. – (Brass Eagle LECTERN, said to be medieval.)

The little town has essentially a plan with parallel streets bordering on long narrow blocks. The streets are narrow too, and interconnected by passages of no more than up to 6 ft width, much like the Rows of Yarmouth. No houses of special merit, but no houses either which are blatantly wrong. The various warehouses with their hoists are the only big buildings.

Near the church two specially noteworthy houses, OSTRICH HOUSE in BURNT STREET, W of the church, with a porch with big shaped gable, a sashed façade, and remains of other windows under the gable-ends, and MARSH HOUSE in MARSH LANE, N of the church, on the way to the station, with seven bays, two storeys, a three-bay pediment, and a hipped roof.

A little to the N of Burnt Street, i.e. the NW of the church, the BUTTLANDS, a very pleasant oblong green lined by trees and with a w side of Late Georgian houses, mostly of three bays, and all attractive. Only one is large, of red brick, with seven bays and a raised three-bay centre. It has four doorways.

Just N of the Buttlands, by Mill Road, the CONGREGATIONAL CHURCH of 1816 with arched windows and a pyramid roof.

From here and a little E of here three or four streets lead to THE QUAY. The Quay is very charming (and could be more charming, if certain debris were cleared up), though again not graced by any outstanding houses. In one of the streets referred to, STANDARD ROAD, a good Georgian brick house of five bays and two and a half storeys with a central Venetian window and no pediment.

WEST CAISTER see CAISTER

WEST RUNTON see RUNTON

* By *Herbert J. Green* (PF).

4010

WEST SOMERTON

St Mary. Round tower with a later octagonal top. This has four
wide lancet bell-openings and four blind ones in the diagonals.
Humble, thatched nave with a s doorway apparently of *c*.1200
and (renewed or new) late c13 windows with Y-tracery. Taller
chancel with big Perp windows including one of five lights to
the e. Perp also the chancel arch. – pulpit. Perp. – screen.
Partly old. With two-light divisions, crocketed ogee arches,
and panel tracery. – paintings. Wall paintings of the late
c14. On the s side St Christopher, also Christ on a rainbow
with two angels. On the n side, hardly decipherable, stories
from the Passion. – plate. Chalice, Norwich-made, 1567–8;
Plate, London, 1799. – monument. Robert Rising † 1797.
With an urn in front of an obelisk.

Windmills. Two tower-mills for drainage. One without sails,
1 m. nw, another still with its sails, $1\frac{5}{8}$ m. wnw.

2020

WESTWICK

St Botolph. Away from the village, in the grounds of the
house. Tall Perp w tower. In 1473 £9 was left towards its
building. Base frieze with cusped lozenges and shields. Decorated sound-holes (cf. St George Norwich). The battlements
re-done in the c19. Perp arcades of four bays with octagonal
piers and double-chamfered arches. The exterior of the aisles
all over-restored (1845). Perp chancel. – font. Octagonal,
with four lions seated on the base and eight flowers and
fleurons against the bowl. – screen. With twelve painted
Saints. One-light divisions with pretty cusping in two tiers in
depth. – plate. Chalice of 1567, Norwich; Paten, undated,
Norwich. – monuments. A series of nice tablets – nice for
stylistic comparison – especially those of 1730, 1772, and 1819.

Westwick House. Seven-bay house of two and a half storeys
with a three-bay pediment. The decoration of the pediment
and the charming apsed staircase with its iron railing (cf.
Stratton Strawless Hall) point to a date *c*.1800.

Westwick Lodges, $\frac{3}{4}$ m. sw. Formerly the entrance to the
grounds. Grey brick with pebble rustication to the s, knapped
flint to the n. Round arch, flanked by pointed niches in three
tiers. Pediment. Small lodges with pointed windows attached.

Lookout Tower, $\frac{1}{2}$ m. e. Grey brick. At the bottom again
pebble rustication. Above circular, with a balcony and an iron
roof.

Old Hall, $\frac{3}{4}$ m. sse of the church. Later c16, of red brick with diaper of dark brick. Not completely preserved, especially largely cut down in height. L-shaped. The hall probably was in the recessed wing, where a pedimented doorway remains. All windows are pedimented too. The projecting part has a gable-end with polygonal angle shafts and windows in three storeys, the top one in the stepped gable. The recessed wing also had stepped gable-ends. One of them is preserved.

WEYBOURNE
1040

Hills to the W rise to 250 ft, to the E to 300 ft and more.

PRIORY and church of ALL SAINTS. The two are so closely interwoven in their buildings that they cannot be separated. The priory was founded early in the C13 for Augustinian Canons from West Acre, but it must have moved into an existing Anglo-Saxon building. Of this remains the ruinous but still very impressive and in any case remarkably large central tower. It has twin bell-openings with triangular heads, blank arcading to their l. and r., and two circular openings above. This tower now has a C14 or C15 window in its E wall, but must originally have been followed by a Saxon chancel. The canons moved in and seem first of all to have extended the building by an inordinately long chancel. They also added a parochial S aisle with circular piers with circular abaci and double-chamfered arches. Two bays of this S arcade are now the N arcade of the parish church; two more bays are blocked and led up to the SW corner of the tower. A C13 doorway also remains. This is re-set in the N wall of the parish church and has dog-tooth decoration. The S doorway of the parish church is of c.1300 or later. Then, in the C15, the parochial premises were enlarged by a W tower (flushwork panelling on the base, sound-holes with pretty tracery, flushwork panelling on the battlements) and a two-storeyed S porch. Brick and flushwork chequer. Niche above the entrance and below a transomed window. – PLATE. Paten, London, 1767; Chalice, London, 1768.

The rest of the priory ruins is inarticulate. In the late C13 or early C14 a large chapel was added to the chancel on the S, and a transept to the N. The E range of the monastic quarters to the N of the N transept was remodelled. But of all that lay round the cloister the remains tell us little. Excavations have, however, revealed the oblong chapter house, the dormitory to its N, the refectory range N of the cloister, and the NW parts of the W range. The present house cuts into this range and

projects far to the w of it. About 300 ft N of the church are the
foundations of another building belonging to the priory. It was
oblong and quite long.

WINDMILL. To the E. A derelict tower-mill without sails.

WHITLINGHAM see p. 293

WHITWELL see REEPHAM

WHITLINGHAM see p. 293

WHITWELL see REEPHAM

4000
WICKHAMPTON

ST ANDREW. Norman chancel, though the exterior indicates an
E.E. date, and the E window is Perp. Internally one can see
the Norman splays of two windows converted externally into
lancets. Also the outer E wall l. and r. of the Perp window
shows clearly that there had been two lancets, and one must
assume an E.E. E wall with three, or rather five, stepped individual lancets. Yet the internal surrounds make Norman
windows probable here too. The nave dates from c.1300 or a
little later and is distinguished by its designer's liking for
heads as hood-mould stops. They are very charming, e.g., l.
and r. of the s doorway. The doorway has continuous chamfers. The N doorway is simpler. w tower Dec to Early Perp.
The bell-openings and the windows below them are Dec, but
the doorway (traceried spandrels) and w window Perp. Flushwork panelling on the base and the double-stepped battlements. Seated figures as pinnacles. – PULPIT. Jacobean. –
BENCHES. One end is exhibited in the chancel, which does not
fit in with any other in the county. Could it be Jacobean? –
SOUTH DOOR. A foliated cross in ironwork round the knocker;
C14. – PAINTINGS. The Three Quick and the Three Dead,
one of the few examples of this allegory surviving complete. –
St Christopher. – Also eight scenes in two tiers, set in architectural frames. They are the Seven Works of Mercy and the
Resurrection to fill the corner. All of the late C14. – PLATE.
Chalice, Norwich, 1567; Paten Cover, unmarked. – MONU-
MENT. In the chancel against the N wall a pair of sumptuous
recesses containing the effigies of a Knight and a Lady, evidently of the late C13. His legs are not yet crossed; he holds
his heart; she wears a wimple. The architectural forms are
ornate but pre-Dec. Big round arches, cusped and subcusped,
on short shafts with foliage capitals already turning nobbly.
The E capital has a hare (?) and a bird. Crocketed gables, and
under one of them a sexfoiled and two small quatrefoiled
circles. Buttress shafts with finials l., r., and centre.

WINDMILL. A drainage mill without sails, 1 m. E.

WICKMERE

St Andrew. Round tower with Dec bell-stage and flushwork
battlements of rubble and squared stone. The W wall of the
nave is of the same build as the tower. Dec windows in chancel
and S aisle. The pretty clerestory windows, though wholly
renewed, are also supposed to represent the original, Dec,
state. They are alternatingly of two ogee lights and circular
with a cusped quatrefoil (cf. Cley, Great Walsingham). Perp
S porch with flushwork front. The arcades inside are of three
bays, with octagonal piers and double-chamfered arches, the
N arcade being earlier than the S arcade. Pretty broad Perp corbel of an image tabernacle in the N aisle. Perp, excessively restored Sedilia and Piscina in the chancel. – FONT. Octagonal,
Perp, with, on the underside of the bowl, faces. – SCREEN. Of
one-light divisions, without surviving tracery, but with four
surviving painted panels. – PAINTING. Two panels with
donors from another screen, fitted into the pulpit. – SEATING.
Some minor Perp and Jacobean work. One end has an inscription. – SOUTH DOOR. With fine C14 ironwork. – PLATE.
Chalice of 1567–8, Norwich; Paten belonging to this; Paten,
London-made, of 1727. – MONUMENTS. Standing Elizabethan
wall-monument with sarcophagus with detached columns and
back wall with arch between the columns (to William Dix?).
Only three small kneeling figures are left. – Two very handsome cartouches, one of 1698, the other of 1768. – Fifth Earl of
Orford † 1931. By *Esmond Burton*. Sarcophagus with recumbent effigy.

WIGHTON

All Saints. A big church with a tall W tower of *c*.1300 (see
the doorway and the bell-openings) crowned by a parapet with
panelled battlements also displaying shields. Perp aisles, clerestory, chancel, and two-storeyed S porch. The aisle windows
show a preference for straight lines instead of the curves of
gables. The S porch is higher than the aisle. The chancel has a
five-light E window with embattled transom. Behind it lay a
low E vestry whose E wall survives. The interior has arcades of
six bays with quatrefoil piers, the foils somewhat squashed and
endowed with fillets, and slim diagonal shafts with fillets too.
The capitals are polygonal. The whole is exactly as at Great
Walsingham, except that the arches are double-hollow-chamfered. This church, probably of the C14, was added to the
tower so that the S arcade stood in line with the former S wall

or s arcade, but the N arcade was pushed farther N. The old
roof-line as well as the exterior show this. – FONT. On two
steps. Octagonal, with a panelled stem and a bowl with shields
exhibiting the emblems of the Trinity and the Passion, St
Peter, St James, St Paul, and also three crowns and two kinds
of crosses. – CHEST. With traceried front. – STAINED GLASS.
Original pieces in the tracery lights of the s and N aisle windows. – Also in the middle of each of the aisle windows a
mid-C19 Saint. – PLATE. Norwich-made Chalice, 1567–8;
Elizabethan Paten Cover; Flagon and Paten, 1672; Paten,
1674; large London-made Chalice, 1677; Flagon, 1677.

IRON AGE ENCLOSURE. Rectangular in form, with rounded
corners and measuring 210 by 180 ft, this seems to be comparable with Warham Burrows (see Warham St Mary). It
contains later Roman occupation material.

4010   WINTERTON

HOLY TRINITY. The church possesses an impressively tall
tower, c.130 ft high, the work of some donor filled with the
hubris of prosperous Norfolk merchants in the C15. The tower
had been built in the C14, as the tower arch, tall enough as it
is, the sound-holes, and the bell-openings show. Then, in the
C15, a new bell-stage was added, with three-light Perp windows, and a new parapet on top with twelve pinnacles, the
eight intermediate ones being figures. The early C14 is otherwise represented in the church by the vestry doorway and the
easternmost N window of the aisle. The rest of the evidence is
Perp and obscured by a drastic restoration of 1877–8 (*H. J.
Green*) – with one exception, the N annexe to the chancel, which
has small slit-like lancet windows exclusively and must be of
the C13. Was it built as an anchorite's cell and converted into
a vestry when the doorway was built? Also, must the Dec NE
window referred to be explained by the existence of C14 aisles
with arcades swept away when the nave was given its present
34 ft width? One would assume that that happened in the C15,
as in a number of other cases in Norfolk, but the windows are
here as in the chancel all Victorian. The s porch is another
Perp showpiece, ashlar-faced in front, with a prettily detailed
flushwork base and a doorway with one moulding decorated
with flowers, shields, heads, etc. Niches l. and r. On the upper
floor two front windows with a niche between. – PLATE.
Chalice and Paten, made in London, 1731.

HOTEL HERMANUS. A conspicuous feature of the seaside aspects of Winterton are the *rondavels* built as adjuncts to this hotel. Such *rondavels* in such a relation to a hotel are a South African speciality, and the name of course bears this out.

WITTON
3030
3½ m. ENE of North Walsham

ST MARGARET. In the N wall high up two circular windows with double splays, evidently Anglo-Saxon. The SW quoin of the nave made of big blocks of carstone is no doubt Saxon too, and the round tower may be. The Sedilia in the chancel tell of a rebuilding of the chancel in the C13. Dog-tooth decoration. The rest of the chancel too much restored in 1875 to be of value. However, E of the chancel arch remains of windows of a chancel before the chancel arch and the aisle arcades were built. S aisle early C14, elementary. The arcade is of five bays, with octagonal piers and double-chamfered arches. The clerestory with circular windows could belong to the same date, but is all new. The roof is probably later. Arched braces, wall-posts, and longitudinal arched braces. – FONT. Simple, octagonal, with panelled stem and quatrefoiled bowl. – BENCHES. Low, with poppy-heads, rather damaged. – BOX PEWS in the S aisle. – PLATE. Almsdish, London, 1813. – MONUMENTS. John Norris † 1734, a conventional tablet of its date, whereas the tablet to Mrs Norris † 1769 is very remarkable. It is so asymmetrical as to appear one half of a composition. A cherub on the l. holds, and points to, an oval cartouche placed, not upright, but diagonally. On the r. books (Sterne, Shakespear, the Bible, and Sherlock). A half-pediment at the top with an urn.

BARROW. A penannular ditch-encircled barrow with central cremation near North Walsham has been shown to have been enlarged subsequently with a new outer ditch; there were seven secondary urned burials.

WITTON
3000
5 m. E of Norwich

ST MARGARET. Nave and chancel and, originally, a W tower. Its former existence can be seen by the tower arch and the stair-turret. Now there is a polygonal bell-turret instead, probably of the C17. The chancel was rebuilt in 1857. The original details of the church point to the early C14. – FONT. Octagonal, C14. With a whole pattern book of tracery patterns.

– STAINED GLASS. One s window signed by *W. Warrington,*
1857. – PLATE. Chalice, Norwich, 1697. – MONUMENTS.
Brass to Juliana Anyell, *c.*1500, a 15 in. figure, by the entrance
door. – John Penrice † 1844. With his head in profile.
WITTON HOUSE. Early C19, grey brick, with a low hipped roof.
s front with a bow window. Entrance side with porch.

0040

WIVETON

ST MARY. The best view of Cley church is to be had from the
churchyard at Wiveton, also of the distant windmill and the
sea, and of Blakeney church behind the trees. Both Wiveton
and Cley were ports for sea-going vessels at the time that their
churches were built. That at Wiveton is essentially Perp, and
is characterized by the sameness of the tracery pattern in the
large windows, a pattern that still has certain Dec elements
and may suggest a date *c.*1375 or 1380. The w tower is not
high. It has ashlar buttresses and flushwork decoration on the
battlements. Baroque pinnacles. The bell-openings prove a
date *c.*1300 for the structure of the tower (Y-tracery), but the
w window is Perp, the first of the design referred to. It recurs
in the N aisle and the s aisle windows. The chancel however is
of the early C14. The E window has four-light intersected
tracery. The large-scale flushwork panelling with blank windows on the E and part of the s wall is most unusual and, if it
is as early as the E window, belongs to the first examples of
flushwork decoration recorded (cf. Ethelbert Gate, Norwich,
1316). Five-bay arcades, Perp. Piers with elongated section (four shafts, four long, shallow hollows, with four thin
diagonal shafts set in them) and four-centred arches. The
tower arch matches, and the chancel arch is at least in the
same style. The aisle windows are set in blank arches allowing
for seats below the windows. The clerestory is later Perp. It
has an E window. Roof with long wall-posts, longitudinal
arched braces, and arched braces up to the ridge. – FONT.
Stem with tiny nodding ogee arches (C14?); bowl plain. –
SCREEN. Under the tower arch, with one-light divisions and
ogee arches. A little panel tracery above them. – CHANDELIER.
Of brass, mentioned in a terrier of 1760. – PLATE. Parcel-gilt
Chalice without marks; London-made Paten of 1725 and
Flagon of 1727. – BRASSES. William Bisshop, priest, † 1512,
a 16 in. figure (in the chancel); Thomas Briggs(?), *c.*1540, a
skeleton in a shroud, 21½ in. long (in the nave); George
Brigge † 1597 and wife, 2 ft 8½ in. figures (by the pulpit).

BRIDGE. A single-arch medieval bridge. Pointed arch, ribbed underneath with five ribs.

WIVETON HALL, ¾ m. NW; i.e. ½ m. NE of Blakeney church. The combination of a mid-C17 house, still Jacobean in style, and placed so as to face E and W, with a larger house of 1907–9 by *Sir Guy Dawber* which faces N and S and represents the same style, but in an improved – really improved – fashion. The old house is not big. It has dates 1652 and 1653 on the hall doorways. It is H-shaped, with a porch to the E. Shaped gables with quadrants and an ogee top. All windows with pediments, resulting, owing to the size of façades available, in a somewhat crowded effect. Curious the W side of the S wing where, owing to the placing of the staircase, the windows are set in a stepped way. To the W, in the middle of the hall, chimneybreast. So the porch entrance and the W exit are not in line.

WOLTERTON HALL   1030

Built by Horatio Walpole, Sir Robert Walpole's brother, in 1727–41. The architect was *Thomas Ripley*, a protégé of the Walpoles and the architect of the Admiralty in London. He had been working at Houghton from 1722. The house was begun therefore only six years after Houghton and represents the same style in its interiors, though of course in more modest forms. Externally it is in the late C17 tradition, and not demonstratively Palladian like Houghton. Seven by three bays, two and a half storeys. Of beautiful rosy brick above a rusticated ground floor of Portland stone. Three-bay pediment with carving to the entrance as well as on the garden side. Originally on the entrance side an open staircase seems to have led direct to the hall on the first floor. Now one enters on the ground floor. On the garden side *George Stanley Repton* in 1828 etc. added the arcading all along the front and the two open staircases up to the terrace above it, a successful feature. Less successful is the Palladian wing added by Repton on the l. of the entrance side. It is of three bays with a fourth rising as a pedimented Palladian pavilion. The original house has very little external enrichment, the most notable being perhaps the Venetian window on one of the short sides. Inside, there are many fine fireplaces, some carved by *Richard Fisher* of Yorkshire, mostly of white marble and coloured agate, and of chaste classical stucco ceilings. The staircase has a balustrade of lyre-shaped wrought-iron units and runs right to the top of the house.

CHURCH. The parish church has disappeared, except for the round tower opposite the entrance side of the house.

GROUNDS. According to Mr Peter Willis's researches these were originally laid out by *Charles Bridgeman*.

WOODBASTWICK

3010

ST FABIAN AND ST SEBASTIAN, a dedication unique in England. Much restored by *Sir G. G. Scott* in 1878–9. W tower with battlements and pinnacles renewed by him. The windows of the nave Perp, of the chancel of the early C14. The interior has a tie-beam roof with kingposts and fourway struts. Scott very nicely marked off the sanctuary by a pair of posts against the walls carrying a tie-beam on arched braces with tracery. – SCREEN. One-light divisions, ogee arches, panel-tracery above them. – BENCHES. Four old ones with poppy-heads. – PLATE. Elizabethan or earlier Paten; Chalice, London-made, 1748.

WOODBASTWICK HALL. 1889 by *Ewan Christian*. Elizabethan, of red brick, large and gabled, with an asymmetrically placed tower. Inside several chimneypieces of *c.*1725 from Wricklemarsh, Blackheath, London (J. Harris).

Pretty GREEN with estate housing, old houses, and a wellhouse.

WOOD DALLING

3020

ST ANDREW. C13 chancel, see the N wall with single lancet windows and the small priest's doorway. Also of the C13 the nave and aisles – basically. This is proved by the E responds of the arcades and the base of the SW respond. The rest of the arcade is a rebuilding of the C14. Four bays, octagonal piers, double-chamfered arches. The N doorway presumably belongs to the same phase. Dec the chancel E window with flowing tracery, one chancel S window, and the angle Piscina. Finally the Perp W tower, tall and much renewed. It cuts into the S aisle W window, i.e. must be later than the aisle. The doorway has fleurons in continuous mouldings, the window a transom abnormally high up. The sound-holes are patterns of flowing tracery or of rose-window type. Clerestory and aisle windows also Perp. Perp S porch two-storeyed. In the façade a niche between the two one-light windows (cf. Salle). – SCREEN. Bits re-used in the stalls. – BENCH ENDS with poppy-heads. – PLATE. Parcel-gilt Paten of the later C15 or early C16 with the monogram of Christ set in a wavy band; sexfoil depression. – Paten inscribed 1753. – MONUMENTS. Effigy of a Priest, very much re-tooled. – Brasses to Robert Dockyng, *capellanus,*

† 1465 (11 in. figure), (to Simon Bolwar † 1504, to John Crane
† 1507), to John and Thomas Bulwer † 1517 and 1518 (two
children only left, standing on the corners of the inscription),
to Edward Warcop † 1510 (a chalice); all near the pulpit.

WOOD DALLING HALL. An Elizabethan brick house with a
front with three gables and a lower gabled porch. Polygonal
buttresses at the angles. Fine decorated circular finials and a
group of two excellent decorated circular chimneyshafts. At
the back the former staircase projects polygonally. Porch doorway with a four-centred head. Original front DOOR. Mullioned and transomed windows of stone.

WOOD NORTON
0200

ALL SAINTS. Perp chancel with priest's doorway and angle
Piscina of c.1300. Perp nave, the windows with a preference
for straight lines instead of the curves of arches. Perp s porch.
The w tower above the ground-stage of c18 brick with arched
bell-openings and battlements. – FONT. Big, plain, probably
C14. – FONT COVER. Plain, C17, with a dove on top. –
STAINED GLASS. In the w window some original fragments.
The e window (1875) by *Charles A. Gibbs*.

ST PETER, ½ m. SE. Traces of the medieval church (c.1300) in
a brick barn of MANOR FARM, a farmhouse of the C17 with a
shaped gable.

WORSTEAD
3020

ST MARY. Externally one of the dozen or so grandest Norfolk 12b
parish churches, internally lacking in inventiveness. The
church was begun in 1379 and apparently built in one campaign. It is c.130 ft long, and the w tower 109 ft high. The
tower is a splendid piece. It starts with two flushwork friezes
(in the upper no flint left) and goes on with tall blank flushwork
arcading. w doorway with quatrefoiled niches in the spandrels.
Four-light window still with flowing tracery. Sound-holes
with tracery. Bell-openings of only two lights with Perp
tracery but a framing of ballflower – an interesting mixture of
Dec and Perp. Decorated battlements. Pinnacles of 1861.
Dec chancel, very probably earlier than 1379. The tracery is
cusped-intersected and reticulated. The aisles with flushwork
base friezes and parapet friezes. Flushwork on the buttresses
too. The windows of each aisle alternate between two designs,
both Perp. Splendid s porch of two storeys with sw turret.
The parapet with flushwork chequer. The entrance has
fleurons in two orders of jambs and arch. In the spandrels

tracery and shields. Three niches with a frieze of shields below. Side windows with Dec tracery. Tierceron-star-vault inside. On the N side no porch, but a freely decorated doorway. Fleurons in the hood-mould, shields and tracery in the spandrels, a small frieze with shields over. Clerestory later, with double the number of windows as there are bays below. Two flying buttresses were later inserted on each side to help to support the roof. Also later than the church the two-storeyed N vestry. Flushwork friezes on base and parapet. The vestry is assigned to the mid C15.

The interior, to say it again, is not up to the exterior. The octagonal piers and hollow-chamfered arches are unimaginative, run-of-the-mill work. But the roof is fine. It is a later improvement; for the late C14 roof-line is still visible above the tower arch. The roof stands on tall wall-posts connected by longitudinal arched braces. Hammerbeams with traceried spandrels. One-bay chancel-chapels with very rough mouldings. Chancel roof with arched braces. In the aisles many bases for images, also two l. and r. of the altar in the N chapel.

FURNISHINGS. FONT. On three steps, the second and third decorated, the third cross-shaped. Panelled stem, bowl with very cusped quatrefoils. – FONT COVER. Of the Perp canopy-type, with the parts set radially or fin-wise. Thin, damaged. – REREDOS (N chapel). A wooden frame and a frieze of cusped quatrefoils below. – SCREENS. Four screens are in the church. The rood screen is dated by inscription 1512. It is very tall and has one-light divisions with cusped ogee arches. The coving is preserved. Foliage trail on the top rail. Against the dado sixteen painted Saints. Carved spandrels. – The S and N parclose screens have ogee arches with delicate tracery in two tiers in depth. Ribbed coving. Top rail with quatrefoil frieze. Four painted Saints. – The tower screen is connected with the tower GALLERY, which rests on arched braces with tracery carved in the spandrels. The screen has a date 1501 and is similar to the parclose screen. On the dado copies of *Reynolds*'s New College windows painted in 1831. – STALLS. With poppy-heads. Two arms with faces. – BOX PEWS. With high back walls. At the rounded corners quadrant pilasters. – VESTRY DOOR. Traceried. – PAINTING. A painted canopy on the nave E wall, and similar painting in the easternmost arch of the S arcade. – PLATE. Paten, Norwich, 1567; Chalice, Norwich, 1650; Paten on foot, London, 1722; Flagon, London, 1732. – BRASSES. John Alblastyr † 1520, a figure of

only 7½ in. in length, in front of the road screen which he
gave. – Civilian, *c.*1500, 23½ in. (chancel floor). – John Yop,
*c.*1410, *c.*9 in. (chancel floor).

Excellent group of houses to the NE of the church, including one
late C17 house of five bays with shaped gables, and one partly
Jacobean (with remains of mullioned windows) and partly of
*c.*1690 with brick quoins.

BAPTIST CHAPEL, Meeting House Hill, 1½ m. N. Built in 1829.
A substantial two-storeyed building with low hipped roof.
Good brickwork. Arched doorway.

WINDMILL, 1¼ m. NE. Brick tower-mill. The cap preserved.

WROXHAM
2010

ST MARY. Norman s doorway, barbaric and glorious. Three
orders of colonnettes with decorated shafts, two shaft-rings or
thick bands, also decorated, decorated capitals, decorated
abaci and arches with zigzags, roll mouldings, a chain motif,
and a plaited, beaded band. In the chancel a Dec window,
otherwise mostly Perp. The W tower still faces the open country. It has traceried sound-holes and flushwork panelling on
the battlements. Inside extraordinarily raw arcades. Three
bays, octagonal piers without any capitals, four-centred arches.
Cox suggests a C16 date, Cautley calls them 'modern'. Nave
and chancel roofs with arched braces. – SOUTH DOOR. The
iron plate for the knocker probably C13. – SCULPTURE.
Alabaster panel of the Holy Family (vestry). – STAINED
GLASS. W and E windows with the monogram of *Wailes*, the
latter also with the date 1851. – MONUMENTS. Many tablets,
the prettiest that of Daniel Collyer, 1774. Grey, brown, and
white marble. With an urn in front of an obelisk. It is surprising to find this graceful tablet dedicated to the memory of a
man who is called 'serious, sensible, successful'. – TRAFFORD
MAUSOLEUM, in the churchyard. 1831 by *Salvin* (A. P. Baggs
and D. M. Young), but looks decidedly High Victorian.
date. Serious no doubt, and in its way successful, that is in a
correct, rather cold later C13 style.

MANOR HOUSE, SE of the church. An irregular building with
stepped gables. Under one of them three pedimented windows of five lights with a transom, four lights with a transom,
and three lights. Under the neighbouring gable smaller pedimented windows. Inside the house an inscription panel is kept
with the date 1623.

YARMOUTH *see* GREAT YARMOUTH

GLOSSARY

Particular types of an architectural element are often defined under the name of the element iself; e.g. for 'dog-leg stair' see STAIR. Literal meanings, where specially relevant, are indicated by the abbreviation *lit*.

For further reference (especially for style terms) the following are a selection of books that can be consulted: *A Dictionary of Architecture* (N. Pevsner, J. Fleming, H. Honour, 1975); *The Illustrated Glossary of Architecture* (J. Harris and J. Lever, 1966); *Encyclopedia of Modern Architecture* (edited by Wolfgang Pehnt, 1963); *The Classical Language of Architecture* (J. Summerson, 1964); *The Dictionary of Ornament* (M. Stafford and D. Ware, 1974); *Illustrated Handbook of Vernacular Architecture* (R. W. Brunskill, 1976); *English Brickwork* (A. Clifton Taylor and R. W. Brunskill, 1977); *A Pattern of English Building* (A. Clifton Taylor, 1972).

ABACUS (*lit*. tablet): flat slab forming the top of a capital; *see* Orders (fig. 17).

ABUTMENT: the meeting of an arch or vault with its solid lateral support, or the support itself.

ACANTHUS: formalized leaf ornament with thick veins and frilled edge, e.g. on a Corinthian capital.

ACHIEVEMENT OF ARMS: in heraldry, a complete display of armorial bearings.

ACROTERION (*lit*. peak): plinth for a statue or ornament placed at the apex or ends of a pediment; also, loosely and more usually, both the plinths and what stands on them.

ADDORSED: description of two figures placed symmetrically back to back.

AEDICULE (*lit*. little building): architectural surround, consisting usually of two columns or pilasters supporting a pediment, framing a niche or opening. *See also* Tabernacle.

AFFRONTED: description of two figures placed symmetrically face to face.

AGGER (*lit*. rampart): Latin term for the built-up foundations of Roman roads; also sometimes applied to the ramparts of hill-forts or other earthworks.

AGGREGATE: small stones added to a binding material, e.g. in concrete. In modern architecture used alone to describe concrete with an aggregate of stone chippings, e.g. granite, quartz, etc.

AISLE (*lit*. wing): passage along-side the nave, choir, or transept of a church, or the main body of some other building, separated from it by columns, piers, or posts.

AMBULATORY (*lit*. walkway): aisle at the E end of a chancel, sometimes surrounding an apse and therefore semicircular or polygonal in plan.

AMORINI: *see* Putto.

ANGLE ROLL: roll moulding in the angle between two planes, e.g. between the orders of an arch.

ANNULET (*lit*. ring): shaft-ring (*see* Shaft).

ANSE DE PANIER (*lit.* basket handle): basket arch (*see* Arch).

ANTAE: flat pilasters with capitals different from the order they accompany, placed at the ends of the short projecting walls of a portico or of a colonnade which is then called *In Antis*.

ANTEFIXAE: ornaments projecting at regular intervals above a classical cornice, originally to conceal the ends of roof tiles.

ANTEPENDIUM: *see* Frontal.

ANTHEMION (*lit.* honeysuckle): classical ornament like a honeysuckle flower (*see* fig. 1).

Fig. 1. Anthemion and Palmette Frieze

APRON: raised panel below a window-sill, sometimes shaped and decorated.

A.P.S.D.: Architectural Publications Society Dictionary.

APSE: semicircular (i.e. apsidal) extension of an apartment: *see also* Exedra. A term first used of the magistrate's end of a Roman basilica, and thence especially of the vaulted semicircular or polygonal end of a chancel or a chapel.

ARABESQUE: type of painted or carved surface decoration consisting of flowing lines and intertwined foliage scrolls etc., generally based on geometrical patterns. Cf. Grotesque.

ARCADE: (1) series of arches supported by piers or columns. *Blind Arcade:* the same applied to the surface of a wall. *Wall Arcade:* in medieval churches, a blind arcade forming a dado below

windows. (2) a covered shopping street.

ARCH: for the various forms *see* fig. 2. The term *Basket Arch* refers to a basket handle and is sometimes applied to a three-centred or depressed arch as well as to the type with a flat middle. A *Transverse Arch* runs across the main axis of an interior space. The term is used especially for the arches between the compartments of tunnel- or groin-vaulting. *Diaphragm Arch:* transverse arch with solid spandrels spanning an otherwise wooden-roofed interior. *Chancel Arch:* w opening from the chancel into the nave. *Relieving* (or *Discharging*) *Arch:* incorporated in a wall, to carry some of its weight, some way above an opening. *Strainer Arch:* inserted across an opening to resist any inward pressure of the side members. *Triumphal Arch:* Imperial Roman monument whose elevation supplied a motif for many later classical compositions.

ARCHITRAVE: (1) formalized lintel, the lowest member of the classical entablature (*see* Orders, fig. 17); (2) moulded frame of a door or window (often borrowing the profile of an architrave in the strict sense). Also *Lugged Architrave*, where the top is prolonged into lugs (*lit.* ears) at the sides; *Shouldered*, where the frame rises vertically at the top angles and returns horizontally at the sides forming shoulders (*see* fig. 3).

ARCHIVOLT: architrave moulding when it follows the line of an arch.

ARCUATED: dependent structurally on the use of arches or the arch principle; cf. Trabeated.

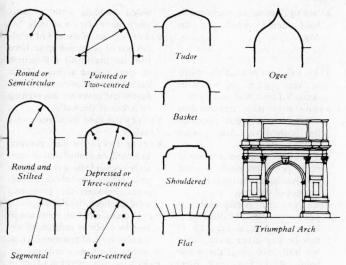

Round or Semicircular

Pointed or Two-centred

Tudor

Ogee

Round and Stilted

Depressed or Three-centred

Basket

Shouldered

Segmental

Four-centred

Flat

Triumphal Arch

Fig. 2. Arch

ARRIS (*lit.* stop): sharp edge at the meeting of two surfaces.

ASHLAR: masonry of large blocks wrought to even faces and square edges.

ASTRAGAL (*lit.* knuckle): moulding of semicircular section often with bead-and-reel enrichment.

ASTYLAR: term used to describe an elevation that has no columns or similar vertical features.

ATLANTES (*lit.* Atlas figures, from the god Atlas carrying the globe):

male counterparts of caryatids (q.v.), often in a more demonstrative attitude of support.

ATRIUM: inner court of a Roman house; also open court in front of a church.

ATTACHED: *see* Engaged Column.

ATTIC: (1) small top storey, especially within a sloping roof; (2) in classical architecture, a storey above the main entablature of the façade, as in a triumphal arch (*see* fig. 2).

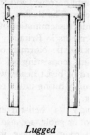

Lugged

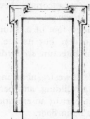

Shouldered

Fig. 3. Architrave

AUMBRY: recess or cupboard to hold sacred vessels for the Mass.

BAILEY: area around the motte or keep (qq.v.) of a castle, defended by a wall and ditch.

BALDACCHINO: free-standing canopy over an altar supported by columns. Also called *Ciborium* (q.v.).

BALLFLOWER: globular flower of three petals enclosing a small ball. A decoration used in the first quarter of the C14.

BALUSTER (*lit.* pomegranate): a pillar or pedestal of bellied form. *Balusters:* vertical supports of this or any other form, for a handrail or coping, the whole being called a *Balustrade*. *Blind Balustrade:* the same with a wall behind.

BARBICAN: outwork defending the entrance to a castle.

BARGEBOARDS: corruption of vergeboards. Boards, often carved or fretted, fixed beneath the eaves of a gable to cover and protect the rafters.

BARROW: burial mound; *see* Bell, Bowl, Disc, Long, and Pond Barrow.

BARTIZAN (*lit.* battlement): corbelled turret, square or round, frequently at a corner, hence *Corner Bartizan.*

BASE: moulded foot of a column or other order. For its use in classical architecture *see* Orders (fig. 17).

BASEMENT: lowest, subordinate storey of a building, and hence the lowest part of an elevation, below the main floor.

BASILICA (*lit.* royal building): a Roman public hall; hence an aisled building with a clerestory, most often a church.

BASTION: one of a series of semi-circular or polygonal projections from the main wall of a fortress or city, placed at intervals in such a manner as to enable the garrison to cover the intervening stretches of the wall.

BATTER: inward inclination of a wall.

BATTLEMENT: fortified parapet, indented or crenellated so that archers could shoot through the indentations (crenels or embrasures) between the projecting solid portions (merlons).

BAYS: divisions of an elevation or interior space as defined by any regular vertical features such as arches, columns, windows, etc.

BAY-WINDOW: window of one or more storeys projecting from the face of a building at ground level, and either rectangular or polygonal on plan. A *Canted Bay-window* has a straight front and angled sides. A *Bow Window* is curved. An *Oriel Window* projects on corbels or brackets and does not start from the ground.

BEAKER FOLK: late Neolithic settlers from western Europe named after a distinctive type of pottery vessel found in their funerary monuments (often round barrows) and their settlements. The Beaker period saw a wider dissemination of metal implements in Britain.

BEAKHEAD: Norman ornamental motif consisting of a row of bird or beast heads with beaks, usually biting into a roll moulding.

BELFRY: (1) bell-turret set on a roof or gable (*see also* Bellcote); (2) room or stage in a tower where bells are hung; (3) bell-tower in a general sense.

BELGAE: Iron Age tribes living in north-eastern Gaul, from which settlers came into Britain between 100 and 55 B.C. and later. These immigrants may not have been numerous, but their impact on material culture in southern Britain was marked.

BELL BARROW: early Bronze Age round barrow in which the mound is separated from its encircling ditch by a flat platform or berm (q.v.).

BELL CAPITAL: see fig. 7.

BELLCOTE: belfry as (1) above, sometimes with the character of a small house for the bell(s).

BERM: level area separating ditch from bank on a hill-fort or barrow.

BILLET (lit. log or block) FRIEZE: Norman ornament consisting of

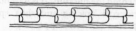

Fig. 4. Billet Frieze

small half-cylindrical or rect-angular blocks placed at regular intervals (see fig. 4).

BIVALLATE: (of a hill-fort) defended by two concentric banks and ditches.

BLIND: see Arcade, Balustrade, Portico.

BLOCK CAPITAL: see fig. 7.

BLOCKED: term applied to columns etc. that are interrupted by regular projecting blocks, e.g. the sides of a Gibbs surround (see fig. 11).

BLOCKING COURSE: plain course of stones, or equivalent, on top of a cornice and crowning the wall.

BOLECTION MOULDING: convex

moulding covering the joint between two different planes and overlapping the higher as well as the lower one, used especially in the late C17 and early C18.

BOND: in brickwork, the pattern of long sides (stretchers) and short ends (headers) produced on

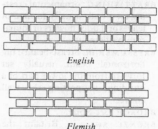

English

Flemish

Fig. 5. Bond

the face of a wall by laying bricks in a particular way. For the two most common bonds see fig. 5.

BOSS: knob or projection usually placed at the intersection of ribs in a vault.

BOW WINDOW: see Bay-window.

BOWL BARROW: round barrow surrounded by a quarry ditch. Introduced in late Neolithic times, the form continued until the Saxon period.

BOX FRAME: (1) timber-framed construction in which vertical and horizontal wall members support the roof. (2) in modern architecture, a box-like form of concrete construction where the loads are taken on cross walls, suitable only for buildings consisting of repetitive small cells. Also called Cross-wall Construction.

BOX PEW: pew enclosed by a high wooden back and ends, the latter having doors.

BRACE: subsidiary timber set diagonally to strengthen a timber frame. It can be curved or straight. *See also* Roofs (3) and figs. 22–6.

BRACKET: small supporting piece of stone, etc., to carry a projecting horizontal member.

BRATTISHING: ornamental cresting on a wall, usually formed of leaves or Tudor flowers or miniature battlements.

BRESSUMER (*lit.* breast-beam): big horizontal beam, usually set forward from the lower part of a building, supporting the wall above.

BROACH: *see* Spire.

BRONZE AGE: in Britain, the period from *c.* 2000 to 600 B.C.

BUCRANIUM: ox skull used decoratively in classical friezes.

BULLSEYE WINDOW: small circular or oval window, e.g. in the tympanum of a pediment. Also called *Œil de Bœuf*.

BUTTRESS: vertical member projecting from a wall to stabilize it or to resist the lateral thrust of an arch, roof, or vault. For different types used at the corners of a building, especially a tower, *see* fig. 6. A *Flying Buttress* transmits the thrust to a heavy abutment by means of an arch or half-arch.

CABLE MOULDING: originally a Norman moulding, imitating the twisted strands of a rope. Also called *Rope Moulding*.

CAIRN: a mound of stones usually covering a burial.

CALEFACTORY: room in a monastery where a fire burned for the comfort of the monks. Also called *Warming Room*.

CAMBER: slight rise or upward curve in place of a horizontal line or plane.

CAMES: *see* Quarries.

CAMPANILE: free-standing belltower.

CANOPY: projection or hood usually over an altar, pulpit, niche, statue, etc.

CANTED: tilted, generally on a vertical axis to produce an obtuse angle on plan, e.g. of a canted bay-window.

CANTILEVER: horizontal projection (e.g. step, canopy) supported by a downward force behind the fulcrum. It is without external bracing and thus appears to be self-supporting.

CAPITAL: head or crowning feature of a column or pilaster; for classical types *see* Orders (fig. 17); for medieval types *see* fig. 7.

CARREL: (1) niche in a cloister where a monk could sit to work or read; (2) similar feature in open-plan offices and libraries.

CARTOUCHE: tablet with ornate frame, usually of elliptical shape and bearing a coat of arms or inscription.

Angle Buttresses   *Diagonal Buttresses*   *Setback Buttresses*   *Clasping Buttresses*

Fig. 6. Buttresses

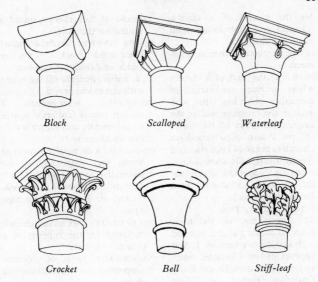

Block   Scalloped   Waterleaf

Crocket   Bell   Stiff-leaf

Fig. 7. Capitals

CARYATIDS (*lit.* daughters of the village of Caryae): female figures supporting an entablature, counterparts of Atlantes (q.v.).

CASEMATE: in military architecture, a vaulted chamber, with embrasures for defence, built into the thickness of the wall of a castle or fortress or projecting from it.

CASEMENT: (1) window hinged at the side; (2) in Gothic architecture, a concave moulding framing a window.

CASTELLATED: battlemented.

CAVETTO: concave moulding of quarter-round section.

CELURE OR CEILURE: panelled and adorned part of a wagon roof above the rood or the altar.

CENOTAPH (*lit.* empty tomb): funerary monument which is not a burying place.

CENTERING: wooden support for the building of an arch or vault, removed after completion.

CHAMBERED TOMB: Neolithic burial mound with a stone-built chamber and entrance passage covered by an earthen barrow or stone cairn.

CHAMFER (*lit.* corner-break): surface formed by cutting off a square edge, usually at an angle of forty-five degrees.

CHANCEL (*lit.* enclosure): that part of the E end of a church in which the main altar is placed. Except in cathedral and monastic churches, usually applied to the whole continuation of the nave E of the crossing.

CHANTRY CHAPEL: chapel, often attached to or inside a church, endowed for the celebration of masses for the soul of the founder or others.

CHEVET (*lit.* head): French term

for the E end of a church (chancel and ambulatory with radiating chapels).

CHEVRON: zigzag Norman ornament.

CHOIR: (1) the part of a church where services are sung; in monastic churches this can occupy the crossing and/or the easternmost bays of the nave; (2) the E arm of a cruciform church (a usage of long standing though liturgically anomalous).

CIBORIUM: canopied shrine for the reserved sacrament or a Baldacchino (q.v.).

CINQUEFOIL: see Foil.

CIST: stone-lined or slab-built grave. If below ground, covered with a protective barrow. It first appears in late Neolithic times and was also used in the Early Christian period in West Britain.

CLADDING: external covering or skin applied to a structure, especially framed buildings (q.v.), for aesthetic or protective purposes.

CLAPPER BRIDGE: bridge made of large slabs of stone, some making rough piers, with longer ones laid on top to make the roadway.

CLASP: see Industrialized Building.

CLASSIC: term for the moment of highest achievement of a style.

CLASSICAL: term for Greek and Roman architecture and any subsequent styles inspired by it.

CLERESTORY: upper storey of the nave walls of a church, pierced by windows. Also applied to high-level windows in domestic architecture.

CLUSTER BLOCK: multi-storey building in which individual

blocks of flats cluster round a central service core.

COADE STONE: artificial (cast) stone made from c. 1769 by Coade and Sealy in London.

COB: walling material of clay mixed with straw and gravel.

COFFERING: arrangement of sunken panels (coffers), square or polygonal, decorating a ceiling, vault, or arch.

COGGING: a decorative course of bricks laid diagonally as an alternative to dentilation (q.v.). Also called Dogtooth Brickwork.

COLLAR: see Roofs (3) and figs. 23–6.

COLLEGIATE CHURCH: church endowed for the support of a college of priests.

COLONNADE: range of columns supporting an entablature or arches.

COLONNETTE: in medieval architecture, a small column or shaft.

COLOSSAL ORDER: see Order.

COLUMN: in classical architecture, an upright structural member of round section with a shaft, a capital, and usually a base. See Orders (fig. 17).

COLUMN FIGURE: in medieval architecture, carved figure attached to a column or shaft flanking a doorway.

COMPOSITE: see Orders.

COMPOUND PIER: a pier consisting of a bundle of shafts (q.v.), or of a solid core surrounded by attached or detached shafts.

CONSOLE: ornamental bracket of compound curved outline (see fig. 8).

COPING (lit. capping): course of stones, or equivalent, on top of a wall.

CORBEL: block of stone projecting from a wall, supporting some

Fig. 8. Consoles

feature on its horizontal top surface. *Corbel Course:* continuous projecting course of stones or bricks fulfilling the same function. *Corbel Table:* series of corbels to carry a parapet or a wall-plate; for the latter *see* Roofs (3) and figs. 22–5. *Corbelling:* brick or masonry courses built out beyond one another like a series of corbels to support a chimneystack, window, etc.

CORINTHIAN: *see* Orders (fig. 17).

CORNICE: (1) moulded ledge, projecting along the top of a building or feature, especially as the highest member of the classical entablature (*see* Orders, fig. 17); (2) decorative moulding in the angle between wall and ceiling.

CORPS-DE-LOGIS: French term for the main building(s) as distinct from the wings or pavilions.

COTTAGE ORNÉ: an artfully rustic building usually of asymmetrical plan. A product of the late C18 and early C19 picturesque.

COUNTERSCARP BANK: small bank on the downhill or outer side of a hill-fort ditch.

COUR D'HONNEUR: entrance court before a house in the French manner, usually with wings enclosing the sides and a screen wall or low range of buildings across the front.

COURSE: continuous layer of stones etc. in a wall.

COVE: a concave moulding on a large scale, e.g. in a *Coved Ceiling*, which has a pronounced cove joining the walls to a flat central area.

CRADLE ROOF: *see* Wagon Roof.

CREDENCE: in a church or chapel, a side table, or often a recess, for the sacramental elements before consecration.

CRENELLATION: *see* Battlement.

CREST, CRESTING: ornamental finish along the top of a screen, etc.

CRINKLE-CRANKLE WALL: wall undulating in a series of serpentine curves.

CROCKETS (*lit.* hooks), CROCKETING: in Gothic architecture, leafy knobs on the edges of any sloping feature. *Crocket Capital: see* Capital (fig. 7).

CROMLECH: word of Celtic origin still occasionally used of single free-standing stones ascribed to the Neolithic or Bronze Age.

CROSSING: in a church, central space at the junction of the nave, chancel, and transepts. *Crossing Tower:* tower above a crossing.

CROSS-WINDOWS: windows with one mullion and one transom (qq.v.)

CROWSTEPS: squared stones set like steps e.g. on a gable or gateway; *see* Gable (fig. 10).

CRUCKS (*lit.* crooked): pairs of inclined timbers, usually curved, which are set at bay-length intervals in a building and support the timbers of the roof (q.v.). The individual cruck is known as a blade. *Base:* blades which rise from ground level to a tie- or collar-beam upon which the roof truss is carried; in timber buildings they support the walls. *Full:* blades rising from ground level to the apex of a building; they serve as the main members of a roof truss and in timber buildings they support the walls. *Jointed:* blades formed from more than one timber; the lower member normally rises from ground level and acts as a wall-post; it is usually elbowed at wall-plate level and jointed just above. *Middle:* blades rising from half-way up the walls to a tie- or collar-beam upon which the roof truss is supported. *Raised:* blades rising from half-way up the walls to the apex. *Upper:* blades supported on a tie-beam and rising to the apex.

CRYPT: underground or half-underground room usually below the E end of a church. *Ring Crypt:* early medieval semi-circular or polygonal corridor crypt surrounding the apse of a church, often associated with chambers for relics.

CUPOLA (*lit.* dome): especially a small dome on a circular or polygonal base crowning a larger dome, roof, or turret.

CURTAIN WALL: (1) connecting wall between the towers of a castle; (2) in modern building, a non-load-bearing external wall composed of repeating modular elements applied to a steel-framed structure.

CURVILINEAR: *see* Tracery.

CUSP: projecting point formed by the foils within the divisions of Gothic tracery, also used as a decorative edging to the soffits of the Gothic arches of tomb recesses, sedilia, etc.

CYCLOPEAN MASONRY: built with large irregular polygonal stones, but smooth and finely jointed.

CYMA RECTA and CYMA REVERSA: *see* Ogee.

DADO: the finishing of the lower part of an interior wall (sometimes used to support an applied order). *Dado Rail:* the moulding along the top of the dado.

DAGGER: *see* Tracery.

DAIS: raised platform at one end of a room.

DEC (DECORATED): historical division of English Gothic architecture covering the period from *c.* 1290 to *c.* 1350. The name is derived from the type of window tracery used during the period (*see also* Tracery).

DEMI-COLUMNS: engaged columns (q.v.) only half of whose circumference projects from the wall. Also called *Half-Columns*.

DENTIL: small square block used in series in classical cornices, rarely in Doric. In brickwork *dentilation* is produced by the projection of alternating headers or blocks along cornices or string courses.

DIAPER (*lit.* figured cloth): repetitive surface decoration of lozenges or squares either flat or in relief. Achieved in brickwork with bricks of two colours.

DIOCLETIAN WINDOW: semi-circular window with two mullions, so-called because of its use in the Baths of Diocletian in Rome. Also called a *Thermae Window*.

DISC BARROW: Bronze Age round barrow with an inconspicuous central mound surrounded by a bank and ditch.

DISTYLE: having two columns.

DOGTOOTH: typical E.E. decoration of a moulding, consisting of

Fig. 9. Dogtooth

a series of squares, their centres raised like pyramids and their edges indented (*see* fig. 9). *See also* Cogging.

DOME: vault of even curvature erected on a circular base. The section can be segmental (e.g. saucer dome), semicircular, pointed, or bulbous (onion dome).

DONJON: *see* Keep.

DORIC: *see* Orders (fig. 17).

DORMER WINDOW: window standing up vertically from the slope of a roof and lighting a room within it. *Dormer Head:* gable above this window, often formed as a pediment.

DORTER: dormitory; sleeping quarters of a monastery.

DOUBLE PILE: *see* Pile.

DRAGON BEAM: *see* Jetty.

DRESSINGS: smoothly worked stones, used e.g. for quoins or string courses, projecting from the wall and sometimes of different material, colour, or texture.

DRIPSTONE: moulded stone projecting from a wall to protect the lower parts from water; *see also* Hoodmould.

DRUM: (1) circular or polygonal wall supporting a dome or cupola; (2) one of the stones forming the shaft of a column.

DRYSTONE: stone construction without mortar.

DUTCH GABLE: *see* Gable (fig. 10).

EASTER SEPULCHRE: recess, usually in the wall of a chancel, with a tomb-chest to receive an effigy of Christ for Easter celebrations.

EAVES: overhanging edge of a roof; hence *Eaves Cornice* in this position.

ECHINUS (*lit.* sea-urchin): ovolo moulding (q.v.) below the abacus of a Greek Doric capital; *see* Orders (fig. 17).

E.E. (EARLY ENGLISH): historical division of English Gothic architecture covering the period *c.* 1190–1250.

ELEVATION: (1) any side of a building; (2) in a drawing, the same or any part of it, accurately represented in two dimensions.

EMBATTLED: furnished with battlements.

EMBRASURE (*lit.* splay): small splayed opening in the wall or battlement of a fortified building.

ENCAUSTIC TILES: glazed and decorated earthenware tiles used for paving.

EN DELIT (*lit.* in error): term used in Gothic architecture to describe stone shafts whose grain runs vertically instead of horizontally, against normal building practice.

ENGAGED COLUMN: one that is partly merged into a wall or pier. Also called *Attached Column*.

ENGINEERING BRICKS: dense bricks of uniform size, high crushing strength, and low porosity. Originally used mostly for railway viaducts etc.

ENTABLATURE: in classical architecture, collective name for the three horizontal members (architrave, frieze, and cornice) above a column; *see* Orders (fig. 17).

ENTASIS : very slight convex deviation from a straight line; used on classical columns and sometimes on spires to prevent an optical illusion of concavity.

ENTRESOL : mezzanine storey within or above the ground storey.

EPITAPH (*lit.* on a tomb): inscription in that position.

ESCUTCHEON : shield for armorial bearings.

EXEDRA : apsidal end of an apartment; *see* Apse.

EXTRADOS : outer curved face of an arch or vault.

EXTRUDED CORNER : right-angled (or circular) projection from the inner angle of a building with advancing wings, usually in C16 or C17 plans.

EYECATCHER : decorative building (often a sham ruin) usually on an eminence to terminate a park or garden layout.

FASCIA : plain horizontal band, e.g. in an architrave (q.v.) or on a shopfront.

FENESTRATION : the arrangement of windows in a building.

FERETORY : (1) place behind the high altar where the chief shrine of a church is kept; (2) wooden or metal container for relics.

FESTOON : ornament, usually in high or low relief, in the form of a garland of flowers and/or fruit, hung up at both ends; *see also* Swag.

FIBREGLASS (or glass-reinforced polyester (GRP)): synthetic resin reinforced with glass fibre, formed in moulds, often simulating the outward appearance of traditional materials. GRC (glass-reinforced concrete) is also formed in moulds and used for components (cladding etc.) in industrialized building.

FIELDED : *see* Raised and Fielded.

FILLET : in medieval architecture, a narrow flat band running down a shaft or along a roll moulding. In classical architecture it separates larger curved mouldings in cornices or bases.

FINIAL : decorative topmost feature, e.g. above a gable, spire, or cupola.

FLAMBOYANT : properly the latest phase of French Gothic architecture where the window tracery takes on undulating lines, based on the use of flowing curves.

FLÈCHE (*lit.* arrow): slender spire on the centre of a roof. Also called *Spirelet*.

FLEUR-DE-LYS : in heraldry, a formalized lily, as in the royal arms of France.

FLEURON : decorative carved flower or leaf.

FLOWING : *see* Tracery (Curvilinear).

FLUSHWORK : flint used decoratively in conjunction with dressed stone so as to form patterns: tracery, initials, etc.

FLUTING : series of concave grooves, their common edges sharp (arris) or blunt (fillet).

FOIL (*lit.* leaf): lobe formed by the cusping of a circular or other shape in tracery. *Trefoil* (three), *quatrefoil* (four), *cinquefoil* (five), and *multifoil* express the number of lobes in a shape. *See also* Tracery.

FOLIATED : decorated, especially carved, with leaves.

FORMWORK : commonly called shuttering; the temporary frame of braced timber or metal into which wet concrete is poured. The texture of the framework material depends on the imprint required.

FRAMED BUILDING: where the structure is carried by the framework – e.g. of steel, reinforced concrete, timber – instead of by load-bearing walls.

FRATER: *see* Refectory.

FREESTONE: stone that is cut, or can be cut, in all directions, usually fine-grained sandstone or limestone.

FRESCO: *al fresco:* painting executed on wet plaster. *Fresco secco:* painting executed on dry plaster, more common in Britain.

FRIEZE: horizontal band of ornament, especially the middle member of the classical entablature; *see* Orders (fig. 17). *Pulvinated Frieze* (*lit.* cushioned): frieze of bold convex profile.

FRONTAL: covering for the front of an altar. Also called *Antependium*.

FRONTISPIECE: in C16 and C17 buildings the central feature of doorway and windows above it linked in one composition.

GABLE: (1) area of wall, often triangular, at the end of a double-pitch roof; *Dutch Gable*, characteristic of *c.* 1580–1680: *Shaped Gable*, characteristic of *c.* 1620–80 (*see* fig. 10). *Gablet:* small gable. *See also* Roofs.

GADROONING: ribbed ornament, e.g. on the lid or base of an urn, flowing into a lobed edge.

GALILEE: chapel or vestibule usually at the W end of a church enclosing the porch.

GALLERY: balcony or passage, but with certain special meanings, e.g. (1) upper storey above the aisle of a church, looking through arches to the nave; also called tribune and often erroneously triforium; (2) balcony or mezzanine, often with seats, overlooking the main interior space of a building; (3) external walkway, often projecting from a wall.

GALLERY GRAVE: chambered tomb (q.v.) in which there is a little or no differentiation between the entrance passage and the actual burial chamber(s).

GALLETING: decorative use of small stones in a mortar course.

GARDEROBE (*lit.* wardrobe): medieval privy.

GARGOYLE: water spout projecting from the parapet of a wall or tower, often carved into human or animal shape.

GAUGED BRICKWORK: soft brick sawn roughly, then rubbed to a smooth, precise (gauged) surface with a stone or another brick. Mostly used for door or window openings. Also called *Rubbed Brickwork*.

GAZEBO (jocular Latin, 'I shall gaze'): lookout tower or raised

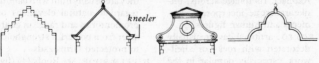

Crowstep   Kneelered   Flemish or Dutch   Shaped

Fig. 10. Gables

summer house usually in a park or garden.

GEOMETRIC: historical division of English Gothic architecture covering the period *c.* 1250–90. *See also* Tracery. For another meaning, *see* Stair.

GIANT ORDER: *see* Order.

GIBBS SURROUND: C18 treatment of a door or window surround,

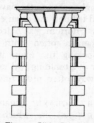

Fig. 11. Gibbs Surround

seen particularly in the work of James Gibbs (1682–1754) (*see* fig. 11).

GOTHIC: the period of medieval architecture characterized by the use of the pointed arch. For its subdivisions *see* E.E., Geometric, Dec, Perp, Flamboyant.

GRANGE (monastic): farm owned and run by members of a religious order.

GRC and GRP: *see* Fibreglass.

GROIN: sharp edge at the meeting of two cells of a cross-vault; *see* Vault (fig. 32).

GROTESQUE (*lit.* grotto-esque): classical wall decoration in paint or stucco adopted from Roman examples, particularly by Raphael. Its foliage scrolls, unlike arabesque, incorporate ornaments and human figures.

GROTTO: artificial cavern usually decorated with rock- or shell-work, especially popular in the late C17 and C18.

GUILLOCHE: running classical ornament of interlaced bands forming a plait (*see* fig. 12).

Fig. 12. Guilloche

GUNLOOP: opening for a firearm.

GUTTAE: *see* Orders (fig. 17).

Hagioscope: *see* Squint.

HALF-TIMBERING: archaic term for Timber-framing (q.v.). Sometimes used for non-structural decorative timberwork, e.g. in gables etc. of the late C19.

HALL CHURCH: medieval or Gothic Revival church whose nave and aisles are of equal height or approximately so.

HAMMERBEAM: *see* Roofs (fig. 26).

HEADER: *see* Bond.

HENGE: ritual earthwork with a surrounding bank and ditch, the bank being on the outer side.

HERM (*lit.* the god Hermes): male head or bust on a pedestal.

HERRINGBONE WORK: masonry or brickwork in zigzag courses.

HEXASTYLE: *see* Portico.

HILL-FORT: later Bronze Age and Iron Age earthwork enclosed by a ditch and bank system; in the later part of the period the defences multiplied in size and complexity. Varying from about an acre to over fifty acres in area, they are usually built with careful regard to natural elevations or promontories and range in character from powerful strongholds to protected farmsteads.

HIPPED ROOF: *see* Roofs (1) (fig. 21).

HOODMOULD: projecting moulding above an arch or lintel to throw off water. When the moulding is horizontal it is often called a *Label*. *See also* Label Stop.

HUSK GARLAND: festoon of nutshells diminishing towards the ends.

HYPOCAUST (*lit.* under-burning): Roman underfloor heating system. The floor is supported on pillars and the space thus formed is connected to a flue.

ICONOGRAPHY: description of the subject matter of works of the visual arts.

IMPOST (*lit.* imposition): horizontal moulding at the springing of an arch.

IMPOST BLOCK: block with splayed sides between abacus and capital.

IN ANTIS: *see* Antae.

INDENT: (1) shape chiselled out of a stone to match and receive a brass; (2) in restoration, a section of new stone inserted as a patch into older work.

INDUSTRIALIZED BUILDING (system building): the use of a system of manufactured units assembled on site. One of the most popular is the CLASP (Consortium Local Authorities Special Programme) system of light steel framing suitable for schools etc.

INGLENOOK (*lit.* fire-corner): recess for a hearth with provision for seating.

INTARSIA: *see* Marquetry.

INTERCOLUMNIATION: interval between columns.

INTRADOS: *see* Soffit.

IONIC: *see* Orders (fig. 17).

IRON AGE: in Britain, the period from *c.* 600 B.C. to the coming of the Romans. The term is also used for those un-Romanized native communities which survived until the Saxon incursions especially beyond the Roman frontiers.

JAMB (*lit.* leg): one of the straight sides of an opening.

JETTY: in a timber-framed building, the projection of an upper storey beyond the storey below made by the beams and joists of the lower storey oversailing the external wall. On their outer ends is placed the sill of the walling for the storey above. Buildings can be jettied on several sides, in which case a *Dragon Beam* is set diagonally at the corner to carry the joists to either side.

JOGGLE: mason's term for joining two stones to prevent them slipping or sliding by means of a notch in one and a corresponding projection in the other.

KEEL MOULDING: moulding whose outline is in section like that of the keel of a ship (fig. 13).

Fig. 13. Keel Moulding

KEEP: principal tower of a castle. Also called *Donjon*.

KEY PATTERN: *see* fig. 14.

KEYSTONE: middle and topmost stone in an arch or vault.

Fig. 14. Key Pattern

KINGPOST: *see* Roofs (3) and fig. 22.

KNEELER: horizontal projection at the base of a gable. *See* Gable (fig. 10).

L ABEL: *see* Hoodmould. *Label Stop:* ornamental boss at the end of a hoodmould.

LACED WINDOWS: windows pulled visually together by strips of brickwork, usually of a different colour, which continue vertically the lines of the vertical parts of the window surround. Typical of *c.* 1720.

LACING COURSE: one or more bricks serving as horizontal reinforcement to flint, cobble, etc., walls.

LADY CHAPEL: chapel dedicated to the Virgin Mary (Our Lady).

LANCET WINDOW: slender pointed-arched window.

LANTERN: small circular or polygonal turret with windows all round crowning a roof or a dome.

LANTERN CROSS: churchyard cross with lantern-shaped top usually with sculptured representations on the sides of the top.

LAVATORIUM: in a monastery, a washing place adjacent to the refectory.

LEAN-TO: *see* Roofs (1).

LESENE (*lit.* a mean thing): pilaster without base or capital. Also called *Pilaster Strip.*

LIERNE: *see* Vault (fig. 33).

LIGHT: compartment of a window.

LINENFOLD: Tudor panelling where each panel is ornamented with a conventional representation of a piece of linen laid in vertical folds.

LINTEL: horizontal beam or stone bridging an opening.

LOGGIA: gallery open along one side of a building, usually arcaded or colonnaded. It may be a separate structure, usually in a garden.

LONG BARROW: unchambered Neolithic communal burial mound, often wedge-shaped in plan, with the burial and occasional other structures massed at the broader end, from which the mound itself tapers in height; quarry ditches flank the mound.

LONG-AND-SHORT WORK: quoins consisting of stones placed with the long sides alternately upright and horizontal, especially in Saxon building.

LOUVRE: (1) opening, often with lantern over, in the roof of a building to let the smoke from a central hearth escape; (2) one of a series of overlapping boards or panes of glass placed in a window to allow ventilation but keep the rain out.

LOWER PALAEOLITHIC: *see* Palaeolithic.

LOZENGE: diamond shape.

LUCARNE (*lit.* dormer): small window in a roof or spire.

LUGGED: *see* Architrave.

LUNETTE (*lit.* half or crescent moon): (1) semicircular window; (2) semicircular or crescent-shaped surface.

LYCHGATE (*lit.* corpse-gate): roofed wooden gateway at the entrance to a churchyard for the reception of a coffin.

LYNCHET: long terraced strip of soil accumulating on the downward side of prehistoric and medieval fields due to soil creep from continuous ploughing along the contours.

MACHICOLATIONS (*lit.* mashing devices): in medieval military architecture, a series of openings under a projecting parapet between the corbels that support it, through which missiles can be dropped.

MAJOLICA: ornamented glazed earthenware.

MANSARD: *see* Roofs (1) (fig. 21).

MARQUETRY: inlay in various woods. Also called *Intarsia*.

MATHEMATICAL TILES: facing tiles with one face moulded to look like a header or stretcher, most often hung on laths applied to timber-framed walls to make them appear brick-built.

MAUSOLEUM: monumental tomb, so named after that of Mausolus, king of Caria, at Halicarnassus.

MEGALITHIC (*lit.* of large stones): archaeological term referring to the use of such stones, singly or together.

MEGALITHIC TOMB: massive stone-built Neolithic burial chamber covered by an earth or stone mound.

MERLON: *see* Battlement.

MESOLITHIC: 'Middle Stone' Age; the post-glacial period of hunting and fishing communities dating in Britain from *c.* 8000 B.C. to the arrival of the Neolithic (q.v.) communities, with whom they must have considerably overlapped in many areas.

METOPES: spaces between the triglyphs in a Doric frieze; *see* Orders (fig. 17).

MEZZANINE: (1) low storey be-

tween two higher ones; (2) low upper storey within the height of a high one, not extending over its whole area. *See also* Entresol.

MISERERE: *see* Misericord.

MISERICORD (*lit.* mercy): shelf placed on the underside of a hinged choir stall seat which, when turned up, supported the occupant during long periods of standing. Also called *Miserere*.

MODILLIONS: small consoles (q.v.) at regular intervals along the underside of the cornice of the Corinthian or Composite orders.

MODULE: in industrialized building (q.v.), a predetermined standard size for co-ordinating the dimensions of components of a building with the spaces into which they have to fit.

MOTTE: steep mound forming the main feature of C11 and C12 castles.

MOTTE-AND-BAILEY: post-Roman and Norman defence system consisting of an earthen mound (motte) topped with a wooden tower within a bailey, with enclosure ditch and palisade, and with the rare addition of an internal bank.

MOUCHETTE: *see* Tracery (fig. 31).

MOULDING: ornament of continuous section; *see* e.g. Cavetto, Ogee, Ovolo, Roll.

MULLION: vertical member between the lights in a window opening.

MULTI-STOREY: modern term denoting five or more storeys. *See* Cluster, Slab, and Point Blocks.

MULTIVALLATE: (of a hill-fort) defended by three or more concentric banks and ditches.

MUNTIN: vertical part in the framing of a door, screen, panelling, etc., butting into or stopped by the horizontal rails.

NAILHEAD MOULDING: E.E. ornamental motif consisting of small pyramids regularly repeated (see fig. 15).

Fig. 15. Nailhead Moulding

NARTHEX: enclosed vestibule or covered porch at the main entrance to a church.

NAVE: the middle vessel of the limb of a church w of the crossing or chancel and flanked by the aisles.

NECESSARIUM: see Reredorter.

NEOLITHIC: term applied to the New Stone Age, dating in Britain from the appearance of the first settled farming communities from the continent c. 4000–3500 B.C. until the beginning of the Bronze Age. See also Mesolithic.

NEWEL: central post in a circular or winding staircase; also the principal post where a flight of stairs meets a landing. See Stair (fig. 28).

NICHE (lit. shell): vertical recess in a wall, sometimes for a statue.

NIGHT STAIR: stair by which monks entered the transept of their church from their dormi-

tory to celebrate night services.

NOGGING: see Timber-framing.

NOOK-SHAFT: shaft set in the angle of a pier or respond or wall, or the angle of the jamb of a window or doorway.

NORMAN: see Romanesque.

NOSING: projection of the tread of a step. A Bottle Nosing is half-round in section.

NUTMEG MOULDING: consisting of a chain of tiny triangles placed obliquely.

OBELISK: lofty pillar of square section tapering at the top and ending pyramidally.

ŒIL DE BŒUF: see Bullseye Window.

OGEE: double curve, bending first one way and then the other. Applied to mouldings, also called Cyma Recta. A reverse ogee moulding with a double curve also called Cyma Reversa (see fig. 16). Ogee or Ogival Arch: see Arch.

ORATORY: (1) small private chapel in a church or a house; (2) church of the Oratorian Order.

ORDER: (1) upright structural member formally related to others, e.g. in classical architecture a column, pilaster, or anta; (2) especially in medieval architecture, one of a series of recessed arches and jambs forming a splayed opening. Giant or Colossal Order: classical order

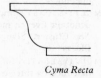

Cyma Recta

Cyma Reversa

Fig. 16. Ogee Mouldings

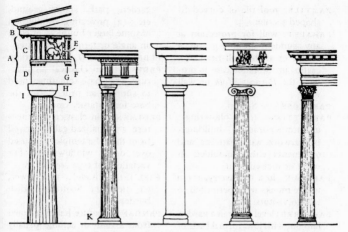

Fig. 17. Orders (Greek Doric, Roman Doric, Tuscan Doric, Ionic, Corinthian) A Entablature; B Cornice; C Frieze; D Architrave; E Metope; F Triglyph; G Guttae; H Abacus; I Capital; J Echinus; K Base

whose height is that of two or more storeys of a building.

ORDERS: in classical architecture, the differently formalized versions of the basic post-and-lintel (column and entablature) structure, each having its own rules for design and proportion. For examples of the main types *see* fig. 17. In the *Composite*, the capital combines Ionic volutes with Corinthian foliage. *Superimposed Orders:* term for the use of Orders on successive levels, usually in the upward sequence of Doric, Ionic, Corinthian.

ORIEL: *see* Bay-window.

OVERDOOR: *see* Sopraporta.

OVERHANG: *see* Jetty.

OVERSAILING COURSES: *see* Corbel (Corbelling).

OVERTHROW: decorative fixed arch between two gatepiers or above a wrought-iron gate.

OVOLO MOULDING: wide convex moulding.

PALAEOLITHIC: 'Old Stone' Age; the first period of human culture, commencing in the Ice Age and immediately prior to the Mesolithic; the Lower Palaeolithic is the older phase, the Upper Palaeolithic the later.

PALIMPSEST(*lit.* erased work): re-use of a surface. (1) of a brass: where a metal plate has been re-used by turning over and engraving on the back; (2) of a wall painting: where one overlaps and partly obscures an earlier one.

PALLADIAN: architecture following the examples and principles of Andrea Palladio (1508–80).

PALMETTE: classical ornament like a symmetrical palm shoot; for illustration *see* fig. 1.

PANELLING: wooden lining to interior walls, made up of vertical members (muntins q.v.) and horizontals (rails) framing panels (*see* linenfold; raised and fielded). Also called *Wainscot*.

PANTILE: roof tile of curved S-shaped section.

PARAPET: wall for protection at any sudden drop, e.g. on a bridge or at the wall-head of a castle; in the latter case it protects the *Parapet Walk* or wall walk.

PARCLOSE: *see* Screen.

PARGETTING (*lit.* plastering): in timber-framed buildings, plasterwork with patterns and ornaments either moulded in relief or incised on it.

PARLOUR: in a monastery, room where monks were permitted to talk to visitors.

PARTERRE: level space in a garden laid out with low, formal beds of plants.

PATERA (*lit.* plate): round or oval ornament in shallow relief, especially in classical architecture.

PAVILION: (1) ornamental building for occasional use in a garden, park, sports ground, etc.; (2) projecting subdivision of some larger building, often at an angle or terminating wings.

PEBBLEDASHING: *see* Rendering.

PEDESTAL: in classical architecture, a tall base sometimes used to support an order; also, the base for a statue, vase, etc.

PEDIMENT: in classical architecture, a formalized gable derived from that of a temple, also used over doors, windows, etc. For variations of type *see* fig. 18.

PEEL (*lit.* palisade): stone tower, e.g. near the Scottish–English border.

PENDANT: feature hanging down from a vault or ceiling, usually ending in a boss.

PENDENTIVE: spandrel formed as part of a hemisphere between arches meeting at an angle, supporting a drum or dome (*see* fig. 19).

PENTHOUSE: subsidiary structure

Broken

Open

Segmental

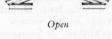

Scrolled

Fig. 18. Pediments

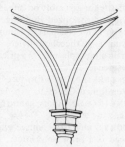

Fig. 19. Pendentive

with a lean-to roof; in modern architecture, a separately roofed structure on top of a multi-storey block.

PERISTYLE: in classical architecture, a range of columns all round a building, e.g. a temple, or an interior space, e.g. a courtyard.

PERP (PERPENDICULAR): historical division of English Gothic architecture covering the period from c. 1335–50 to c. 1530. The name is derived from the upright tracery panels used during the period (see Tracery).

PERRON: see Stair.

PIANO NOBILE: principal floor, usually with a ground floor or basement underneath and a lesser storey overhead.

PIAZZA: open space surrounded by buildings; in the C17 and C18 used erroneously to mean an arcaded ground floor, especially adjoining or around an open space.

PIER: strong, solid support, usually round or square in section. See also Compound Pier.

PIETRA DURA: ornamental or scenic inlay by means of thin slabs of stone.

PILASTER: representation of a classical column in flat relief against a wall. *Pilastrade:* series of pilasters, equivalent to a colonnade. *Pilaster Strip: see* Lesene.

PILE: row of rooms. The important use of the term is in *Double Pile,* describing a house that is two rows thick.

PILLAR: free-standing upright member of any section, not conforming to one of the Orders.

PILLAR PISCINA: free-standing piscina on a pillar.

PILOTIS: French term used in modern architecture for pillars or stilts that carry a building to first-floor level leaving the ground floor open.

PINNACLE: tapering finial, e.g. on a buttress or the corner of a tower, sometimes decorated with crockets.

PISCINA: basin for washing the communion or mass vessels, provided with a drain; generally set in or against the wall to the S of an altar.

PLAISANCE: summer house, pleasure house near a mansion.

PLINTH: projecting base beneath a wall or column, generally chamfered or moulded at the top.

PODIUM: continuous raised platform supporting a building. In modern architecture often a large block of two or three storeys beneath a multi-storey block covering a smaller area.

POINT BLOCK: high block of housing in which the flats fan out from a central core of lifts, staircases, etc.

POINTING: exposed mortar jointing of masonry or brickwork. The finished form is of various types, e.g. *Flush Pointing, Recessed Pointing.*

POND BARROW: rare Bronze Age barrow type consisting of a

circular depression, usually paved, and containing a number of cremation burials.

POPPYHEAD: carved ornament of leaves and flowers as a finial for the end of a bench or stall.

PORCH: covered projecting entrance to a building.

PORTAL FRAME: in modern architecture a basic form of construction in which a series of precast concrete beams, placed in pairs to form 'portals', support the walls and roof. The upper part of each beam is angled up to where they meet at the roof ridge.

PORTCULLIS: gate constructed to rise and fall in vertical grooves at the entry to a castle.

PORTICO: a porch, open on one side at least, and enclosed by a row of columns which also support the roof and frequently a pediment. When the front of it is on the same level as the front of the building it is described as a *Portico in Antis* (Antae q.v.). Porticoes are described by the number of frontal columns, e.g. Tetrastyle (four), Hexastyle (six). *Blind Portico:* the front features of a portico attached to a wall so that it is no longer a proper porch.

POSTERN: small gateway at the back of a building.

PRECAST CONCRETE: concrete components cast before being placed in position.

PREDELLA: (1) step or platform on which an altar stands; hence (2) in an altarpiece, the horizontal strip below the main representation, often used for a number of subsidiary representations in a row.

PREFABRICATION: manufacture of buildings or components

off-site for assembly on-site. *See also* Industrialized Building.

PRESBYTERY: (1) part of a church lying E of the choir where the main altar is placed; (2) a priest's residence.

PRESTRESSED CONCRETE: *see* Reinforced Concrete.

PRINCIPAL: *see* Roofs (3) and figs. 22, 25.

PRIORY: monastic house whose head is a prior or prioress, not an abbot or abbess.

PROSTYLE: with a free-standing row of columns in front.

PULPITUM: stone screen in a major church provided to shut off the choir from the nave and also as a backing for the return choir stalls.

PULVINATED: *see* Frieze.

PURLIN: *see* Roofs (3) and figs. 22–5.

PUTHOLES or PUTLOCK HOLES: holes in the wall to receive putlocks, the short horizontal timbers which scaffolding boards rest on. They are often not filled in after construction is complete.

PUTTO: small naked boy (plural: putti. Also called *Amorini*.)

QUADRANGLE: rectangular inner courtyard in a large building.

QUARRIES (*lit.* squares): (1) square (or diamond-shaped) panes of glass supported by lead strips which are called *Cames*; (2) square floor-slabs or tiles.

QUATREFOIL: *see* Foil.

QUEENPOSTS: *see* Roofs (3) and fig. 24.

QUIRK: sharp groove to one side of a convex moulding, e.g. beside a roll moulding, which is then said to be quirked.

QUOINS: dressed stones at the

angles of a building. They may be alternately long and short, especially when rusticated.

RADIATING CHAPELS: chapels projecting radially from an ambulatory or an apse; *see* Chevet.

RAFTER: *see* Roofs (3) and figs. 22–6.

RAGGLE: groove cut in masonry, especially to receive the edge of glass or roof-covering.

RAIL: *see* Muntin.

RAISED AND FIELDED: of a wooden panel with a raised square or rectangular central area (field) surrounded by a narrow moulding.

RAKE: slope or pitch.

RAMPART: wall of stone or earth surrounding a hill-fort, castle, fortress, or fortified city. *Rampart Walk:* path along the inner face of a rampart.

REBATE: rectangular section cut out of a masonry edge to receive a shutter, door, window, etc.

REBUS: a heraldic pun, e.g. a fiery cock as a badge for Cockburn.

REEDING: series of convex mouldings; the reverse of fluting.

REFECTORY: dining hall of a monastery or similar establishment. Also called *Frater.*

REINFORCED CONCRETE: concrete reinforced with steel rods to take the tensile stress. A later development is *Prestressed Concrete*, reinforced by wire cables which can be stretched to induce compression in the tension area of the concrete before it is loaded.

RENDERING: the process of covering outside walls with a uniform surface or skin for protection from the weather. *Stucco*, originally a fine lime plaster worked to a smooth surface, is the finest rendered external finish, characteristic of many late C18 and C19 classical buildings. It is usually painted. *Cement Rendering* is a cheaper and more recent substitute for stucco, usually with a grainy texture and often left unpainted. In more simple buildings the wall surface may be roughly *Lime-plastered* (and then whitewashed), or covered with plaster mixed with a coarse aggregate such as gravel. This latter is known as *Roughcast*. A variant, fashionable in the early C20, is *Pebbledashing:* here the stones of the aggregate are kept separate and are thrown at the wet plastered wall to create a decorative effect.

REPOUSSÉ: decoration of metalwork by relief designs, formed by beating the metal from the back.

REREDORTER (*lit.* behind the dormitory): medieval euphemism for latrines in a monastery. Also called *Necessarium.*

REREDOS: painted and/or sculptured screen behind and above an altar.

RESPOND: half-pier bonded into a wall and carrying one end of an arch.

RETABLE: altarpiece, a picture or piece of carving standing behind and attached to an altar.

RETROCHOIR: in a major church, the space between the high altar and an E chapel, like a square ambulatory.

REVEAL: the inward plane of a jamb, between the edge of an external wall and the frame of a door or window that is set in it.

RIB-VAULT: *see* Vault.

RINCEAU (*lit.* little branch) or

Fig. 20. Rinceau

antique foliage: classical ornament, usually on a frieze, of leafy
scrolls branching alternately to
left and right (*see* fig. 20).

RISER: vertical face of a step.

ROCK-FACED: term used to
describe masonry which is cleft
to produce a natural rugged
appearance.

ROCOCO (*lit.* rocky): latest phase
of the Baroque style, current in
most Continental countries
between *c.* 1720 and *c.* 1760, and
showing itself in Britain mainly
in playful, scrolled decoration, especially plasterwork.

ROLL MOULDING: moulding of
curved section used in medieval
architecture.

ROMANESQUE: that style in architecture (in England often called
Norman) which was current in
the C11 and C12 and preceded
the Gothic style. (Some scholars
extend the use of the term
Romanesque back to the C10 or
C9.) *See also* Saxo-Norman.

ROMANO-BRITISH: general term
applied to the period and cultural
features of Britain affected by the
Roman occupation of the C1–5
A.D.

ROOD: cross or crucifix, usually
over the entry into the chancel.
The *Rood Screen* beneath it may
have a *Rood Loft* along the top,
reached by a *Rood Stair*.

ROOFS: (*1*) *Shape:* for the external
shapes and terms used to describe them *see* fig. 21. *Helm:*
roof with four inclined faces
joined at the top, with a gable
at the foot of each. *Hipped* (fig.
21): roof with sloped instead of
vertical ends. *Lean-to:* roof with
one slope only, built against a
vertical wall: term also applied
to the part of the building such
a roof covers. *Mansard* (fig. 21):
roof with a double slope, the
lower one larger and steeper than
the upper. *Saddleback:* the
name given to a normal pitched
roof when used over a tower.
See also Wagon Roof.

(*2*) *Construction:* Roofs are
generally called after the principal structural component, e.g.
crown-post, *hammerbeam*, *kingpost*, etc. See below under
Elements and figs. 22–6.

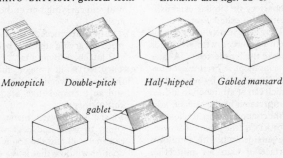

Monopitch   Double-pitch   Half-hipped   Gabled mansard

gablet

Hipped   Hipped with gablet   Mansard

Fig. 21. Roofs: external forms

A *single-framed* roof is constructed with no main trusses. The rafters may be fixed to a wall-plate or ridge, or longitudinal timbers may be absent altogether. A *common rafter* roof is one in which pairs of rafters are not connected by a collar-beam. A *coupled rafter* roof is one in which the rafters are connected by collar-beams.

A *double-framed* roof is constructed with longitudinal members such as purlins. Generally there are principals or principal rafters supporting the longitudinal members and dividing the length of the roof into bays.

(3) *Elements: Ashlar piece.* A short vertical timber connecting an inner wall-plate or timber pad to a rafter above.

Braces. Subsidiary timbers set diagonally to strengthen the frame. *Arched braces:* a pair of curved braces forming an arch, usually connecting the wall or post below with the tie- or collar-beam above. *Passing braces:* straight braces of considerable length, passing across other members of the truss. *Scissor braces:* a pair of braces which cross diagonally between pairs of rafters or principals. *Wind-braces:* short, usually curved braces connecting side purlins with principals. They are sometimes decorated with cusping.

Collar-beam. A horizontal transverse timber connecting a pair of rafters or principals at a height between the apex and the wall-plate.

Crown-post. A vertical timber standing centrally on a tie-beam and supporting a collar purlin. Longitudinal braces usually rise from the crown-post to the collar purlin. When the truss is open lateral braces generally rise to the collar-beam, and when the truss is closed they go down to the tie-beam.

Hammerbeams. Horizontal brackets projecting at wall-plate level on opposite sides of the wall like a tie-beam with the centre cut away. The inner ends carry vertical timbers called hammerposts and braces to a collar-beam.

Hammerpost. A vertical timber set on the inner end of a hammer-beam to support a purlin; it is braced to a collar-beam above.

Kingpost. A vertical timber standing centrally on a tie- or collar-beam and rising to the apex of the roof where it supports a ridge.

Principals. The pair of inclined lateral timbers of a truss which carry common rafters. Usually they support side purlins and their position corresponds to the main bay division of the space below.

Purlin. A horizontal longitudinal timber. *Collar purlin:* a single central timber which carries collar-beams and is itself supported by crown-posts. *Side purlins:* pairs of timbers occurring some way up the slope of the roof. They carry the common rafters and are supported in a number of ways: *butt purlins* are tenoned into either side of the principals; *clasped purlins* rest on queenposts or are carried in the angles between the principals and the collar; *laid-on purlins* lie on the backs of the principals;

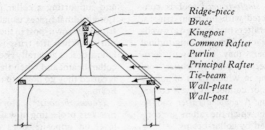

Ridge-piece
Brace
Kingpost
Common Rafter
Purlin
Principal Rafter
Tie-beam
Wall-plate
Wall-post

Fig. 22. Kingpost Roof

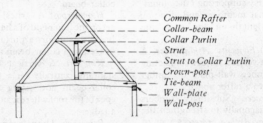

Common Rafter
Collar-beam
Collar Purlin
Strut
Strut to Collar Purlin
Crown-post
Tie-beam
Wall-plate
Wall-post

Fig. 23. Crown-post Roof

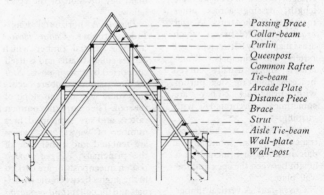

Passing Brace
Collar-beam
Purlin
Queenpost
Common Rafter
Tie-beam
Arcade Plate
Distance Piece
Brace
Strut
Aisle Tie-beam
Wall-plate
Wall-post

Fig. 24. Queenpost Roof

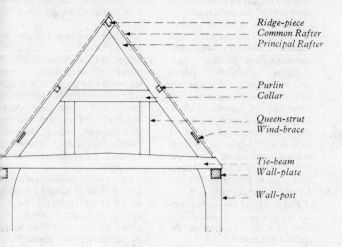

Ridge-piece
Common Rafter
Principal Rafter

Purlin
Collar

Queen-strut
Wind-brace

Tie-beam
Wall-plate

Wall-post

Fig. 25. Queen-strut Roof

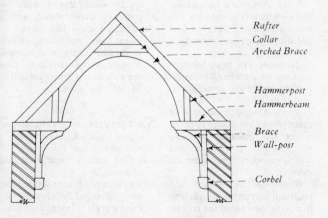

Rafter
Collar
Arched Brace

Hammerpost
Hammerbeam

Brace
Wall-post

Corbel

Fig. 26. Hammerbeam Roof

trenched purlins are trenched into the backs of the principals.

Queenposts. A pair of vertical, or near-vertical, timbers placed symmetrically on a tie-beam and supporting side purlins.

Rafters. Inclined lateral timbers sloping from wall-top to apex and supporting the roof covering. *Common rafters:* rafters of equal scantling found along the length of a roof or sometimes interrupted by main trusses containing principal rafters. *Principal rafters:* rafters which act as principals but also serve as common rafters.

Ridge, ridge-piece. A horizontal, longitudinal timber at the apex of a roof supporting the ends of the rafters.

Sprocket. A short timber placed on the back and at the foot of a rafter to form projecting eaves.

Strut. A vertical or oblique timber which runs between two members of a roof truss but does not directly support longitudinal timbers.

Tie-beam. The main horizontal, transverse timber which carries the feet of the principals at wall-plate level.

Truss. A rigid framework of timbers which is placed laterally across the building to carry the longitudinal roof timbers which support the common rafters.

Wall-plate. A timber laid longitudinally on the top of a wall to receive the ends of the rafters. In a timber-framed building the posts and studs of the wall below are tenoned into it.

ROPE MOULDING: *see* Cable Moulding.

ROSE WINDOW: circular window with patterned tracery about the centre.

ROTUNDA: building circular in plan.

ROUGHCAST: *see* Rendering.

RUBBLE: masonry whose stones are wholly or partly in a rough state. *Coursed Rubble:* of coursed stones with rough faces. *Random Rubble:* of uncoursed stones in a random pattern. *Snecked Rubble* has courses frequently broken by smaller stones (snecks).

RUSTICATION: treatment of joints and/or faces of masonry to give an effect of strength. In the most usual kind the joints are recessed by V-section chamfering or square-section channelling. *Banded Rustication* has only the horizontal joints emphasized in this way. The faces may be flat, but there are many other forms, e.g. *Diamond-faced*, like a shallow pyramid, *Vermiculated*, with a stylized texture like worms or worm-holes, and *Glacial* (frost-work) like icicles or stalactites. *Rusticated Columns* may have their joints and drums treated in any of these ways.

SACRISTY: room in a church for sacred vessels and vestments.

SADDLEBACK: *see* Roofs (I).

SALTIRE CROSS: with diagonal limbs.

SANCTUARY: (1) area around the main altar of a church (*see* Presbytery); (2) sacred site consisting of wood or stone uprights enclosed by a circular bank and ditch. Beginning in the Neolithic, they were elaborated in the succeeding Bronze Age. The best known examples are Stonehenge and Avebury.

SARCOPHAGUS (*lit.* flesh-consuming): coffin of stone or other durable material.

SAUCER DOME: *see* Dome.

SAXO-NORMAN: transitional Romanesque style combining Anglo-Saxon and Norman features, current *c.* 1060–1100.

SCAGLIOLA: composition imitating marble.

SCALLOPED CAPITAL: *see* fig. 7.

SCARP: artificial cutting away of the ground to form a steep slope.

SCREEN: in a church, structure usually at the entry to the chancel; *see* Rood (Screen) *and* Pulpitum. A *Parclose Screen* separates a chapel from the rest of the church.

SCREENS or SCREENS PASSAGE: screened-off entrance passage between the hall and the service rooms in a medieval house.

SECTION: two-dimensional representation of a building, moulding, etc., revealed by cutting across it.

SEDILIA: seats for the priests (usually three) on the S side of the chancel of a church; a plural word that has become a singular, collective one.

SET-OFF: *see* Weathering.

SGRAFFITO: scratched pattern, often in plaster.

SHAFT: upright member of round section, especially the main part of a classical column. *Shaft-ring:* ring like a belt round a circular pier or a circular shaft attached to a pier, characteristic of the C12 and C13.

SHARAWAGGI: a term, first used *c.* 1685 in Sir William Temple's *Essay on Gardening*, which describes an irregular or asymmetrical composition.

SHEILA-NA-GIG: female fertility figure, usually with legs wide open.

SHOULDERED: *see* Arch (fig. 2), Architrave (fig. 3).

SHUTTERED CONCRETE: *see* Formwork.

SILL: (1) horizontal member at the bottom of a window or doorframe; (2) the horizontal member at the base of a timber-framed wall into which the posts and studs (q.v.) are tenoned.

SLAB BLOCK: rectangular multi-storey block of housing or offices.

SLATE-HANGING: covering of overlapping slates on a wall, which is then said to be *slate-hung. Tile-hanging* is similar.

SLYPE: covered way or passage, especially in a cathedral or monastic church, leading E from the cloisters between transept and chapter house.

SNECKED: *see* Rubble.

SOFFIT (*lit.* ceiling): underside of an arch (also called *Intrados*), lintel, etc. *Soffit Roll:* roll moulding on a soffit.

SOLAR (*lit.* sun-room): upper living room or withdrawing room of a medieval house, accessible from the high table end of the hall.

SOPRAPORTA (*lit.* over door): painting or relief above the door of a room, usual in the C17 and C18.

SOUNDING-BOARD: horizontal board or canopy over a pulpit; also called *Tester*.

SOUTERRAIN: underground stone-lined passage and chamber.

S.P.A.B.: Society for the Protection of Ancient Buildings.

SPANDRELS: roughly triangular

spaces between an arch and its containing rectangle, or between adjacent arches. In modern architecture the non-structural panels under the windows in a framed building.

SPERE: a fixed structure which serves as a screen at the lower end of an open medieval hall between the hall proper and the screens passage. It has a wide central opening, often with a movable screen, between posts and short screen walls. The top member is often the tie-beam of the roof truss above; screen and truss are then called a *Spere-truss*.

SPIRE: tall pyramidal or conical feature built on a tower or turret. *Broach Spire:* starting from a square base, then carried into an octagonal section by means of triangular faces. The *Splayed-foot Spire* is a variation of the broach form, found principally in the south-eastern counties, in which the four cardinal faces are splayed out near their base, to cover the corners, while oblique (or intermediate) faces taper away to a point. *Needle Spire:* thin spire rising from the centre of a tower roof, well inside the parapet.

SPIRELET: *see* Flèche.

SPLAY: chamfer, usually of a reveal.

SPRING or SPRINGING: level at which an arch or vault rises from its supports. *Springers:* the first stones of an arch or vaulting-rib above the spring.

SQUINCH: arch or series of arches thrown across an angle between two walls to support a super-structure of polygonal or round plan over a rectangular space, e.g. a dome (*see* fig. 27).

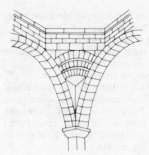

Fig. 27. Squinch

SQUINT: hole cut in a wall or through a pier to allow a view of the main altar of a church from places whence it could not otherwise be seen. Also called *Hagioscope*.

STAIR: *see* fig. 28. A *Dog-leg stair* has parallel zigzag flights without an open well. *Newel stair:* ascending round a central supporting newel (q.v.), called a *Spiral Stair* when in a circular shaft. *Well Stair:* term applied to any stair contained in an open well, but generally to one that climbs up three sides of a well with corner landings, e.g. the *timber-framed newel stair*, common from the C17 on. *Flying Stair:* cantilevered from the wall of a stairwell, without newels. *Geometric Stair:* flying stair whose inner edge describes a curve. *Perron* (*lit.* of stone): external stair leading to a doorway, usually of double-curved plan.

STALL: seat for clergy, choir, etc., distinctively treated in its own right or as one of a row.

STANCHION: upright structural member, of iron or steel or re-inforced concrete.

STEEPLE: tower together with a

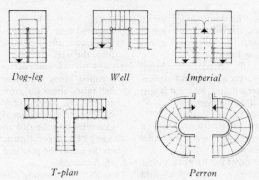

Dog-leg   *Well*   *Imperial*

T-plan   *Perron*

Fig. 28. Stairs

spire or other tall feature on top of it.

STIFF-LEAF: type of E.E. foliage decoration. *Stiff-leaf Capital: see* fig. 7.

STOUP: vessel for the reception of holy water, usually placed near a door.

STRAINER: *see* Arch.

STRAPWORK: C16 and C17 decoration used also in the C19 Jacobean revival, resembling interlaced bands of cut leather.

STRETCHER: *see* Bond.

STRING COURSE: intermediate stone course or moulding projecting from the surface of a wall.

STRINGS: two sloping members which carry the ends of the treads and risers of a staircase. Closed strings enclose the treads and risers; in the later open string staircase the steps project above the strings.

STUCCO (*lit.* plaster): *see* Rendering.

STUDS: subsidiary vertical timbers of a timber-framed wall or partition.

STYLOBATE: solid platform on which a colonnade stands.

SWAG (*lit.* bundle): like a festoon (q.v.), but also a cloth bundle in relief, hung up at both ends.

SYSTEM BUILDING: *see* Industrialized Building.

TABERNACLE (*lit.* tent): (1) canopied structure, especially on a small scale, to contain the reserved sacrament or a relic; (2) architectural frame, e.g. of a statue on a wall or free-standing, with flanking orders. In classical architecture also called an *Aedicule*.

TABLET FLOWER: medieval ornament of a four-leaved flower with a raised or sunk centre.

TAS-DE-CHARGE: stone(s) forming the springers of more than one vaulting-rib.

TERMINAL FIGURE: pedestal or pilaster which tapers towards the bottom, usually with the upper part of a human figure growing out of it. Also called *Term*.

TERRACOTTA: moulded and fired clay ornament or cladding, usually unglazed.

TESSELLATED PAVEMENT:

mosaic flooring, particularly Roman, consisting of small *Tesserae*, i.e. cubes of glass, stone, or brick.

TESTER (*lit.* head): bracketed canopy over a tomb and especially over a pulpit, where it is also called a *Sounding-board*.

TETRASTYLE: *see* Portico.

THERMAE WINDOW (*lit.* of a Roman bath): *see* Diocletian Window.

THREE-DECKER PULPIT: pulpit with clerk's stall below and reading desk below the clerk's stall.

TIE-BEAM: *see* Roofs (3) and figs. 22–5.

TIERCERON: *see* Vault (fig. 33).

TILE-HANGING: *see* Slate-hanging.

TIMBER-FRAMING: method of construction where walls are built of interlocking vertical and horizontal timbers. The spaces are filled with non-structural walling of wattle and daub, lath and plaster, brickwork (known as nogging), etc. Sometimes the timber is covered over by plaster, boarding laid horizontally (weatherboarding q.v.), or tiles.

TOMB-CHEST: chest-shaped stone coffin, the most usual medieval form of funerary monument.

TORUS: large convex moulding usually used on a column base.

TOUCH: soft black marble quarried near Tournai.

TOURELLE: turret corbelled out from the wall.

TOWER HOUSE: compact medieval fortified house with the main hall raised above the ground and at least one more storey above it. The type survives in odd examples into the C16 and C17.

TRABEATED: depends structurally on the use of the post and lintel; cf. Arcuated.

TRACERY: intersecting ribwork in the upper part of a window, or used decoratively in blank arches, on vaults, etc. *Plate tracery: see* fig. 29(*a*). Early form of tracery where decoratively shaped openings are cut through the solid stone infilling in a window head. *Bar tracery:* a form introduced into England *c.* 1250. Intersecting ribwork made up of slender shafts, continuing the lines of the mullions of windows up to a decorative mesh in the head of the window. *Geometrical tracery: see* fig. 29(*b*). Tracery characteristic of *c.* 1250–1310 consisting chiefly of circles or foiled circles. *Y-tracery: see* fig. 29(*c*). Tracery consisting of a mullion which branches into two forming a Y shape; typical of *c.* 1300. *Intersecting tracery: see* fig. 29(*d*). Tracery in which each mullion

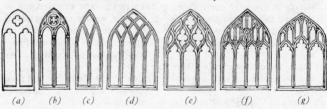

(a)   (b)   (c)   (d)   (e)   (f)   (g)

Fig. 29. Tracery

of a window branches out into two curved bars in such a way that every one of them is drawn with the same radius from a different centre. The result is that every light of the window is a lancet and every two, three, four, etc., lights together form a pointed arch. This treatment also is typical of *c.* 1300. *Reticulated tracery: see* fig. 29(*e*). Tracery typical of the early C14 consisting entirely of circles drawn at top and bottom into ogee shapes so that a net-like appearance results. *Panel tracery: see* fig. 29(*f*) and (*g*). Perp tracery, which is formed of upright straight-sided panels above lights of a window. *Dagger:* Dec tracery motif; *see* fig. 30. *Mouchette:* curved version of the dagger form, especially popular in the early C14; *see* fig. 31.

Fig. 30. Dagger

Fig. 31. Mouchette

TRANSEPTS (*lit.* cross-enclosures): transverse portions of a cross-shaped church.

TRANSITIONAL: transitional phase between two styles, used most often for the phase between Romanesque and Early English (*c.* 1175–*c.* 1200).

TRANSOM: horizontal member between the lights in a window opening.

TREAD: horizontal part of the step

of a staircase. The *Tread End* may be carved.

TREFOIL: *see* Foil.

TRIBUNE: *see* Gallery (1).

TRIFORIUM (*lit.* three openings): middle storey of a church treated as an arcaded wall passage or blind arcade, its height corresponding to that of the aisle roof.

TRIGLYPHS (*lit.* three-grooved tablets): stylized beam-ends in the Doric frieze, with metopes between; *see* Orders (fig. 17).

TRIUMPHAL ARCH: *see* Arch.

TROPHY: sculptured group of arms or armour as a memorial of victory.

TRUMEAU: central stone mullion supporting the tympanum of a wide doorway. *Trumeau Figure:* carved figure attached to a trumeau (cf. Column Figure).

TUDOR FLOWER: late Gothic ornament of a flower with square flat petals or foliage.

TUMBLING or TUMBLING-IN: term used to describe courses of brickwork laid at right angles to the slope of a gable and forming triangles by tapering into horizontal courses.

TUMULUS (*lit.* mound): barrow.

TURRET: small tower, usually attached to a building.

TUSCAN: *see* Orders (fig. 17).

TYMPANUM (*lit.* drum): as of a drum-skin, the surface between a lintel and the arch above it or within a pediment.

UNDERCROFT: vaulted room, sometimes underground, below the main upper room.

UNIVALLATE: (of a hill-fort) defended by a single bank and ditch.

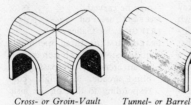

Cross- or Groin-Vault   *Tunnel- or Barrel-Vault*   *Pointed Barrel-Vault*

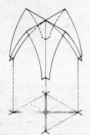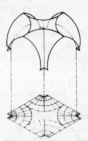

Quadripartite Rib-Vault   *Fan Vault*

Fig. 32. Vaults

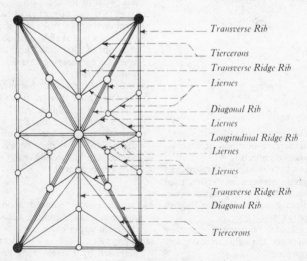

Transverse Rib

Tiercerons

Transverse Ridge Rib

Liernes

Diagonal Rib

Liernes

Longitudinal Ridge Rib

Liernes

Liernes

Transverse Ridge Rib

Diagonal Rib

Tiercerons

Fig. 33. Vaulting ribs

UPPER PALAEOLITHIC: *see* Palaeolithic.

VAULT: ceiling of stone formed like arches (sometimes imitated in timber or plaster); *see* fig. 32. *Tunnel-* or *Barrel-Vault:* the simplest kind of vault, in effect a continuous semicircular arch. *Groin-Vaults* (usually called *Cross-Vaults* in classical architecture) have four curving triangular surfaces produced by the intersection of two tunnel-vaults at right angles. The curved lines at the intersections are called groins. In *Quadripartite Rib-Vaults* the four sections are divided by their arches or ribs springing from the corners of the bay. *Sexpartite Rib-Vaults*, most often used over paired bays, have an extra pair of ribs which spring from between the bays and meet the other four ribs at the crown of the vault. The main types of rib are shown in fig. 33: *transverse ribs, wall ribs, diagonal ribs*, and *ridge ribs*. *Tiercerons* are extra, decorative ribs springing from the corners of a bay. *Liernes* are decorative ribs in the crown of a vault which are not linked to any of the springing points. In a *Stellar Vault* the liernes are arranged in a star formation as in fig. 33. *Fan-Vaults* are peculiar to English Perpendicular architecture in consisting not of ribs and infilling but of halved concave cones with decorative blind tracery carved on their surfaces.

VAULTING-SHAFT: shaft leading up to the springer of a vault.

VENETIAN WINDOW: a form derived from an invention by

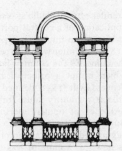

Fig. 34. Venetian Window

Serlio, also called a Serlian or Palladian window. The same motif is used for other openings (*see* fig. 34).

VERANDA(H): shelter or gallery against a building, its roof supported by thin vertical members.

VERMICULATION: *see* Rustication.

VERNACULAR ARCHITECTURE: design by one without any training in design, guided by a series of conventions built up in a locality (Brunskill).

VESICA: oval with pointed head and foot, usually of a window or tracery.

VESTIBULE: anteroom or entrance hall.

VILLA: originally (1) a Romano-British farm or country house. The term is one of convenience and covers a wide spectrum of sites, ranging from humble farmsteads to sumptuous mansions associated with large estates. Various architectural traditions, including both classical and vernacular, are evident in villas, but all display some pretension towards fundamental Roman standards. (2) the C16 Venetian type with office wings, derived from Roman models and made grander by Palladio's varied application of a central portico. It became an important type in C18 Britain, often with the special meaning of (3) a country house which is not a principal residence. Gwilt (1842) defined the villa as 'a country house for the residence of opulent persons'. But devaluation had already begun, and the term also implied, as now, (4) a more or less pretentious suburban house.

VITRIFIED: hardened or fused into a glass-like state.

VITRUVIAN OPENING: door or window which diminishes towards the top, as advocated by Vitruvius, book IV, chapter VI.

VITRUVIAN SCROLL: running ornament of curly waves, on a classical frieze (see fig. 35).

Fig. 35. Vitruvian Scroll

VOLUTES: spiral scrolls on the front and back of a Greek Ionic capital, also on the sides of a Roman one. *Angle Volute:* pair of volutes turned outwards to meet at the corner of a capital. Volutes were also used individually as decoration in C17 and C18 architecture.

VOUSSOIRS: wedge-shaped stones forming an arch.

WAGON ROOF: roof in which closely set rafters with arched braces give the appearance of the inside of a canvas tilt over a wagon. Wagon roofs can be panelled or plastered (ceiled) or left uncovered. Also called *Cradle Roof.*

WAINSCOT: *see* Panelling.

WALL-PLATE: *see* Roofs (3) and figs. 22–5.

WARMING ROOM: *see* Calefactory.

WATERHOLDING BASE: type of early Gothic base in which the upper and lower mouldings are separated by a hollow so deep as to be capable of retaining water.

WATERLEAF CAPITAL: *see* fig. 7.

WEALDEN HOUSE: medieval timber-framed house of distinctive form. It has a central open hall flanked by bays of two storeys. The end bays are jettied to the front, but a single roof covers the whole building, thus producing an exceptionally wide overhang to the eaves in front of the hall.

WEATHERBOARDING: overlapping horizontal boards, covering a timber-framed wall, most common after the mid C18.

WEATHERING: inclined, projecting surface to keep water away from wall and joints below. Also called *Set-off.*

WEEPERS: small figures placed in niches along the sides of some medieval tombs. Also called *Mourners.*

WHEEL WINDOW: circular window with tracery of radiating shafts like the spokes of a wheel. *See also* Rose Window.

INDEX OF PLATES

INDEX OF ARTISTS

INDEX OF PLACES

Mannington, 43, 191
Marsham, 193, 390
Martham, 193
Matlask, 194
Mautby, 194
Mayton, 195
Melton Constable, 40, 54, 59, 63, 64, 195
Metton, 37, 197
Morston, 57, 198, 390
Moulton St Mary, 56, 198
Mundesley, 199
Neatishead, 199
New Catton, see Norwich, 67, 281
North Barningham, 49, 57, 58, 200
North Burlingham, see Burlingham St Andrew, 106
Northrepps, 200
North Walsham, 37, 55, 61, 66, 201
Norwich, Introduction passim 204, 390-2
Ormesby St Margaret, 294
Ormesby St Michael, 64, 294
Oulton, 34n, 295
Overstrand, 68, 295
Oxnead, 53, 55, 297
Palling, see Sea Palling, 45, 312
Panxworth, 297
Paston, 14n, 55, 57, 298
Pensthorpe, 23, 299
Plumstead, 299
Postwick, 23, 299
Potter Heigham, 14n, 41, 45, 299
Rackheath, 300
Ranworth, 22, 47, 48, 55, 300
Reedham, 14, 54, 301
Reepham, 36, 50, 51, 65, 303
Repps, 304
Ridlington, 304
Rollesby, 34n, 39, 55, 305
Roughton, 305
Runham, 306
Runton, 306
St Benet's Abbey, see Ludham, 29, 52, 191
Salhouse, 307

Salle, 37, 39, 41, 46n, 47, 307, 392
Salthouse, 19, 37, 41, 309
Saxlingham (nr Holt), 310
Saxthorpe, 311
Sco Ruston, 311
Scottow, 311
Sea Palling, 45, 312
Sharrington, 312
Sheringham, 14, 15, 64, 68n, 313
Sidestrand, 315
Skeyton, 315
Sloley, 46, 316
Smallburgh, 21, 316
South Burlingham, see Burlingham St Edmund, 26, 106
Southrepps, 316
Southtown, see Gorleston and Great Yarmouth, 66, 137, 149
South Walsham, 317
Southwood, 318
Sparham, 48, 318
Spixworth, 58, 319
Sprowston, 64, 290
Staininghall, 319
Stalham, 38, 60, 320
Stibbard, 320
Stiffkey, 20, 54, 58, 321
Stody, 39, 322
Stokesby, 49n, 322
Stratton Strawless, 58, 323
Strumpshaw, 323
Suffield, 324
Sustead, 324
Sutton, 14n, 325
Swafield, 62, 326
Swannington, 18, 52, 326
Swanton Abbot, 327
Swanton Novers, 327
Taverham, 328
Templewood, see Northrepps, 201
Themelthorpe, 328
Thornage, 47, 56, 329
Thorpe, 63, 67, 291, 392
Thorpe Market, 329
Thorpland, 42, 330
Thrigby, 330
Thurgarton, 53, 330

ADDENDA

(DECEMBER 1961)

p. 86 [Beeston St Laurence, Beeston Hall.] Messrs Baggs and
Young tell me that an engraving of 1780 shows the
building basically similar to what it is now.

p. 96 [Blickling Hall.] A drawing of c.1725 in the Prideaux-
Brune Album shows the N side not open. There are
instead completely irregular structures, one of them
with arched window-lights, i.e. a surviving part of a
house preceding the present one.

p. 103 [Brinton, St Andrew.] The Rev. J. F. Lord draws my
attention to the E.E. double lancet window in the S
wall W of the porch, overlooked by me, and also mentions a plan of 1868 on which in the same wall a
blocked, circular-headed doorway is marked. On the
same plan by the present porch the W limit of 'an older
and smaller fabric' is entered.

p. 109 [Caister, Holy Trinity.] Ready for re-assembly in the
church the parts of the Blennerhasset family monument.
Latest death recorded 1704.

p. 109 [Caister, St Edmund.] Mr D. A. J. Buxton kindly tells
me that tracery and other fragments probably from the
church are in the garden of THE CANNONS, West
Caister.
Also between East and West Caister there is a
thatched BARN belonging to GRANGE FARM, built of
the same bricks as Caister Castle and incorporating
one gun-port from the castle. One end of the barn is a
cottage. Has this always been the case?

p. 117 [Coltishall, St John Baptist.] There was a re-consecration
of the church in 1284.

p. 117 [Coltishall, St John Baptist.] In the chancel lancet a C13
panel of the Virgin and Child. – WEST DOOR. Ori-
ginal, with elaborate tracery. – PLATE. Chalice and

Paten, Norwich, 1567; Paten, 1826. (This addition.
information on Coltishall was given me by the Rev.
John Fellingham.)

p. 127 [Fakenham.] Mr A. Paget Baggs suggests that I should
add the CORN HALL, 1855 by *John Brown*.

p. 133 [Filby House.] White's *Directory* says that the house was
rebuilt in 1833.

p. 137 [Gorleston.] ST PETER THE APOSTLE (R.C.). By *Eric
Gill*, 1938–9. Brick, cruciform, with aisled nave, transepts and chancel. The *leitmotif* the pointed arch. The
arcades are pointed arches, i.e. not piers carrying
arches. So are the windows, i.e. they have no vertical
jambs. Each main window has two plain mullions, i.e. is
tripartite. Steep roofs throughout, also of the low w
porch and the low appendages by the w and E ends.
The crossing tower has four steep gables. The altar
stands under the crossing, and the crossing arches
cross so as to form an octagonal central space whose
diagonals are steep pointed arches, bowing. The church
cost *c.* £6000 to build. – PAINTING by *Denis Teget-
maier* on the E wall of the tower, SCULPTURE on the N
porch wall by *Anthony Foster*, both designed by *Gill*.

p. 139 [Great Snoring, St Mary.] COMMANDMENT BOARD,
16 by 6 ft with paintings of Moses and Aaron, Death,
Judgement, Heaven and Hell.

p. 172 [Horsham St Faith, St Mary and St Andrew.] LECTERN.
Of wood; Perp. With an eagle.

p. 179 [Itteringham, St Mary.] On the N side of the nave the
roofless former Lady Chapel.

p. 193 [Marsham, Bolwick Hall.] Messrs Baggs and Young
comment: C17 interior. Refaced and enlarged early
C19. Grounds almost certainly by *Repton* and still very
charming.

p. 198 [Morston.] Munro Cautley mentions a C17 COLLECTING
SHOE at Morston.

p. 210 [Norwich Cathedral.] Mr A. B. Whittingham, surveyor
to the cathedral, draws my attention to two more fires
which damaged the cathedral, one in 1272, on the